East End Underworld

* *

Chapters in the Life of Arthur Harding

History Workshop Series

General Editor

Raphael Samuel, *Ruskin College, Oxford*

Already published

Village Life and Labour
Miners, Quarrymen and Saltworkers
Rothschild Buildings: Life in an East End
    Tenement Block 1887–1920
People's History and Socialist Theory

Forthcoming

Childhood (2 vols)

Routledge & Kegan Paul
London, Boston and Henley

Raphael Samuel

Tutor in Social History and Sociology
Ruskin College, Oxford

East End Underworld

* *

Chapters in the Life of
Arthur Harding

First published in 1981
by Routledge & Kegan Paul Ltd
39 Store Street,
London WC1E 7DD,
9 Park Street,
Boston, Mass. 02108, USA, and
Broadway House,
Newtown Road,
Henley-on-Thames,
Oxon RG9 1EN
Set in 11/12pt Bembo by
Rowland Phototypesetting Ltd, Bury St Edmunds, Suffolk
and printed in Great Britain by
St Edmundsbury Press, Bury St Edmunds, Suffolk
Plates printed by
Headley Brothers Ltd, Ashford, Kent

British Library Cataloguing in Publication Data

East End Underworld. – (History Workshop Series)
1. Harding, Arthur
2. Crime and criminals – England – London –
Biography
3. London. East End
I. Samuel, Raphael   II. Series
364.1' 066' 0924   HV6248.H16/   80-41511

ISBN 0 7100 0725 6
ISBN 0 7100 0726 4 Pbk

Contents

Preface

Arthur Harding, born in 1886, is probably the last man alive
to have been brought up in the 'Jago', the most famous
criminal slum of late-Victorian London, and the subject of
Arthur Morrison's still widely read fiction, *The Child of the
Jago* (1896). Arthur is only a few years younger than
Morrison's eponymous hero Dicky Perrott, and the first five
chapters of this book offer an alternative view of a district
which has been consistently vilified in London literature ever
since it was pulled down in the 1890s. He grew up to become
a familiar figure in the East End underworld, giving evidence
before the Royal Commission on the Metropolitan Police in
1907, where he was described as the 'king' or 'captain'
of the Brick Lane van-draggers – 'a most slippery and
dangerous criminal' (according to the testimony of a local
police inspector) '. . . the leader of a numerous band of
thieves'. Graduating from pickpocketing and 'shoot-flying'
in his early days to armed hold-ups and 'protection', he was a
well-known local 'terror', 'looking after' the market stallholders and the street bookies, and taking some part in racecourse wars and struggles for territorial supremacy. In 1911
he served a five-year sentence for his part in the 'Vendetta
Affair' and in 1915 was sentenced to a further five-year spell
in jail.

  In different phases of his life, Harding was a cabinet-
maker, a street trader and a wardrobe dealer and these
Chapters have been constructed to show the relationship of
organized crime to the more hum-drum economy of south-
west Bethnal Green. Through Arthur's life and that of his
family one can follow the changing fortunes of East End
people from the desperate hand-to-mouth conditions of the
late nineteenth century to those neighbourly securities
celebrated in Michael Young and Peter Willmott's *Family and*

Kinship in East London and Peter Townsend's *Family Life of Old People*. These *Chapters* shed light on some of the main aspects of East End life – back-street enterprise; family industries; politics (Arthur was at one stage a supporter of Sir Oswald Mosley, and he helped to organize strike-breaking convoys in 1926); and popular culture. Among the many themes to which the reader is introduced are the relationship of the underworld and the local working-class community; the collusive understanding established between villains and the police; the effects of the criminalization of street betting; and the relationship of Jews, non-Jews and what Harding calls 'half-Jews' in the neighbourhood of Brick Lane.

These *Chapters* have been drawn from tape-recorded reminiscences taken over a six-year period. The story of how they came to be constructed – and of the battle of wills entailed in the making of them – is contained in a companion volume (*East End Underworld: South-West Bethnal Green*) to which the interested reader is referred. The volumes can be read separately, but they are closely and indeed organically linked. The other volume situates Arthur's life both in a local context – the moral and social peculiarities of south-west Bethnal Green – and, more generally, in the political economy of crime. It also contains passages in Arthur's life which only emerged after these *Chapters* had been completed, and when I undertook a fresh phase of both recordings and research. The discussion of the narrative itself may help to alert readers not only to the value of this text – as a testimony to a way of life that had seemed to be beyond human recall – but also to some of the complexities concealed by the words on the page.

In the course of what has been a very long project I have incurred many debts. They are acknowledged in the preface to the companion volume.

Raphael Samuel

Prefatory note

The words in this narrative are Arthur Harding's, but they have been drawn from a mass of tape recordings taken over a period of six years, from 1973 to 1979. The difficulties of such a text, and the problems involved in constituting it, are discussed in a companion volume: *The East End Underworld 1: South-West Bethnal Green*. In the course of what has been a very long project I have incurred many debts. They will be acknowledged in the companion volume, but I would like, here, to express my gratitude to the Nuffield Foundation, whose generous grant gave me the time off teaching to put this narrative together; and to John Mason, who did the great bulk of the library work for the corroborative footnotes attached to the text. The companion volume, a study of Bethnal Green from the early nineteenth century to the First World War, will be published later this year or next. It draws on a further cycle of recordings with Arthur Harding, but is mainly based on printed and manuscript sources, and the oral testimony of other survivors from these times. The contents are as follows:

1. The weavers' parish; 2. Culture and environment; 3. Backyard industries; 4. Penny capitalism; 5. The dialectics of waste; 6. Business and crime; 7. The political economy of crime; 8. Crime and community; 9. Clan formation; 10. Sexual order; 11. Ideology and politics; 12. The voice of the past?

Raphael Samuel
January 1981

Acknowledgments

Photographs 8 and 9 are reproduced by permission of the Greater London Council Photograph Library.

1 Inside the Jago

In the last quarter of the nineteenth century there were some 6,000 people[1] – men, women and children – who lived in the Nichol. The district was bounded by High Street Shoreditch and Hackney Road on the north and Spitalfields to the south. It was made up of many alleys and courts. The principal streets were Boundary Street, the main playing street, Old Nichol Street, New Nichol Street, Half Nichol Street, The Mount – where the old clothes dealers were – and the only street with shops – Church Street. Arthur Morrison in his novel called it 'The Jago'.

The Nichol was something like a ghetto. A stranger wouldn't chance his arm there, but to anyone brought up in it every alley was familiar. The Nichol was a place on its own, you didn't go into other territory. You could go into the cake shop and say, 'Got any broken biscuits, mister?', or into the pudding shop and ask for a pie-crust or say, 'Got any cold pudding?' and they'd say, 'How much have you got?' and you'd say, 'A halfpenny', and they'd say, 'All right, give us that', because they knew you. Everybody knew the children belonged to the Nichol and everybody was kind to the children. There was hardly any traffic – the children could go anywhere and have no fear of anything. The coal carts didn't go fast. The chimney sweeps, they knew everybody. And so the result was that it was a close-knit community and everybody knew everybody.

The whole district bore an evil reputation[2] and was regarded by the working-class people of Bethnal Green as so disreputable that they avoided contact with the people who lived in the Nichol. Some people would have liked to build a wall right round it, so that we wouldn't have to come out. They put everything that was needed inside. They put the mission hall there – the Ragged School[3] in Old Nichol Street. They put the hospital there – the Mildmay Hospital[4] in Austin Street; and they put the school there, the Nichol School,[5] so the kids wouldn't have to come out and be a nuisance. There was a police station in Church Street,[6] opposite Turville Street, and there was Father Jay's church, Holy Trinity, in Old Nichol Street. It was a big red brick church which was bombed out in the war. It stood right in the middle of the Nichol. At the door of the church you used to get jam puddings when you came out of school at midday – the housekeeper made roly-polys and the kids used to line up. A penny could buy a dinner but if you didn't have one she would give it to you. Father Jay was a big, smiling man, a six-footer – I think he had been a boxer.[7] At the end of Bethnal Green Road there was Macpherson's, where you went in and got your bottle of medicine.[8] It was a medical mission run by Scotch people. The Mildmay was Church of England, the Mission was more Nonconformist – I used to get a bit of clobber there when they had sales on. You went there on a Sunday to learn about the Christian religion.

In the Nichol there seemed to be a wall enclosing you. Boundary Street round to Virginia Road and Austin Street – beyond you was out of the Nichol. The people had to go shopping either in the Brick Lane, Church Street, or the High Street Shoreditch. The children went to school either at Rochelle Street or Castle Street School which was in Austin Street.[9] In Virginia Road lived the mother of a young man named Baker who was hanged at Carlisle with two others named Rudge and Martin for the murder of two policemen, while escaping from Netherby Hall[10] where they had committed a robbery. Mrs Baker never opened her shop again. Years later I learnt the name of the fourth man involved in the murder; he was never caught.

I was born on 27 November 1886 at No. 4 Keeve's Buildings, Boundary Street. We had one small room in a three-storeyed tenement which contained twelve rooms, let to twelve different families. Keeve's Buildings were built as tenements, a sort of barracks. There was a street door, but it was always kept open: it was a great 3-inch thick door. There was a basement which was supposed to be for a wash-house, for washing dirty linen, but as it was in complete darkness it was only used by homeless people at night as a shelter from the cold. The yard was only about 12 foot wide – just enough to put the dustbins in each side. Nobody was responsible for the cleaning of the place; they wouldn't pay nobody. There was a wooden staircase, they weren't buildings like we know them today. Each room had an ordinary panelled door (cost about 2*s* 6*d* if it cost that). Just an ordinary flimsy door that you could kick open. They had a lock and key, but there was scarcely any fear of anybody breaking into them. There was nothing of value to lose. They had a wooden wainscoting right round the wall, it was about 3 feet high – it had been painted once. I can remember that my father got some paint from somewhere and it caused a bit of trouble from the other people. They said we'd driven the bugs into their room. The water tap on each landing was three or four stairs below the level of the floor, in a sort of alcove, about 5 feet wide; and then two rooms on either side, two back rooms and two front rooms. The rent wasn't very expensive at all – about 3*s* a week for a room.

The houses in Boundary Street were three storeys high. They only ran on one side of the street. The shops on Shoreditch High Street backed on to the other, especially Jeremiah Rotherham's, where they unloaded goods and all the rest of it. Even today the left hand side of Boundary Street going down from Church Street is a blank. There's no shops of any description – never has been any shops there.[11]

Half Nichol Street was of varied architecture, they didn't comply with one set of rules. There was courts and alleyways as well. A court was a bit of a place where the architect and the builder had got into such a state that there was a part empty. There'd be houses all round the square. Originally the idea was to have a bit of a garden for people, but when space and land began to fetch good money the landlords sold the part of the gardens to developers and built these little alleyways and courts in it. They had to congest the buildings to a small dimension because they never had the space available. That's what happened to Nichol Street and Half Nichol Street. New Nichol Street was a more up-to-date affair. The houses were only two storeys high and a bit more ornate, they put a round top to the windows.

My young sister Mary was born round New Nichol Street in Charlotte's Buildings. That was where my aunt Liza had her shop, and where her beerhouse stood.[12] It was an ordinary thoroughfare, just wide enough for a horse and cart. The houses were built so close together that you could put a rope across the road and hang the washing on it. Everything was on a miniature scale, there was nothing huge about it.

In a court you'd get a small entrance and then it widened out where they built the cottages. Some had two front houses so you had a couple of rooms over an archway: the archway was built about 6 foot wide so you could get a barrow through, and the top rooms was where somebody lived. You went through it into the court, and depending on how big the square was, you'd get perhaps seven houses, about 8 foot to 10 foot wide. They weren't very big.

Then there were the alleyways, they weren't very pleasant places, they'd just been slung up. They were very dark. You'd have about six houses, three on each side, down an alleyway. Why they built them I don't know, except there was so many people homeless, they had to build somewhere for them to live in.

The courts were just a breathing space, enough for a few barrows, donkey barrows and all that. Wherever there was any free space they stuck up sheds for the donkeys. There was plenty of costermongers about. A lot of these courts were used mainly for sticking up sheds, like they stick up garages today.

It was very crowded in the Nichol, every little space was built on. It appears that before the railway extended to Liverpool Street, some people would have two rooms – they could afford it and the rent was much lower. But when they started pulling the houses down along the route of the Great Eastern Railway, all those people were thrown out, evicted: they paid them 30s or something. Well, they had to have somewhere to live, and the landlords started letting out one-room tenements.

Turville Street ran from Church Street to Mead Street and ended near Castle Street School. The houses were mostly of the tenement type of three storeys. The Mildmay Medical Mission had its beginnings in Turville Street. This street with the French name owes its origin to the French silk weavers, because you could see the weavers' rooms at the top of the houses. There were two half turnings which led to Mount

Street. At the corner of Turville Street and Old Nichol Street was a large corner shop which sold everything that the people of the Nichol might need. It was the only shop in Turville Street and was owned by my aunt Eliza. My uncles Arthur and Jim lived at the shop, or at the beerhouse on the other corner,[13] which the family also owned. The cottages in the turnings were very old, two rooms and a scullery downstairs, one large room upstairs which was usually the bedroom for the family; the toilet was outside in a small garden. They did not have weavers' windows.

Turk Street was at the top of Brick Lane. There weren't many shops, but there was an old clothes market on Sundays. The old girl, old Mother Morgan, she had a shop in Turk Street,[14] selling old clothes, next to the 'Duke of York';[15] she made a packet of money, and bought property round in Essex Street, Hoxton, furnished rooms. The Morgans were Romanies. Them and the Smiths and the Harpers, another mob from the Nichol, they were all hawkers, going round with a little pony and cart, or barrows. There was another family of Morgans, a different one, who had a couple of cows, in the dairy, off of Nichol Street. Even when I was grown up and married they had two cows in Bethnal Green, they used to milk 'em there – my wife used to go every night to buy hot cow's milk from the dairy.

The high heaven of everything in the Nichol was Church Street where all the shops were. The whole place was crooked, even those who kept shops. Church Street, now called Redchurch Street, starts from High Street Shoreditch. The 'White Horse' pub stands on one corner, and on the other corner was a big men's and boys' tailor shop, known as Lynn's. This tailor's shop extended to Boundary Street where I was born. On each side of Church Street there were food shops, used mostly by the people of the Nichol. The first was a fish and chip shop right opposite Boundary Street; the people would send the children for 'a penny bit and haporth' – one penny bit of fish and a halfpenny worth of chips or fried potatoes.[16] This was the usual dinner and supper meal.

Next to the fish shop was a small timber yard,[17] where the one-room cabinet-maker bought his timber: mostly white wood, very easy to work with. On the corner of Ebor Street which led to Bethnal Green Road was a pub outside of which stood a street bookmaker waiting for punters to bet their fancy on horses; also a paper boy selling the *Star* which cost ½*d* like most of the papers.[18] I remember there was another racing paper like the *Star* – it was called the *Echo* at ½*d*. On the next corner stood a small coffee shop,[19] cup of tea, two slices of bread and margarine: 2 pence, old currency. Cup of tea 1*d*, bread and bloater 3*d*. Lunch 4*d*: meat, two veg's and a piece of jam tart.

Just along the street stood Burdett's fish shop.[20] Bloaters, smoked haddocks, kippers and most cheap herrings like mackerel, eels, etc. This shop was famous all over the Nichol and Bethnal Green. Old Charles Burdett, whose family owned the shop, was often to be seen on a fine day sitting outside the shop; his age was some sixty years or more although in the 1890s it was a rare sight to see an elderly person in the Nichol, unless they were in the workhouse uniform. In his youth old Charles had been a burglar. While engaged in his profession he was discovered by a vigilant policeman and in attempting to escape he fired at his pursuer. The police constable was not hit, the burglar was caught and came up for trial at the Old Bailey and the judge said to him: 'As the PC's life was spared so shall yours be, you will go to penal servitude for life.' Old Charlie paid his debt to society and after some twenty years was released on licence. May I say that old Charlie never got into any further trouble and was a lovable old chap who was well liked by all the children in the Nichol. Opposite the shop was a small Salvation Army chapel, on a fine day it was not unusual to see a bonnie Salvation Army lassie sitting by his side. Passing along Church Street there was another pub in the middle of the street called the 'Crown' which is still there. This pub was well known for being the meeting place for the bird fanciers who would bring their birds down to the pub at weekends with a big silk handkerchief over the cage: then the competition for best singing birds would start and last for many hours.

On the corner of the next street, Camlet Street, was a wardrobe dealer's shop which sold second-hand clothing of all kinds, from babies' first garments to men and women's clothing, there were several shops of this description. Passing along you come to Club Row which is much wider than the other streets. At the Bethnal Green end of Club Row stood the 'Knave of Clubs' pub, and on the other corner was MacPherson's the dispensary for the sick poor – they could obtain medicine for their illnesses or get a letter for hospital.

The north side of Church Street began from Fox's the chemist who sold every kind of medicines and cures for every kind of illness, also furniture polish and varnish, and the dangerous liquid called methylated spirits which tasted like whisky. Next to the chemist stood Weber's the pork butcher. This cook shop was the best in the locality and was very popular with the Nichol inhabitants who were able to buy very good cooked food at very cheap prices. Next was a doctor's shop, Dr Rogers. He was a very tall man; he wore a high silk hat and morning coat and always dressed in black. His fees were 6d if you went to see him; 2s 6d for a visit to your home. These fees included medicine or pills. A newsagent was next to the doctor's surgery. On the corner of Mount Street was the pub called the 'Black Dog'. Mount Street was the end of the Nichol and ran as far as Virginia Road.

Passing along Church Street towards Shoreditch we pass more food shops. On the corner of Turville Street was a pub called the 'Dolphin' – this was right opposite the old police station. From Turville Street to Club Row there were shops – a barber's shop, dining rooms, a baker's, and the undertakers on the corner of Club Row. On the other side of Club Row was a large grocer's shop selling very cheap tea, sugar, etc. There were several wardrobe shops selling cheap second-hand ladies' and gents' clothes, especially children's clothes.

We have now reached Camlet Street where there was a corner shop named Butcher's. Here, the children would buy a large bag of broken biscuits for ½d or 1d. Cake was sold at about 2d per pound. This shop was a God-send to the hungry children of the district. Next to Butcher's was the pudding shop; hot pies a penny each, jam roly-poly pudding penny a portion.[21] This shop also sold a kind of leg of beef soup for 1½d a jug full.

Still in Church Street, and opposite the 'Crown' and Charlie Burdett's – was a building that had once been a doss-house, but was now used by the Salvation Army.[22] The people of the

Nichol who attended the services were able to take home large jugs of good soup instead of jugs of beer. Next to the soup kitchen was a rag-and-bone shop where the kids would take old rags and get a few coppers for food.

You could say that Shoreditch High Street was our Champs Elysées. It was a prosperous market place with stalls and shops on both sides of the street; they catered for a large population of many thousands. It used to be a big market even on a week day, right up to about 1910.[23] There were many pubs on both sides of the street. On the left-hand side going towards Liverpool Street Station was St Leonard's Church whose bells ring out the famous chimes of Bow Bells which can be heard all over the East End. A few yards from the church was a pub called 'The Gun'; from this pub in 1888 the terribly mutilated body of Mary Kelly, the last known victim of Jack the Ripper, was buried.

There were no stalls on this side of Shoreditch High Street, but shops and pubs, and also the 'London' music hall which had two performances six days a week.[24] All the most famous artists appeared there twice nightly. Marie Lloyd and others would often patronise the refreshments bars. Next to this famous music hall was the firm of Jeremiah Rotherham, which today is one of the largest wholesale drapers in the East End. Several shops further along led to Church Street. A large pub on the corner was the beginning of the largest store in the East End.[25] It was called Hopkins and Peggs and occupied the whole length of the front from Church Street to Bethnal Green Road. The large staff all wore black dresses and the gents wore morning coats and striped trousers and slept on the premises.

On the right-hand side of Shoreditch High Street – going towards Liverpool Street Station – was the 'Kings Arms' pub. Then there was a large billiard saloon, and outside this was the beginning of the market stalls.[26] First in pride of place was a large fruit stall belonging to a family called the Bellinghams. The family were noted for the fine fruit they sold. Somebody told me that when Shoreditch Borough Council did away with the stalls in Shoreditch High Street she committed suicide. Next to the fruit stall stood one of the noted jellied eel stalls belonging to the Mitchells. These eel stalls were well patronised by the crowds of ordinary people who could always be found along Shoreditch High Street up to midnight. From the Nichol there was only the courtway to get to the High Street, what they called the Bonnet Box Court, because of the ladies' hat shop on the corner – the Bonnet Box.[27] And there was a passage called Boundary Passage – it is still there – which used to be the getaway when they snatched the parcels from Hill's the tobacco people. It's on some of the maps. It is just a narrow place, and Hill's used to be on the corner of New Inn Yard. The lads used to wait up there and when a fellow came out with a big parcel of tobacco, they used to snatch the parcel and run through the passage.

The children of the Nichol would hang about the High Street seeing if they could fiddle something off the stalls. If they could pinch anything, they'd pinch it. If they had anything over they'd sell it to the neighbours. A tin of blacking, that'd be 2d – they'd sell it very likely for ½d. They'd steal fruit – anything to eat. But the ones from the criminal families would always have a wee bit of a bag with 'em. A pair of shoes, hanging up outside the bootshop, was easy to cut down. So they got into the habit of only hanging one shoe out. They'd bring back what they could lay their hands on, wrapped in a roll of paper – anything that was worth money. When the stallholders saw them they'd say, 'What you doing there?', perhaps the child would reply, 'Come on, it's only a couple of specks.' A cockney's a very sensible person. What's he going to run after a kid for? To give him a slap? Everybody would be setting about him if he did. The stallholder would be serving the customer, he'd be in the front, and the kids would be round the back; one would get the fruit from under the cover and put it in a bag; the other would walk away with it. Twos and threes used to do it together, sometimes more than that. If an owner had three or four kids hanging round his stall, he'd got to keep an eye on what was happening under them, to know what was going on. Girls and all used to be at it. They were very nimble. Anything they could lay their hands on. There were no stores like Woolworth's in those days; if you wanted to pinch anything you had to go for the stalls.

Opposite the 'London' music hall in Shoreditch High Street was the famous pub the 'Jane Shore',[28] where my Dad worked, for 2s daily from 6 a.m. until midnight. The large

entrance hall to the bars had big mosaic pictures on the walls
and floors. They portrayed the various incidents in the life of
the unfortunate mistress Jane Shore. The pub was built over
the spot where, tradition says, the body of Jane Shore was
found. The small children would play in the corridor. From
the 'Jane Shore' to New Inn Yard was a line of penny shows
like in a fairground, and there were many freaks and laughable
shows. At the corner of New Inn Yard was a large tobacco
shop owned by Hill's Tobacco Co. In the doorway was a large
wooden statue of a Red Indian with a naked light for a
cigarette, so that a customer could light his pipe. During the
lunch interval the crowds were very dense, made up of the
white-collar brigade, listening to the pedlars of various
medicines which would cure all ills.

By Holywell Lane, which faced Bethnal Green Road, you
could see a large shop which sold mens' and boys' clothes,
called Alexander's. Men's suits sold at 18s which was a week's
wages for the lower paid people; boys suits from 6s 11d to 7s
6d. From Holywell Lane to the 'Royal Standard' theatre[29] in
Norton Folgate you would pass three pubs next to each
other;[30] then you would see 'Shoreditch's Hat Shop', re-
nowned for the splendid hats they sold to the music hall artists
and the actors from the 'Royal Standard'. It was owned by a
German, I think, a big well-dressed man.[31] He must have
made a packet – all the comedians used to buy their hats there.

Outside the hat shop, in the road, stood a large figure of
wood, representing the figurehead of an old-time wooden
fighting ship. It was painted in vivid colours. My father, when
not working, was often to be found outside the hat shop,
doing odd jobs for the owner. Next to the hat shop stood a
'Pearce and Plenty' tea shop. Cup of tea a halfpenny, slice of
bread and marge a halfpenny, and one could buy a three-
course lunch for 4d. Over the shop was a bagatelle room for
customers to enjoy games. Next to the Pearce and Plenty
dining rooms was the 'Royal Standard' theatre. In this famous
theatre some of the great melodramas of the age were
dramatised for the people of the East End. Prices for admission
were very popular: 1s, 9d, 6d, were good seats and the gallery
was well patronised at 3d admission. One could buy drinks –
beer and spirits were at popular prices. Next to the theatre was

yet another pub on the corner of a street. Across the main road was Great Eastern Street, which was opposite Commercial Street.

The trams ran up to Liverpool Street Station along Shoreditch High Street. They ran along rails and were drawn by a pair of horses; the speed was about 10 or 12 miles an hour. Some of them came from Tottenham. The buses, also horse-drawn, ran from Walthamstow along the Lea Bridge Road. The driver, sitting on top, was well dressed in heavy top coat and hard hat, with a very long whip which was never used. The bus had no fixed stopping places like today but stopped when signalled.

After crossing Great Eastern Street you continued your walk towards Liverpool Street for a drink in 'Dirty Dick's',[32] at the corner of Middlesex Street, commonly known as Petticoat Lane. There were twenty-two pubs along Shoreditch High Street, between St Leonard's Church and Liverpool Street Station.

My mother was born in Norfolk on 5 November 1856 and died in Bethnal Green on 1 January 1942. She used to work in an eel shop in the capital, Norwich. Her name was Milligan, Mary Anne Milligan. I've sometimes thought she might have had some Irish blood. When she was well boozed she used to sing Irish songs: 'Bold Robert Emmet who died with a smile', all that kind of thing. It was a famous song with her – who he was I haven't the faintest idea. And I can remember, years later, going into a wake to pull her out, after Mrs Abbot died in Gibraltar Gardens. They was all sitting round drinking beer.

Her father was an agricultural labourer whose wages were so small that the parish had to give him a small sum from the rates to augment his weekly wage, and then when the farmer discovered it he lowered his wage. I remember my sister talking about that. He was a great big man and my sister used to tell me that Mummy wouldn't dare say a bad word in front of him. The only time I saw him was in Hoxton workhouse, where he died. It was when I was at Dr Barnardo's. My mother wanted to show me off in the uniform – it was a very smart uniform – and she took me there. He was sitting on a bare form. He seemed a country-speaking man, a rough agricultural labourer with knotted hands. He couldn't get a job when he came to London and they spent their last years in the workhouse. His wife, my granny, was a small woman, a little short woman about 5 foot. She only had one eye when I saw her, the other was closed up. The workhouse was in Wilmers Garden, Hoxton – the 'Land of Promise'[1] they used to call it. I went to see her in the infirmary. She was in bed but there was nothing wrong with her. She said to me, 'You look like a soldier.' It was the only time I saw her. I think the poor old chappie died from doing nothing. He must have been forty or fifty when they came to London, and there was nothing for him there.

Some time about 1875 the family had to migrate to London because they could not live on the starvation wages that were paid for labour in Norfolk. They moved to Hoxton, which was about the worst bloody place they could have gone to. But there you are, they had to survive and to go where rents were cheap. My mother was about eighteen when they came. She had several sisters and they all settled down in the roughest part of Hoxton, in Wilmers Gardens and Falkirk Street. None of them had any money or we would have been out to tap them. I didn't have much to do with them. Aunt Caroline had a bit of a reputation. She was well known in Hoxton. One of her sons was a bit of a terror. She lived in Wilmers Gardens – the roughest street in Hoxton, where the lodging houses were.[2] The people there were very poor and lived in tenement houses, three storeys high. Outside her house, in 1896 or 1897, there was a murder. A policeman was arresting a drunken man just outside my aunt's house and one of the crowd who had gathered there stuck a knife into the policeman's back and killed him. The policeman clung to the man who he was arresting for being drunk and disorderly and when the whistles was blown and other police arrived he still had him in his grip. They arrested him for the murder. He was innocent – the man who really did the murder was someone known as 'Warhorse' but my aunt was too frightened to go up and give evidence, even though she's seen what happened. I kept away from her after that.[3]

One of my mother's other sisters, aunt Harriet, became posh, select. She married a police sergeant and lived in the buildings next to Bethnal Green police station, in Wilmot Street.[4] My elder sister was named after her. She was a steady, Christian woman, far superior to my mother. But she was very kind to me – never upbraided me for getting into trouble. I saw her regularly even when I was a man. Even when I come out of prison she still saw me. She was specially fond of me. Her daughters were all college girls. They had a good education – one was a cashier at Gardiner's, the big store in Whitechapel. I said to her one day, 'Is there any chance of me coming up there for a job?' She said, 'You keep away.' It was meant as a joke but I think she was frightened. The daughters kept religiously away from me, because I had a reputation as a terror.

After she came to London, mother found employment in a rag factory, sorting rags. This was a very filthy work because the rags were collected from the poorest districts and had to be sorted into the different qualities and colours. The wages were higher than in the factories, but it was a dirty, filthy job. Mother worked there until she met my father. She was about twenty years of age when she first met him, and he was about thirty. They met at 'Dirty Dick's', the pub opposite Liverpool Street Station, on Bishopsgate.

The Hardings, my father's family, had come from Cornwall, somewhere down Helston Way, and they established themselves first in the Borough, then in Spitalfields, making baskets. They were mixed up with market work. There were four brothers and two sisters. Aunt Liza was the eldest, and when the parents died she became head of the family. She was a spinster and remained so for the rest of her life. The parents both died at the age of fifty-seven.

The family were well known in the Nichol for breeding dogs. They specialised in a very small black-and-tan terrier which was sold by its weight. This wee little dog was worth its weight in sovereigns and could be carried about in the pocket of a greatcoat. Uncle Lark and uncle Jim done the breeding. They sold them in the pubs. We used to have them under glass cages in Keeve's Buildings, but my father didn't go in for breeding: he was more of a horse-racing man. My father was the youngest in the family. He was born in Pearl Street, Spitalfields, behind the 'Cambridge' music hall.[5]

The Hardings were well-to-do by Nichol standards. They were the 'kings' down there, the chief owners, the richest people round that way. Years ago I used to talk to people who knew the Nichol, they knew what they were talking about, and they said the Hardings had control of the whole place. They owned a pub and several drinking shops, also a large general store which sold most everyday requirements. All the family were illiterate, and were typical of the people who lived in the Nichol. The brothers had been in trouble with the police over drinking hours and had been fined some hundreds of pounds.

There were six brothers in the family. The only ones I was really familiar with was my uncle Arthur and my uncle Bill.

My uncle Albert was in the wood-carving line. He lived in Bethnal Green Road, poor old devil, even when he was over eighty. I can see him now, carrying bits of furniture about. He used to carry work about from one place to another. The sons became very expert carvers – uncle Albert used to collect the cameo legs for them to carve on chairs and wooden bedsteads and drawer fronts for the china cabinets. Their workshop was in Approach Road.[6] They only carved for the top people, doing exhibition work. Uncle Albert was the respectable one of the brothers; he kept himself quiet, never mixed with the others. The sons wouldn't have anything to do with me – my name was too much in the papers for any of them. For years they lived by Victoria Park and then they moved out Gipsy Hill way – they're in the phone book there. Very posh people.

Uncle Bill lived down Chambord Street, off Brick Lane. I don't know what he done for a living. He died very young of consumption – always coughing. I can see him now, standing on the corner of Gossett Street, coughing away. There wasn't much life left in him. His wife was a hawker. She had a stall in Brick Lane, at the Turk Street end. She used to take her stand there on Sunday mornings, selling old clothes. She was one of them women who didn't mix, didn't go on the booze. They were a big family, but all her sons were killed in the First World War. The mother used to go over to Belgium where they were buried – the villagers made a memorial for them.

Uncle Jim. He was the craftiest one of the lot. He never done any bloody work, so far as I know, all his life. Never. Anything that wasn't work, he was in it. He lived on his sister Liza. He was in charge of one of her grocery shops. You could get anything off of him when you went round: my sister Mighty could wheedle things out of him, she'd say, 'Mother said that she'd bring round the money tonight,' but she was never able to pay. That was ordinary. But the old girl never sponged on them – as a family we was entitled to help. Uncle Jim never married or had a family. He belonged to Liza's shop, he and Uncle Arthur and Liza. They all three mucked in together. He was the oldest of the brothers, and the only one who had a beard. I used to think he was in charge, later I learnt that it was really Liza. They used to get a lot by fiddling with the dockers. They got a lot of cheap tea and sugar from the dockers – they'd bring it in underhand – and sometimes they used to get whisky: that was what uncle Arthur got time for, selling unlicensed whisky.

Uncle Jack lived to a great old age, but I don't know much about him. All his sons was in the dog business, breeding dogs and selling them, on a Sunday morning market. He made a living by buying and selling dogs down Club Row – to any publican who wanted to buy a terrier. He had a big white beard in his old age. I used to see him about once a year. He lived Hoxton way, towards St Luke's.

Uncle Arthur was a very smart man – I was named after him. They used to call him 'Lark' because he was ever so nice-looking. He never done no work. He had the shop and the pub, together with aunt Liza. But when it came to a raid, he had to carry the can. He was the one in charge of all the drinking business in the Nichol, and he was always getting into trouble with the police. He had a bad name with the police and I think it was his record stuck against me when I came up for trial the first time. Once he was fined £500 for selling drink illegally.[7] He said, 'I'll do prison instead', and so he was sent there for six months. His drinking shop was in Half Nichol Street. I used to go up to him to get a few coppers. He wasn't an old man or nothing when he died, about thirty or forty – he must have had cancer or something, just dropped dead.

My aunt Liza was a very shrewd woman. She had that sharp business manner. No foolishness about her. As a matter of fact I don't ever remember getting a penny off her. She used to frighten me. My sister Mighty took after her – she was a good business woman and very shrewd. Aunt Liza used to call me 'Prince' – they all called me 'Prince'. She never condemned me. Sometimes she would say to me, 'What have you been up to?' but she wouldn't tell me off for getting into trouble.

Aunt Liza's original shop was at the corner of Mead Street and Mount Street.[8] It was just an ordinary house with a shop front. The pub was nearby and the door at the back was open so that if there was a chap the police were looking for, he could always get out. The dockers used to come into the shop with what they knocked off – they'd come in with pocket loads of tea which they had pinched. She would weigh it and give them a price for it – then she used to make it up into bags, using a sheet of old newspaper. They used to bring it in on a Sunday morning, when the market was on. It was a pretty decent-sized shop with a great stock of things in it. The people used to line up. A lot of it was done 'on the slate'. People would go in and say, 'Can you let me 'ave a loaf? My old man's got a day's work coming tomorrow.' Aunt Liza had everything anyone could require – bacon, bread, tea, sugar. Not fish or nothing like that – you had to go to Burdett's for that. Coal was a very profitable business. It cost about tuppence for fourteen pounds, 10*d* a hundredweight. She sold it in a shed round the side, not where they came in for food, but in a separate place. She also sold paraffin, candles and all that sort of thing. Candles was still of great use. They were a necessity. If a man didn't have candles he had nothing.

They pulled the shop down when the Nichol was destroyed. It was one of the last buildings to go, in 1895.

Uncle Tom was aunt Liza's proposed husband, though they never got married. He had a pub called the 'Jack Simmons'[9] in Church Street. She used to keep company with him and they were pally – she was his fancied woman if you know what I mean – but she didn't live with him. Uncle Tom was a betting man. He looked like a betting man, and like all the racing men he had plenty of gas, plenty of talk. He mixed with the prize fighters and he used to go away racing with the three-card trick. He lived in Turville Street, one of the turnings off Church Street. The 'Jack Simmons' was at the corner of Church Street and Ebor Street. It was the most famous pub in the East End of a Sunday morning. All the top Johnnies were in there, the prize fighters, and some of the music hall artists. It had a great big bar at the front, with a little private bar round at the side. Of a Sunday morning they used to do a rare old trade. The boxers and the prize fighters and the racing people used to go in there. All the rogues and villains – the three-card mob and all that lark. I used to go round to get pennies for sweets, that's when I used to see them. Later it was turned into a Jewish Synagogue.

When I came out of Borstal aunt Liza had a big house at the Bethnal Green Road end of Church Street. The back part was in Church Street, the front part in Bethnal Green Road. Aunt Liza lived there, and uncle Arthur, and I think they let some rooms out. My father was using the basement as a workshop – he was doing some carving, but he never did much bleeding work there. Then uncle Arthur started living with a woman in Hollybush Gardens[10] – very nice woman, we used to call her aunty. My aunt Liza went to live with them eventually. She had the top floor. And uncle Jim went with them. In the end they all lived in Wilmot Street, Bethnal Green.

Aunt Mary Anne – my father's other sister – was quite different. She wasn't much good at looking after herself. For a long time she lived with her daughter, and at the end she lived with aunt Liza in Wilmot Street, when she moved to Bethnal Green.

My father was fond of the ladies. He had two wives and he already had some five children before he married my mother. At that time he was known as 'Flash Harry'. There were three boys and two girls by his first marriage and they were called my step-brothers and step-sisters. My mother had the supervision of a couple of the youngest of them – 'cos the mother had gone away and left the lot of them. The others went to relatives in Hoxton. George and Dick were the two my mother looked after. They were ten, twenty years older than me. Dick was the eldest of the step-brothers. He worked round at St Luke's for Shoreditch Borough Council. I never knew him till about 1920, when we were down Gibraltar Gardens. But we became very friendly then. They came to my wedding and they were at my father's funeral. They came to my sister's parties, and on her outings and they were at my wedding – whenever there was any family business they were around. Dick and his wife Frances, they were like part of the family. One of the girls, Liza, came to visit us a lot when we lived in Queen's Buildings. She was pretty shrewd. She didn't live with us then but she had a lot to do with bringing up my sister Mighty. They were firm friends and when we were in Queen's Buildings she would come down to buy clothes off her. As a matter of fact she married the caretaker of the

Mission where we used to go to get our breakfast. His name was Buck. Her second marriage, she married a singer, Tom Davis. He used to earn quite a lot of money. He went to concerts, at the working men's clubs, but he'd get as much singing outside the pubs in Brick Lane – he could collect 5s round a crowd. But what he earned he'd drink: he didn't last long.

One of my father's sons made a name for himself. Harry Rich. He was older than me – they used to hang his old clothes on me and later on in years my father used to go off to touch him, he used to give my father clothes and money. He had a big house in Brixton, all the music hall people lived there. I can remember going over there as a kid, when my father was touching him for money. Rich was only his stage name. He was a famous comedian and he and a Jewish chap used to work together, called themselves Rich and Rich. It was a bit of a turn, like Morecambe and Wise. When he was in the Nichol he used to go to Father Jay's club and that's where he used to learn the tricks of the trade. He started off at Father Jay's – he had a great big club underneath Holy Trinity. He married a girl out of the Nichol – a big family in the greengrocery line – they had a stall and were a bit on the flash side.

In the 1900s he was getting £18 or £19 a week which was a lot of money for those days. At Christmas time he used to play Mother Goose in the pantomimes. He was in a clique with Marie Lloyd,[11] Alec Hurley,[12] and all that crowd – they used to use Johnny Cooney's pub in Hanbury Street.[13] They all met up when they were playing the local halls like the 'Paragon'[14] on Mile End Road, the 'Pavilion'[15] in Vallance Road or at the 'London' in Shoreditch High Street. I remember the browns coming up in the pub there. Marie Lloyd, she could knock them back. All the London ones kept together – Johnny Cooney used to have signed photos of Marie Lloyd, Harry Champion and the others hanging behind the bar. From Johnny Cooney's they used to go to the 'Seven Stars' in Brick Lane and the 'Flower Pot'. Marie Lloyd had her daughter with her, a nice girl. Harry Rich was a nice fellow, very free with his money. When he died in 1914 he was one of the top stars, earning £100 a week. But he killed himself with drink – whisky. He used to part with all his money. His son was called

Lenny – I named my own son after him. He went on at the 'Olympia' in Shoreditch, but when the war broke out he joined the navy and went down in one of the battleships that was sunk. Sarah, the daughter, she married in the show-business field and went to America where she founded a show-business family.[16]

3 Home life

Soon after her wedding my mother met with a street accident. A runaway milk cart knocked her down and seriously injured her hip. She was taken to Bart's hospital where the doctors wanted to amputate her leg but she refused. She remained a cripple for the rest of her life. No compensation.

Soon after this misfortune my father sold his pub and they went to live in Boundary Street. They rented a room at No. 4 Keeve's Buildings, where I was born.

Because she was a cripple, mother couldn't go out to work. Instead she used to take in work for Bryant and May's, making matchboxes.[1] Every day she made eight gross of matchboxes $2\frac{1}{2}d$ a gross, $1s$ $6d$ a day. She was fagged out when she had made her eight gross, poor old dear. Bryant and May supplied the labels and the pieces of cardboard. She had to buy the paste out of what she earned; she'd make a big saucepan full of it – flour and water and a bit of soap – a big basinful of it and a big brush to put it on. When she had finished the boxes she would throw them on the floor until they dried which took about a couple of hours. They weren't the safety boxes of today. There were strips of sandpaper to stick on. The work was paid daily but you didn't get paid until you took the matchboxes into the receiving depot in Bacon Street.[2] My sister Mighty used to do that for her, and sometimes father.

Mother suffered continuous pain from her diseased hip. How she was able to carry on the work of a housewife, bring up her children, and make a living, is something I can only guess at. Victorian husbands of the working class were very ignorant and brutal in their treatment of their women, and during my early years I often saw the results of a row upon my mother's face. At the age of thirty her hair was grey and she looked old and worn and sad. She was an object of pity to the ladies who dispensed charity.

Mother lost her first child when it was two years nine months. In October 1882 my sister Harriet was born – later known as Mighty. I was the next, in 1886, then came Mary and George. The room we lived in was very small – 12 foot by 10 foot – and it was the only room we had. There was an old kitchen table, about 18 inches wide but with two flaps. Mother used that for working most of the time. There was a fireplace with a small oven at the side and a flat top to boil a kettle of water on, or the fish (my father was fond of haddock and herrings, we lived mostly on that). We had these straw mattresses, horrible bloody things – two of them made a bed; they were about 6 to 8 inches wide. There were no gas fittings or anything like that. For light we had a sixpenny lamp which used to hang on the wall, a paraffin lamp which you renewed with a pint of paraffin every two days. There was an old chest of drawers made out of tobacco barrels. By the side of the stove was a large cupboard for the coke or coal – the bottom was used as shelves for storing food. If father was at home he would sit in the Windsor chair and the kids – that was me and Mighty – would squat on the floor, or sit on the orange boxes. Mother couldn't sit on them because of her bad hip – she had a Windsor chair too. Orange boxes were in great demand then. Cost nothing – they were only too glad to give 'em to you. The only thing the old man would do to them was pull the nails out at the end. They were useful for storage too, because they had two compartments, and if there were too many you could use them for firewood. My cot was an orange box when I was born – I heard mother speak about it.

The chief ornament in the room was a picture of Queen Victoria hanging over the mantlepiece. And there was a coloured holograph of the Crucifixion. The frame was worth more than the picture. It was vivid, with the red blood streaming down and all the rest of it. It made a great impression on me at the time, but I often wondered afterwards why it was there – my dear mother had no idea about religion.

Our home in Keeve's Buildings was very crowded. The floor being the drying ground for the matchboxes, there was no room to move about. Everything was done in a single room. The matchboxes had to be spread out to dry and you couldn't afford to tread on them. I used to be put in a box

outside the door, or sent into the street with my sister Mighty.
My mother monopolised the table with the paste for the
matchboxes – if you wanted to eat she might give you a
couple of slices of bread and you'd go out and eat it on the
doorstep – there was no room for you inside. Many a time I'd
have my food in the street. That was a common occurrence.
Immediately you got home from school at 4 o'clock you were
naturally a wee bit hungry. But mother would be busy at the
table, and the floor was covered with matchboxes. You
couldn't go in while the performance was going on, so directly
I got in she would say 'Get out'. Sometimes she would chuck
me something to eat – she would give me perhaps a couple of
slices of bread, put it on a saucer and say, 'Go on outside,' and
I'd eat it on the street.

One time my mother took to sack-making. It was terrific
hard work. Used to wear a palm, made of leather. Put a big
needle through – it wasn't cotton, more like tarry string.
They were coal sacks and my father used to take them into the
firm he was working for at the time, somewhere in Shoreditch. It might have been all right for a man, but it was a
terrible job for a woman – especially a half-nourished one.
Sometimes they'd come cut out and you'd have to sew them
up. But there were no sewing machines – had to do 'em all by
hand, and it was very strong canvas. My father would hire a
barrow to take them in.

If my mother didn't have money to spare, for food or for the
rent, she would send to aunt Liza's. That was only a couple of
minutes away, in Half Nichol Street. If my father was ever
short of anything, he'd go round to her and say, 'When the
kids come in, let 'em have something, I'll see you after.' And
my mother would say to my sister, 'There's no coal, Mighty,
go round and see aunt Liza and take the oil can.' My sister says,
'Where's the money?' 'That's all right, tell 'er I'll see 'er later.'
It was three farthings for a pint of oil – and you had to buy a
new pint every two days. Coal was a shilling a hundred-
weight, but we never had a hundredweight of bleeding coal –
we couldn't afford it. My sister would take the orange box
round with a rope to pull it back and she would get fourteen
pounds of coal. Sometimes Liza would bawl my father out and
tell him she wasn't getting paid: ''Ere Harry, where's the

money? The kids have been round today and I haven't had a penny.' But she never refused us.

The predominant idea was paying the rent. That was the first and last duty of everybody, to pay that rent, 'cos you knew how damned hard it was to find another room. So the rent came first. What came next was insurance, a penny a week for each of us. For funerals. One thing they dreaded was that the parish would take them. So they paid. Every child was paid for. Eventually there were four of us so it was fourpence a week. The funeral of my little brother – the one I never saw – cost thirty shillings. Thirty shillings. Thirty shillings was like a million pounds to them.

My mother was a forager. God bless her, she foraged all her life, that's how she brought us up. She got a good few bob off the people in the Mission.[3] She would tell the hard–luck story so as to get herself in. Well it was a true story. The whole thing was having your poverty well known to the people who had the giving of charity. They noticed that mother was a dead cripple, and that father was a loafer, and that she had children to bring up. And so she got on the list for any of the gifts which came from wealthy families, to distribute among the poor. They made out she was 'deserving'. They were always asking whether we was good children or not, and whether we were clean, and whether we went to Sunday School.

The whole idea was to get your nose in, so that they'd know the poverty you was living in. If you wasn't poor you had to look poor. The clothes you wore had to be something that didn't fit – so that they would give you some, so that you could get something that did fit you, for your Sunday best. But you had to be clean and that was easy – soap and water didn't cost a lot of money.

There were ladies who used to come round from the wealthy part of London. My mother used to be on the top of the list, being a cripple, that appealed to them. The children had to be all lined up for the ladies to look at, and if you were clean you got more money. The old man used to read the Riot Act to us, telling us how to behave and all the rest of it. The most vivid memory I have of the Nichol was the lectures the old man used to read out to us. 'They'll be round today,' he'd say, 'Now mind you behave yourself.'[4]

The teachers at the school used to communicate with these charitable people, and if you didn't go to school they'd put in a bad word for you. They'd say, 'No good encouraging them, they don't send their children to school; they don't intend them to get on well.' It was a good way of getting the children to go to school. My mother, poor old dear, didn't much care if we went to school or not. But she knew it was the law of the land, that she could be punished if we didn't go to school, and she liked to be well in with the Mission. There was always a few bob to be got from them, provided you were well behaved.

Mother used to pinch a lot of clothes at the church sales. Three or four of them used to go, it was a sort of holiday. Didn't cost anything because they used to pinch the clothes and they might get 5 or 10 bob out of it. They got to know when there was a good jumble sale on. A man would come round and say, 'Here, girl, I'll tell you where there's a lovely sale on.' They'd lift more than they paid for. My mother, Liz Steadman, and two or three other ladies from the Nichol, they'd get information about where the sales was and they'd get there. It cost nothing to go in. Mother used to go up with a bag. I've been up many times with her – my sister Mighty and I. Mother used to say, 'Those things are sent down to the churches to be *given* to us, not to make us pay for them.' She thought it was right to pinch them – the clothes were sent for the people, not so that the old rector could get another bottle of whisky. Mother would get a good big load and fetch them out and I'd put them in the sack outside. They used to sell 'em to the wardrobe dealers down the Lane – in the old clothes market. Men's clothing were very saleable, though good children's clothes were worth money too. They didn't trouble about women's clothes at all.

The Mission gave us our breakfast, and it also got us to school. Rochelle Street School was right next to where the Mission was, they practically adjoined each other – there was a passage which led from one to the other. If you went into the Mission for breakfast you were practically in the school – there was only one way out and that was into the school. You couldn't get away from it. They didn't tell you to go to school – they gave you a breakfast and then you were in. You went in there to have a jolly good breakfast and all the buildings being attached you thought it was all one establishment.

The day worked out like this: at seven o'clock you had to line up for breakfast and by the time you were finished it was half past eight and the old school gates were wide open to welcome you. It was a good breakfast. You got a great big bowl of milk – pure milk, it wasn't this prefabricated stuff you get today – because all round the Nichol there were cows. And you had as much bread as you could eat, dipped into the milk. The mission was an enormous place, with long tables and great big murals round the wall, pictures of the Crucifixion, feeding the five thousand and all that. We used to have a hymn and a 'Thank God from whom all mercies flow' and then they'd say, 'Now children don't be late for school.' That was the clever part of it, it was so arranged that by the time you'd finished eating the school gates would be open to welcome you. Everybody was contented because they'd had a good meal, and you did the lessons with a better spirit because you weren't hungry. It made the children more trusting.

You earned your ticket[5] for the breakfast by going to Sunday School, which was also held at the mission. If you missed Sunday School there would be no breakfast for a week. Mother had us up early for it, washed us and made us look clean. The business started about half past nine and then you'd go again in the afternoon. Mind it wasn't like in church. There weren't sermons or any of that business. We wasn't there long – about an hour and a half. If you kept 'em there too long then the children would be naughty. You didn't get no breakfast of a Sunday – you had that at home – but they gave you a ticket for the breakfasts next week. As you came out at the end, they gave you your ticket.

Everybody in the Nichol went to Sunday School. Morning and afternoon. Twice in the day. The hymns didn't make much impression on me, but the Bible did. 'Jesus loved little children.' They was all very kindly people, the teachers, men and women. When I look back I wonder why they done it – there must have been something in it for them. The thing that made a vivid impression on me was the great pictures that were round the wall – Christ feeding the five thousand and all the rest of it; coming up to Jerusalem for the Passover. They were not ordinary pictures but great big murals, half the size of the wall. Every summer there was a Sunday School outing to Chingford; they had a place for children there, at the 'Queen Elizabeth', where they gave you tea and buns.

Apart from breakfast, you had to trust to luck for your meals. It was no good going home for lunch when you came out of school, because your mother wouldn't have time to cook anything, even if there was anything to cook. You went to Father Jay's, by Holy Trinity. The old Irish housekeeper there, she used to make great big jam puddings. You left school at 12 noon and you had to be there quick because if you were a bit late they were all given away. Mostly it was the children who went to bread and milk breakfasts in the morning. You got a big lump of jam pudding, but if Father Jay was out of puddings you had to go and forage. At that time, many people had more empty days than dinner days.

If you had a penny or a halfpenny you could go into the shops. In Church Street, by the school, there was Butcher's the cake shop where you'd get a great big bag full of broken pieces of cake for about ½d or 1d. Sometimes, if you didn't have any money, he'd give 'em to you. Next door to that was a pudding shop where everything cost a penny. 'Got any cold pudding, guv'nor?' the children would say. You could also go to the fried fish shop and get a haporth of fish and a haporth of potatoes. You'd ask for a haporth and a haporth and you'd get a meal fit for a king. It was not far from the school, you could go round the corner, squat on the pavement and eat it. At the fish shop, there would always be a crowd of kids – those that had got a penny from their parents. If you didn't have the penny – that is if your mother hadn't give it to you – you had to use your brains. I would sometimes go to my aunt's shop. I'd say, 'I haven't got nothing for dinner, you know', and she'd say, 'There, go and get yourself a bit of fish and taters.' She was always a standby – she had money. Or we would wait outside the shop and cadge – 'Got a 'apenny governor, got a 'apenny for a bit of fish?' Outside all the eating shops you used to do that sort of thing. Outside the fish shop you'd say, 'Give us a tater, give us a tater, missus.' Some of them would call you a bad name – 'Get out, yer bleeding so and so.'

The chief meal was supper. My mother would put a big

stew on. She used to buy sheep's heads – every poor person used to buy sheep's heads and tripe, all that kind of thing, you never see them in the butcher's shops now. There was a stall in Brick Lane that used to sell them till eleven or twelve at night. Mother would say to Mighty, 'Run down the Lane and get us a sheep's 'ead.' Then there would be a halfpennyworth of pot herbs – turnips and onions and carrots and sometimes a bit of swede – and what you called 'bits' which they got from the butchers. Whatever it was went in it. I don't ever remember being hungry at night. And there'd be a big saucepan, with some left to hot up for the next day. The stews we had contained everything that was good for the body and it must have given us wonderful staying power. Because it's an extraordinary thing that four of us, brought up under the most awful conditions, are still alive today. And my mother and father lived till they were very old.

Our salvation when we had money was the pork butcher's, because there were so many luxuries there which you could get for a halfpenny or a penny. They sold them hot or cold, when they was cold they was cheaper. Sometimes, about 1 p.m., my sister would go round to where the German butcher was in Church Street and she would get a couple of cold faggots. Perhaps she'd take one up to mother and the other one – with a couple of bits of bread around it – we would eat as a sandwich. A faggot was better cold than hot because you could cut them up. They were glorious, the smell was worth it alone, it was as good as eating them. You'd cut them up and put in two slices of bread and eat them like a sandwich. My mother would sometimes make a stew of them, put in a few potatoes and onions and all the rest of it. It smelled lovely, gorgeous. Years later I walked all the way from Cardiff to London, and when I got home the first thing I did was to send for two cold faggots.

When I was young I didn't see much of father. He wasn't home much and when he was at home you tried to keep out of his way. He only lived for himself. I don't remember him at all when we were at Keeve's Buildings. I remember him more at Bacon Street, when we moved there. I used to go to Hughes's[6] in Brick Lane – and Jackson's[7] in Hare Street, to get him haddocks. He'd buy them when he came home with a few bob. Good haddocks, cost 3*d* a time. He'd give us the head and tail – there were three of us to feed.

Father was a bully. He used to knock my mother about, so I was told. But in later life he was terrified of me – he called me the 'big fellow'. This was when he had lost his strength.

Father was a well-dressed beau when my mother married him. He went with the 'Jack Simmons' racing mob, and was known as 'Flash Harry'. He had a pub too, and was quite well off. But by the time we lived in Keeve's Buildings he wasn't much good to anyone, even himself. He had a job for a time as potman at the 'Jane Shore' in Shoreditch High Street. Then he worked for a hat shop in Shoreditch[8] running errands, and waiting outside the shop.

Later he took up cabinet-making, making overmantels. It didn't require much wood. You bought the wood all cut and planed – you could buy it to the inch required. All you needed was glue to stick it together, you didn't need to plane it. The moulding you bought for 2*s* a hundred feet. It didn't require much skill. When they were finished they were only worth 10*s* each. He made them in my aunt Liza's house, corner of Church Street and Bethnal Green Road. They gave him the cellar. I used to go round from Bacon Street to take him a jug of tea, but I never gave him any other kind of help.

His eyesight was deteriorating and perhaps that was why he gave it up – or because he was too lazy to earn a living. After that he turned to cadging.

When we moved from Bacon Street to Queen's Buildings father turned a bit religious. Instead of hanging about the 'Jane Shore' he started hanging round the Lord Shaftesbury Mission[9] in Gosset Street which was only about 50 feet or yards from our home. He divided his time between doing something there and minding the baby at home – my younger brother George. The people in charge of the Mission gave him a ticket to go round the restaurants to see what they would give him in leavings. I used to go round with him. I used to carry the bag for him. It was a Saturday job which I detested – cadging for food: I would sooner have pinched it. I was never no good at cadging. It wasn't just scraps of food – might be half a leg of lamb or a ham-bone. It was food that was good to look at and good food for a hungry family. They were wealthy restaurants – there was a couple in Bishopsgate and another by Threadneedle Street. They took a pride in it. Probably told the vicar they were helping the poor people of the East End. Got them another niche in the book up in Heaven, if they got there. He became gradually dependent on the alms of the visiting ladies.

I had no respect for my father – no feeling at all. He wasn't really an invalid. It is true his sight became bad – in the end he went completely blind and got a pension – but that was only through neglect and ignorance. By the time I was nine or ten he had become a confirmed part of the casual poor, depending upon alms from the rich, and remained so for the rest of his life. A few years later we threw him out of the house and he went to live with a sister. He wasn't really religious. The only time I saw him say a prayer was just before he died in 1930. It was in St Clement's, Mile End Road. He was about eighty-five or eighty-six when he died. He'd been living apart from us for a long time.

The strange legacy that my father's family left to all their offspring was their political beliefs. They were all true-blue Conservatives, quite simple. The Conservatives were rich and powerful and they distributed large gifts to their supporters. The Radicals and Liberals were too poor, they were out to get something for themselves so what was the good of voting for them? These political beliefs have remained with all the off-spring of those uncles and aunts from the Nichol. With my family and my brother's and sister's family, I can say that all who hold our name vote Conservative.

I was brought up more by my sister than I was by my mother. My earliest recollection is of being taken round by her. Later she used to take me on errands and to look after me in the street. She and her friend Toffee were my chief play-mates in the Nichol – we used to get rid of our energy by going into empty houses. Then when she began selling lemons in the market she had a bit of money and she would buy me treats sometimes, and take me to the theatre. When my mother began drinking she kept the house together.

My sister Harriet was called Mighty by all the family. We never called her by any other name. She was born in 1882, when mother and father were living in Half Nichol Street.

(She was only ten months old when her younger brother, Henry Thomas, died, 3 August 1883.) When I was born in 1886 she was some four years old and no doubt this event was welcome because she had someone to fondle and love. My earliest recollection of her is wheeling and pulling me about in an old orange box, to and from the market. Mighty did all the errands for mother. Aunt Liza who had the corner shop would always be generous to Mighty when she came to the shop. She also did the shopping in Brick Lane. When she was about eleven she would do all the running about with the match-boxes, taking them to the Bryant and May depot in Bacon Street. My mother used to make eight gross a day and Mighty would carry them down. She would go down there regularly every afternoon, and after she came back she would go out shopping. Friday was what they called the double day – you had to have double the money to provide for both the Saturday and Sunday and that would mean two trips to Bacon Street with the matchboxes, one early in the morning and the other about 8 o'clock at night. When Mighty was a little child my father used to take the matchboxes in, but in the time I remember it was always Mighty who did this. She wrapped them up in an old sheet or blanket – there were a lot of them to take but they weren't too heavy to carry. You can say that three days a week Mighty, instead of going to school, would hop it. My mother came to some arrangement with the school inspector. They didn't want to summon her, my mother being a cripple, so they made this special arrangement – twice a week she went to school and the other days she had off.

The whole of the Nichol was a safe area for children to play in – there was no motor traffic about, no fast carts, only the milkman. Boundary Street was our main playground. The whole of one side was a blank wall, at the back of Jeremiah Rotherham's and the shops on Shoreditch High Street. If we went to Half Nichol Street or New Nichol Street, it would be, 'Get back to your own bloody turning.' But in Boundary Street we had the place to ourselves.

We used to play tramcars there. You would get as many as a dozen children at it, both boys and girls – my sister was part of the crew. Often there would be three or four different lots of children racing each other. The tramcars were made of barrows, two of them tied together. Barrows were very plentiful round the Nichol. You could pinch them. The kids used to say to each other, 'Got a barrow? There's one round the corner, why don't you go and get it?' Two of these barrows fixed together and you had a lovely tramcar. You jammed the two shafts together and tied 'em round with a bit of rope, and that was it. Or you tipped one barrow up and put the other one underneath it. They'd turn the barrows round so that the shafts faced each other, then jammed the two shafts together and tied 'em round with a bit of rope. Then all you had to do was to keep the front part of the barrow with its nose up clear of the roadway, and with the children pushing behind you could get up quite a speed, with one fellow sitting in the middle as the driver or the conductor.

It was playing tramcars that I had my accident. There must have been seven or eight of us at the time, quite easily. I was behind pushing. They wanted to get rid of me – I must have been one of the villains trying to tip the lot up, which was one of the things that used to happen. I suppose I must have been putting my weight on the back, trying to tip the lot up.

Anyway I run away from the barrow and crashed right into the unloading bay, where they were taking goods into Jeremiah Rotherham's. There was a small crane there, swinging a barrel of butter. It swung out and gave me a crack on the head and down I went. A man carried me up to the hospital and that's all I can remember. I was six at the time, and they said I might die of it when I was twenty-one. My father, who was a schemer, got a solicitor to start an action and I was awarded a small sum of compensation – they'd had the red flag flying in front of the van, to warn pedestrians, which is why the damages were so small.

A man named White Nob (his real name was Daniels) used to give the children rides in Boundary Street. He had a roundabout, all gaily painted, with little flags flying. There were about six seats. You'd get five minutes for a halfpenny a time. There were little chairs and he used to spin it round himself – he didn't have no mechanical controls. A donkey would pull it along when he took it to the fairs, but it didn't do anything else. He'd put the kids on – or the mothers – and then he'd spin it round. 'Course, he didn't charge a halfpenny a time when he went over Hampstead Heath, he charged twopence or threepence then. He'd put it up on Boundary Street because there was no traffic to interfere with him.

Later on, when he moved to Gibraltar Gardens, I got to know him better. He lived at the bottom house and walked the donkey through to the back. He was a peculiar character, but he was liked by the children. I've seen him pick a child up and put it on when he found that the mother hadn't any money. He was a character on his own, he was. I think he was a Romany. His wife was a snuff-taker, she didn't go out with him.

The other playgrounds weren't as quiet as Boundary Street. You had the grounds at St Leonard's Church, Shoreditch, the church yard – you could roam about there. But they used to usher us out. You'd get the chap who was in charge after you. Then there were the timber yards. You could play at see-saw there, but it was a bit risky, a child would come off at the top – and you were always being shooed away.

Then there were the watchmen's fires. You could always find a fire where they were digging up, and you'd see a crowd of kids round, wherever there was a fire. They'd start an old song, a very old song. Kids were always singing and perhaps the watchman would say, if he was one of the kinder blokes, 'Come on, kids, give us a song.'

Then there were the 'backs'. They were at the back of some workshops. Princes Court was at one end, Satchwell Rents at the other. They was a good size, as big as a street, easy. It was an old burial ground, never been built on, not even today. They used to say it was the burial ground for the plague – great pits where they bunged the bodies in. On Guy Fawkes night the children used to make a bonfire there. They'd go to Spitalfields Market and get as much wood as they liked – firewood, old orange boxes, all that sort of thing. They'd pile it all up, and add some old rags. The police never used to interfere.

There was another 'backs' further down Brick Lane, just round the back of Bacon Street. It was entirely enclosed by houses all round. This 'backs' lay in the middle. But there was a little passage where the children used to get through to play. When the fairs wasn't there the kids would be in there playing. But it was a pretty dangerous place because there were a lot of bricks lying around and the kids would aim them at each other.

The fairs used to come there for winter, towards the end of September after they'd done their tour of the country. They settled down in the 'backs' for the winter. There'd be about fifty caravans there when the dark nights drew in. Really it was like a parking place for them. They'd start coming about the end of October, that's when their season finished. The caravans of years ago were one-horse caravans, and usually they had a dog tied underneath when it was on the road. They always made a fire outside when they camped there. They had none of these up-to-date caravans that you see today. It was right in the centre of a row of houses, this enormous gap, all ruins. A lot of the kip-house wallahs – elderly ragged men – would come to sit around the fire: a little bit of warmth was like a good meal to them. There was a roundabout, coconut-shies, roll down the penny and all that sort of thing.

When they started to pull down the Nichol there were plenty of places to play. Empty buildings. Me and my sister and her friend Toffee we used to go to all the empty houses.

There were hundreds of them in the first stage of being demolished. Some people left their things behind – you'd break
everything. The girls were looking for something they could
take home. The boys, they would break the windows. My
sister would get cups and saucers and give them a good wash.
Our turning, Boundary Street, was the last turning the developers left. And we played in the ruins – about 1901 there
was a vast area of desolation where the Bandstand and Calvert
Street are today. That was our ideal playground.

There was no life in Boundary Street, where we lived. The
nearest place for amusements was Shoreditch High Street,
which ran down the west of the Nichol. From 12 o'clock to 2
o'clock each day there was vast crowds there for the market.
And in the evening there were the penny shows and eel-and-
pie shops. On one side there was big stores, some were equal
to Selfridges, very big stores, where the girls used to live in,
like they were in an orphanage. On the other side there were
the market stalls. A lot of them were what we call 'fly
pitchers' – they didn't have a regular stand but found a vacant
place and put up their show for a time. There was plenty of
fruit stalls there where you could get an apple or something
like that. We used to go in twos and threes – not more because
people would notice you. Billy Warner and Wally Shepherd
were always at it – they hopped off school regular, as a matter
of fact they couldn't bloody read or write, either of them,
when they reached school-leaving age. One would go in front
and ask, 'How much is oranges?' while the others would get
round the back and pinch them. Or we'd pick up fruit when
the stalls had packed up.

All along there were the shows, the penny shows. Probably
my sister would take me along while I was young. Every shop
that went empty in Shoreditch High Street had a little show in
it. There'd be posters outside – my sister used to read them to
me. 'Come and see the greatest marvel in the world, a donkey
with its head where its tail ought to be.' You'd see people
coming out of them, some laughing, some with a bit of a
naughty look on their face, and you'd want to go in and see
what was there. And when you got in all you would see was a
donkey with its face turned into the door and its tail in the
feeding box. There was the great head-hunters of Borneo:

'Come and see the War Dance', 'Come and see the scalps'. And there was the magic lantern business, all in the pitch dark – they'd put slides in 'em. Another show we had was the india-rubber lady – she pulled her skin off and pulled it over her head – I never found out how they done that. And there was the Two-Headed Lady. My sister would say, 'Let the little baby in,' and they'd let me go in.

We went to Hoxton market as well – Billy Warner and me. I had an aunt lived down one of the streets there, though I never found out where she lived. Billy Warner would never go to school – he'd go scrounging instead. Food was a very great attraction to him. There was always droves of kids in Hoxton market – lots of kids from the Nichol went there. There was a great Mission there,[1] where the children went. I remember one Christmas I went to see my half-sister, she lived in Brunswick Square nearby – about 10 o'clock on Christmas morning. The whole area was covered with big pork pies – the kids took a couple of bites at them and threw them away. They'd been to a Christmas party at the Mission and among the things they gave them coming out was a big pork pie and oranges and apples. At that period children were really hungry, but they'd stuffed themselves so much at the party that they could afford to throw the stuff away.

When I was very young they say I was always reported for being lost. I can remember going into the Kingsland Road police station.[2] They used to make a fuss of you there. They knew that you was hungry. And so they'd give you a slice of bread and jam. Sometimes the policeman would carry you, sometimes he would walk you back home. When I got lost my mother would say, 'Mighty, go and fetch him, he's in the police station.' It wasn't far away – across Austin Street, through Union Street and there you are. The inspector used to say, 'Tell your mother, I'm not having him in here no more!'

When you got lost there was always someone who would say 'Where do you live?' That would start two or three of them getting round to help. Then a policeman would take you home – he'd be glad enough to get the time off, instead of getting someone in the Nick for drinking, which was a very much harder job. It wasn't bad waiting in the police station, they usually had a couple of toys, that was a regular thing.

Billy Warner and Wally Shepherd were the two pals I was always with. We was always up to bloody mischief. In later life, they both got knocked out in the First World War.

Billy Warner was a Didicai, a gipsy that had settled down. His father and his uncle used to play the 'Crown and Anchor', going about with the boards. He lived in Half Nichol Street. Wally Shepherd lived in the same place as myself, Keeve's Buildings. We were quite pally. Billy Warner went to Father Jay's.[3] That's where he learnt to box. He would have made a good boxer but he was killed in the war. He looked a gypsy. All his people looked gypsy. They was on the dirty side if you know what I mean. The other brother worked in Spitalfields Market all his life; the father was always in and out of prison. He had another brother who was also a boxer, he lived to quite a good old age.

Once we got lost by Tower Bridge. Wally Shepherd said to me, 'I bet you I'll get onto the top of the bridge when its goin' up!' I said to him, 'Well, we'll see.' But he never got to the top – he said the police used to come running to pull him down. 'If we see you round here again, we'll take you inside.' The first time we went to Tower Bridge we got lost. I was about seven or eight at the time. Someone must have told a City policeman and he lumbered the two of us somewhere up Aldgate way. They wanted to know why we weren't at school. Wally Shepherd came out with it at once. 'My sister's got measles,' he says. 'Me mother and father's got measles, and we can't go to school.' If you had measles you were supposed to be isolated.

We often used to go to Tower Hill. You didn't pay nothing. Outside they were all hollering and hooting – there'd be a crowd gathered round the speakers. There was a villainous trick we played – a bloody dangerous trick – pinning a sheet of paper on to a bloke's back and setting light to it. They had plenty of mischief in them, Wally and Billy.

There was two places where you could go bathing in summer. Victoria Park,[4] where there was a great big proper place – the Bathing Lake. There wasn't anyone in charge to safeguard life or anything, but you very rarely got anyone drowned there, because there were a lot of grown-ups around. You didn't pay anything but it was a long way away.

The other place for bathing was the canal, which is where we went from the Nichol. The nearest canal to the Nichol was the Regent's Canal at Haggerston, opposite the hospital in Kingsland Road – what we used to call the 'Cut'. I was about eight when I first started going there. When I was eleven I got slung in.

The canal was a penny ride on the tramcar, but it was a straight run from the Nichol, all the way up the Kingsland Road, so the way to get there was to climb up on the tailboard of a cart. If it was a van the driver couldn't see you. With an open cart he was always liable to say 'Get off there', but he's got to stop to get you off and if he's always stopping he won't keep to his timetable, so sometimes they didn't trouble. Some would let you be, others would hit out with the whip. It was a straight run from Shoreditch, but it might take three or four changes of cart before you got there. Sometimes you'd get a lift half the way and walk the rest.

At Kingsland Road you could get over the wall and go down the side of the towing path. In the summer a lot of kids would go bathing there. They went in as they were born – taking all their clothes off. The police didn't stop it – perhaps they thought it would give them a good wash. It was forbidden – there were notices saying it was Private Property – but they never took no notice of you. Victoria Park was free, but the children preferred the canal. Children are like that. If they can go somewhere for nothing, they'll go to the place that's harder, where there's that wee bit of danger. At Kingsland Road they were breaking the law – but on a hot summer's day there was droves of children there, all along the banks at Haggerston.

I nearly lost my life over that canal. There was nobody to protect a child from danger, and children at that period were very rough in their ways. There'd be quite a pressure for a bigger boy to throw a smaller boy in the deep part. That was what happened to me. The boy who did it was far superior to me in strength. It was only a few yards from the road and somebody dived in and got me out. I was nearly at the end. The third time I was going down he pulled me out and they tipped me upside down in the pub (there was a pub just opposite). Then the stretcher came and they took me to St

Leonard's Hospital. I was in there a week, they say, unconscious. Bassy Lynch was the one that pushed me in. He was a
bit of a villain – lived in Keeve's Buildings or Bacon Street. It
was just before I went into Dr Barnardo's. He was a bit of a
villain and he pushed me in. He died in the canal himself, later
on, he got drowned there.

The only older person who took me out was my sister. I
never been out with my father in all me life. He never took me
out anywhere. He was a man that lived for himself alone. We
never had no contact with him whatsoever and he didn't
care at all. And there was thousands like him about, you
know. I never knew my mother go out – she couldn't walk
much.

When I was quite young, about six or seven, Mighty started
taking me to the old Britannia in Hoxton Street.[5] Once a week
she took me, 'cos they changed the programme every week.
Tuesday, always Tuesday. Most people go on a Monday, but
she went always on Tuesday, and I'll tell you why. Tuesday
was market day in Roman Road, so she'd have the stuff down
there and she'd do pretty well. So she was able to have an extra
shilling or so. They used to come round with cakes in the
gallery, penny and halfpenny cakes or oranges, and she used to
buy me 'em – you know, them round hard cakes. I forget
what they called them. And she used to go with a bag-load of
fruit – not monkey nuts nor nothing like that – apples and
oranges. Good stuff. It was one perpetual feast all the night. It
cost threepence to get into the gallery. Sometimes there used
to be my sister, her friends and me. I was the male one
amongst them, and I think they used to smuggle me in between them. They never went up the 'Standard' as far as I
remember, always the 'Brit'. They had a better class of play at
the 'Standard', but it wasn't so near as the 'Brit'.

It was quite a big place, the 'Brit'. And it was a place which
catered and provided good entertainment for the people, un-
educated people, who was glad to be relieved of the monotony
of being in the same place every day for twenty-four hours a
day. It started about 7 o'clock, right up to about 11 o'clock at
night. It used to be 12 o'clock sometimes. They only had the
one play. I can remember there used to be the tragedies of
G. R. Sims[6] and the Melville Brothers.[7] I've got them all

mixed up in my mind – 'The Girl that Took the Wrong
Turning', 'The . . . Woman . . . in London', 'Scotland
Yard'[8] and all that sort of thing – vivid melodramas. It was all
very excitable. And we used to hoot and boo, and one thing
and another. And wait outside for the villain to come out.
There was plenty of fighting – had to be plenty of villains in it.
Otherwise it didn't go down. Well, it was all real life to me,
y'know: it was an education in itself – gave you an idea of how
the other half lived.[9]

They was a good lot of actors in it – good class actors. Mrs.
Lane, she looked like the Queen Victoria to me, and dressed in
the same way with the high-backed dress. Louisa Peach was
always the heroine. I've often tried, thinking about old times,
to picture her. To me today she looks like one of them old
faded has-beens what you see round Streatham, you know,
retired and living on small means. The hero was Algernon
somebody,[10] and the villain's name was Steadman, W. G.
Steadman. He was a dark man, I don't know why all villains
had to be dark. And a moustache, nice moustache and bushy
eyebrows, sort of thing – whether they was false I don't
know. He used to wear a silk hat, a long frock coat, you know,
and he used to have a walking stick or an umbrella. That was in
case anybody set about him outside. Used to walk right down
Hoxton Street. And he used to get on a tramcar to take him up
to Bloomsbury. They was sort of middle-class people, well-
educated people but they wasn't in the Shakespearian class,
you know.

When the play was over Mighty used to lumber me round
the back to watch 'em come out. My sister would follow them
to where they got a tramcar or a bus to take them home – try
to get near them and touch their clothes. The actors and
actresses used to love it. People from the audience would
follow them down the road. I've seen 'em offer 'em a drink,
you know – 'Have a drink, my dear, do you good after all that
hard work – bloody scoundrel, knocking you about like he
did.' They would talk as if it had actually happened. 'Oh, I'm
so glad you're alive. I though you was dead.' And the men
used to say to the villain, you know: 'Why didn't you 'it 'im on
the head with a 'ammer?'[11]

We had another place round in Pitfield Street, about five

minutes away from the 'Brit' – a music hall called the 'Variety'.[12] It was so small that you could see all the paint on the actors' faces, they was right up close to you. The children could call them names, 'Look at him with the black eye.' 'Look at all the red round his mouth.' For anybody who wanted a lark the 'Variety' was better than the 'Brit'. The children used to do as they liked there. Some of them never even used to pay. They used to dodge the pay-desk, just like bloody monkeys.

Sometimes my sister used to take me to the 'Cambridge' music hall in Commercial Street, Spitalfields – perhaps because the play at the 'Brit' had already been on before. But the 'Cambridge' wasn't a favourite – it was too near the Nick – the Commercial Street Police Station; just across the road, and you was in.

Of all places of amusement, the 'Foresters' in Cambridge Heath was the best.[13] They used to have one performance on a Monday, because the costermongers had the day's holiday on a Monday and they used to go up there with bags of specs. And directly anybody come on that was not good, they used to pelt the life out of them, you know. Sometimes they didn't give the man a chance; if the first few minutes didn't go off good, whallop! I didn't start going there till I was about fifteen.

5 Totting and busking

When I was about six or seven years of age, I used to go to Spitalfields market and collect waste potatoes. A lot of us kids would go together, through the Wheler Street arch. When you came home from school mother would say, 'Go and see if you can get some potatoes. Take that sack and I don't want any specky ones.' Or a child would say, 'I'm going over the market, are you coming?' They'd take a little barrow; the father might make 'em one – an orange box with a couple of pram wheels underneath to help it along. It made an ideal cart. That was one of the chief things for a boy, years ago, to have a cart. The market porters were friendly – they would tip the sack of potatoes out, knowing the kids would come over. There were some good cockneys up at the market, when they saw us they would shout, 'Here's the kids, come over 'ere.' They were real market people – they knew the kids was hungry. You might get half a bag of potatoes, even tomatoes, but potatoes were more valuable than tomatoes because they were something you could cook easy. When you got home you'd sort them out. You'd run home and shout, ' 'ere you are mother.'

The market was also good for firewood. There were heaps of old orange boxes all piled up. You'd tie them together and drag them home, tied together by a lump of string. An orange box would sell for ½d or even a penny a bundle, selling it around the houses as firewood. Houses always had a copper. People had to do their own washing at home – you had to boil the clothes to really get the dirt out of them. Every house had a copper.

You could also get firewood from the saw-mills, where the lumps of wood came off the plane. The girls would go round the saw-mills – they wouldn't let the boys in there. The mothers would say, 'You let the girls go over there.' The girls went by themselves and the boys went by themselves.

Boys also used to go down to get coke from the Haggerston gasworks. It was in Great Cambridge Street, a decent way away. They had to line up there very early, about 7 or 8 o'clock in the morning. It was cheap fuel and you would carry it away on carts. Elderly people would buy it off you. An old woman would say, 'Oh I wish you'd go and get me some coke – I'll tell you what I'll do, I'll give you 3*d* if you will bring me a sack.' A boy would do anything for 3*d*. Some people didn't have as much as threepence, so they'd give a penny or a penny halfpenny.

Saw-mills where they cut the wood up and planed it were everywhere. If you was a regular, you'd get lovely lumps of hardwood, what they cut off for the cabinet-makers' planks. That was mostly for the fire of a night-time, to keep the fire going. You put them on the fire and then banked them up with coal dust – you didn't want them to burn, just to heat. The chips were good for burning under coppers. It would save a lot of money on coal. They didn't charge anything, they was only too glad you had come to take it away, but they insisted you couldn't select – you had to take whatever they said. Put it in sacks and wheel it home on a cart. These lumps of wood from the saw-mills were very saleable.

It was only the saw-mills you went to. You couldn't get much wood from the cabinet-makers – they used all the spare wood they had to keep the fire burning. Coopers were no good for wood, because the barrels wasn't good burning material – they'd been soaked with one thing and another. And another thing was, if they were oil barrels, they were bloody dangerous – they would set the chimneys alight.

Children would steal coal from the coal vans. It was some-thing which made a mother happy, when a child brought something home: instead of a bashing they'd get an extra lump of pudding at dinner. Thieving coal was a frequent occurrence in the Nichol and when the coalman came round he had a big boy sitting on the back of the van to keep an eye on it, and bully the children away. But many of them came round alone. If somebody on the first floor said, 'Bring me a bag of coal', the coalman would have to go up and that left the van at the mercy of the street urchins. Anyway one who came along could help himself. It was best to do it when the cart was stationary, when the back of the van was down. The coalman wasn't worried.

I never knew anybody charged with stealing coal, only from shops where they kept it outside – like coal shops. The oil shop Arthur Morrison talks about in *Child of the Jago*, they had coal outside. I have just a faint remembrance of that shop, it was off Church Street on the corner of Club Row,[1] 'cos I often went there to get a bag of coal, or paraffin oil or something like that for my mother. They had to be small bags, 7 lbs or 14 lbs, otherwise you'd have needed some sort of transport to carry 'em. If a shopkeeper found a boy taking coal, he wouldn't charge him or give him over to custody even if he knew his name, it would cause more trouble than the coal was worth. And if the policeman caught him, he wouldn't charge him, he'd say, 'I'd sooner lose the bag of coal than cause trouble.'

Food was one of the chief items that boys of that kind would go after, 'cos it was easily saleable to the small corner shops. A small box of margarine or butter was saleable, and it was something that a boy could easily carry. They'd get that from a van. It was quite easy: all they had to do was lift the tailboard down and take it. Jeremiah Rotherham's, the big provision people, they used to have vans loaded up with provisions. They had a shed along there, at the top part of Boundary Street, where there used to be about eight or nine vans being loaded. Well, them vans, the children used to watch 'em as if they contained a treasure. It was quite easy for a boy to lift a small box of butter, or eggs, or even one of the small rolls of cheese. That was very frequent; it got so bad that the school authorities started complaining about the number of boys it kept away. I remember my mother talking about it and saying they shouldn't be allowed to have a place like that down there.

Pinching things from vans was easy.[2] They'd go at a very slow pace, 8 to 10 miles an hour, and a lot of goods was taken by barrows; the man would pull the barrow along and a boy could go behind and take a parcel off. There were always parcels being sent from one firm to another. There was a draper's at the top, where we used to live in Gibraltar Gardens,[3] it was a wholesale place, and they used to send out a tremendous amount of stuff. An old fella used to pull the barrow and of course it was unprotected entirely and it was quite easy for a child to walk behind and take a parcel. They wasn't tied down, they wasn't that heavy – it was quite easy for even a small child to take them. Boys of fourteen or even less than that were employed to take goods around like that, a cheap way of transit, you see. I've seen boys of that age taking a barrow to cattle market with a store-keeper's goods on it, through the back streets of Hoxton, well it was quite easy for a boy to lift one or two parcels off. They was always three or four boys together and I would give 'em a hand and it was quite easy, if it was an elderly person pulling the barrow, to take three or four parcels, one at a time.

A lot of that used to go on in Sclater Street. It was a road that was frequently used. Not being a main road the drivers avoided a lot of traffic and it was a quicker way to get to the top of Cambridge Heath – to Whitechapel and Roman Road. The railway vans used to go that way, and some of them never had van guards. If you were to read the evidence of the Royal Commission [Royal Commission on the Metropolitan Police, 1906] there was a large number of Bethnal Green tradespeople who went to the Commission about the number of times they'd seen van-dragging take place even by young boys.[4] That was the evidence given at the opening of the Royal Commission. Sclater Street was quiet. There wasn't any fear of accidents happening. The vans went along there very slowly, and there was a large number of coffee shops and dining rooms where they could stop and have a meal. Only the railway van with expensive transport in would have a van guard, mostly they was supposed to keep an eye on them from the windows of the dining rooms. The lads had no fear of detection – there wasn't any police out that way, they were in the main road. Sugar came in big cases, at least a hundred-weight – it wanted some lifting, but if you made a hole in them you could scoop the sugar from the road. They'd leave a trail of sugar till somebody drew the attention to it.

Some of the boys went thieving off the Jews. There was a Jews' market right under Brick Lane arch, where the 'Greeners' had their stalls. When the market filled up mischievous boys would grab things from the stalls. And they would steal from the Jewish women. It was a common practice when a woman would walk past with expensive combs in their hair, they never wore a hat, but they had their wig on.

They grabbed the comb out of the hair and sometimes they pulled the wig off with it and run away with it.

Kids always had a sharp pen-knife with them, and they'd work those shops that left things outside. They'd nick anything that was small – little kids' rubber shoes, they was about 1s a pair; a pair of boots from outside the shop, used to have 'em hanging on a string; little girls' things like socks. The girls didn't carry penknives, but the boys always carried them, very handy with fruit to cut the bad part of it. Children would also steal from the oil shops. They'd go in and say, 'A pint of paraffin oil.' The man had to go out the back, 'cos they were duty bound to keep the oil right out the back as a safeguard, and while he was off, out went Charlie with whatever he'd pinched – a scrubbing brush, a broom head, all that kind of thing, even a small saucepan or a pail. Very saleable stuff – those things were always useful at home.

From the stalls they'd take apples and all that kind of thing. They'd have to be very careful, directly the enemy appeared on the front. Mrs Barrington, she had the first fruit stall right opposite St Leonard's and she sold good fruit. But she lived round in Virginia Road, close to the Nichol, and her couple of sons would chase 'em out of it. You could only get behind her stall, you couldn't get in front, because the apples were piled on top of each other to make a nice show. They served you from the back, like Brussels sprouts, beautiful ones in front and all the crap behind. Well, they'd get in a position behind. They'd concentrate on peas and that, so that they could put 'em in their pockets easy. If they were caught they would tell the biggest pack of bloody lies – 'My mum bought these for me yesterday and told me to take them back to the shop.' And the public would all take the kids' part. All them little tricks, children is remarkable how quick they learn all the things they shouldn't know, especially cockney kids, they are very sharp. Quick-witted enough to have excuses for anything.

There was a place in Shoreditch that was as bad as the Nichol. It was called Norfolk Gardens,[5] and ran out into the Curtain Road, opposite Jeremiah Rotherham's. Those Gardens was very, very old, 'cos Shakespeare had the first theatre there.[6] Over there you'd see a battle royal between the two groups of kids, one from Norfolk Gardens and one from the

Nichol. The Garden kids went along Shoreditch High Street, nicking the same as us. Norfolk Gardens finished up with the stalls by the 'Standard' theatre. They never touched the book stalls, they was no good to them y'see, or the jellied eel stalls – they were after what they could sell quick. Socks, that kind of thing. The boys of the older age group went on the rampage down the Bethnal Green Road, thieving – it was a living for 'em – those that never went to school, or anything like that.

The children of the Nichol were far superior to a normal child coming of a respectable family. The poverty had sharpened their wits. When Dickens described Oliver Twist, he didn't describe him properly. Oliver Twist could never have existed because he wasn't able to help himself. But a child that can move about and is a reasonable age, say eight or nine, can survive because it's got the instinct to survive – he'll thieve, or he'll beg off passers-by. You could get a few rags out of the dustbins and take them to Green's the dealers – you'd get a copper or two like that.

Begging was a common thing. What we used to do was nothing but begging: 'Carry your bag, sir?', 'Carry your bag, Madam?', 'Oh, kind lady, let me carry your bag for you'. And she'd give you 3d to get rid of you, at Liverpool Street. If you saw a child begging in Liverpool Street it was something you'd have to admire for its dexterity – it was clever the way they played on a human being. If they said, 'Go away,' he'd say, 'You wouldn't say that, Madam, to a starving child, would you?' They wouldn't leave 'em, they'd have their palm out. 'I haven't got anywhere to sleep tonight, would you like to see me sleep on a cold winter's night out on the street?' The writers of that period, even Dickens, never made proper use of children – how clever children are. Some children are born actors, there's no argument about it, they can cry at will. All they had to do was see someone well-dressed coming along and they'd turn the tap on: 'I've had nothing to eat all day.' The bloke would give a tanner to get rid of 'em, in case people come along and think it's one of his own kids. Mind you, they were judges of character. They knew the right 'uns from the wrong 'uns and they picked the one that looked a real, right mug. In Shoreditch High Street they'd wait for the posh ones to go in the shops on the other side: 'I'm lost and I've had nothing to eat all day.'

During the Guy Fawkes season all the kids would hang about the streets. The season started in October – it lasted nearly two months. Me and my sister and her friend Toffee – we used to go out together. No good around the Nichol, couldn't get nothing round the Nichol – you had to go out to Shoreditch High Street. You gradually walked up till you got to Liverpool Street which was the Mecca of all things wealthy. Some of the kids didn't even have a Guy, but people would give to a child, and even in those times you could get a lot of money.

Liverpool Street Station was the best place to beg, 'cos you got all the country people coming up, frightened of what they might meet. It was only five minutes from the Nichol. My sister Mighty, she used to take me up there, when I was about seven or eight. When I was about twelve years of age – come out from Dr Barnardo's – I used to go there carrying luggage. You didn't carry it far – inside the station that's all. You might wait a little way out. She'd get off a bus, or out of a hansom cab or something, and you'd say, 'I'll carry your bag, Madam.' And you'd pick it up, carry it in there and you'd get 3d or 6d, usually a threepenny bit – but that was a lot of money, easy earnt. You didn't give them a chance to say no.

The police were very strict on children round the station – the railway police would tell you to clear out. But nobody interfered with you in the pubs. When I was about twelve I used to go round the pubs selling – all the pubs on Bishops-gate, there were twenty-two of them. I worked them with my toys. I used to do very well at 'Dirty Dick's' because the Spitalfields porters were good with their pennies. Mostly I sold German toys. You could buy them in Houndsditch and sell them for a penny.

Some children went busking at the theatres. Any song that was popular. Well I tell you what was favourite, and that was singing hymns – what they learned in the Ragged School Mission – 'Onward Christian Soldiers' – you'd get the queues keeping time. People liked to listen to a good hymn, a good tune y'know. When the Boer War was on it was all them old war songs like 'Tommy Atkins', 'Rule Britannia' – they sung all them songs. They wouldn't give a lot, a penny would be a lot – they'd throw it in the hat. There might be three kids go out together, two collecting and one singing. The 'Standard' in Norton Folgate was the best theatre for that.

You'd get a better class of people than at the 'Brit'. There was what you call the poor working class, those that never worked, the casual unemployed, they went to the 'Brit'. But at the 'Standard' you had the respectable poor – doorkeeper, stallkeeper or one of them jobs on the City Corporation, anything that put you a step higher up the ladder than the casual poor. They were a wee bit higher and they knew it. The copper was in their pocket to give. Poor people are the best givers in the world, you know. The poorer you are, the more generous you are.

At the 'Standard' the queue would stretch right round from Norton Folgate into Great Eastern Street. There was a little short turning in Great Eastern Street where the crowd lined up for the gallery, and the kids used to do their little acrobatic tricks there. Somersaults and jumping over each other, leap frog – anything to attract attention. Some of them done nothing, they just simply went and started cadging along the queue – telling tales with a cap in hand: 'I ain't had nothing to eat', 'Mummy and Dad's in prison or the workhouse and we're all on our own, and my little sister's over there, she's crying.' This was a part of everyday life, in some cases it was true.

A performance started at 7 p.m. – the kids were up there performing, turning cartwheels while the crowds was waiting to go in. The kids used to go over and over in somersaults, put the hat down in the middle. You know you can't be done if you don't ask – the police never used to take no notice, 'cos the police station then was in Kingsland Road, not Old Street. It was an elementary way of getting round the law, 'cos if you're giving value for money you're not begging – that's why the buskers do all that kind of nonsense.

Children would also go selling at the theatres. At the 'Britannia' the only thing they sold was the oranges and cakes – what they could eat in there. Nuts, the management used to ruck about, the shells being on the floor and all that. The cakes came from Dean's[7] – it was a big confectioners, a wholesale place in Brick Lane. They used to sell 'em with a basket round the queue, halfpenny a time. They were round cakes, hard as iron. In Scotland, they call them oat cakes.

Another thing they sold up at the 'Brit' was 'Brompton's Cough Tablets'. They also used to go round the pub selling them. The winter months in London was full of smoke, fog – people had the English complaint, bronchitis, wholesale, coughing all the time. Brompton's tablets was the one that dealt with all chest complaints. They was good, there was twenty-four of these little tablets in a packet. They cost 8d a dozen and you sold them at a penny a packet, so you earned 4d out of every shilling. Brompton's were a good seller, but you had to have capital to buy them. The kids used to get 'em wholesale from a shop the top of Bethnal Green Road there, just by the police station.[8]

Another thing they sold outside was trotters. 'Penny each, trotters.' The children bought them from the stall – there was an old girl who stood outside the pub selling them, and they'd go round to the 'Brit' – 'Here's your trotters, ladies, two for 1½d, have that big one for a penny.' They'd carry 'em round on a tray, perhaps some of 'em had a string round their neck like when they had the basket with the oranges. That was the best seller, along with the Brompton's Cough Cure.

Oranges they used to sell, boys and girls used to sell 'em. I knew a woman used to employ 'em up there – give 'em a hundred and they'd be two or three a penny. They used to earn out of 'em. Some of 'em used to get specks over the market and then go back to the woman and say: 'They wouldn't buy 'em, look they're specks.' I don't say they done it regular, but it was a little side business. They'd be about nine or ten. Mrs Wilson, who employed a lot of 'em, used to live down the Gardens. She used to do well. She had four or five of them at it, mostly at the 'Cambridge' music hall. She was a Norfolk woman; she lost her husband in the South African war; she had a pension; she was a cunning cow she was.

The 'Pavilion' at Whitechapel, they used to sell there and all – apples and oranges mainly. Some were employed to do it and some of them went on their own; some of them were embryo shopkeepers.

It was quite exhilarating to see the kids earning money. A lot of 'em being choir kids, they could speak quite all right.

A child who could carry a brush and a pail could always earn money by sweeping the pavement, for say a doctor. 'Let's go round to the doctor's', they would say. They'd sweep the pavements there for the patients to come in. The boys would go round to the posher parts of town, or up the upper part of Bethnal Green, specially round Victoria Park Square, where there were some very nice houses. They'd play truant from school, it was always an excuse: 'Why weren't you at school yesterday?' 'Well sir, I went and swept the old lady's pathway,' and it'd be considered a genuine excuse. It was the same type as what you see today who go up to Liverpool Street on Guy Fawkes day. They used to be at least four or five of 'em together, they'd say: 'You do that one Jimmy and I'll do this one.' It's the same thing as singing carols in the Christmas time. Up Barnet Grove, along Bethnal Green, by the Post Office, all private houses, with all decent, respectable people there, they'd always be prepared to give a child a copper or two, 'cos even at that time a halfpenny was money. So there was always children especially the rough 'uns who wanted to go out and earn. They'd just borrow mother's broom.

Some of the girls used to go out step cleaning – three or four of them together. Even up to a few years ago they'd do that. Young girls up to twelve or fourteen, sixteen years of age, would go out lighting fires for the Jewish people. There was a place called 'Jews' Island' in the top part of Brick Lane, just by Prince's Court. Davis, the Jewish builders, had built these places specially for Jewish people only. There were workshops at the back. Round there they'd come and clean the steps. In some of the three-storey houses, like tenement houses, the tenants would all combine together to make up, say, a shilling to give a girl to clean the stairs. Even poor Jewish people would. Mostly Saturdays, the girls would come round – no schooling you see. They'd light the fire, do pretty well, they could go up the pictures afterwards, or up the 'Brit' or the 'Standard'. Maybe the very poor mothers would say: 'Here, take the pail, get out and try and get some money.' It could be that the dinner depended on the amount the child earned.

People didn't give them a lot of money, but they could earn

half-a-crown in sixpences. Just cleaning the step, lighting the fire and giving the stairs a rub over.

Those girls had an upbringing that prevented them from ever being interfered with. They were taught the facts of life very early by the married women. The result was that they wasn't easy prey for anybody. Girls always kept together, that was a strict injunction from the mother: 'Who you're going with?' 'I'm going with Mary White.' 'Don't allow yourself to be pulled into a room – keep together where you can always be together.' So that prevented any nonsense. They always went as a group and remained as a group, wouldn't stand for no nonsense. If one saw someone chatting up one of 'em, she'd say, ''Ere piss off, get out of it.' Those girls were as pure as the day they was born.

6 Bacon Street and Queen's Buildings

We were some of the last ones to be put out of the Nichol.[1] We settled down in Drysdale Street, a little turning at the back of Old Street police station, in Hoxton. It was about 1895 I think. It was a three-storey house, and we had one room in the front. I can remember it very vividly. There was a pub opposite – the 'Red Cow' – the 'Blue Cow'[2] – something like that. And there was a wood-yard there.[3] I can remember that because there was a horse and cart standing outside and I got a potato or an apple and I was feeding it and it bit half my bloody fingers off. All round them streets there were small cabinet-makers (a cabinet-maker could have a room and turn the work out from there, good cabinet-makers and all) and I screamed and my finger was all pouring with blood – part of it was hanging – and one of these cabinet-makers went and got his glue-pot and glued the bandage on (for years after the top part of my finger was a different colour from the rest, though there's no sign of it now). I remember the pub too. I remember sneaking in there with my sister Mighty looking for my mother and father. We went in and there was the two of them knocking whiskies back. I found out, many years after, that they'd been up to the county court to get the money which was compensation for my accident. It was only ten pounds, but it was a fortune to them.

We got slung out of Drysdale Street because we were three children, and a fourth coming, and there wasn't supposed to be any at all. I remember that quite well. It was rainy, a January day. The first night we were homeless and settled down under the Brick Lane arch for the night. There were others laying there, with sheets of newspaper on the pavement and old coats to cover them. It was the common thing both at Brick Lane arch and Wheler Street, the two railway arches. The Wheler Street arch was the more crowded because it was longer and bigger. The police walked down the right-hand side, the people slept on the left. About 5 a.m. the dockers and market porters began going to work. They looked at mother who was pregnant and my two sisters – Mighty who was nearly fourteen and Mary who was four – and some threw down money. One of them, a big fellow, spoke to my father and told him of a room to let in Bacon Street,[4] which was only a few yards away. He said to Dad, 'Say Patsy Connors sent you.' (Afterwards I found out that Connors was a well-known dockers' family from the Nichol; they lived about four doors away from us in Bacon Street.) He gave Mighty his lunch and said 'share it among the kids'. When it was light, Dad and Mighty went to the house and told the woman that Patsy Connors had sent them for the room that was to let. She told Dad to move in at once. So we had found a haven of rest – No. 37 Bacon Street.

Bacon Street was just as bad as the Nichol. There was no difference. We still all lived in one room. And now there were six of us, because two days after we moved in my brother George was born. So now there was six of us – my younger sister Mary, my older sister Mighty, baby George, mother, father and myself. The only change is that we were farther away from the school. We were three storeys high and my mother scarcely went out at all, because of the pain of having to climb the stairs. We had no street door, because the part that should have been the yard, or garden, they built a workshop in it, and the workmen had to carry their work right through from the yard to the back.[5] All we had was a chest of drawers, a couple of Windsor chairs, the old kitchen table, couple of orange boxes, and a big bed.

There were no washing facilities at Bacon Street and getting the water was difficult because we lived at the top of the house and the tap was in the yard. The most terrible instrument of torture that was ever invented for a poor family was the great big bath what they done the washing in. It stood on two chairs and all the family washing went in. They'd stand for hours, washing – hard, terrible hard work. We did our washing in that bath, stripping down like the miners. There was a different mentality at that time than there is today. Today people look at anybody they can with a bad mind, an evil mind. But at that time there was no shame. 'Cos many a time when I was a boy my mother and my sister used to wash their selves with practically nothing on 'em. It was nothing to me.

They carried that bowl, that great big bath full of water out, and they had all the strain on their internal stomach muscles to carry it out to empty it. They emptied it out in the yard. And that's what caused all the bloody trouble, that bath. They didn't have the patience, or didn't have the time to empty it gradually with pails of water. They wanted to empty the lot. Seventy-five per cent of the working people of the age, of the time of what I'm talking about, had hernias. 'Mothers' cramp' they called it. They was hard-ruptured because of overlifting.

Underneath us lived a family named Ward that had a fish stall in Brick Lane market. A man and a woman. They sold kippers and bloaters and they used to keep them under the bed. The smell was continuous so you very rarely noticed it. They only had one room and all they had on that stall went into the room because you couldn't trust it out in the yard – the people would be knocking it off. They only had a barrow – a barrow and a board – but Mr Ward fancied himself, and thought that being a stall-keeper he was a cut above the layabouts: he reckoned himself a tradesman even though he did it all from a single room. In the back room at the top there was an Irish family called Lynch. Mr Lynch was a tall man with a club-foot; he used to walk with those special heavy boots; he had a shoeshine box at the top of Gibraltar Walk and used to clean your boots for threepence. I used to give him sixpence: we'd moved away by then, but he still had his shoe-box there.

Mrs Lynch, his wife, was a big powerful Irishwoman, a very clean woman. She went about charing. They had four sons and one daughter and these sons were all of a military type, big-built but too bloody lazy to work. The youngest one got drowned in the canal. The second son became a burglar – not a big burglar, more a housebreaker than a burglar. He had two or three years in prison. I remember I once saw him in Brick Lane (a few years later, after we'd moved away) and I said, 'You don't look well, why don't you go over to London Hospital?' He was yellow – some disease had turned him yellow – and he died of it in London Hospital. The third son went to the South African War and never came home no more.

And the fourth one simply disappeared. I don't know what happened to him but I know that his name was Bobby and that he and another fellow called Cassel were always in and out of the army, joining different lots. They joined a Scotch regiment and got transferred to India and both of them deserted and made an overland journey and got back to this country. The daughter was left with a baby by a scoundrel and the baby was born blind, a girl. For many years afterwards I used to see her, in fact until quite recently. Somebody at the London Hospital took an interest in them and found them a place.

There was a couple of families down below. One was a Jewish man in his forties – he became quite wealthy afterwards; he got on in the world, but he was a very nice man, he fitted in. He had a shop underneath and three children growing up. They occupied the bottom part of the house and I think he bought interest in the rooms. He used to sell anything he could buy at the sales – old clothes – and he had a stall outside.

The Connors – the family who had helped us get to Bacon Street – lived three or four doors along. Most of them were dockers. Opposite there was a little block of buildings and in it a family of the name of Isaacs who made ice-cream out in the back. It was good ice-cream, hard stuff. They would cut it up with the knife. They sold it in halfpennyworths and penny-worths. The big freezer was in the middle of the yard – there was a big back-yard there with workshops and all – and then they had a barrow to take it out with.

There were also some Italian people in Brick Lane who made ice-creams.[6] They were very friendly. They used to let me in their yard. I used to watch them at work. They called the father 'Padrone'. They had about six labourers came from Italy and they used to get a shilling a week and what they made, and they'd save enough money and after years of work they used to go to Italy and buy a plot of land. Nice fellows, though they had a bit of a temper – the type who would get weapons if you done anything to them. They used to go out in the summer with the ice-cream barrows and in the winter with hot chestnuts and baked potatoes. There were only two rooms, but they had a yard round the back of Granby Street where they used to put the baked potato cans and chestnut cans when they come home – because they wasn't allowed to leave them outside the shop. It was only a small shop – a shop for sweets and cigarettes.

In Bacon Street there was a chap named Silkie. He was a character. He knew everybody's business. He was what we used to call a 'half-wide mug'. He wanted to make out he was a crook but didn't want to take the risks. He had a very tricky way of talking. He hung about on the fringe of the gangs.

There was another family in Bacon Street called the James's.* The sons are still there. I knew the father and mother quite well; they went round the city buying tea chests and packing cases. They knew exactly the sizes and the firms that required packing cases. They bought them off the importers and sold them to the exporters. The father was a real nice man, but the sons were villains – they went in for putting the 'frighteners' on people. They went in for stealing. They'd buy and steal cases full of goods and pretend to go in and get the empty cases and come out with the full ones which they'd sell. During the war they made a stack of money out of waste paper.

Just round in Chilton Street in the turning that leads up to Bethnal Green Road from Bacon Street, there was a woman named Thompson. She had a front room with a great big roller in it – a mangle – and she used to charge so much a dozen to mangle the washing and she used to be at that all day long doing the washing for people. Very cheap, about 1d a dozen or something like that. I think she had a daughter with her. There was plenty of people who would do a bit of washing 'cos even sixpence was a valuable bit of money. Nearly every poor quarter had people with mangles then. What interested me was that it was such a huge machine. They had to dry before they were mangled, wet things would clog the machine up. If a woman took a dozen things in and was washing them for say 6d a dozen she'd have to have a wringer there – perhaps it would be the same woman done the washing and the mangling.

Everybody had a different method of getting a living, some got it in a marvellous bloody way. Some women did sack-making. In the Nichol my mother had made coal sacks but it was so hard she turned it up because there was no sewing

* Fictitious name.

machines at that time. They made the coal sacks for different firms – it's possible she made them for Charrington's, the big coal people.[7] It was very hard work.

Then in Bacon Street she started making market bags – using old flour sacks and cutting them up. My sister used to go round the bakers' shops and buy them. The bakers had no use for them. They cost about 1d or 2d each. She'd buy a dozen and then cut them up and make market bags for the people out shopping. It was my sister first discovered the possibilities of flour bags. In the market they went for 3d each. A good strong bag would last for years. She always made them very strong so the handle wouldn't break off. They was a good source of income.

Other forms of work people used to do? Some of them would make Christmas cards, Christmas decorations. I've seen them making paper chains to go across the ceiling. There was different things you could earn a shilling at. I knew people used to make dolls and fluffy things for the Christmas trade. Old fur coats they made them of, some of them were diseased – they shouldn't have been made into children's toys.

Then you had people looking after children for a living, people taking in children. But years ago there was plenty of child murders and people was afraid to trust their children with other people. There was the notorious Mrs Dyer.[8] She killed about ten of them – she got hanged at Reading – and people remembered those things.

Artificial flowers, that was a common thing. And you'd see them making wreaths for the funerals. People made packets of money at it. They used to go down to Covent Garden more than Spitalfields because that was a flower market, buy the flowers and make the wreaths. In the East End there were funerals galore. Mondays was a special day. People would say, 'Go round to Mrs So-and-so and she'll make you a couple of wreaths.' You'd go round there and say, 'How much would you make me a wreath for?' and she'd say, 'What do you want?' and she'd mention the different flowers, 'cos she would know what was cheap and what was expensive at different times of the year. And then she'd say, 'Well I can make you one for 10s 6d and a bigger one for a pound.' 'Gates of Heaven' that would be 50s. 'Gates of Heaven' was a sort of pearly gates with

St Peter and all that. And if it was a child, the mourners might tell them he was fond of a dog or something like that – so they'd make the wreath in the form of a dog.

You'd be surprised at the amount of money they spent on wreaths. They'd pawn their husband's suit to get a wreath. On Keeve's Buildings when anybody died no matter who – husband, wife or daughter – they'd have a collection for the wreaths: that's a regular thing still today in the East End of London.

You didn't need a shop to make wreaths. They'd know how to make wreaths wherever you lived, especially Hoxton, plenty of people in Hoxton make wreaths even today. Most of them got a living flower-selling. I remember there was Mrs Kelly round the back of Shoreditch Church: she was the one I used to patronise when I wanted a wreath. She had a big flower shop right opposite the Mildmay Hospital. Country Billy Smith's wife had a stand in Moorgate, outside the tube, selling flowers during the day and after the morning she'd pack up and go home and start making wreaths. She lived in Falkirk Street, Hoxton. I knew her in Bacon Street. They called him Country Billy Smith but he came from Birmingham. He was a docker but a very lazy docker and she used to get him a living. She was a very good flower-seller. The Cooks and the Hands, they were all flower-sellers. They were from the same family, and they lived in a shop on the corner of Barnet Grove. Mrs Cook done the wreaths in Chambord Street when we lived in Queen's Buildings, she was always making wreaths round there.

We remained at 37 Bacon Street for some five years. From here we began to lay the beginnings of our future prosperity. When we moved there we had nothing – just a mattress and a big chest of drawers, a kettle, a saucepan and some crocks in the drawers. It was easy to fit on to a barrow. We had no bed then, just straw mattresses (they were ideal breeding ground for bugs). Few bedclothes. I don't ever remember sheets. They were unheard of. Just a couple of blankets tied up and bunged on top.

Then Mighty started to work. When she reached the age of fourteen she went to work at the offices of Lipton's, the grocers's, in City Road.[9] She was paid 7s 6d weekly for cleaning the offices. She started at 7 a.m., worked to 9 a.m. then left and went back again from 5.30 to 7.30. After she finished in the morning she would go and sell lemons in the Roman Road market, in Bow, which at that time was a better class of market than the one in Bethnal Green Road, though it was further away to travel to. She used to buy the lemons by the sackful in Spitalfields market which was only a hundred yards or so from where we lived. She would get 300 for next to nothing. I used to go and carry them for her and she would sell them three a penny, or four a penny. She used to go down Spitalfields very early in the morning, sometimes 5 or 6 o'clock. She used to hire the barrow from Goldfine's – that was a Jewish man who had a business hiring out barrows to the stallholders in Brick Lane. He was a straight man, a very nice man, he fell in with the district.

I don't know what gave her the idea of starting up with a barrow. Mighty took the mother's part. All through my early life she was more a mother than anybody because she provided the means by which we were able to get on in life.

When she first went with the lemons she started in Bethnal Green Road, but there was a good market down Roman Road on Tuesdays and she started going there. At that time the people who had a stall in Roman Road, at Bow, were a wee bit over the ones in Bethnal Green Road. That part of London was the upper working class – what they called 'the respectable working class' – the sort of people who went to church on a Sunday. Lower-middle-class people. Mighty used to stand outside a big flour shop – a corn chandler's. She fell into the right hands. On the other corner was a big fruiterer's, Clarke's.[10] They used to do a tremendous trade. One morning someone tried to turn my sister away but Mr Clarke said, 'What did you send her away for?' And he called her back and said, 'Come on, Missie, sell your lemons out there.' He had his own stall pulled down so that she could stand there. That was the goodness of the man, because she did well there, and he never let anyone go in her place.

The business progressed. Soon she was selling not only lemons but other savouries – mint, sage, and also market bags. Then my mother started up in the Roman Road and took a stall opposite Mighty's. They used to make good money and me and my sister Mary went up to help them. The driver on the No. 8 bus (a horse-drawn bus with an open top – you needed a mackintosh) got to know them and he would pull up right on the corner so that my mother, who was crippled, could get out. Later my younger sister Mary married a conductor on the No. 8 bus. The Rothschilds had the buses then – they gave a golden sovereign to their employees at the end of the year.

On Saturday nights we would finish about 12.30 to 1 o'clock. That was an unruly hour, with drunken people coming out of the pub. My sister was about fourteen or fifteen, which is a very dangerous age for a girl. But no one would trouble her. Children was very much respected in the East End. And we'd sit on that barrow eating faggots and pease pudding – what the old German butcher saved for us on Saturday nights – and no one bothered us. That faggot and pease pudding was a luxury. You sat and ate there and the world was at peace. You took no notice of people going along singing, or the policemen who were probably struggling with someone who wanted to fight.

It was my sister's stall. But when my mother came down she used to take charge. You've got to remember this, that young or old the mother was the top Johnny in the family. What she said was law. All the money you earned went to her and she would share it out.

Directly we got to Bacon Street my mother gave birth to my brother George. She got a lot of charity. Ladies from the West End used to come up, she being a cripple, and they gave her clothes, and they talked about getting me adopted. But I left home and started sleeping rough. I was nine at the time. It was no good: we couldn't all sleep in that room and everyone's attention was going on the new baby.

I wasn't on the street very long. There were some tenements in Sclater Street, mostly with Jewish people. They were very friendly and they let you sleep on the landing. The stairs were nice and I kipped there a couple of nights, then gradually worked my way round. In Bacon Street there were workshops, Jewish workshops, where they used to work to 12 at night. I used to go there a bit but the staircases weren't good, not proper staircases, you slept on the landing. And I used to get in the watchman's hut, round Spelman Street, Vallance Road, round the fire. It wasn't anything out of the ordinary; there were hundreds of kids roaming about the streets. Some of the watchmen wasn't so good and you had to give them a wide berth, but some would let you sleep by the fire and they would give you a bit of their supper. And there was Great Eastern Buildings, off Vallance Road: there were buildings there you could sleep on. I got very lousy and dirty by myself. But my mother was too ill to trouble.

Then the police took me in and I was taken to Stepney Causeway, to Dr Barnardo's.[11] I'd been sleeping rough for about three weeks. They found me in an empty house off Whitechapel Road: there were a lot of ins and outs by Old Montague Street. It was about 2 o'clock in the morning. They had a lantern. They said, 'Why don't you go home, haven't you got no home?' And naturally I put on that I didn't have no home. When I got to headquarters they put an investigator on it and they went round (it wasn't too far from Stepney Causeway to Bacon Street). When they found out the conditions my parents were living in, they sent me to Leopold House[12] in Burdett Road, corner of Mile End Road, a penny tram ride from home.

Dr Barnardo's seemed to occupy the largest part of my childhood from nine till I was nearly twelve years old. We were allowed out on Saturdays about 1 o'clock and I went home and stayed a few hours, first to Bacon Street and then to Queen's Buildings in Gossett Street when we moved there. My sister used to give me 2d. She'd come back with me, half the way anyway, and then at Green Street they used to have sweets, 8 ounces a penny. You'd take 'em in and share 'em with the boys.

In the last time at Bacon Street things started improving. My sister was going out and earning money and after I left Dr Barnardo's, I started earning money myself, going round the pubs. I was giving my mum 10s a week and my sister was giving her more because she was getting on in the world, she had money of her own. We were just beginning to realise the possibilities of the future. When we came we had nothing, just a mattress and a big chest of drawers, a kettle and a saucepan. It was easy to fit on to a single barrow. After my sister started at

Lipton's we bought this couch – a sofa – it was a terrific struggle getting it up through the window. When we moved from Bacon Street, it took two carts to move us.

In 1902 we moved to Queen's Buildings,[13] in Gossett Street, about half a mile away. They were old buildings, but very much better than anything we had been used to. At Bacon Street, the front door was always open, because there was a cabinet-maker's at the back and they had to get through. At Queen's Buildings we had our own front door, all to ourselves. When you went in, you shut it. For the first time, we had two rooms – a front room, a back room and then a scullery. And we had our own water tap – in the Nichol we shared the one on the landing. And we had our own toilet. It was a paradise. A toilet in the yard, but it was your own toilet. No one else had access to it. There was a gas mantle that lit up the corridor – all the rooms were lit by gas. At Bacon Street it was all paraffin. That was our first contact with gas, though we didn't have a gas cooker till we moved to Gibralter Gardens. I don't remember any lino. We never had nothing on the floor because my sister used to scrub the floor regular. We got rid of the bloody mattresses when we got round to Queen's Buildings, they was alive with vermin. We bought another completely different thing, a chair-bedstead. Completely new, with different material, it had black trimmings. We only had the one. I remember, this is a strange thing, even so late as when I come out of Borstal, I was sixteen, seventeen years of age, my sister was twenty. And we both slept in the same narrow bed. She slept at the top and I slept at the bottom, and the two kids, my sister Mary and George, slept with my mother in the big bed.

At Queen's Buildings they were the more respectable working class, the higher ranks. We were a wee bit higher in the social ladder. We paid 7s 6d rents – at Bacon Street the rents was much smaller, 2s 9d or 3s. My mother said we'd have to look a bit more respectable – 'respectable' was the word everybody used. When we moved to Queen's Buildings we had to make a show going in, because the people were more posh round there. So we got this chair-bedstead – it was the first proper bed we had, before then the children had to sleep on the floor. I think mother bought a couple more chairs; and we also bought a wash hand-stand. We had the room to put things in – the wash-stand went in the scullery. Really we didn't know what scullery meant until we went to Queen's Buildings. On the mantlepiece we had a couple of ornaments. We had a clock, a china clock, and two vases to match. That was the pet decoration. The vases on each side, and the clock in the middle. A set. Didn't cost a lot – 12 or 15 bob, say. You bought 'em in the shops. A 'china set': it used to be a stock gift for a wedding. With the curtains, it made a sort of shrine of the mantlepiece. Later on we got lace curtains for the front windows, 'cos people could all see us as they went by. That was later on. I remember going and fetching them from Caledonian Road. Once, my father was sitting by the fire nursing the baby and he set light to them.

But the drawback of Queen's Buildings was that we had a pub nearly opposite, and mother started to drink. What with the pain in her leg and the hard life she'd had it's no wonder she took it up. But it was a very terrible business. It was a terrifying thing, women drinking. Not just sipping – they used to drink like bloody navvies. They used to collect on a Monday, about four or five of them – I remember seeing my little brother and sister playing in the sawdust in the pub corridor. Mother used to drink at the 'Queen's Head' which was right opposite where we lived in Gossett Street, and it was a terrible job to get her home. How she got the money was the Saturday takings and the few shillings my sister gave her and the five shillings I gave her from my job in New Inn Yard, so she could afford a couple of days on the booze. Why she turned it up was the Habitual Drunkards Act which the government brought in – that frightened her – she might have been put away in a home. When I came out of Borstal, I terrified the publican to stop serving her.

Mighty was now the mainstay of the family. She was the main breadwinner because she had a fixed job and she was earning money at the stall. But mother was the paymaster – we were so obedient that we gave her all our wages. Mighty was my mother's total slave – if she'd been a slave she would have been better off. She earned money but she didn't want it for herself – that was a remarkable thing about her all her life, she was always doing things for other people. When my father left home she cared for him and looked after him and paid for his funeral when he died.

Father was just an encumbrance. He was an old man now – sixty – and he stopped more at home, nursing the baby. There was nowhere else for him to go. I saved his life once. He had the baby in his arms and he went to light his pipe and there was a lot of lace about the mantlepiece and it caught alight. For a time he hung about the hat shop in Shoreditch High Street, doing errands. He stopped drinking – he didn't have money to go to the pub. My father was getting frightened now that I was getting more of a man. He could swear – every word out of his mouth was swearing – but he couldn't fight for toffee. Later he went with his sister to live in Wilmot Street until she slung him out. In the end my sister Mighty bought a house for him down Roman Road and he lived with her there.

7 Criminal apprenticeship

When I left Barnardo's I started earning money. Nothing regular, because I was supposed to be going to school. But I started selling things in the pub and also helping my sister on her stall. And I used to go up to Liverpool Street Station, carrying bags.

There weren't many jobs for school leavers. You couldn't get a job in the breweries – they was all Home Counties people, great big country fellows from places like Norwich and Ipswich. It was a job for life once you were in, but you couldn't get in if you were local. Allen and Hanbury's,[1] the druggists at the top of Bethnal Green Road – that was a good job, well paid and all. It was a safe job. You were there for the rest of your life as long as you didn't misbehave yourself. It was a good job, a clean job, you learnt a lot. Later, about 1904, they started a print works locally, but you had to have a special recommendation from the headmaster. Boys leaving school could get on the railways as van guards or van boys. And they were in great demand for street cleaning – in the years when horse traffic fouled the streets. These boys wore a uniform and were permanently employed by the City Corporation. They worked from a big yard in Stay Lane, Houndsditch. They used to dodge in and out of the traffic like monkeys sweeping up the dung, and were known as 'shit rakers' or 'sparrow starvers'. It was a job for life, and was much sought after, because as the boys grew older they were raised to a higher position. My nephew Benny, he started as a cleaning boy and he finished up as a messenger in the Stock Exchange. He's still there. At the Stock Exchange, all the messengers were recruited from members of the cleaning department.

There was nothing safe in cabinet-making – you'd got to be a first-class man to work for people like Maple's or Harrod's. Otherwise cabinet-making was no bloody good at all – too much hard work, slave labour, kids wouldn't stick it.

The first job I got was down Hoxton Market, in a kind of mill.[2] That's all I can remember of it, looms and that sort of thing – a mill like they have in Lancashire – there were wheels going round all the time. They were making some kind of fabric. My sister and her friend used to take me there first thing of a morning – it was right by where she worked at Lipton's. They used to drag me out of bed to get me there by 7 o'clock. I only lasted about three days – I can't remember much about it.

The next job I had was in the cabinet-making business. Atkins's[3] in Church Row, Bethnal Green, not a stone's throw from where I lived. I saw a notice, 'Boys wanted for Sand-Machines', and in I went. I knew the foreman and he knew me, because he belonged to the neighbourhood, and I got the job. I was there for about a month and earned 8s a week. It was a big firm. They made all sorts of furniture, but deck-chairs mostly. They were proper business people, eventually they moved to a place out at Wembley.

It was while I was working there that I got involved with the police for disorderly conduct. I got off but the policeman who arrested me had gone to Atkins's to see if I worked there. One of them said, 'You don't work at Atkins's,' and I saw him talking to the foreman. I thought I was bound to get the sack so I didn't go back.

Before working at Atkins's I had had a brief spell in the army. I joined on 27 November 1900. I was only fourteen years old, but I was well built and could pass for seventeen. At this time a wave of patriotism was sweeping through the country. Great Britain was at war with the Boers, and the country needed more troops and I joined up. I went to Angel Lane, Stratford East, and joined the Royal West Kents. I was sent to Maidstone, Kent, which was the training depot for the regiment. I believe I was in the fourth battalion.[4]

The weeks I spent at Maidstone training as a soldier were well spent. I was used to discipline from the two and a half years in Leopold House. The uniform was a red tunic and blue serge trousers, with a red stripe down the seam. For church parade, which we attended every Sunday in full dress and spiked helmets, white belts and blue cuffs on tunic. We marched through the town to the Garrison Church, which was decorated with the battle honours of the Regiment back from active service. Church parade always reminded me of the boys of Leopold House marching to church service every Sunday morning, with the band playing stirring tunes and marches.

The weeks passed and I was just getting over the initial stage of training when I was called before the CO, who asked me my age. He said, 'How old are you?' I replied, 'Eighteen, sir.' The CO informed me he had received a letter on behalf of my parents stating I was only fourteen years old, too young for the army. So my parents had taken action to bring me back to the East End. I was fourteen and I could earn wages, so I was an asset which my father did not intend to give up lightly. Too young for the army, but not too young for prison.

After leaving the army I went back to life as a street Arab, hanging about street corners at night and making a nuisance of myself to the police. I was a bit on the flash side – a wee bit superior to my fellows. I was well versed in reading and writing from my time in Barnardo's. I was a good scholar and people looked up to me.

The first time I was arrested I had just turned fourteen. We were standing on the corner of Bacon Street and Brick Lane, about 11 o'clock at night, larking about – anyone came along you might knock his hat off, that sort of thing. A policeman came down the Lane – they used to have a point policeman – and he was making his way down the middle of the road a bit sharpish. The boys said, 'He's after trouble,' and hopped it, running off down Bacon Street. I didn't follow them. The policeman came up to me and said, 'Why didn't you run away like the others?' I said, 'Why should I run away from you?' Now I was a wee bit posh and he thought I was being saucy. 'I'll have you for obstruction,' he said. 'Come along with me to the police station.' So he took me up to the one in Commercial Street. I wasn't charged with obstruction but with being a suspected person. I think they suspected I was a deserter from the army, because they had seen me before in my uniform. When the case came before the Worship Street magistrate's court the case collapsed.[4] The magistrate asked the policeman, 'What was he doing?' so he said: 'Well, he had been in the army and I suspected him of running away.' 'Oh, I see, that's another thing. And had he run away?' 'No Sir, he'd been discharged, under age.' The Boer War was still on and the magistrate was a wee bit sympathetic, he treated me with respect and dismissed the charge of suspected person. I was discharged on 10 April 1901.

My next attempt to get into the army took place within a few months of my discharge from the Royal West Kents. I went to the same enlistment office at Angel Lane, which at this time was the chief recruiting depot for the East End. There were some six or more recruiting sergeants in their full dress uniform, complete with medals. Being in close proximity to the docks, the depot did a brisk business for recruiting the unemployed. This time I enlisted in the Royal Fusiliers stationed at Hounslow Heath, Middlesex. The huts in which the battalion were quartered had been erected on the Heath and it was very cold in them, especially at night. After a week or two I developed a very bad cough which disturbed the other men in the hut during the night, so I was ordered to go and see the MO.

The medical officer examined me, and after a few questions regarding my age told me I was too young, and also that I was medically unfit. I was discharged the same day. This incident finally ended my intention to be a soldier and serve the Queen. After this set-back I went looking for a job to learn a trade.

My first job was at a glassblower's[5] in Hanbury Street, Brick Lane, just by the Salvation Army. There were about twenty men working there. The firm made medicine bottles and jars. I worked underneath the furnaces, clearing clinkers. I had to have a big rake to pull the clinkers out. I must have been potty to take it on. One day a ruddy great hot clinker fell on my arms, and I had to go to hospital. I've still got scars on both my arms. I was in the London Hospital about a week, and after I come out I never went back to the job. There was not a penny compensation.

After trying my hand at two or three other jobs, I finally started work at a cabinet-maker's in New Inn Yard, Shore-ditch, Butler's and Sons.[6] Nine months I worked there. I was learning to be a cabinet-maker, doing odd jobs, sandpapering up, scraping, running errands. Butler's were big cabinet-makers. This firm made every kind of furniture from coal scuttles to bedsteads with canopies. They did beautiful work, coal scuttles with little carved doors, bedsteads with twisted posts. There were good workmen there. Everybody had got his own bench. If it was a long bench they had a couple of men working, one on one side and one the other side. They didn't change places. Monday they had fresh timber. They used to mark their work out and go to the mill, all that sort of business. On a Friday night they worked right through the night to get the work out for next day – doing what they called a 'ghoster'.

I used to go out and get the men their dinners. They ate their meals where they worked, on the benches. I used to go and get steak 'n kidney puddings in the coffee shops in Great Eastern Street. At the end of the week you'd get a tanner off each one of them, for running to get their errands. I made a little extra on it, because I found out a place where I could get beefsteak puddings for fourpence when they gave me fivepence apiece for them. It was simple. They didn't get robbed. They got what they wanted and didn't have to pay any extra. I learnt all the tricks of the trade there at Butler's. Anything which the firm sent me for I used to find a way of getting something out of it. If they sent me out for 100 feet of moulding I'd get 80 feet. They didn't know the difference, they didn't measure it up. I used to *earn* there, that's why I stuck it. I gave my wages to mother, but anything extra I kept for myself. It was while working there that I got into trouble and was put in prison.

The boys with whom I associated had not reached the stage when they could be called criminals or, in modern legal jargon, juvenile delinquents. Most of these boys like myself earned a few shillings selling newspapers or carrying luggage at Liverpool Street Station. Some worked for the City Corporation as street cleaners. When we were not at work we were tearaways. We used to frequent Clark's coffee house which was near the railway arch in Brick Lane, which was opposite Hare Street and quite close to Club Row. A lot of thieves hung out there. We used to watch them follow the carts. They would lift the goods off the back quite openly – sometimes a bale of cloth, or a large side of bacon, or some boxes of eggs. It was comparatively easy work: the vans were drawn by horses and their speed was not more than ten miles an hour. Often we used to watch them and sometimes we would give them a hand. I was unlucky enough to be caught at it by the police.

It was early in February 1902. The time was about 8.30 p.m., the street was dark, being badly lit by gas lamps. A large horse-drawn cart was slowly passing along in the roadway, loaded with large bales of rags which were bulging out at the sides. Nobody could mistake the large bales for anything but what they were – rags. I noticed a man walking behind the cart, and attempting to pull one of the bales off. It was One-eyed Charlie, the leader of a well-known gang of thieves who frequented Clark's coffee shop. He seemed to be having some difficulties in clearing the sack from the ropes, but eventually got it down on the road. Charlie recognised me as one of the young boys belonging to Brick Lane and asked me to give him a hand with the sack. I did so willingly. Suddenly, from nowhere, a policeman appeared and blew his whistle. He seized Charlie by the arm and they began struggling. Eventually he was taken to Commercial Street police station and charged with stealing a bale of rags, valued at 18s. I ran off, but unfortunately the policeman who had arrested Charlie recognised me and the next day I was arrested. I was taken to Commercial Street police station and put in a cell for the night. No food was given me and no one was sent to tell my mother where I was.

The next morning I was taken by Black Maria to Worship Street magistrate's court. When the time came for me to appear the jailor led me to a large dock where I stood to attention. The clerk of the court read out the charge and asked me to plead 'guilty' or 'not guilty'. I pleaded 'not guilty'. PC Stevens then had a conversation with the magistrate which was quite unintelligible to me. The magistrate then remanded me to appear the next week with Charles Walker. No bail. The trial eventually took place on the 4 March 1902 at the North London Sessions, Clerkenwell. There were two judges at that court. In No. 1 a Mr O'Connell[8] was the chairman. He had the reputation of being a humane judge. No. 2 court was presided over by a lawyer named Mr Loveland Loveland,[9] a man devoid of sympathetic impulses. In Holloway, where I had been held on remand, the old timers advised me to plead guilty because then I would come up before Mr O'Connell, who had a good reputation among old offenders. Unfortunately I did not take their advice but pleaded 'not guilty' and came up before Mr Loveland Loveland. The case lasted about an hour. I was so scared that I could not speak the words 'not guilty' when called. Walker received three years penal servitude, and I, being a first offender, was given twelve months hard labour.

I was sent to Wormwood Scrubs and placed in an empty cell. The first thing I noticed was that I had no bed to sleep on. Some eminent Christian with the love of Christ in his heart had ordained that we were to sleep on a plank of wood. He had also made hard work our daily fare. In the first month we were employed every day picking oakum. It was a painful task which made the fingers sore, and sitting on a wooden stool for hours on end can be very painful. The next month we were sewing coalbags. After that the work was easier – mailbags. We were unlocked for an hour's exercise each day, but the only other time we were let out was to go to chapel. This happened once a day and twice on Sunday. The congregation numbered 500 or more and the warders sat on a raised platform facing them. The congregation joined in the service with great enthusiasm and I was amazed at the fervour. The whole atmosphere was like the 'Edinburgh Castle'[10] meetings I had been to in Limehouse, when I was a Barnardo boy. I could not join in – I was filled with bitterness against the warders and the prison governor and all those who had locked me up. I got ill from the stuffy atmosphere of the cell and with the help of a young prison doctor I was able to have a little more time in the prison grounds, getting a job carrying coal to different furnaces.

On 18 January 1903 I was released. I was given a gratuity of ten shillings – a gold half sovereign – and given back my clothes. At the gate there was a lady who gave me a tract and a ticket for a free breakfast. 'God bless you,' she said (the text, in red letters, was 'I say unto Ye, that he that is without sin, let him cast the first stone').

The first weeks of my liberty were spent helping my sister in Roman Road. The stall was a now prosperous business, but mother was spending every shilling earned on drink, so that we were worse off than we were before. There was no home life for us. Mother was taken in for being drunk and disorderly, but this did not stop her. There was no possibility of regular employment, so I tried the recruiting office again. This time I tried to enlist in the Royal Marines. But after a medical examination I was rejected as unfit and advised to go into hospital.

Soon I began to associate with my old friends, hanging about the corners of Brick Lane. Under the railway arch the Jewish people had a little clothes market. We pinched things from there and we also went about stealing their chickens. We thought they were fair game.

My closest pal at this time was a boy named Peaky. He came out of the Nichol, same as me, but his mother and father were on the respectable side – the father was a collar and tie man and worked for the Port of London Authority, supervising goods in the warehouses. They lived in Turville Street and when that was pulled down they moved to Chambord Street right by Queen's Buildings. Peaky went to the Rochelle Street school, like me, but he was always on the missing side. He would go up to Liverpool Street, carrying bags or begging. In the pudding shop you'd always see him having a good lush-in; he would lay out twopence or threepence at a time. While I was away in prison, he was in Reform School for playing truant. When I come out of doing my twelve months I palled up with him again. We both wanted to be van boys and tried to get a job on the Great Eastern Railway, but they expected you to read and write and Peaky couldn't even sign his name. And they wanted you to produce a 'character' either from school or somewhere else. So we gave that up. Once or twice I took Peaky home to try to learn him the alphabet, but it was hopeless, he didn't want to learn.

Peaky and I were pals. What I got I shared with him. He looked up to me as a sort of defender. But it was through me that he got into trouble. One day, about eleven weeks after I'd come out of Wormwood Scrubs, we were back in Brick Lane watching a game of 'piemen'.[11] I was around Bacon Street with my pal Peaky. It was dinner hour for the printers and they were playing pitch the toss. One of the young fellows had a watch and chain. 'He's got a kettle,' I said to Peaky, 'I'll try to get it.' I took it out of his pocket. It was quite simple, I just put my hand up and swivelled it off. Just as I'd got it in my hand, he tumbled to what was happening and said, 'Give me my watch back.' I laughed and gave the watch to Peaky and we walked away. The boy followed us, crying. It was a silly thing to do – he was a boy who worked at the printworks and he knew the two of us. Well, he done a thing I never thought he would do – he went to the police and Peaky and I were arrested. The police found us in Clark's coffee shop.

Our case came up on 10 April 1903 at the North London Sessions, Clerkenwell Green. We just stood in the dock. Neither of us opened our mouths. He gave me twenty months and Peaky nine months.

The Borstal system was introduced while I was serving my sentence. I did three months at Wormwood Scrubs with the 'old offenders'; then I was transferred to a place near Rochester, in June 1903. We were the first Borstal Boys and the governor, a Mr Western, was keen to make the new system a success. He would visit the lads in their cells and urge them to do well in a trade. He was always immaculately dressed – he seemed to have a different suit on every day. We were also permitted more library books and the more backward lads were taught to read and write. I read *Oliver Twist* – that was the first time I came in contact with Dickens. You weren't kept in a cell. Every day there were physical exercises out of doors and these had a beneficial effect on my health which had suffered from the close confinement of Wormwood Scrubs. And I learnt a good deal of woodwork. I had described myself as a cabinet-maker so I was put into the carpenter's shop – in later years I always went to the carpenter's shop when serving time in jail.

I was discharged from Borstal in September 1904 and went back to Bethnal Green. I had no 'prospects' but I had supreme confidence in my ability to survive. Borstal had made me fitter, stronger, taller. I was no longer a kid, and when I went back to my old associates I found that I was something of a hero. I had had a good education at Dr Barnardo's. I was more intelligent than the other boys. I had a reputation for being tough. And I was the only one in the younger age group to have done time. They began to look up to me as a sort of leader.

There was a crowd of us went together, and what I told them to do they would do because they trusted me and perhaps because they were now a wee bit afraid of me. We youngsters began to mix more with the older thieves. There were about a dozen of them who used to hang out at Clark's. They were six or seven years older than us. But we used the same coffee shop and so we became known to them. The young lads looked up to the 'Heads' as they called the older thieves, and some of them helped to carry stolen goods. You could say the older ones were the first eleven team, and me and my pals were the second.

I learnt pickpocketing from a chap I'd met at Wormwood Scrubs. His name was Edward Spencer.[12] He was four years older than me and a real criminal. He thieved all his life. He was a real bloody villain, a complete criminal. He'd turn his hand to anything. His father worked for the Port of London Authority and his mother was respectable – they lived in Canrobert Street, Bethnal Green. He went thieving all over the place – him and a crowd of others. In the early years he used to go what they called 'shoot-flying' – stealing watch chains by getting hold of them in the street and tugging. They would go into a street with a lot of turnings and when they'd made their catch they would shoot down the turnings – that's why they called it 'shoot-flying'. They also called it 'blagging'. About four of them used to do it, regular of a morning, just like going to business. They worked where the City toffs were – Broad Street, Finsbury Square.

I learnt about pickpocketing just like the Artful Dodger in Dickens. The other fellows were much older and took a real pride in their work. Spencer wouldn't let me go with him, but he told me how it was done and helped me to practice. Women were the easiest to take from. They didn't have handbags then, but used to have pockets at the back of their skirts. It was easy to cut them away – they didn't even notice what had happened. Whoever invented these pockets must have been a whizzer. Wallets were more difficult because they were kept in breast pockets, and shoot-flying you had to be ready to run. Pickpocketing men and women were two completely different lines. The Jewish boys, down in Whitechapel, were very good whizzers, but they only went in for women.

Spencer's lot only went in for men, and One-eyed Charlie's gang were the same – though mostly he was a van-dragger – he wasn't a clever thief at all.

Soon I had my own little team. Mostly we went pick-pocketing about Whitechapel and Petticoat Lane, where the crowds were, for the market. Sometimes we would take a little ride out, say to Peckham. And we used to go to market places like Whitecross Street in Finsbury and Leather Lane, Holborn. You went to market places because that's where people were in crowds. I was the gaffer. I looked after the others, always got them to do the pickpocketing. When they got it they would give it to me and I would do the selling and the sharing out of the proceeds. People trusted me. Holiday times – holiday Mondays – we would go to New Cross or to Deptford where there was a big fair on the Broadway. You could sneak something here, there and everywhere when there was a fair on. We never used to go to Hampstead Heath. That was because it was in Middlesex and the judge at Middlesex Sessions – Sir Ralph Littler – was the hottest judge in England.[13] My friend Spencer got six years from him for attempting to steal a watch at White City. He gave a man fourteen years for breaking a window and stealing a bottle of whisky. He said he would make Middlesex so safe that a man could hang his watch and chain on a lamp post and nobody would take it.

In 1906 I teamed up with some Jewish boys and we went on some pickpocketing expeditions to different parts of the country. Later they gave up pickpocketing in favour of running girls on the street, and I lost track of them. I was a great favourite among these Jews. I was in charge of the operations – they did the pickpocketing. They were dressed like Eton College boys with big wide collars and they looked very innocent. They wasn't the rough type at all. They was on the small side, and they looked so nice that nobody would suspect them. And they had the gift of the gab when they got into trouble.

There were five Jewish boys in the gang – I was the only 'Yok'. Asher was about the same age as me. His real name was Lazarus and his parents lived down Gossett Street, just a few yards away from us in Queen's Buildings. That's how I got to know him. We lived a few yards from each other. The parents were poor Russian Jews, good, honest, hard-working people.

Another was Jackie Shinebohm. He was a very clever pickpocket – so nice-looking that nobody suspected him. He was fourteen or fifteen when we first met up. I picked him up round the coffee stall at the top of Bethnal Green Road. I said to him 'What are you at?' and he said, 'I'm a whizzer' (pickpocket). So I knew you could trust him and he was clean. He had no parents or nothing – sometimes he used to sleep at my place in Gibraltar Gardens. Jackie got killed in Ireland in 1922. He was there with a gang of pickpockets, four or five of them. They'd got the police straightened up so that they wouldn't interfere with their business, and he was talking to a couple of Dublin CID chaps and it seems the Sinn Feiners spotted him and put a tail on him. They followed him to the hotel where he was staying and shot him dead. It was just an honest mistake. They thought he was a spy.

Then there was Eisenberg, better known as Long Hymie. He came from the Argentine and was a year or two older than me. When I met him he was chasing two other Jewish chaps – there'd been a row about the cutting-up of a robbery they'd been in together and they attacked him with a hammer. Well he went for them and I gave him a hand. Long Hymie was a fine-built boy – very brave fellow – never knew what fear was. Not a bad looker either. But I was always afraid he might shoot a policeman. What every crook is afraid of is getting involved in a murder case and in the end that's why I had to break away from him. He was too dangerous. In the end I gave him the sack and he stayed down Flowery Dean Street.

Years later Long Hymie got caught burgling a house at Enfield. He was working with a jubber – an iron bar which they used to force the door open – and he nearly killed the policeman who caught him. He got three years and they deported him from the country, sent him back to Argentina. He left his wife and a boy behind him. He was good to his wife, but she told me she never heard from him again.

Albie Symons was another of our gang. Me and him were dead pals. He came with us when we were in Brick Lane but I never took him away with us on our expeditions. His father,

who was a tailor in Bethnal Green Road, said, 'Arthur, don't
get him into trouble,' so I didn't take him pickpocketing.

I can't remember the names of the others.

We would go away for two or three weeks at a time. Often
we went to the Welsh towns. They had a market there once a
week, in each town, where they sold faggots and pease pudding. In 1904 I went to Swansea with Asher and Long Hymie.
We were very nearly caught at Port Talbot, a couple of big
Welsh coppers were coming for us but we got away across the
railway line.

We kept away from Liverpool – they were said to have the
hottest police force in the world.

Once we went to Buxton in Derbyshire. There was a festival on and the King was staying there with the Earl of Derby.
We thought we would do well because they were a good class
people. It was a place like Bath.

Jewish people were the safest people to stop with. They had
bad memories of the police in Russia and weren't fond of
giving them information. You could trust them because they
had a verb in Yiddish 'Thou shalt not' – they were not supposed to injure another person. Jewish people were very
homely, and they did not seem to mind that I was a 'Yok'. At
Swansea we stayed with the Davises. Lovely people – they
lived down a basement. He was a cabinet-maker. She had a
young boy and I used to give him boxing lessons. They were
brainy intelligent people. Mrs Davis said to me once, 'If I had a
daughter, I would let you marry her, Arthur,' she said, 'I think
you're lovely.' She meant it. At that time I could be very
vicious, but I could also be kind.

The first time we went away we got a steamer by Hayes
Wharf at London Bridge and sailed from there to Newcastle. It
was a lovely run – all the way to Newcastle for five shillings.
We thought we were very brave being out at sea. From there
we went to various towns working the markets – at that time
there were markets in every town. We also went to the races at
Morpeth. That was a New Year's Day. I'll always remember it
because I'd got hold of a Kruger sovereign and I couldn't
change it. So I went to a bookmaker and he tried to do me out
of it.

When we were in Manchester we went out pickpocketing in

threes: one person would do the pocket-picking while the other two kept a look-out. There were six of us altogether and we all slept in one room. We stopped with some Yiddisher people in Cheetham Hill, almost opposite Strangeways prison. They took us to a Jewish theatre there, at James Street down Manchester, Piccadilly. But they were all speaking in Yiddish so I couldn't understand.

We hit a lot of trouble in Manchester. There was a woman and her daughter looking in at one of the shops and Jackie Shinebohm went for them. What he forgot was that the woman could see the reflection in the window. The daughter saw him taking out of the mother's pocket – very good-looking she was – and she was so surprised that she stood stock still. Jackie started to push his way through the crowds and I was just about to follow him when I began to realise that something had gone wrong. I could see the woman and her daughter talking and I realised that I'd have to stop the mother and daughter running after him and shouting 'thief'. The daughter picked me out. 'You was with him,' she said. I said, 'What do you mean, what's 'e done?' 'Stole my mother's purse.' I said, 'I didn't see him take anything.' I was stalling to stop her shouting out. A crowd started gathering round and a man belonging to the store came up and said, 'There's two detectives standing over there, CID men. Shall I get them?' So I says, 'Yes', and they come up. The daughter said, 'Oh no, I never accused you of stealing my purse. But we thought we saw you with the boy who did it.' The detective said to her, 'Where's the boy?' She said, 'Right down there' – pointing round the corner. Well I got talking to the detective and I fetched out my documents and we all finished up good friends. In the end he gave me his card – Caversham Road police station – and told me to look out for the scoundrel. 'Would you know him again if you saw him?' he said. So I said, 'Yes, I would.' So he told me that if I saw the boy I was to call the nearest policeman.

The next day Asher got arrested: a detective bagged him at Boot's. So I said, 'Let's clear out, this is getting too hot.' He would have given the same address as me. So we got out of Manchester and went up north. Asher got three months.

By about 1909 or 1910 we were getting older and wiser. Some of the boys turned from pickpocketing to running women on the streets. I turned to snide-pitching – i.e. changing false money. I went with a different group of boys – all English – and different groups on different expeditions. You kept changing partners in the coining line, because if you got off and the others were 'done' people would think you had 'dropped' on them (i.e. squealed).

We would go away from London for about a couple of weeks at a time. My sister Mighty used to parcel the coins up for us. She would send them from the Post Office at the top of the road, very carefully packed. I used to tell her a couple of days beforehand where we'd be on a certain day. So she knew where to send them. We never told anyone else where we were going or what we were doing.

Snide-pitching was very much safer than pickpocketing. Provided you knew the law you could be quite safe – you took the necessary precautions and it was very difficult for them to get a conviction. If you were caught it had to seem like an accident – you couldn't afford to be caught with a little store of bad coins on you. There ain't no charge if you've only got one false coin. The one who took in the snide had only that on him, so if he was caught it seemed like an accident. And if you've got the gift of the gab you can talk yourself out of anything, even murder. It doesn't matter what the evidence is against you. It's no offence to be caught with a bad coin on you unless you've been told by a shopkeeper that they're bad and you still try to change it. And you can always put up the defence that you had ten shillings on a horse and the bookmaker paid you out with bad money. It was no offence to have a certain number. They have to prove that you knew they were bad coins.

£1 worth of half-crowns cost us 4s. £1 worth of 2s cost 5s because the 2s pieces were more difficult to make. The 4s pieces were the cheaper. They went very well in Wales where people used them to save up. You used to buy them from the maker. We had a marvellous maker called Simms. It was the greatest secret where he made them. No one knew where he lived. I used to meet him in the street, and at a different place each time. He was the finest maker of coins you ever saw. He used to make *old* 2s pieces. He smuttered them to make them look old.

Billy Holmes was also a source of supply. He was a good all-round thief – van-dragger, burglar, coiner. He made bad *old* coins – people somehow thought that a false coin was always a new one – but he used to make bad 1862 2s pieces. He used to smut them. Even people who thought they were in the know were deceived by them. Shopkeepers in those days were on the look-out for false coins. They thought they could tell them by the ring. But you could take in one of Billy Holmes's coins and bang it down on the counter and it would make a lovely ring. Billy used to melt a halfpenny in the pot, or a farthing, and it gave them that special ring. He used to use white metal. His real masterpiece was the 4s piece – it didn't have the George and Dragon on it like the 5s piece so it was easier to imitate. We could even use that one in Post Offices. I knew him because he was carrying on with a young woman down the Gardens.

The chief difficulty for the makers was to find buyers whom they could trust. Billy Holmes had a chap working for him who would bring the coins down to us and when we were away he would post them to us in a parcel.

Once we were in Oxford going along the road. There were four of us, me and Bob Wheeler and Stevie Cooper and Gus Davies. We got off at a country station near Oxford, but somehow the police got on our tail. I saw a couple of them in the bushes and said, 'We're being followed.' I sent Gus Davies and Bob Wheeler ahead with the coins and told them to dump them.

Suddenly a horse and trap came up and a superintendent or somebody like that got out and then they all came out from behind the bushes. Talk about a pantomine – I never knew there were so many coppers in the country. I knew I had to bluff because once they got us in the Nick they could be on to the blower and then we would be done for. I was wearing a straw hat and one of the policeman said, 'What are you doing about 'ere?' I said, 'We're on 'oliday, taking a walkin' 'oliday, tourin' the country.' He said, 'What's your two friends doing here?' – pointing to the other two. I said, 'They're no friends of mine, they just asked me what time the train comes in.' So he said, 'You're suspected of counterfeit, would you mind turning out your pockets?' So I did. If you say 'No' then they've a right to take you on to the police station, but if you allow them to do it there and then they've no reason to 'stop, search and detain'. So I pulled all the sixpences and coppers out of my pockets and put them in my hat. He said, 'You've got enough money on you, 'aven't you?' I said, 'Well, you can't go on 'oliday unless you 'ave money.' He said, 'But they're all sixpences and shillings.' I said, 'I know, 'cos if you've got no small change in the country, and you try to give 'em a sovereign, they don't have no change.' 'Well, you're a bit right there,' he said. Anyway the train was due and he let me and my friends go. So we bought our tickets and got on the train. Then at the next station we got out. I said to Stevie, 'Out of it. If they pinch the other two they will be waiting for us.' So we got out at Beaconsfield, and came home another way.

The other two never came home. The police found the coins under a milk churn and they were arrested at Paddington. As I came down the Gardens I saw two policemen – Brogden and Dessent[14] going round to Gus's house to tell the people he lived with that he'd been arrested out in the country for counterfeit coins. They looked at me as they passed and said 'We'll be seein' yer' but they didn't do anything else. The squeak came from a shopkeeper: he must have given a description of us.

The last snide-dropping trip I made away was with two chaps from Hoxton named Joey Jones and Charlie Halworth. Halworth was a married man, though young; the other fellow Jones lived around Turin Street. We were putting down 4s pieces. Halworth was caught because he run away and left his wife and she made enquiries. Somebody told her that he'd run away with me. So she went down and asked my sister where I was and she told her, little knowing what she was doing. Then she went to Old Street police station and told them that he was in the west of England. Scotland Yard put two and two together and got on to the police at Usk where we were and they went into the Post Office, opened the parcels and found all those lovely four-bob bits which my sister had sent. They caught Charlie and he got ten years – I've never seen him since. Jones got about three or four years. I'd already come home, but that put paid to coining as far as I was concerned.

Simms the maker got caught a little afterwards. He got five years for it.[15] After the war he got a pension from the army and he never did any work after that.

In 1908–9 I served another twelve-month sentence. It was a trumped-up business – I got twelve months for being a suspected person down Brick Lane.[16] Under the Habitual Criminal Act once you had had two convictions on indictment they could get you a third time simply for being a suspected person.[17] These small sentences I had as a boy thus counted against me. So I was done under the Prevention of Crime Act. (The policeman who brought the charge soon afterwards dropped dead.) While I was in Pentonville, serving my time, the Borstal Association got in touch with me. They had a high regard for me and they wanted to help me make a new start. So they tried to get me out of England. They paid my fare to Cardiff to find a berth on a ship – they had a home there for boys who were going to sea.

On arrival, I went to a house in the Tiger Bay area, to stay until arrangements were completed for my departure from England. The house was a large boarding house of several rooms, where you could get bed and breakfast for 2s 6d. Resident in the house were a number of Borstal boys who were waiting for a ship. The place was run by a man and his wife, and it was obvious that whatever ship you sailed on, the captain and crew would know you were a jailbird or Borstal boy.

The boarding house keeper received pay from the Borstal authorities; he also received the first three months' pay in advance of the boy who went to sea. So it was a very profitable trade. All this did not appeal to me. I could see the racket that was carried on, and I wanted no part of it. The boarding house keeper looked a real right villain, and I quit. The next morning I set off for London, starting at noon, and making my way by road. I walked all the way home. That was the last time I tried to break free of Bethnal Green.

8 Gibraltar Gardens

When I came home from Borstal in 1904 I found that the family had moved. They'd been slung out of Queen's Buildings because they never paid rent. If you missed a week at 7s 6d a week there would be 15s to pay the next week. My mother had been on the booze and they'd never had the money. So they were slung out. They found a couple of rooms in Gibraltar Gardens, in some big tenement houses at the bottom – what they called 'The Buildings'. The rest of Gibraltar Gardens were cottages, two up and two down. A lot of people from the Nichol had settled there, it was only a few streets away.

Gibraltar Buildings were three tenement houses with twelve rooms in each place and were some 100 years old. Even in 1904 they were in the last stages of dilapidation. There was a basement or cellar in each tenement where the tenants could wash their dirty linen, but as the cellar was in complete darkness it was never used, only by homeless persons. This place was to be my home; the rooms were very small. The front room some 12 feet by 9 feet, the back room smaller. My mother rented two rooms at the top of the tenement. These two rooms were as bad as any in the Nichol. One can only guess at the pain mother suffered when she climbed the stairs, owing to her diseased hip. She must have been very hard pressed to take them on. In Gibraltar Buildings lived the dregs of the East End. The inhabitants of these filthy dens were families who had sunk beneath the terrible burden of poverty, disease and hopelessness. Not a night passed without the drunken screams and violent fights of the human animals who had long ceased to live the decent industrious lives of working folk. Even right up to modern times, round Gibraltar Buildings, they never had no form of gas or electric light. The police had to put a special lamp-post at the top so as to throw some light on the Buildings, but there were always fights going on there, and the police gave the inhabitants a wide berth – they had a very bad character, and the people in the rest of the Gardens did not mix with them.

Soon after coming out of Borstal I got involved in a fight with the family who lived below us – the Collinses. They were very quarrelsome, especially when they come home from the pub. The brother of the wife – a man named Stone – was a real terror: he had served a seven-year sentence for stabbing. They were the terrors of the Gardens. Everybody was scared of them. One night they started shouting up the stairs filthy abuse at my mother; they were drunk and wanted trouble. I went downstairs and told the man what I thought of him in the only language they understood. Words led to blows and, being young and fit, I gave the man a good hiding.

That night, my eldest sister told me an astonishing story which was supported by my young sister and brother. It appeared that one night the husband and wife had rushed into mother's room, dragged her from bed and brutally assaulted her so that when the police arrived and a doctor examined my mother, she was taken to the hospital for treatment. Husband and wife were arrested and charged with causing grievous bodily harm; both were remanded on bail for a week. The following week mother refused to prosecute and the case was dismissed.

This story enraged me. I went potty. And the next day I belted them up – including Stone, the one who was a terror. There was a bit of a barney. I pulled them out and I bashed them up. I could fight like a lion even though I was young and they were no match for me. They brought a case against me and I was arrested but when I came up before the police court, Mr Cluer,[1] the magistrate, was on my side. He said: 'You did what you should have done and I'm dismissing the case.' That was the first time I came up in front of Mr Cluer – several times afterwards I came before him and he discharged me. The funny thing was that in later years I worked with young Billy Collins as a wardrobe dealer (all the Collinses were wardrobe dealers). At the final I liked him, and never let the old sores stop it. He was only a little boy of eight at the time.

Jimmy Norrey lived on the floor below – he and his wife

had the front room on the second storey. Jimmy used to be the 'spotter' for likely jobs in pawnbrokers and jewellers and he would plan the getaways. That was how he got his living. His brother Ginger was a character from the Nichol. He was a 'tapper' – people used to drop him when there was a job because he had a reputation as a terror. Jimmy worked with George King's mob.[2] Georgie and his brother Billy were both screwsmen, both done time for it, pawnbrokers mostly. Jimmy Stickwell worked with them too. He was an engineer who lived in Bethnal Green. He wasn't really a crooked man at all, but he worked with Kingie's gang and he invented a bolt-cutter[3] which they used – it's still in use today. Now this bolt-cutter it could cut through a pawnbroker's grille in half an hour. Then all they had to do was smash the window (if you put a sheet of paper over there was no noise), take the glass out and then help yourself. Jimmy wasn't a tearaway or anything like that. He was respectably married. In 1908 he got a twelve-month sentence and that was the finish of him – he never went back to burglary. If he'd patented his bolt-cutter he could have made a fortune.

I soon put a stop to mother's drinking. She was a wee bit frightened of me and the publicans were too, because I was known in the neighbourhood as a terror. Well, when she started her tricks again – going out of a Monday for about three days on the booze – I thought there's only one way to stop this. 'I'll go after her.' I never touched my mother but I forced her to come back home. And the publicans knew for a cert that if they served her too much they were in for a barney. I would say, 'Here, if you serve my mother again I'll smash yer bleedin' house up.' I used to say things like that. 'I'm not having that gang coming in here.' So gradually I drove her further afield. In the end she got frightened by the Habitual Drunkards Act.

Soon things got better and we began to reap the benefit of more progressive times. My sister had started a sort of money-lending business and in Gibraltar Gardens it prospered. She had started it with lace curtains when we were in Queen's Buildings, buying lace curtains in Caledonian Road, and selling them to the neighbours for weekly payments. She used to sell them very cheap, about 2s 6d a pair. People might want two pairs of curtains and they'd pay 1s a week or 6d if they didn't have money to buy them. She used to let them out finally when she was in the money. Not hire purchase, they just rented them. But my sister was very good to them.

In Gibraltar Gardens she started dealing in drapery. Everything for the house. Like bedding and bedsheets and pillow slips and all that kind of thing. She sold clothing too on credit: men's shirts and suits of clothes, from Bernard's the tailors, down in Brick Lane. Men used to go there and be measured up, but they would pay my sister and she would give the money to the tailor. My sister had a great business. Moss de Jong, the big drapery people, in Houndsditch, thought the world of her because she paid them regular in cash. She got everything from them, blankets, sheets, shirts for the men and she used to let them out at about 1s a week. They were a big Jewish firm and very good friends to us. You could buy anything there – socks for the old man, aprons, sheets. Then Wickham's[4] in Mile End Road – a great big store that used to belong to Barker's – she used to do a tremendous amount of business with them through Provident cheques. She earned a lot of money on that. With Wickham's, the cheque cost 21s and she charged them 22s and Wickham's gave her 1s 8d for every one she sold. So we got 2s 8d in the pound. People would come and say 'Give me a couple of Wickham's cheques' and they would pay back 1s a week until they'd paid 21s. For a pound cheque they could purchase anywhere in the shop. It took them 21 weeks to pay it all off. It was a profit-making business. Once people had paid the 1s deposit they could go to Wickham's and get anything they wanted. It was a big store like Selfridge's or Harrod's. She never let 'em overdo it because if a person gets too much in debt you get nothing – they'd go somewhere else. It's like a publican: he prefers a steady customer who spends two or three bob every night. One day he says 'Could you lend us a pound Jack?' and the publican thinks, 'If I refuse, he won't come to the house again', and perhaps he gives it, but that's the worst thing he could do because the fellow will keep out of there now, because of owing the money.

When we moved to a cottage down Gibraltar Gardens, my sister used to have loads of stuff in the front room. People would come in there, and pick a pair of curtains, take 'em away and give her a shilling. Women would say, 'I could do with some curtains', and my sister would say, 'Come and have a look.' 'How much?' 'Shilling a week.' Sometimes I would go down to the cattle market in Islington to fetch them home – that was another place where she got them.

My sister still had her stall down Roman Road, and when I came out of Borstal I went out to give her a hand on Saturdays and Sunday morning. But then I became more dominant, and started travelling all over the country. Between us we did well and when I got the rest of my money from the county court – the old compensation for the accident – we had money to buy furniture. What with one thing and another we moved out of the Buildings and got one of the cottages in the Gardens – a place with a large forecourt at the front. At last we had a whole house to ourselves. That must have been about 1906 or 1907.

The rent for Gibraltar Gardens was 7s 6d, for four rooms. But he was a good landlord, and now that my mother had stopped her drinking bouts we did not fall behind with the rent. We had a big forecourt in front, big garden and there was plenty of room inside. I had a bedroom of my own. My sister used to sleep upstairs with my mother, my younger brother used to sleep downstairs in the back bedroom with me. We were quite comfortably off. Things were going pretty well for us when we moved there. To start with we painted the whole place out. And we replenished everything. New beds, new furniture, new everything we got. We gave away the old stuff, or burnt it.

It was the first home where we had linoleum. We bought it down the Lane. Used to be a fellow who sold it there on a Sunday morning, half-a-crown a yard. Of course, it's improved greatly in quality now. I remember the fellow well, his name was Mills. He got killed up in Walton Street one day by a chap who hit him in the jaw. He earnt so much money that he drank a bottle of whisky a day. He was in that pub just off Walton Street, on the corner by Devonshire Place – it was a Mann and Crossman's pub, I forget the name – and he insulted a paper seller who had his stand there and the paper seller hit him on the jaw and he went down dead. That was many years ago. Mills was a great big fellow but he was a dead liberty-taker, and that was how he met his end. Don't know where he got the lino from, but he earnt a lot of money out of it. He used to stand there and sell rolls and rolls of it, half-a-crown a yard, great big rolls, people used to come from the country to take it home.

Gibraltar Gardens was an L-shaped cul-de-sac or alley with the entrance some 6 feet wide, in the Bethnal Green Road. On one side was the GPO sorting office, on the other side of the entrance was the vicarage – a large, twelve-roomed house, where the vicar and his wife lived, together with an only child. They never came down the Gardens. It seemed that the Council were not proud of the Gardens and had encouraged the builders to hide the Gardens from the public view so that not even the sunlight could brighten the gloom. The whole court or alley was about 100 years old, built about the same period as the Nichol. It was surrounded by the backs of two timber yards and a large block of workshops. The only entrance to the alley was in Bethnal Green Road. A pub in Gibraltar Walk, 'The Gibraltar', had made a small passage into the Gardens so that the people could get their beer from the 'Gib'. This passage formed a perfect escape route for the many thieves who began to rob passers-by of their purses, gold chains and other valuables – run through the Gardens, then through the passage shutting the door and so stopping all pursuit by the police or others. Some early Victorian humorist must have named this alley after the barren rock in the Mediterranean. It must have been the same sardonic person who named the entrance to Hoxton Workhouse 'Land of Promise'.

One woman down the Gardens used to specialise in confinements – a woman belonging to the neighbourhood who was expert in that kind of business. That was one of the Barclays, Alice Barclay – Carly I called her. She was a married woman. Her husband used to sell racing cards. They was dead ignorant. She exceeded herself one day. Her sister had had three or four children very quick and she was called in by her sister to do away with the child – instead of that she done away with her. The sister died a terrible death – I know that because the doctor told me. Carly being ignorant and trying to fiddle about with instruments, she made a terrible mess of it, and when the doctor come he took one look and said, 'Good

God! Ambulance at once!' But it was too late. It was when they
had children quick that they looked for help from somebody.
But it was a very dangerous proceeding entirely. Thank God
my wife never had anything to do with that although we had
children every two years.

There was also a man in Brick Lane who was suspected of
doing away with babies if you paid him enough. He had a
chemist shop in front and you went right through to a little
surgery at the back. He sold stuff for doing away with babies. I
don't know for sure, but they used to say he was handy for
anything like that, for an abortion.

Another character down the Gardens was Mrs Casey. She
lived nearly opposite me. She was a great Irish woman. She
was continuously washing – that was her main source of living. She was disliked by everyone down there because she had
a very foul tongue. Even the police was afraid to go down
there if she was standing at the door. I've heard her rollock the
police up, even a sergeant. He'd come down delivering sum-
monses and when he come by, he got as far away from the
door as he could to get by her. She was a regular customer for
the children for the chips, 'cos she was continuously washing.
I liked the woman a lot – she was continuously working. I
never saw her with a hat on or a coat. She had a boy and a girl.
They was lazy children, not the type to go getting wood, the
girl got married about sixteen. An American soldier took her
back to America with him and the boy, he got married early
and got away from her.

There was a woman in nearly every street of the East End of
London who got a living taking neighbours' things to the
pawn shop. The pawn-shop broker would lend her more than
he would an ordinary customer on the goods because he knew
that she would get 'em out again on Saturday – he trusted her.
He didn't want to be lumbered up with a shop-load of stuff
that wasn't going to be redeemed. He'd sooner do business
with her, than a person who fetched a load of stuff in there and
didn't intend to redeem 'em. We had a woman like that in
Gibraltar Gardens, Mrs Taylor, she used to take all the parcels.
She lived just round by the Gardens. She was well-known.
And so was her husband – we used to call him 'Old Taylor'.
He was a right 'un. Not a violent man, but he knew all the

tricks of the trade. And could they drink, the two of them! If you ever wanted to find them, you just made a round of the pubs.

The sixteen cottages in the Gardens were owned by two different landlords. On the right of the court were seven cottages, on the left were nine more owned by the same landlord as the Gibraltar Buildings.[5]

Our first house in the Gardens was the cottage at No. 5 but by the time we left the Gardens – in 1930 – we owned four or five houses there. I had one, my brother had one, my mother had one, my sister had one and the other was let to my brother's daughter, Mary Davis. In the end we practically owned the Gardens.

At No. 5 we had lodgers. My mother had a girl with her in the top room, after my sister Mighty married and moved to No. 3. For some years she would give lodging to young women who were homeless and they would stay with mother until they found a husband and set up home together. Later, when I married and moved into No. 3, she took in a middle-aged couple. He was a typical Yorkshire man, she was a Romany. We called him Ginger Tom. He paid 5s a week for the room. He was a docker at the Surrey docks and when work was scarce he would play, or rather run, a 'Crown and Anchor' board at the docks. He was very clean in his personal appearance. He was the sort of person that you would call untrustworthy. She was a gypsy who was a good wife and very clean in her habits and home. They had no children but she would be pregnant at times and then become normal again. They were lodgers for some years.

I used to put up pals when they had nowhere else to go. Jackie Shinebohm slept with me in the back room. I would put him up when we come home from our provincial expeditions. I didn't put him up regularly – only when he had no other place to go.

At that time a lot of boys used to stay out of a night-time – even shopkeepers' sons – and if they didn't have anywhere to stay I would take them home. That's how I met up with Jackie Shinebohm. He didn't have no parents. Another boy I picked up, quite a nice Jewish boy. It was a peculiar thing, he could talk well, but oh, was he dirty. My Lord, he looked as lousy as a cuckoo. I said, 'Cor Blimey, you need a wash', so he went to the baths and I got him a change of underclothes. I didn't take him out thieving, but I took him home and gave him a place in my mother's back room. He impressed me very much, he was so lively and intelligent and I couldn't understand why he'd got in such a condition. Years later, in the 1920s, we were at a race course in Essex, Chelmsford – three or four of us had gone there to play the spinning jenny and we'd straightened up the police. I saw a couple of Jewish chaps. They was on 'duff' photos – they took a picture, got the deposit on them and then never developed the prints. We was in a buffet when one of them said, 'Don't you recognise me?' and I said, 'No' – he had a lovely suit of clothes on and a lovely smile. He said, 'Think back down the Gardens,' and it was him. He had the gift of the gab and he was getting quite a lot of money at the photo game.

The man who stayed longest with me was Edward Spencer, my evil genius – in 1915 he got me put away for five years because of a robbery he had done. I first got to know him when I left Wormwood Scrubs in 1902. He mixed with the gang at Clark's coffee house and then he came to live in the Gardens. I think the first time he came to live with us was in 1911. He had had a four-year lagging for thieving a wallet at White City – during the Olympic Games of 1908. He served three of the four years and when he came out he needed a fixed address. And so he came to Gibraltar Gardens, sharing the back room with me. He was evil right through. He dressed very magnificent and I always thought he was a woman's man. But when we were in prison together I discovered that he was a homosexual.

9 Cabinet-making

You might say that cabinet-making was the family trade of the Hardings, though only one of them did it regular.

My uncle Albert was a carver. He had a shop in Old Bethnal Green Road. He had three or four sons who were carvers. We used to employ one of them – my cousin Jack – when we had the cabinet-maker's place in Cotton's Gardens. Him and Bill Saville – my partner – was pals. But Jack was a bit on the posh side and he became a very expert carver. He and his brothers used to do the exhibition work – they became internationally known for their carving. They moved right over the other side – Peckham, Gypsy Hill way, they all went over there. After that we never came in contact. It was a different sphere – we remained where we were known in the Nichol and they got right away from it.

My father started making overmantles about 1898. I think he might have had some ulterior motive when I look back on it. We were still living in Bacon Street. I don't think my mother was making many matchboxes at the time, and my sister hadn't really got going with her stall. I'll tell you where the workshop was – on the corner of Church Street and Bethnal Green Road. My aunt Liza had the whole of the house there – it was after they pulled down the shop in the Nichol. Well, underneath was a large basement. So my father put a bench up and started making overmantles. I used to go round there and get the small shelves and take them to the mill. I don't know what money he earned at it.

My first job was at a cabinet-maker's – Atkins in Church Road. They used to make deck chairs and all that sort of thing there. I was on the sanding machine. I think I got 7s 6d a week. It was only a few yards from where we lived.

I was only at Atkins's for a few weeks, but later I worked at Butler's for nine months. They was a big cabinet-makers in

New Inn Yard. They used to make wonderful work, beautiful work. Used to make the bedsteads, the wooden bedsteads, with the canopies, lovely twisted arms. Marvellous. I wish I had the furniture in my house now, the lovely furniture what they made. They were skilled men in there – good workmen.

In 1907 – when I was nineteen or twenty – I started a cabinet-maker's factory in partnership with a man named Bill Saville who had had a long experience of the work. Bill lived in Chilton Street. He worked in a cellar there and made cheap china cabinets. He owed my sister £20. I was only there to get our money back. I put a few quid in, but I could see I wasn't going to get rich so I turned it in.

The first place we had was at the back of a pub in Hare Street – what they call Cheshire Street now – the 'Red Cross'. We took the back part for a workshop, me and Bill Saville and a workman we employed. We took it 'cos the rent was very cheap, 5s a week, something like that. The room was supposed to be a bagatelle room. It belonged to the pub. You had to carry the timber up the side of the pub, through a passageway. We did very well there but they sold the pub. It was one of the pubs done away with by a Liberal Act of Parliament which got rid of of thousands of pubs. After we left, it was turned into the synagogue, 'cos the number of Jewish people was increasing enormously around there.

Then we got a place in Cotton's Gardens. It was in a turning off Kingsland Road, opposite Drysdale Street. It was a factory which had just been built. We had the bottom floor. Upstairs was all in the boot trade. It was a big place – we could have got a dozen makers and their benches in there and it was much more expensive than Hare Street – 15s a week. We only took it because they didn't know us. We had to knock them in the end for five weeks' rent. We never paid anybody for anything. Saville was well known for that – that's why he put my name on the bill. We bought the timber from the place opposite and never paid them. 'Long firm' business. We were able to do it because we looked a posh affair.

Our speciality was making Louis cabinets. They were flash jobs with big mirrors on the sides, and ornaments. Cameo legs, glass all bevelled. They stood at least 7 foot high with the pediment at the top. There was a big pane of glass in the middle, and two kidney-shaped mirrors at the sides, fitted into the wood, and a diamond shape at the bottom. There were two doors underneath with shelves to put in crockery and glasses, all that sort of thing. The whole thing was a gigantic bluff. They were very cheap to make for they looked expensive. I suppose they sold them for about a tenner each. Louis cabinets were made out of whitewood blacked all over; the polishers stained them black and then used to polish them with a varnish, not french polishing but sandpaper and varnish. A wee bit of carving, and that was it.

We had four makers and a couple of polishers. They didn't have no planing to do – the work was all planed and cut at the mill. All they had to do was fit them up. I wasn't much of a cabinet-maker – I'm a carpenter – but there was no hard work in it. Whitewood – they don't use it today – would take the stain and polish easy. The drawer had a bit of carving on the front of it – what they called 'a scratching'. There wasn't any artistic fittings, they was nailed and glued together. The carving cost 5s 6d. I used to get my brother's father-in-law, Mr Gibbs, to do the carving. He was a good carver.

The cabinet would cost some 25s for making, that is 5s for maker, 5s for timber, 5s for polisher and polish, 5s for glass, 5s for carving. Nails was 2d a pound. When completed they were sold to the large wholesalers in the Curtain Road. Each maker would make six cabinets a week. Really and truly they cost us about 27s or 28s to make, and we used to sell them to Hollington's for 32s. I don't think we ever got more than 32s out of them. Hollington's was the last resort. They kept open till 5 o'clock on the Saturday afternoon. The workmen used to wait for us to come back after selling them, so that they could get their wages: they waited just by the railway arch in Kingsland Road, in a pub.

If the work was ordered by a shop you might get 40s or more. But if you had no orders you had to take them out on spec. It was a bare living. No matter how many of them you made, you wouldn't get rich.

Jack Taylor, he'd come round with his pony and cart and he'd say, 'Got anything? – I'm going round Dulwich or Hammersmith,' or something like that. He worked the furniture shops round there. It was a question of transport – he had the pony and cart. He used to go round hawking. Lewisham was a good place. The shopkeepers there would say, 'Well let me have a couple of them, I'll try them,' and he'd probably sell them for 50s apiece. There was an art in selling them to the shops.

Saville did the work, I owned the shop. I helped him to mark the wood out, but the workmen did most of the work. We engaged some six makers and two polishers. Monday no workmen appeared, it seems that Monday was devoted to drinking beer. The day was regarded as a holiday which started by having a sub from the boss – this was the custom in the cabinet-making business. While the men spent their money on drink, we the bosses would buy the timber for the week's work and during the morning we would visit the wholesalers for orders. Tuesday the makers would start work, marking out the wood for the mill to cut and plane. The day's work would end about 7–8 p.m. Most workers would ask for a sub to carry on at home. The rest of the week they would work hard.

It didn't last long – not more than about a couple of months. If we'd had our own horse and vans we could have made a profit. Saville was a man that knew the business right through, but he was too fond of women and you can't mix it – when I was earning money if I'd been out boozing and betting horses I'd never've saved up enough to get meself out of the bloody mess I was in. I set about him and belted him. He went up the nick and got a summons against me and I was given a £10 fine.

Cabinet-makers were very numerous in the East End of London.[1] During the years 1890 and onwards, land developers could be seen in every road where there were houses which had gardens in the rear. The gardens were bought from the landlord and the builders would put up small workshops which were let to cabinet-makers. Blyth Street and Teesdale Street in Bethnal Green were specially built for the Jewish cabinet-makers. The top storey was made for workshops. They were built by a firm named Davis. The houses in Bacon Street was the same. Each tenement had a workshop in the back-yard which had been built on the garden. There was no entrance or exit for the workmen and their work had to be carried through the passage-way of the houses. So one can guess at the filthy conditions of the premises.

Nearly in every street there was chair-makers. They didn't finish the chair, only frames. They sold them in the white to the upholsterers. Mostly birch. You would have a couple of benches. You could stack them on top of each other. There was not much work in it, planing them. The mill done all the work. The upholsterers finished them, polished them, got them ready for market. There were plenty of buyers – people were changing from Windsor chairs to upholstered chairs. Light's in Curtain Road were the big buyers.[2] They bought for the West End. Chair-making was a trade by itself. You didn't move from it to cabinet-making. They kept to that one branch of the business.

Then there were the barrow-makers or wheelwrights. They made barrows and let them out at one shilling a day. I know one man – Goldfine – who made a fortune out of it. Everybody wanted market barrows.

Cabinet-making was a family affair. You brought up your children to it. Then Darling & Son set up in 1902.[3] They was printers. They brought printing to the East End. They took all the boys from St Matthew's. Instead of going into the cabinet-making they went into the print and turned out more respectable. Some of the biggest ruffians out had children who did that. It was a very respectable firm, with commissionaires on the door.

Overmantles was the easiest thing for a man to make. Everybody bought overmantles. It was a new fashion about 1900. The poor always wanted an overmantle. Couldn't have a house without an overmantle. We had one in Queen's Buildings. The bigger the better. Lovely glass in the middle and two side glasses. They was all different types. Some had shelves on, most did, and a canopy at the top, with a big shelf to put little ornaments on, or a clock. The one we had at Queen's Buildings was just a cheap thing, about ten bob I suppose. It looked all right. Polished, not painted. You had two little fasteners on both sides, you put the nail through into the wall, and that was it. They was very ornate, black and gold. Ours was polished walnut. Overmantles wasn't expensive at all.

The cheapest ones were ten bob new in a shop. When you looked at 'em, you couldn't realise how cheap they was.

I knew a lot of overmantle makers, cabinet-makers, you know, who made them. They'd take them on the hawk, round the retail shops, save a shop at Croydon making the long journey to the East End. My father used to make them, used to have 'em gilded and all – he had a craftsman gilder to do it. I made overmantles too. You could make half a dozen at a time. The whole thing was really cheap – a couple of panels, several panes of looking-glass and plenty of stain. You could use any kind of wood and buy a cheap stain. Fox's in Church Street, the chemists, they sold polishes and stains.[4]

Cabinets – like china cabinets or music cabinets – were the same. Polished wood, everything that was made was polished. Veneered, no – you see years ago they had this system of inlaying. They used small instruments and they put a screw through the piece of wood, ½ inch or 1 inch according to how far they wanted the marking to go and then they put a sort of a yellow line in it. Well, that's how they made inlaid furniture. The end of the screw cut into the soft wood, and left a ridge. Then all they had to do was put the inlaid stuff in, and you had an inlaid top, which made it look a very precious thing. It didn't cost nothing. Sold 'em for 8s.

About 1900 the Hackney Furnishing Company started the shilling business – you know, the credit business. You could buy a five-pound home for a shilling a week. 'Five pounds – a hundred weeks to pay,' that's what their adverts said. It stands out in my memory. It was such a huge success that other firms copied. You got a kitchen table, a couple of chairs, a Windsor chair, a bed, and a wash hand-stand. From the business point of view it was a wonderful idea because after a couple had been in it a year or two, they would find something else that they wanted. It might be a wardrobe, or a china cabinet. It was such a wonderful idea because you had to go there, most cases on a Saturday when you had your money in your pocket. If they were decent people they would aspire for a better home than what they had. So, the result was that when they went there they'd probably buy something extra.

The wash hand-stand was really only a wooden top with a round ring in it for the basin and a stand for the jug of water, and then the chamber pot underneath. But some of them was really ornate. They had a composition, like a kind of marble, imitation marble for the top, so that the water when you washed yourself wouldn't sink into the wood and perish it. Composition, it was only composition you know. Not all of 'em, some of 'em just had an ordinary wooden top, cheap like the kitchen table. But they had a little bit of wood at the back so that the bowl wouldn't slip off, or the jug wouldn't slip off. Just a small backing. Some became more ornate; they had a mirror fixed in the middle and side wings and they developed into the three-piece furniture: the sideboard and the wardrobe and the dressing table. In the end you had the dressing table with a lovely mirror in the middle. A bedroom suite was the first furniture I bought when I got married in 1924, to keep the clothes clean of bugs.

The first thing for a couple who could afford it was a wardrobe. Wardrobes were practically unknown when I was a child. You put the same things on the next day. It was a question of sticking them on the chair when you went to bed of a night. If you had any best clothes, you kept them in the pawnshop.

Cabinet-making was a precarious living because of the cut-throat competition of the vast number of out-of-work makers who could be seen in the Curtain Road area every day.[5] If you didn't have the orders you still had to keep your men employed or they would go to work for somebody else, and at the end of the week you'd got to sell them because you depended on that to pay your men out. You'd got no capital or bank account. You'd got to sell on Saturday even if you lost money on what you had made. Rivington Street, Shoreditch, had a number of wholesale firms who bought the finished work. They bought black Louis cabinets which cost some 30s to make. Sometimes the maker would be compelled to sell at a loss. Overmantles would be sold sometimes at 10s each. Many small makers were compelled to pay a hawker to travel with a load of work around London's furniture retail shops to sell at a price which did not leave much profit for his labour. Hollington's were a big firm in Rivington Street.[6] It was run by two brothers. They used to buy it pounds cheaper than what it was worth because they knew the cabinet-makers had to sell their

work on Saturday or Friday in order to have the money to pay
the workmen. Lebuses, they were one of the worst slave-
masters out. I remember pulling the barrow up to their factory
in Worship Street.[7] They had their own factory but they
bought everything.

Bedroom suites were small then, you could get three or
four on a barrow – very small wardrobes, wooden bedstead,
wooden coal scuttles with a tin inside them. Nearly every
cabinet-maker made those. There was plenty of fellows about
who'd do a job for 6d, that was nothing unusual. I knew chaps
who'd take loads of stuff up to the Cattle Market (that was
about eight miles away) for half-a-crown.

Most of these makers depended on buying cheap boards
from the timber-yards. There were plenty of timber-yards
about. At that time there was no three-ply. You went to the
timber merchant and ordered common deal. A 3-inch plank
was ripped down to a bare quarter of an inch so they could get
twelve out of a plank. They used that for the back-board of a
gentleman's wardrobe, or the bottom and panels of a chest of
drawers. For a cabinet you'd buy the timber for about twenty
or thirty at a time. You bought it to a certain width, according
to the shelves you've got in your cabinet, about four or five
inches wide. All you had to do was to fit it up and plane down
the raw edges. You had different patterns for the different
kinds of cabinets, and you'd follow them.

We sometimes used old packing cases. Firms didn't want to
be lumbered with old packing cases. They were glad to get rid
of them. The Kemp family in Bacon Street, they used to buy
these big barrels, great big barrels which had been used to send
over tobacco from America. They used them to make round
tables.[8] All the family was at the same business, a big family, a
lot of brothers. They had proper workshops all round Bacon
Street, Chiltern Street, and they employed people. They were
biggish people, but they used to spend their money on beer, so
they didn't become millionaires. Dealers would get cases from
the city, all they had to do was to take the nails out. Georgie
Berner in Bacon Street, he made a living out of it, he knew
all the firms which had the stuff – this cheap, whitewood
stuff. You could get it yourself, but you had all the trouble
of knocking the packing cases to pieces; pulling out the

nails, filling up the nail holes. It was easier to buy from a dealer.

In the cabinet-making game you were always in debt. You owed the timber-merchant, you owed the glass people. Somebody's got to be done. One week it was the timber-yard, the next it was the glass people, another week the carver, or the people where you went to get the fittings. To survive you had to swindle somebody – you either swindled the timber man or the glass man, or you didn't pay the rent. You'd buy what you could on trust – got it 'on the nod'. One week you'd knock them, the next week you'd pay. The economics of it was not to pay so long as you could get away with it. Say they want to settle on Monday. Well you've no ready money, and so you ask them to wait. You do the same thing with the timber people, the same thing with the glass people, the same with the landlord.

A lot of the cabinet-makers worked at home.

Jimmy Saunders who lived on the Mount was a man who worked for many years in a one-room workshop making wooden brackets for which there was a great demand. Some of his work was very expensive. The brackets were made with a mirror in the middle and shelves held up by pillars. Expensive ones had some good carving. These brackets went in pairs and looked very nice when they had family photographs.

Charlie Cooper was an overmantle-maker.[9] He had a large room in Turin Street, Bethnal Green. He could make a large stock of overmantles for sale to retail shops. The making was easy but the only snag was getting the bevelled glass for the centre piece. Charlie Cooper had a wife who was a good french polisher, so he was able to finish the jobs right out. All they had was a back room in the house in Turin Street with a six-foot bench. The work was easy. You don't want a lot of help making overmantles, they're quite easy to make.

Jimmy Silk, he was a hawker. He had his wife to make the things which he sold at the fairs to children at holiday times, like rattles. Lived in Bacon Street. He made a packet out of her, she was a very hard-working girl. He sold at Hampstead Heath and Deptford Fair.

Joe Barker worked in a single room – on the corner of Club Row, just one room. Not very big about 9 foot square, 'cos they wasn't big cabinets. They was only small cabinets that they made. The height was only about 2 foot and the width was about 20 inches – you didn't need a lot of timber.

Not all the cabinet-makers were poor. The Mitchells became big-class people. They went from the making of 'em to the buying of 'em, sending them all over the world. They were in Bethnal Green Road, at the top of Turin Street. They started round the Mount. There was a lot of brothers. They became pretty wealthy. You wouldn't see them boozing in the public bar, you'd always see them with some customers in the saloon bar. The Taylors was a relation to the Mitchells, but he was more in the selling part of it – they employed him for a time. He had a pony and cart. He was a good seller – he could sell anything.

I knew another cabinet-maker who did well – Meadows, he went to school with me. They had a small shop in Bacon Street – they used to make tables, good, decent-class work. The whole family was in the cabinet business. Good tables, good workmanship. I've seen wardrobes go out of there. They bought proper wood at the timber place. They were a family that I would call 'well-breeched'. The daughters were very respectable. They didn't work at cabinet-making – they was in the print business. One of them married Jack Godwin, who trained the Jewish boxers. The Meadows were English.

The only time I came into contact with Jewish cabinet-makers was when I lived in Bacon Street. They were Russian Jews. And they were *workers* – the only time they knocked off early was on a Friday.

When we moved round Gibraltar Gardens there was two cabinet-makers down there: one was Barclay and the other was old Joe Smith. Jack Barclay made music cabinets. He was a pretty good workman, but he drank. Both he and his wife liked a drop of drink, she was a good goer. He died young of TB. He'd always be round to my sister on a Monday morning to borrow a few bob. He bought cheap wood and inlaid the top and sides with a home-made tool, using white wax, but heating the wax he was able to inlay the work. He could make a dozen music cabinets a week, price £4 16s 0d. This left him some £2 weekly, not hard work. (These same music cabinets, with three shelves, polished and inlaid, are looked upon as antiques today and sold for £4–£5–£6.*) Barclay lived in Gibraltar Buildings where he had a single room. He was just a simple man; a decent chap. I liked him, a very quiet man. He dressed very poorly but he always had a bowler hat – that was unusual for the working class – and he always put on a muffler whatever the weather. When he felt fit enough he'd make a couple of cabinets a day. He'd have to go around fetching the wood. He'd go anywhere he could get it. Orange boxes was ideal. They've got two solid tops and thin sides. They formed the basis of the cabinet and then at the timber-yard they sold what they called 'twelve cut', a 2-inch or 3-inch plank of wood cut into twelve very minute boards. You could buy them very cheap and they formed the back part of the cabinet. The shelves were made of the thin part of the orange box – the sides. You didn't pay nothing for 'em. His music cabinets cost 8s, had four shelves in it and they stood flat on the ground without any legs. It was really a glorified box with shelves put in, but it looked very nice when it was polished. There was usually a walnut stain, 'cos it was the cheapest and it held the best. And then, at the moment it dried, you gave it a coat of varnish and it come out beautiful. Say it cost him 30s for somebody else to get him the orange boxes, and nails and screws and a little bit of inlaid stuff, and a wee touch of glue. He'd make very likely about twelve a week, took 'em to Hollington's at the weekend. He made a fair living at it, but he gradually faded away – he had about eight children when he passed away and the oldest boy he died of consumption when he was about fourteen.

Old Joe Smith made music stools. He had one room down Gibraltar Gardens; he used a basement that nobody used, not big, nothing was on a big scale. The basement was about 12 foot by 9 foot. For these music stools he used orange boxes, same as Jack Barclay. It was good wood, clean, no knots in 'em. He got a little smoothing plane, took five minutes to plane 'em up. Then stain it well, and give it a coat of good varnish. All he had to buy was the four legs. Joe Smith didn't have no one to help him – he had a wife but he was always away from her. He did it all himself.

* 1974 prices.

A french polisher could earn more than a cabinet-maker, even though she was a woman. It was a skilled trade. The cabinet-maker did the work in the white, and the polisher would stain it and varnish and sandpaper. It had to be good work – so beautifully polished that you could see your face reflected in it. The polishers had to polish with a varnish. They made their own rubbers, made a hard ball of wadding and soaked it in polish. It had to be good quality rag so it wouldn't tear. Then they put a linen rubber over it and squeezed the polish through.

French polishers didn't work regularly, but any place would take them on.[10] They might do two different firms in the week. They would only be taken on when the makers had finished their work, usually at the end of the week. A big firm would have a lot of things for them to make up at the end of the week, and they'd want a couple of polishers. On Friday nights they worked what they called a 'ghoster' – that is they worked all night till Saturday morning – 'cos you had to get the work ready to put in the van and up in Shoreditch. They'd want double the pay for that. They earned enough at the end of the week for the whole week. Women were better polishers than men; they had that uncanny touch. My brother's wife was a polisher. Scores of young women went into it. It was hard work, but paying. A lot of them had the work brought to them at home. It was hard work, handling big wardrobes. You had to keep at it, rubbing, it knocked the hands about. Some of the hooligans married french polishers because they knew they would make good money. The husband might do the woodwork and then leave the wife to do the staining. Charlie Cooper, his wife had her own polishing shop in Turin Street. She used to employ girls to work in there. She was steady, earned plenty of money. She had four or six girls working for her all week. People used to fetch the work to her on the barrow. The husband made his own cabinets, but he liked the drink.

Two very well known characters of the early years of the century were named Sam and Mary Holloway. Both were french polishers and very good at their trade. They would work for six months or more and keep off the drink. He would buy himself some nice clothes and his wife Mary would keep herself nice and tidy. Sam Holloway was a little man, some 5 feet high; his wife was double his size and taller, about 5 foot 10 inches or more. They had a big family and were all well known and respected. When Sam and his wife went on the booze then they lit the neighbourhood up. Mary Holloway was completely changed. From a quiet friendly woman she became a real villain. She could stand and fight any man or woman. I once employed Sam and Mary to polish some work, they were good workers but when Mary was drunk she would try to sort me out and shout my name all over the place. All the children were polishers, all the sons and all the daughters, they was brought up to it. We paid the Holloways 5s 6d for a Louis cabinet to be glossed. Mrs Holloway was scared of me and everyone else was scared of her. She was a villain when she was drunk, but all right when she was sober. She was a hard worker.

10 The terrors of Brick Lane

Brick Lane was a hotbed of villainy. Women paraded up and down the streets, took the men to their 'doubles' and sold themselves for a few pence. Thieves hung about the corner of the street, waiting, like Mr Micawber, for something to turn up. In the back alleys there was garotting – some of the brides would lumber a seaman while he was drunk and then he would be dropped – 'stringing someone up' was the slang phrase for it. There were some wild characters about. One of them was 'China Bob'. I believe he was of Jewish extraction. He always carried a small chopper or hatchet in a poacher's pocket of his coat or jacket. He once fought a duel in Dorset Street with a man named 'Scabby'. Coats and shirts off, both had small knives. Both had small wounds when taken to the London Hospital and had their cuts attended to. An enterprising reporter of the *Star* newspaper took some photos of their bodies. May I say that both of these two men were more like animals – and wild animals at that – than human beings. They inflicted terrible injuries on each other. China Bob had many scars and half-healed cuts upon his body, he smelt of decaying flesh. He was found one morning in the gutter in Commercial Street which he had terrorised for so long. He was dead; no one was sorry, no one cared, least of all the police.[1] This was after the First World War.

The man they called 'Scabby' was the same type of character. He would pick his victims from people who showed fear, and make them give him money for protection. One night in a doss-house in Dorset Street Scabby came in with a parcel of fish and chips. He offered the chips round, which was the custom then and still is. But one drunken fool took his piece of fish instead of just the chips and started eating it. Scabby had a knife in his hand, because he was about to cut a loaf of bread. When he realised what had happened he stabbed the man fatally. He was put on trial for murder, pleaded provocation and was acquitted.[2] Later after drinking in the 'Frying Pan', a pub at the corner of Thrawl Street and Brick Lane, he crossed the road, walked into Mother Wolff's, picked up a penny cake and walked out of the shop without paying, after using some threats.[3] He was charged with stealing a penny cake and sentenced to 12 months jail. Such is justice.

Another character who haunted Brick Lane at that time was Biddy the Chiver. She and China Bob were natural enemies – he inflicted injuries upon her with his little hatchet what he carried about in his inside pocket. Biddy would have a go at anything, 'lumbering' a man and all the rest of it – i.e. luring him into some dark alley and then stripping him. There were a lot of people like that. They wouldn't thieve but they would terrorise people. Biddy was an attractive woman, while she was young. She had everything that men admire in a woman except the power to control her evil nature. She easily lost control. I first met her when I went to a party in a friend's house. Our eyes met across a crowded room. I liked the look of her. We talked and I wanted to know more about her. Someone warned me of her reputation for violence, so I left her alone. Biddy lived by making other women pay up to her, know what I mean? She'd terrorise all them people who got a living from lumbering sailors and that kind of thing. Men as well as women were afraid of her. With her, you couldn't be sure you would get away with superficial wounds. Sometimes a knife goes just too deep – or too near a vital spot – they are dangerous things to play with, and Biddy always worked with a knife. Her evil nature had made her notorious. They called her 'Biddy the Chiver' and she lived up to her name. She slashed a woman's face with a broken glass, inflicting nasty injuries. She was acquitted at her trial at the Old Bailey because the witness swore it was an accident.[4]

Years slipped by. She looked what she was. Just like every other woman did at the other end of Brick Lane. She was dark-haired and slim – no superfluous flesh on her – but she wasn't attractive in any shape or form. She had a couple of nasty scars on her face and her reputation was very, very bad. Not many people would associate with her, not even men. She wasn't a desirable sort of person. She lived in Flower and Dean

Street and carried on in the same old way, with small convictions for fighting, but nothing to put her away. Old Smithy owned the rooms and I think he was a wee bit wary of turning her out when she didn't pay her rent. Then she met and married a man who treated her very badly; she was frequently seen with bruises on her face. One day it happened. She went to look for him, found him with another woman and stabbed him to death. She was sentenced to three years for manslaughter, diminished responsibility. She died in Holloway prison.

'Spud Murphy' was another of the half-mad loafers who belonged to Brick Lane and Aldgate, living on the wretched women of Spitalfields. Had a tattoo right across his forehead. At one time he had served in the mercantile marine, but that, it seems, was the only honest work he ever did. He was indicted for the murder of his lady friend, 'Singing Rose', a bride from the other end of Brick Lane.[5] He killed her in a lodging house in the Borough, in Tabard Street. Everyone knew he'd killed her but the judge let him off with a friendly warning: be careful, you may not be so lucky next time. He once asked me how many women Jack the Ripper done in. I have a pretty good idea how many Spud done. The last one was another unfortunate woman at Islington.[6] This time the verdict was guilty and he was hanged at Pentonville prison. He was a mental case, an ignorant, homicidal, mentally sick animal. Sort of chap who would do a lot of harm and who had the tools to do it – like a machine gun.

Jack Parr was a young pickpocket. He had lived in Bethnal Green all his young life. In the first years of this century he could find no suitable employment, so like hundreds of other East End boys he turned to dishonesty. In 1902 he was released from Pentonville prison after serving a sentence of three months as a suspected person. While he was in prison his girlfriend had decided not to renew her friendship with him on his discharge. He pleaded with her to give him another chance, but the girl refused and declared, 'If you don't stop following me I will go to the police station.' Parr said, 'Go on, if you want to "shop" me to the police, go in the nick.' The girl went into Bethnal police station to make a complaint. Parr followed her in and in an instant he pulled a gun from his pocket and shot her dead.[7] He was speedily disarmed. Jack Parr was eighteen years, he was tried, condemned and hanged in Pentonville prison. There was an outbreak of riotous behaviour in the Bethnal Green district at the failure to obtain a reprieve – hooliganism – a boy was stabbed to death in Union Street; no one got done for it. He left an old mother behind.

The 'brides' were mostly down the other end of Brick Lane, where the lodging houses were in Flowery Dean Street. The 'Seven Stars' next to Christ Church School was mostly used by the ladies of the town, and the 'Frying Pan', on the corner of Thrawl Street and Brick Lane, was famous for being the centre of the red-light district. At the beginning of Flowery Dean Street there were the 'doubles' – in the narrow part – where you had furnished rooms. They were paid for not by the week but on a nightly system – same as in Jack the Ripper's time when Mary Kelly used them. Mother Wolff's cook house was in Flower and Dean Street. She was a very famous character and a great service to the homeless people down there. She sold cooked food and she was a godsend to the lodgers in the kip-houses. They were able to buy cooked food at very low prices.

Jimmy Smith owned the lodging houses in Flower and Dean Street. He had a shop there and started by selling coal to the people – just ordinary working-class people – at terrible prices. He had a woman in charge of the furnished rooms side of the business, a Mrs Neville; himself he lived in the Commercial Road, and later he went to Brighton. Jimmy Smith was half-Irish, and his second wife was Jewish. One of the daughters married a Jewish bookmaker. He knocked her about and done all her money in, and eventually he committed suicide. He done every penny of her money in gambling.

I can remember when I was very young he used to walk through Brick Lane, dressed magnificently, and his wife and boy always followed, at a discreet distance, behind. I used to go with young Benny Hall, his step-son. He might have been three or four years older than me, and he had charge of one of the Flowery Dean lodging houses. I used to buy my guns off him (he got them cheap from the lodgers) and in later years, after the First World War, he was the best man at my wedding. His step-father left him £4,000 when he died but he never did much with it – he kept it in the piano, he told me, but he never gave anything away, he was very tight.

Dorset Street had an even worse reputation than Flowery Dean Street. That's where Jack the Ripper done some of his murders. We just used to call it 'the street.' There was such a large number of doss-houses there that they called it 'Dossers' Street' and they abbreviated it again just to 'the street' which is what we called it. There were doss-houses on one side, furnished rooms on the other. McCarty owned all the furnished rooms down there. He was an Irishman, a bully, a tough guy. Marie Lloyd used to see him, because there was a pub round the corner she used to go to. All his daughters were in show business on account of Marie Lloyd. They had plenty of money. McCarty lived down there and Danny Macarthur, and a chap I had some trouble with, Billy Macguire. I went down there and put a stop to some business with a girl.

There were two kinds of girl. Those who went up West mixed with the toffs.[8] They would get as much as 10s a time or even £1 and they would ride home in hansom cabs. Some of them used to hang about Aldgate where the hansom cabs would pull up for them, or they would have their customers from the late buses out of the West End. They would meet them at the coffee stalls 1 or 2 or 3 in the morning.

The girls who stayed in Spitalfields were very poor. That was what you called a 'fourpenny touch' or a 'knee trembler' – they wouldn't stay with you all night. Jack the Ripper's victims were fourpenny touches. Like poor old Mary Kelly. She couldn't pay her rent so, poor cow, she went to the bottom. Even if you stayed all night with the girls like that it was only a couple of shillings.

I was friendly with the girls but I didn't stay with them except once. It was when I was about eighteen. I had just come out of Borstal and I'd heard the boys talking about the women and girls – I hadn't really any idea of that sort of thing. In Sclater Street (Club Row) there was a block of buildings inhabited by the Jewish people, and one of them was a chap we called Fiddler – a man who'd lost his legs serving time in Siberia. I liked him very much and he used to buy a little bit of stolen stuff. He had a room upstairs which he let to a prostitute, a nice, slim, tall girl. She was an English girl, about eighteen years of age. I never knew her name – they used to call her 'Faithful Wedding'. One day, when she was passing by, one of the boys said, 'I'd like to have a go at her.' I said, 'I could have her any time' – you know how you boast about these things. So we had a little bet – about a shilling – and I said, 'I bet I go home with her tonight.' I had no more idea of what it meant than a fly in the ear, but I wanted to be somebody. Next night she must have done well, because about 12.30 she came home in a hansom cab. I went over to her and said, 'Hello, do you want to take me upstairs?' She said, 'Do you really want to come upstairs?' I said, 'Yes.' So we went upstairs – all stone stairs – and went into her room. It was the first time I'd ever been in a room with a bed-covering – she had a sort of eiderdown. I said, 'Will Fiddler know?' She said, 'No he don't know, he's no trouble.' It was the first time I'd ever been in bed with a woman and she had to instruct me. Afterwards we lay there talking and I was trying to convert her. I was saying: 'What a lovely girl you are. Why do you do it? I wish I had a lot of money, I'd take you away.'

When it was all over I felt very bad. I said to her, 'You've made me feel ill.' She said, 'I haven't done anything to you. It's your first experience.' I said, 'It's funny, I feel terrible bad.' She said, 'You'll be all right. I'll see you tomorrow night.' I said, 'I don't think so.' I went out very early next morning, about 5 o'clock, and all my stomach seemed empty. I was so weak I said to myself, 'I'll never go with another one.' I didn't go with her again, but I used to protect her – I never let anyone interfere with her. She talked a little about herself. She come from a good home and she had good manners. I could have got her some time afterwards. I was thinking about her the other night and realised that I wouldn't even recognise her if I saw her. It was done just out of bravado. I always had a lot of sympathy for these girls and stopped people interfering with them.

Some of the brides went with thieves, luring men home and then having them coshed. They could weigh them up and if a man was a chump they would ask £2 or £3 a time.

A lot of garotting went on. Five years and a bashing you got for it – eighteen strokes with the cat. That was the penalty. But a lot of it still went on, by Flowery Dean Street, and in the pubs at the back of Leman Street, and all down the Highway. Even at the 'Fleur de Lis' in Elder Street I've known it done. Not in Bethnal Green. I've never known it done in Bethnal Green. You had to be tall to do it. You would come up to a man from behind, put your arms round his throat, with your fists on his throttle. If it went on for more than a few seconds he would choke, so you had to be skilled. Some of them had a girl working for them – she would get a man well boozed, mix his drinks for him and they'd get him while he was drunk. Some of the Yiddisher fellows along Whitechapel Road did it. Most of them retired – got a job or went to live with a girl. Long Hymie did it, and some of them who went with the Raddies, the Italian mob. I strung a couple up. One was a big Polish fellow. It was outside the 'Ship' in Bacon Street. These Polish fellows – not Jews – used to drink there. They were all cabinet-makers and we was always fighting with them. This man was a big man, always fighting. I done him for £5 and his watch and chain, just after the boozer closed, about 1 o'clock in the morning. He reported it to the Commercial Street police station and they put me in an identity parade, but he was too frightened to point me out.

The thieves at Clark's coffee shop were small-time crooks. Most of them got their time for van-dragging. These young men had never had a chance from the day of their birth until the day of their death in some convict prison or mental asylum. Many of them died in France and Flanders fighting in a war they knew nothing about. I, who admired them, have seen the end of their wasted and worthless lives, and wondered why they were ever born. Of the whole gang only one became a real professional criminal conforming to the characteristics of Cesare Lombroso's ideal criminal. That was Edward Spencer. He was a complete all-round criminal. He was some seven years older than me, and in 1900 had already collected some small sentences for picking pockets, especially in the City. He was one of a gang who took part in most of the robberies in the Bethnal Green part of Brick Lane in the early years of the century. Later, he served two terms of penal servitude for larceny and violence. His last appearance at an Assize Court was at the Old Bailey in the 1930s when he was acquitted for killing a man.[9] Soon after this acquittal, he died in Bethnal

Green Hospital from cancer. Spencer was a well-built man and took a great pride in his appearance. He used to dress magnificent and was called 'The Count'.

Another of the 'first eleven' at Clark's coffee house was Jack Worby, a man of about the same age as Spencer. He was not a violent man, but he was a good pickpocket who specialised in wallets. He got a short term of imprisonment, and after he came out he found honest employment in the fish market at Billingsgate. On the outbreak of war in 1914 he joined up and was killed on the Somme. Jack Worby lived in Bacon Street. He was the uncle of the girl I married.

The leader of the 'first eleven' when I first got to know them was 'One-eyed' Charlie Walker, who lived in a one-room tenement in Quaker Street off Brick Lane. Through an accident he had lost the use of an eye and in 1902, though only twenty-six, he was already in the last stages of TB – he died soon after in prison. Charlie always looked half-starved and very poorly clad. He was considered a dangerous man. The best of the gang were a wee bit scared of him, and we youngsters were also afraid. He always looked hungry.

Steve Cooper, although he associated with the rest of the gang, never took part in stealing or pickpocketing. Cooper was twelve years older than me. He met most of the others in Clark's and the pubs. He was a 'tapper', that is he expected the gang to give him money like most of the street bookies did. Everybody was afraid of him, he was always in trouble with the police. Stevie was very badly beaten up by a policeman from Commercial Street, a very violent man named PC Redman who half killed him and possibly drove him mad. Later on he became potty and when I was somebody I stopped him killing a copper down Brick Lane. Soon after that the police charged him with stealing a gold chain from a man by a snatch. Cooper had been identified by the loser as the man who stole his gold chain. May I say at once he was innocent of the charge. He was sentenced to eighteen months. No one outside his family was sorry. He was sent to Wormwood Scrubs prison to serve his sentence. The dormant insanity which had caused him to act so violently on many occasions became apparent and he attacked a warder and was sentenced to be flogged. He was given eighteen strokes with the lash – the scars were still visible years later when he was dying. When Stevie came out of jail he was a savage.[10] In December 1911 at the Old Bailey, before Mr Justice Avory, he was sentenced to three years penal servitude for firing a revolver at some unknown person.[11] Some time after he attempted suicide by cutting his throat – prompt medical attention saved his life. The prison doctor declared him insane and he was sent to Broadmoor. Finally he was transferred to Claybury Asylum at Woodford. When I visited him in 1915 he was totally insane.

Bob Wheeler was not a thief but he was willing to take his share of the loot. He and Steve Cooper were pals. He committed many assaults upon the police and others but was never convicted, others paid the penalty.

Ginger Norrey[12] was also a cunning fellow. He only appeared when a job was to be done, and disappeared afterwards and would not be seen until another job was to be done. By these evasive acts he escaped every time when there were round-ups for identity parades. He was a very skilled thief.

Nobby West was a fine big fellow. He got a three-year conviction for van-dragging and while serving his sentence at Portland had an accident and lost one eye in the quarries. As far as I know he did not get any compensation for his injuries, but as he was a married man with children, he found work with the borough council and remained on the council until he died.

'Echo', another of One-eyed Charlie's lot, was a chain-snatcher. This man was a small dark-complexioned fellow who took part in most chain-snatching felonies but was never pulled in for an identity parade. I was able to prove conclusively that he was a police informer and was working for the CID.

Billy Warner snatched ladies' bags – mainly in Shoreditch High Street and then running away down the little turnings. He didn't want no one with him – he did them on his own. He would earn a few bob pulling a barrow if he wasn't thieving. He was quite capable of earning. Billy Warner was from the Nichol and he moved to Bacon Street same as me. He came from a Romany family – his uncle was a broad-player. He was four years older than me, but we had been together when I was still a boy, and now I used to meet up with him at Clark's.

Billy was a good fighter with his fists – so was his brother who worked over in Spitalfields market. He got killed in 1915 on the Somme.

Wally Shepherd was also from the Nichol. He was a very smart sneak thief, taking from gas meters in people's houses, or shop tills. He was a loner, not a violent type at all. He died in 1915 in France. Wally Saunders was also from the Nichol – a very smart sneak thief who worked by himself, not a violent type, good family man. Very clean in appearance. He was father to a large family. He died in prison. Two other thieves from the Nichol were Patsy and Tommy Lauchlin. Tommy was born on the same day as myself. His family lived in Old Nichol Street. They were Irish Cockneys. Tommy was a good whizzer who always worked alone. He went down with the cruiser *Exeter* at the start of the war. His brother Patsy was a proper mad Irishman – he was killed with the Irish regiment during the war.

When I came out of Borstal in September 1904 I found that One-eyed Charlie's gang was beginning to break up. Charlie himself died in prison hospital while he was serving his three-years' sentence. Some of the group had married and were settling down to casual work for the council or the docks. One or two had drifted away to the West End, where they were mixed up with the clubs and the ladies of the town. Or they worked as look-out men for the street bookmakers. A few were in prison. The remnants of the old gang joined up with the younger lads, so making a very mixed collection of villains. Spencer served a term of four years for stealing a wallet but when he came out again he joined us, and became a lodger at my mother's house in Gibraltar Gardens.

I also started to recruit some young 'uns. People began to look to me for protection. I'd learnt a lot in prison. I was a good fighter. And they trusted me. I started to take some of the young 'uns home – Tommy Taylor, who was an orphan, Cossor Gilbert, when he didn't want to go back to his mother's. And others. That was how I picked up Jackie Shinebohm. I found him at a coffee stall in Bethnal Green, gave him a home, and took him thieving with us.

We weren't so much a gang as a loose collection of youngsters who had Clark's as their coffee house. We were a collection of small-time thieves ripe for any mischief. We numbered among our accomplishments snide-dropping, counterfeiting, van-thieving, and gold-chain snatching – or, in slang, 'shoot flying'.[13] We were ready to steal anything. Sometimes we went in couples, sometimes alone – it was only when there was a big fight on that we went as a gang.

We didn't go far out of our manor. Pickpocketing or snatching we would go as far as City Road. Tabernacle Street – City Road, Finsbury up to Broad Street station – Great Eastern Street (keeping to the City side) – that was our manor, where the old city toffs were. They would walk out with their gold chains to impress people and you just had to walk towards them and pull the lot out. You'd find them all day long morning to night. One chap thought he would be brave and get his name in the paper – he chased us and he got punched, but you very seldom had to use violence.

When we went out snatching we very seldom got the watch. The chain would break off as you snatched it. But you could get 10s for a chain. They were mostly 15 or 18 carat gold. If you got a pound, you were lucky. Leon Behren – the chap who got murdered on Clapham Common – used to buy them from us. He used to weigh it and test it and give us the money, but I think he was the outside man for Ruby Michaels,[14] the top man in Aldgate for buying anything.

Behren used to hang out at the Warsaw Hotel,[15] which was a cafe at the Whitechapel end of Brick Lane. We would go in there and give him the eye. If he wasn't there you could often find him at a little shoe shop round the corner. Later, I used to sell to a straight chap in Black Lion Yard – where all the jewellers were.

Bill Sutton used to buy them too. He had a big sweetstuff shop in Lever Street, Hoxton.[16] He used to melt them down so that they couldn't be identified. He used to get stuff off the Titanic mob, and he used to take all the stuff from the Bessarabians too. The screwsmen used to go to him if they'd done a big house and got some heavy stuff, or something from a jeweller's. It was just a business like any other. Sometimes he'd have a dabble on his own (i.e. take stolen property and sell it for himself).

A lot of people started using guns about this time. Brick

Lane was getting dangerous. One night, about midnight, I
was standing outside one of the Italian ice-cream shops when a
policeman came by. There were three or four of us there,
including Long Hymie. Long Hymie pulled his bloody gun
out and fired it. The policeman stood there petrified and so did
I. The policeman, who knew me well, came across and said,
'That was a wicked thing to do Arthur!' I said, 'What?' He said,
'That was a wicked thing.' I said, 'It's a toy gun, it was nothing
but blanks.' He said, 'It was not. I 'eard the bullet whistle by
my 'ead. And if you like to come over an' have a look, it's
probably in the shutter.' Phew! although I was young I was
not so bloody young and silly that I didn't realise the seriousness of it. He only had to blow his whistle and we'd have been
well in it. Anyway he didn't. After that we got rid of Long
Hymie. He only wanted to start banging away and we thought
him too dangerous.[17]

I got my first gun about 1904. I remember I fired it in a
crowd against a man named Sawyer. He was a good fighting
man from the Hackney Road, but we were at loggerheads. He
was three or four years older than me. And he went around
with a gang, about six-handed. I was right in front of him so I
don't know how I missed but the bullet went up in the air. I
gave the gun to Berner and he gave it to Jimmy Green, the
fishmonger. It was a crowded Saturday night market in Brick
Lane.

I wanted a gun more for protection than for anything else –
I used it to frighten people. You could buy a gun then for
about 4s or 5s – automatics hadn't come in. I used to get my
gun the other end of the Lane, at the Whitechapel end of Brick
Lane, where all the kip-houses were. Benny Hall kept the
lodging houses at the top end of Flower and Dean Street,[18] and
we remained pals down to the end of his life. I could always get
a gun from him – he used to get them off the lodgers. Some of
them were pinfires – it was a wonder you didn't kill yourself
with them: you had to fire from the percussion cap. When we
started holding up the Jewish spielers in Commercial Road and
Whitechapel I used a Royal Ulster Constabulary revolver
which cost me half-a-crown – it was a good job I never hit
anyone with it – it had the biggest bullets I've ever seen.

In 1908 I was sentenced to twelve months imprisonment

under the Prevention of Crimes Act. I hadn't done anything at all. I was put away as a suspected person. When I came out I was much more vicious in my behaviour. People avoided me like the plague. The police began to give me a wide berth. I started to beat up many of the villains who were regarded as 'terrors'. I was now in the prime of my life and according to the police I was the terror of Brick Lane. I was noted for always carrying a gun and that was the cause of my being famous, but I didn't have to use any weapon to make myself feared. If we'd wanted money we could have made a fortune – everybody in Brick Lane was scared of us. But money wasn't a great influence on me. If my mother and sister was all right, that was enough.

About this time I teamed up with three others – Tommy Taylor, Dido Gilbert and Danny Isaacs. Together we got a reputation for toughness and my name began to be known not only in Brick Lane but as far away as Clerkenwell and the Elephant.

My special friend, Tommy Taylor, mixed with the bullies in Whitechapel and Aldgate, and knew everything that was going on in the way of rackets. Tommy was an orphan boy and a stranger to East London when I first palled up with him. As a kid he'd come away from an orphanage. I made a pal of him and looked after him. I slept out with him. I never took him home. Tommy was an all-round thief, violent and dangerous. He started going down the other end, and living off the brides in Whitechapel. He was what the Jews called a shundicknick (a ponce). In 1915 he died of VD.

Dido lived down Turin Street, what they called the old town of Bethnal Green. He was a worker, not a crook. Only used to come round our house for the fun of it. He worked where they made deck chairs, arm-chairs (I worked there when I was a youngster) at Atkins' in Church Row. He worked there for years, but he was a game one, and if you wanted to go round and sort somebody out you'd take him with you. He'd join in just for the pure love of it, for the excitement. He got fifteen months over the Vendetta case, the shortest sentence. I knew Dido all my life, all his family come out of the Nichol. I'd be about twelve years when I first knew him. I lived in Bacon Street then and he lived in Turin Street, just opposite. I remember the name when I was in the Nichol, the brothers knocking about the street. He wasn't a crook, and after the Vendetta case, I never saw him no more. He probably got killed in the war; he was the type to shout 'Come on boys' and go over the top.

Danny Isaacs lived just round the corner in Bacon Street. His father and mother were ordinary working people, but his sister was on the game. He was just a tough guy, not a thief. I always had him with me because he could fight. He married a girl I used to be friendly with, Emma Holmes. He was an absolute villain to her – knocked her about and he had a terrible hatred of me because I was her first love. When I come out of prison after the Vendetta, about 1916, he thought he'd make himself big by having a go at me. He said that one of the CID blokes had told him that I'd given information against him and got him twelve months. It was a lie. Anyway, I said: 'Get outside, you bleedin' half.' I didn't want any arguments. A couple of days later, he came by, he was a bit winey, he was with some bloody tearaway. When he said something, I punched him, and the chap I was with went to finish him off. I said, 'Leave him alone.' He laid down there, it was in Gibraltar Walk. He was unconscious. The next day his wife came down. It was the first and last time I saw her for many years, she said to me: 'He came home and said you knocked him about.' I said, 'Tell him to keep himself away from down there or he'll get himself in trouble.'

It was about 1910 that we started on the Jewish spielers. There were four or five of us working together – Tommy Taylor, Dido and Danny Isaacs. None of the others had been in prison. When we raided a club, we were all armed; all had orders not to use any weapons unless attacked. When we made a raid on a club, we made everyone stand up, and waved our guns around to show that we were serious. We made them stand up because we thought some of them might have been carrying weapons. They were all crooked men. Two of us covered them with guns while the other two went about searching them. The first one I ever went in, one of the gamblers – Cocky Flatnose, a whizzer out of Commercial Road – said to me 'blag the box', i.e. the banker's bank or owner's kitty. That's how I got to know about the box. After that we always made for the box. There wouldn't be much in the box – £3 or £4. We did it for the excitement as much as for the money.

We'd go in at 6 or 7 at night when it was dark. We always shut the door behind us and then we started. Everyone knew who we were. None of the patrons ever resisted. It's a good job they were all Jewish – if they'd been English there would have been a fight and we might have had to shoot some. But they were too bloody sensible to make any trouble. Yiddisher people make a laugh of it. They said, 'Give them a few bob and get rid of them.'

Once they was waiting for us. We had a lot of our own team in a pub, Mother Wolff's in Whitechapel, and they paid us out.

Soon the big-time gamblers began to stay away from the spielers through personal fears of a shooting match. I got bribed by the big heads at Aldgate to stop it. Ruby Michaels was the top man in Aldgate for everything and the big heads there bribed us to put a stop to it. Ruby Michaels said they'd have to straighten us up. Tommy Hoy was the man who fixed it.[19] He used to work for Billy Chandler on the racecourse. He was reckoned to be the best twister in 'Faro' in the world.[20] This was a Jewish card game. It was said you couldn't cheat at it but he and Billy Chandler used to make a packet out of it. He wasn't Jewish but he used to play both in Whitechapel and in the West End. The big heads knew he knew me and said, 'Keep those kids away because the law is going to mix it for them and we don't want no shooting in those clubs.' So Tommy told me, 'You'd better keep away from there.' They gave us a fiver once or twice, that was all. To tell you the truth I was glad to put a stop to it. A couple of my team were itching to use the guns and I could see it was going too far.

The last time we raided the clubs was after the Houndsditch murders in 1910 – when the anarchists shot the policemen. The City police thought I was helping them – they wanted to find the people who had killed the coppers. But what we was really after was the guns, wonderful guns they was – Lugers – you couldn't get them anywhere.

The spielers made our name. Everybody wanted to know who we was. The Darby Sabini mob[21] was interested – they got up a collection for us when we were at the Old Bailey for

the Vendetta affair. We got friendly with the City Police –
they wanted to put a bit of fear into the Jewish flashboys at
Aldgate. People knew that we were around and we'd got a
name for toughness.

One of our jobs was with the printers in Fleet Street. We
didn't know what it was about, but we got a free meal and £2
or £3 to share out. They wanted to put a stop to the 'blacking' – the printers at the *News of the World* came from Elephant
and Castle way, and they didn't want outsiders coming to take
their jobs. So we teamed up with some men from Billingsgate
and went to give them a hand. All we had to do was to make
ourselves known at the '11 o'clock house'. You didn't have to
use violence – you just let them know you were there. We
didn't know what it was all for, but you got a free meal for it
and you might get a quid or two.

Another place we showed ourselves was at Epsom, on
Derby Day. People would say, 'Go along to the racecourses,
you'll get a few quid, everybody wants to see you.' You'd go
with a racing tout and he'd introduce you to the different
bookies and say 'You know so and so' and he'd mention your
name and the bookmaker would look at you and he'd give you
a couple of quid in the hat. Kipper took me down there in
1910. He was a tick-tack man who lived in the next turning to
me in Bethnal Green, in Turin Street. He dropped dead about
1914 when Johnny Hughes was buried. About eight of us went
down there, all Bethnal Greeners, Tommy Venables was one.
He was in what they called the 'office lark' – they would dress
up and go in pretending to look for a job and pinch wallets.
Besides him there was Tommy Taylor, Cooper, his pal Bob
Wheeler, Emsey (Spencer), and two or three others.

About 1910, just before the Vendetta case started, we went
down to Walthamstow to sort out George King. He had
become the guv'nor down there – all the stall-keepers had to
give him rent. He was interfering with everybody's business.
Crayses the fish people[22] was employing us – they were rich
people and they wanted to get rid of him. We went down
there five-handed. There was Stevie Cooper, Bob Wheeler,
Tommy Taylor, Spencer and myself. So over we went and we
was in the pub – pub opposite Crayses, its a big pub, it's still
there – waiting for him. I was sitting down on the seat – I

never used to drink much – and the other three were standing up, knocking them back and all of a sudden Kingie come in the door with a gun in his hand. In he come, as much as to say, 'Who wants to have a go?' I was sitting right behind him and Taylor was on the other side of the door. I said to him, 'Put it away, put it away, you chump,' and he turned around and he knew he was beat. So he put it in his pocket. He wanted to know what it was all about. He said that what he did was his business, we'd got no right to interfere; 'It's bad enough having the bleeding law after you, not you as well.' We hung it on the Crayses.

That was on a Friday night – I always remember it now. We came home on the train, got in at Bethnal Green junction. I was beginning to think very deeply about it. And I thought, 'Bleeding murder will be done here if we're not careful. Somebody will be getting topped.' Having bad characters, they wasn't particular about whether they found you guilty or not. I thought to myself, 'Blimey, I think I'll get out of it.' I said to them in the train coming home, 'What have I got to worry about bleeding Crayses, the fishmongers, or anybody else.' That night my mother says to me, 'Be careful, you don't want to get mixed up with him. He's a villain.' She knew Georgie King because he come from the Nichol. Big, tall, dark fellow he was.

The next night, Saturday, we was in Clark's. I went in to have tea. The others – Cooper and Spencer and Taylor – they was in the pub, the 'Hare' on the corner of Brick Lane and Hare Street, right opposite Clark's. I was standing outside when all of a sudden I see Kingie coming towards me, walking down Hare Street. I saw him coming down and he crossed the road and he pulled a bleeding gun out. I turned sideways to him, so I wouldn't be a big target, and at that identical moment, when he was looking to see if there was any law about (there were plenty of people about, it was about 5 or 6 o'clock), Taylor come from behind him, stuck a bleeding gun in his back. Course he knew he was beat. He went away under Brick Lane arch.

The others decided to go up to Walthamstow to have it out with him but I began to use my brain and thought, 'I'm not going to be mixed up in this bleeding business.' There were five of them went. They were all loaded up and one thing and another. I said, 'Not me. I'm not getting mixed up in this.' So they went without me.

Well, after the boozers closed that night I went back home, down Gibraltar Gardens. It was about 1 o'clock in the morning. There was several youngsters knocking about at the top – four or five of them – they all turned out crooked in the end. All of a sudden 'Bang, Bang, Bang'. I dashed up the Gardens and Spencer was there holding his mouth – he was bleeding profusely – and there was a fellow laid out in the road – a Russian Jew, Phil Shonck. The Post Office windows was all smashed with bullets and the shop on the corner – a musical shop. Darky the Coon was there and all and one of the Jewish chaps had a crack too. They'd come down there with Kingie to wait on me. Well, all my good resolutions went overboard. I'd still got my gun in my trousers pocket – the Royal Irish Constabulary gun – and when I saw Kingie I went after him. He ran down Kerbela Street, making for Bacon Street, where he lived. I was getting quite close to him when two uniformed policemen came up – on patrol. They were walking gradually though they'd heard the shooting. I was in the middle of the road and they saw me distinctly. They knew me and they saw the gun, but they didn't say nothing. I turned back and went back home. All the mob was there. Spencer had a new gun, Tommy Taylor had a new gun – what's-his-name had a new gun – there were four guns in my house. I told them to make themselves scarce, because the two policemen would have to report the shooting and then they would be after us.

It was Jimmy Watts who got us mixed up in the affair. He had an office down at Mansfield Street, Aldgate, what he used to do a lot of crooked business with. He was supposed to be a Commission Agent. He was a Romany, a Didicai. Jimmy Watts put us on to other jobs but he also tried to lumber me and God knows how many people he sent to penal servitude. He was a police informer – he knew all the top men and it was a top man at the Yard that told me about him.

One day Jimmy Watts asked me to go down Barking way. There was a fellow there – I forget his name – who was a sort of confidence trickster. Jimmy Watts said to me, 'He's got £30,000 in shares.' He said, 'We'll go down his house and get them.' He said, 'He's got a big Alsatian dog, but I've got a fellow who's not afraid of Alsatian dogs. He'll go with you.' I don't know what the shares were, all I knew is that they was valued at a lot of money and we was going to get a good bit of money off of somebody who was going to buy them.

I took a chap from Brick Lane with me, a chap named Charlie Barney who was often with me at that time. He was a relation to Billy Chandler and sometimes went with the Titanics. He wasn't a thief but he could fight. He wasn't frightened of anything so I took him with me. There was Jimmy Watts, this fellow that could punch Alsatian dogs – he was a big fellow, a Romany and all – Charlie Barney and me. So we went into this man's house, a big house, lovely house he had, somewhere over Plaistow way. We had to search the house, but we mustn't let the fellow know or he'd put the dog on us. Jimmy Watts was a cunning bleeder, and he got the fellow to give us drinks. He said, 'I knew you lived here, I just popped in with some of the boys.' Anyway the dog comes in and this Romany chap said to me, 'Have you ever seen a dog go out?' When he hit him the dog went out like a boxer in the ring. Knocked him out. He said, 'Get to work.' I hopped out the back while they tried to bring the dog to. Me and Charlie Barney made out we was going to the toilet. The bloke was more interested in his dog than he was in us. So we turned the place over and found the papers underneath a mattress. Well the dog came to and started barking, and Charlie Barney was so frightened that he threw the shares away, chucked the bleeding lot over into somebody's garden.

The next night we was in the pub on the corner of Mansford Street, Aldgate – a Mann and Crossman's – when all of a sudden in comes the fellow. He come into the bar with his hand in his pocket. I got near him and when I got close I crammed his hand in his pocket – it wasn't a gun, but he had a tool there. So there was a bit of an uproar. But he was a wee bit timid, this fellow, and he said, 'I'll buy them back off you.' I never heard no more about it.

11 Jews and half-Jews

In the Nichol there was a few Didicais[1] and Irish, but you never saw a Jew. All that you knew about them was what you learnt in the Mission. I don't think I ever saw a Jew until we moved to Bacon Street. Suddenly you saw them everywhere. Hundreds of thousands had come to England in the 1890s[2] and you would still see them coming from the London docks: they came in horse brakes and some of them had white sheepskin coats. They were very poorly dressed – you never saw them in suits except on Shabbas.

There weren't many Jews up our end of Brick Lane – it was all English from Bethnal Green Road down as far as Truman's brewery. But the Jews took part in the Sunday morning market. Under the railway arch in Brick Lane some of the richest Jewish families in the country had their start. And some of the Jews came to work at the cabinet-making shops in Virginia Road, Austin Street and Columbia Road – mostly younger men. They used to work till late at night – 8 or 9 of a winter's evening. They would walk back home in the middle of the road, down Brick Lane. You had some Jews living round the bandstand, on the Boundary Street estate – they could afford the higher rents.[3] And there was a little colony of Jews in Jews' Alley, at the top end of Brick Lane. My sister and her friends used to go round to clean their stairs on a Shabbas. The houses had been built by Jewish builders for the Jews. There were workshops at the top for the tailors, shops on the ground floor and rooms to let which were entered from the back. Kid Lewis,[4] the boxer, lived there. He worked as a cabinet-maker at Prince's Court which runs from Jews' Alley into Old Nichol Street. Blyth Street, Bethnal Green, was like Jew's Alley – built by the Jews for the Jews.

The big concentration of Jews was at the other end of Brick Lane. The last turning in Brick Lane before Whitechapel High

Street was Old Montague Street. It began with a large pub on the corner and continued with small shops up to Black Lion Yard where the diamond shops were – some of them acted as fences. There was a market there, mostly composed of barrows, where the smells was of raw fish and poultry both live and dead. The shops were very small and the street was so narrow that when a cart wanted to come through there was often a row and the language became very forceful. At this period it was predominantly a Jewish district. Moishe the Gonnoff,[5] the most famous Jewish pickpocket of that time, lived in Old Montague Street, near to the jewellers. He worked the Petticoat Lane market, but he also used to come up Brick Lane and when he appeared all the stallholders would say, 'Watch out, here comes Moishe the Gonnoff.' He never caused us any trouble – he worked on his own.

Most of the Jews lived in the drums off Whitechapel, and all the little dives off Petticoat Lane. Whitechapel Road was their high street. It was always full of people, very noisy. The spielers were there – the Jewish gaming houses; and the theatres – the 'Pavillion' was very popular with the Jews.[6] There were a lot of Jewish boxers at the 'Wonderland',[7] which was almost opposite the London Hospital. Most of the boxers there were Jewish. Kid Lewis fought there and Cockney Flat-nose, and also my friend Cossor Gilbert. All the young fighters would go up there – they were paid ten bob for six rounds. There was a load of Jewish boxers there. They used to fight there on a Saturday night. Jacobs was the owner. I think there were two brothers.

The 'Pavilion' was a music hall and playhouse at the corner of Vallence Road. I saw my first Jewish play there. It was called *Humanity* and I can always remember the impression it made on me: 'If you cut us, we bleed, if you starve us we die, if you hurt us we cry.' Near the 'Pavillion' was a big coffee shop where the Jewish whizzers met – the expert pickpockets. One of them was a very good whizzer called Barney Bach. The Midget came from there too, though he wasn't Jewish. He was a very good wallet-getter, who joined up with the Titanic mob in Hoxton. In later years the pickpockets mostly degenerated into 'shundicknicks' – living off the white girls. The Rubin brothers went in for garotting. They sent girls out 'on the batter' and lumbered the men they brought in. In the end they were hanged for killing a sailor. It was a miserable affair, which happened in 1912. At the Old Bailey one brother turned King's Evidence against the other, and the chief witnesses against them were the girls.[8]

Whitechapel Road was alive with thousands of people. All the shops and stalls were open on a Friday night and Shabbas. Jews and Cockneys all mixed together. But most of them were Jewish. It stretched all the way from Petticoat Lane and Aldgate, to Charrington's brewery and the London Hospital, a good mile. The Jewish shops stayed open on Friday night and Saturday, in spite of the Shabbas.

During the day the tailoring workers would assemble in Whitechapel Road, close to Black Lion Yard. You would see groups of them walking up and down – the police kept them on the move. I used to say, 'What are they hanging around like that for?' – they looked as though they were on strike. They were waiting for the master tailors who wanted workmen. When a master came down they would say: 'Want a trousers machinist? Want a buttonholer?' Most of the Jewish tailoring business was done in private streets. They used to take the work home and you'd see men with trousers or waistcoats over their arms making their way to the West End. A lot of the work was done for the West End tailors.

The first we had to do with the Jews was stealing. They were passionately attached to 'enas' – chickens. They were always buying and selling them, especially on a Sunday, and we used to steal them from the yards. Later I got to know some of the Jewish boys in Brick Lane. They took to me – they looked on me as a sort of protector. And the mothers would ask me to keep their boys out of trouble. The older Jewish people always took a fancy to me when we went on our expeditions: Mrs Davis in Swansea had more faith in me than in the Jewish boys.

I came to have great sympathy with the Jews when I learnt about their persecutions in Russia. I didn't change my view even when I went with Mosley's crowd. I always look back on what a wonderful people they were. They had a very hard struggle. It was pitiful how they tried to keep up appearances on the Shabbas. The rich Jews took advantage of the poor Jews and made them work for next to nothing. Every room was turned into a workshop.

Most of the Jews kept to themselves. They didn't branch out into more Englishified districts, except if it was to take a market stall there, or go round peddling. They prided themselves on being 'froom' (orthodox). The Great Synagogue at the corner of Fournier Street was always crowded, but some of the younger ones gravitated towards the English and became real tearaways.

Joe Goodwin was Jewish, and his brother – they came out of Brick Lane. But he married an English girl named Meadows, and Alf Goodwin, his brother, married her sister – nice-looking girls they were. Joe was the finest trainer of boxers in the country. He trained champions. His brother was also a boxer; he had great big cauliflower ears. Jack Goodwin's gym was in Hanbury Street,[9] later he moved up the West End. He used to have some very good fighters. There was no distinction between Jewish people like the Goodwins and us. You didn't talk about being Jewish or English.

My special pal, Cossor Gilbert, was a Jew. Me and Cossor had been brought up practically together. He was about the same age as me, and we were good friends, but he always had that wee bit of fear of me; he'd do what I told him to do. As a matter of fact I gave him a lodging many times in my own house in Gibraltar Gardens. Me and him used to sleep together in the night. Cossor was more at home with the Yiddisher boys but he also came with us. Any trouble we had he'd say 'count me in'. He wasn't a thief but he would always help out in fights.

I liked Cossor. He was very comical and to me he was a person totally different to anybody, he had such charming ways with him. My two sisters would give him anything, not the physical thing, but anything else. My mother liked him too. He was a very kind sort of fellow. Somebody would say, 'Want a job pulling a barrow down the road?' and Cossor would say, 'Certainly, anything to oblige.'

Cossor and me was kids together. I'd be about eleven or something when I first knew him. He only lived round the corner to me in Hare Street, when we lived in Bacon Street. He was always one of the crowd of boys that hung about Brick

Lane. There were four or five of us went together. We used to sleep out of a night, different buildings and all the rest of it. Sometimes, we would get over the backyards and steal the 'enas' – the chickens – sell 'em up the road. You earned a couple of bob, used to share it out, 6d was a lot of money. We used to live like that.

His parents were nice people, just good, decent, working people. But Cossor wanted to be away from the Jewish type of life, going to synagogue, keeping holidays and all that. He broke away and lived mostly with the 'Yoks'. His mother used to come round and ask me to fetch him home – there were several Jewish mothers used to come round and ask me to help them get their boys back.

Most Jewish people at that time used to send their children to the Free School in Middlesex Street; and they used to dress them in corduroy suits, to distinguish them. Well, he wouldn't have none of that. His brother went, his brother was a wonderful dancer, a lively dancer he was. But Cossor was a bit backward in education – he didn't go much to school. Cossor was one of those chaps who couldn't settle down. He knocked about Brick Lane, sometimes he'd do a job. Like an old Jewish cabinet-maker got to send a wardrobe somewhere for a certain time. He'd pull the barrow down to Curtain Road, and earn himself a couple of shillings – well, he could always do that.

What happened to him in the early part of his life was that at the age of about fifteen he went in for boxing and become a good boxer. The 'Wonderland' was the first place where he boxed, used to get 10s for six rounds. But they had to have plenty of the red stuff flying about otherwise they didn't get paid. They give 'em 10s, half a sovereign, but if they didn't make the blood come out – nose bleeding or mouth cut – they got a bit of a warning that they wouldn't be employed again. The customers had to be satisfied. Anyway, he became a good boxer, but like a good many more boxers that I knew, he would take a drop: he had that terrible habit of letting people bet on him to go down. When the promotors got to know that he didn't get many jobs. I used to say to him, if he was short of money 'come over to Lea'. They used to have a big fair there Holiday Monday – a bloke would offer to take on anybody in the crowd, but when the showman saw Cossor they would say, 'Here's two quid, now get out of it.' People would bet on him winning; Posh Reed would bet him, Tommy Hoy used to bet him, he was a bookmaker down there. These people would say 'Are you trying?' and if he said 'Yes', I'd know he would win.

Cossor drifted into being a 'shundicknick'. He left home and went to live with one of the girls in Flower and Dean Street, down the other end. He used to call her Laura. She was a country girl, just an ordinary English girl who had left home and got stuck in the East End with the others. She was a nice girl. Unfortunately her reputation wasn't that good. She lived by prostitution. I mean they all did down there, and Cossor lived on her. After being thrown out of the 'Wonderland' he didn't have no recognised form of living. Nobody's tried more than I did to keep him away from the other end, I even took him home. But he'd say, 'You've gotta live – she was at it before I knew her.' See what I mean, the logic of it? 'I can't make her different,' he would say. In the end he did it regular. Off of Brick Lane there was different streets, and in many Jewish houses they'd have a furnished room where they didn't ask any questions. Somebody would say to him, 'Cossor I'll tell you where there's a furnished room, nice people, they don't want to know.' And he'd say, 'All right.' He got took in for living off immoral earnings of a girl down there and I didn't have him no more after that. It was a bad thing to be convicted for – it gives a man a bad name. That was practically the end of my association with him – about 1911. In my opinion there's nobody can equal the person who lives on the immoral earnings of a woman. There's people who live on the wealth of their wife, if they marry a rich girl. That's a different kind of thing, but I haven't got much room for that either. If I went into a pub and I saw a man in there that I knew was commonly called a 'ponce', I couldn't drink with him, I'd have to insult him. I'm talking about years ago. Today I wouldn't even speak to him.

Cossor got five years for killing a chap in Brick Lane. It was during the First World War, in 1915. He was standing on the corner of Flower and Dean Street when he saw an American sailor knocking a girl about, because she wouldn't go with him. Cossor said to the sailor, 'Why don't you let the girl alone?' And he said, 'What's it to you?' One thing and another, there was an argument and the sailor pulled out a knife, course they carried knives. Cossor got it away from him and in the struggle stabbed the man to death.

Cossor was indicted for murder, and murder at that time meant the rope, no quarrel about it, no recommendation for mercy. And I thought to myself, 'He hasn't got a bloody chance, what with that conviction against him for living off a woman's immoral earnings.' He said to me afterwards, 'I was sure I'd get topped'. He says to me, 'I used to imagine a line where the trap was and practise stepping into the trap.' He pictured himself in the condemned cell. When he come up for trial at the Central Criminal Court, Wensley had them instructed that they should go for the capital charge but they reduced the charge of murder to manslaughter and he got five years' penal servitude. To him it was like a death blow. I think the only time he'd done any time was three months.

I saw him in Parkhurst while he was serving his time. His head had gone wrong, boozing I suppose and one thing and another. He thought he saw the murdered man looking through the cell window at him. This is official, it's in the records – he went crazy, raving mad and they had to put him in the padded cells. But the doctor knew that I knew him and he asked me to go and have a talk with him. He recovered, and when he got out after serving his sentence he seemed to be all right. But there was just that wee bit of difference, there was that wee bit of something not there. He didn't want to mix with the old type of people that hanged about, like Jackie Berman and Long Hymie. He went down to the docks; I think there was a dock strike on at the time and he got himself a job as a docker. Nobody knew what really happened to him, but he was found dead in the river. Whether he was cracked on the head and thrown in I don't know. Everybody liked him except the people who threw him in; he could have done it himself, but I doubt it.

Down Watney Street some of the Jews married the Irish and they produced some right terrors. Usually it was the Irishman who married the Jewess, and the children inherited the worst qualities of both. They were half and half as I used to call them – they had a Jewish name but an Irish character. Old

Benny Hall was one – he had a Jewish mother and an Irish father. Dodger Mullins and Timmy Hayes[10] were right specimens. I used them as strikebreakers in 1926, when I was employed by the Mansion House, and they recruited some of the Watney Street Irish. But I detested the two of them. They were ignorant as bloody hell and brutal with it. They got themselves a name by being terrors. Dodger lived by tapping people for money. They gave it him because they were frightened. I once watched him kick a little white dog to death. 'It bit me,' he said. He didn't look Jewish. Charlie Horrickey was another typical half-breed, as ignorant as hell, though he was never dangerous. In 1926 we were both charged with cutting Moey Levy's throat after a barney in Whitechapel Road. Horrickey got three years but I was acquitted.

Jack and Dolly Marx had a wee bit of Jewish blood in them, but otherwise to all intents and purposes they were just East End people. Brother and sister, they were two of the worst characters I ever knew. Jack Marx was a remnant of another generation – when they used to fight with bare fists. He'd been a real terror. Jack Marx was old enough to be my father and his mob were twelve, twenty years older than me. They used to play the boards – 'Crown and Anchor', the three-card trick. They were also proper bruisers – the last of the Mohicans. I liked Jack Marx but Spencer and I gave evidence against him at the Old Bailey and that finished him. Sometime about 1907 he and several other chaps got mixed up in a riot in Westminster. I don't know what the trouble was about, but there was a lot of damage done and some very heavy sentences dished out. They went after another gang – something to do with Covent Garden.[11]

Dolly Marx, his sister, was very violent – she got seven years jail for her part in the Westminster riot.[12] She was on the game, and she wasn't bad looking, but she went in more for lobbing people – what they call lumbering. She was very violent towards other women and to people like myself. She would think nothing in a pub of having a row, picking up a glass and smashing it into someone's face. And she could really fight – Dolly had a terrible record for inflicting injuries on other people. At that time they used to take women prisoners sentenced to penal servitude from Holloway to Aylesbury.

They had a terrible business trying to get her to put on convict clothes – she stripped herself stark naked. That was the type she was. She was reckoned at the time to be one of the worst women in London.

After she came out of prison Dolly married a well-known boxer, and her son became a well-known boxer too – Arthur Howard, he lived down Gibraltar Gardens.

The man who governored the whole Jewish underworld was Edward Emmanuel.[13] He was the Jewish Al Capone – everything was grist to his mill – he got in the spieling business and through that with the racing. He used to fix the boxing fights and all – I remember when there was a fight between Cockney Cohen and young Joseph of Aldgate. Well there were thousands on the match: two Jewish chaps fighting each other and thousands of Jewish people betting. Cockney Cohen was the favourite; he was regarded as the top man of the two. Edward Emmanuel wanted Cohen to lay down: they tried to pay him to take the drop, but Cohen refused. Somebody stuck a knife in him. I can't remember whether the fight took place.

I got involved with Edward Emmanuel because of four sisters, the Bradshaw* girls. Nice-looking girls they were, out of Spitalfields. I was with Esther, another was with 'Jew Boy' Stevens – the CID man at Commercial Street – and the third went with Edward Emmanuel. The oldest – Polly – was married to Long Hymie. Esther was a lovely girl and Edward Emmanuel had her after I left her, 'cos as a matter of fact I wasn't too fond of women. But in the end she left him, and he went down to live in Brighton.

Edward Emmanuel had a group of Jewish terrors. There was Jackie Berman. He told a pack of lies against me in the Vendetta case – he had me put away. Then there was Do-Do. He was a cunning gentleman – I don't know where he lived – he was a good fighter, not a boxer, but a good 'terror'. Bobby Levy – he lived down Chingford way – and his brother Moey. Bobby Nark – he was a good fighting chap. In later years all the Jewish terrors worked with the Italian mob on the race course. Bobby Levy worked with them. So did Bobby Nark.

*Fictitious name.

The Narks were a famous Jewish family from out of Aldgate. Bobby was a fine big fellow though he wasn't very brainy. His team used to hang out in a pub at Aldgate on the corner of Petticoat Lane. I've seen him bash a bloke's hat over his face and knock his beer over. He belonged to the Darby Sabini gang – that was made up of Jewish chaps and Italian chaps. He married an English lady – stone rich – they said she was worth thousands and thousands of pounds. He's dead and gone now.

Ruby Michaels was the most noted receiver of stolen property. He was the biggest buyer of stolen jewellery in East London. His headquarters was the 'Three Tuns' in Aldgate. He had several front men – Leon Behren, the man who got killed in 1911, was one of them. They picked the stuff up from the daylight screwsmen at the spielers, and took it to Ruby at the pub. Anyone who had any diamond rings to sell, they took it to him, and the buyers came from all over the world. In Portland I met a crook who had come all the way from America to buy something off Ruby.

We used to see Behren at the Warsaw restaurant in Osborne Street, at the bottom of Brick Lane. The watch-chains we used to pinch, we'd go there and sell them to him. With gold chains he used to pay you 27s 6d an ounce for 9 carat gold and 56s for 18 carat, and about £4 for 22 carat, but that was very rare. You'd go to him and he'd go to Ruby Michael's and get how much it was, cut half of it off and give it to you. If you got two or three customers a day he would do well; he earned 10s each out of them. It was a precarious living. He tried to keep up an appearance of being rich to encourage people to trade with him, so that if somebody made a haul they would take it to him. He used to wear a £5 piece on his gold watch and chain and he had an astrakhan collar and coat. He looked a proper Yid.

When things were hard we used to go down there, two or three of us, to see if we could catch him on the hop, but he was too bloody fly. Many times we waited on him to have his watch and chain and £5 piece, but he kept away from dark turnings, he knew all about it.

All these small-time fences took the really valuable hauls to the big-time buyers of stolen property. The wealth of these buyers could be counted in thousands of pounds, not so the little French Jew, who was supposed to own property; his wealth consisted of his personal jewellery and a few sovereigns.

About 1908 or 1909 we started to hear of anarchism.[14] The old Jews used to talk about it. They wanted to turn the world upside down, to change everything. It was all anarchism in those days. You never heard the word communism. That came in much later – I think it was when they wanted to be more respectable – I've got an idea that the word 'anarchist' frightens people. There was a big anarchist meeting place in Jubilee Street.[15] It was like a theatre. It could hold 1,000 people easily. It had small rooms where you could take on classes – anyone who wanted to learn Hebrew or English – and two big halls: I think in later years they were turned into a boxing arena. They used to have plays there connected with the anarchist business, communism and all that, mostly about Russia. Up our end there was a pub in Hanbury Street where the anarchists used to go – the 'Sugar Loaf' – and a Jewish restaurant in Sclater Street, Gardstein's mob were using it in 1910 just before the Houndsditch murders.

In the Warsaw Hotel they were always talking politics. The old Jewish people, the elders used to get in there – the 'old rabbis' as I called them – and they used to be talking about the times, you know, the world as it went round: English people don't do it like that, not as far as I know, they go in a pub and get drunk. In the Warsaw restaurant they used to talk about anarchy and all this sort of thing. They had a way of emphasising their arguments, using their hands – they got very excited over politics. They missed Russia, and they were always talking about it. That's all they seemed to talk about in those Jewish restaurants, politics and Russia. When I went in there to find Behren, they were always talking.

Fiddler was an anarchist – he used to buy things off us, same as Behren, but he worked on his own. He used to tell us about Russia – he had lost his legs in Siberia and walked about on wooden legs. He lived just by Clark's coffee house and went to the Jewish restaurant in Sclater Street, not the Warsaw Hotel but another one. When Gardstein's mob arrived he told us they were refugees on the run from the police.[16] That's why they had our sympathy. Fiddler regarded me as a protector. We called him 'Fiddler' because he knew how to fiddle about here and there – how to get rid of stolen property. He would help women too who were down and out, putting them up in his place. If she had something to sell he would say 'Go and pawn it' and advise her how much to ask. Lots of little advice. I don't think it matters what nationality you are, you will always find people like that who are really human.

The Warsaw hotel was the headquarters of Gardstein, the leader of the gang who murdered the city policeman at Houndsditch in 1910. It was also where Steinie Morrison met Leon Behren on 31 December 1910 – the night when he was murdered on Clapham Common. We used to take our things to Leon Behren in the Warsaw hotel, and he lived in Jubilee Street, only a few yards from the anarchist club. I don't know whether he was mixed up in it, but Steinie Morrison was – he was still a red-hot anarchist when I knew him in Parkhurst prison. He would have liked to have killed the warders, but in the end they killed him.

We were on nodding terms with some of Gardstein's mob. They were part of the landscape in Brick Lane. They used to go to the restaurant in Sclater Street next to the 'King's Arms'. It was also near Clark's coffee shop where I and my friends would meet, so we had many opportunities of becoming acquainted with them. They used to have two or three lovely girls with them, all good lookers, nice, shapely girls, all blond. I couldn't talk plainly to them, they didn't understand much, but you could make yourself understood. I never knew the mob were bloody armed, that they carried pistols about with 'em. One day one of them pulled me away, it must have been a row over his girlfriend: I gave him a right-hander and he went down, cor blimey I never knew how near I was to getting a bullet in me.

The top fellow – Karl Gardstein – used to go to the Warsaw restaurant in Osborne Street – that was the bottom end of Brick Lane, between Old Montague Street and Whitechapel. I first saw them about 1909 or 1910. The most peculiar thing about them was that they always walked in the road, never on the pavement. I can see the idea, if anyone's lying in wait for you to arrest you, they wouldn't wait out in the road, they'd wait in a doorway, they could see in the road. They always marched along in the roadway with their womenfolk in the middle of them; they numbered sometimes as many as twelve or fifteen people, men and girls – the girls were good-lookers, gypsy-style: we would have liked to be friendly with them. We knew they were crooked, but we were told they were on the run from the Russian secret police; that fact alone gained them our sympathy. They had to live, they had to pay their lodgings, and they needed the money for their politics when all's said and done. That's why they did these robberies.

Gardstein was the head of the mob, George Gardstein, some called him Karl, he was smart, a good looker, about twenty-six, twenty-seven. He was the gaffer, the top man. He lived in Grove Street, Commercial Road, he had a bride, she was one of the girls they used to be with, she went raving mad, poor dear, finished up in a lunatic asylum. He spoke English not too badly. He was a nice chap.

One of Gardstein's mob I got to know well – Milly, a blonde girl. She was in at the killing of the policeman at Houndsditch and she got two years for being a suspected person. I hid her for a few days after the murder. Fiddler told me about her one morning. He said he had her in his flat and asked me if I could help. She only knew a couple of words of English – I couldn't understand what she was saying, but she appealed to me as a young woman in trouble. I took her back to Gibraltar Gardens and my mother put her up. When the hue and cry was on my mother and sister wanted to get rid of her. They made a ruck of it so I took her to someone in Commercial Road. But the police got hold of her and she was brought up at the Old Bailey with the others. She got two years. All they could convict her for was that she had made tea for the others. They had lived in Exchange Buildings for some days before the raid and used the women to convince the neighbours they were ordinary people. That was Milly's job – they never accused her of shooting the policeman. She only got two years but she had been so bashed about by the police at the station that she went potty. They certified her and she was sent off to an asylum. One of Wensley's mob told me that she died there. A tragic way for a life to be done away with.[17]

Wensley of 'H' Division, because the alien gang were domiciled in the East End. The police always put in that extra bit of zeal when hunting down the killers of their comrades.

On the 2 January 1911 the police were in possession of information which suggested that some of the gang were in hiding in a room in Sidney Street, Whitechapel. The scene of the last act in this tragic story of the Houndsditch murders was set in a sordid street opposite the famous tavern, the 'Blind Beggar', in Whitechapel Road, E.1. A few yards east of the famous London Hospital and nearly opposite where General Booth started his Salvation Army crusade.

The 'siege' of Sidney Street – which ended in the blowing-up of the anarchists – became famous all over the world.

One of the raiding party told this fantastic story to the *Evening Standard* in 1966. He was my old enemy, Det. Sgt J. Stevens, nicknamed 'Jew Boy' by the underworld, now ninety years of age. He said, and I quote: 'I went to the London Hospital and attempted to get a doctor to supply me with a drug so that I could dope the suspects in the house at 100 Sidney Street. While in the house I saw "Peter the Painter".' He did not explain why they did not arrest him. I expect 'Jew Boy' had been dreaming when he told that story to the *Evening Standard*. Det. Sgt Jack Stevens, aged ninety-one, died on Christmas Eve 1967, so he went to a higher court.

My informant who took part in the first attempt to enter the house gave me the story which I believe entirely. No. 100 Sidney Street, E.1. was a three-storey tenement house let out in rooms to Jewish emigrant families who could only speak Yiddish. The attempt to evacuate the families from the house by sending in a Yiddish-speaking Jew to explain matters caused a good deal of commotion, which unfortunately alerted the suspects who realised something was on. The families of people were evacuated and the house was empty except for the two suspects who appeared to be asleep. The street door was open, which is common with all these tenements which contained several families.

About 7 a.m. a large furniture van called a pantechnicon drawn by two horses stopped outside 100 Sidney Street.[18] Inside the van were twenty or more armed plain-clothes police from the City police and 'H' Division Metropolitan police, most of these men were members of the CID and were getting on in years. Some had families. Uniformed police from the City and Metropolitan were drafted into the surrounding streets so that a complete cordon was drawn around the block of houses containing 100 Sidney Street.

Inside the van, the raiding party of CID men were addressed by DDI Wensley, who had assumed command. He told the men that it was proposed to call upon the two suspects to surrender, as the place was surrounded by the police, so as the suspects might be asleep it was proposed that the raiding party should leave the cover of the furniture van and throw stones at the windows of the house, so as to make the men look out, and then call them to surrender. Wensley made no attempt to knock on the door of the room and question the men. These two suspects were Russians and used to Russian police methods. We did not give them any chance to explain.

This plan did not meet with the approval of the majority of the CID men and none wanted to be a dead hero. But amongst the party was the CID man who was DDI Wensley's Sergeant, Det. Sgt Leeson, and he knew well that the 'Governor' expected him to show an example. He volunteered for the stone-throwing. So, leaving the protection of the van, he started to throw some stones at the windows; immediately shots were fired from the house and the brave Sergeant Leeson fell, shot in the chest. Several of his comrades rushed to his aid and he was pulled through the passage of a nearby house and carried over the walls to the London Hospital, where immediate medical attention saved his life.[19]

Meantime, the furniture van was driven away with most of the raiding party inside. So ended the foolish plan to frighten two scared and desperate men to surrender, and that was the only action that the police took to arrest the two suspects. The rest of that day was taken up by men of the Scots Guards having a little shooting exercise and waiting for the Royal Horse Artillery to arrive with their guns, while Mr Winston Churchill watched the so-called battle and conferred with the police chiefs.

Det. Sgt Leeson was the first casualty on that disastrous day; before the day ended others would die, the just and the unjust, because firemen became casualties when they finally put the fire out, all because an incompetent policeman was in charge. Guards from the Tower, guns from Richmond. The whole business sounds like a comic opera.

The two men should have been taken alive to stand trial, if there had been sufficient evidence to justify committal. Many other suspects, men and women, were arrested and committed for trial on the weakest of evidence, in some cases on no evidence at all. Some were even convicted and sentenced to long terms. But the Court of Criminal Appeal would not tolerate this kind of panic justice and quashed every conviction for lack of evidence to justify conviction.

In regard to the legendary character, Peter the Painter, no one ever saw him, none would or could swear to his existence, yet the national press made him such a real person. There were reports from all parts of the world that he had been seen here, there and everywhere. Det. Sgt Leeson was promoted to Inspector and pensioned off. He is on record as saying, 'I saw Peter the Painter in a railway carriage in Australia.' How he knew 'Peter' was a mystery because no photograph was ever proved to be the mysterious unknown 'Peter the Painter'. Others swore he was poor old Joe Stalin from Russia.

The only Peter among the mob that I knew was the least offensive of the gang I remember, he remained in the district and I often saw him many years after these events had been forgotten. He had become an honest man, so I 'forgot' him.

One fact stands out plain for all to see. DDI Wensley arrested and charged everyone he could, had them committed for trial although he was never able to find even a gun that was used on that fatal night in December 1910. I believe he arrested some ten people; the men and women were all tried and acquitted.

Browne and Kennedy, the two vicious killers of PC Gutteridge, were both as dangerous as any of the aliens who took part in the Houndsditch murders. Both men were armed when arrested, but through good police work they were taken without anyone getting injured. In August 1966, three CID men were shot dead within a couple of minutes by three armed men.[20] All three murderers were arrested without a shot being fired. Yet in 1910, these two men, who were only suspects, aliens in a strange land, were forced to give battle to hundreds of police and some 100 Scots Guards.

Shortly after the siege of Sidney Street, Leon Behren was murdered.[21] His body was found on Clapham Common. According to the story in the underworld he was murdered because he was a police informer who had helped them make arrests after the Houndsditch murders. The man who was arrested for the murder – Steinie Morrison – had acted unwittingly as the decoy, but he had neither taken part in the execution nor known it was to take place. This was also the story which Morrison told me when I got to know him in Parkhurst prison.

It must be remembered that the Houndsditch killers were also burglars and they had 'fences' who bought their stolen property. These fences were their danger. The only persons who could positively identify them were the persons who had bought their stolen jewellery. At this point, Steinie Morrison enters into the story. Morrison was known to Gardstein and Leon Behren. He was the contact man between the gang and the fences, so he was going to earn good commission. It is true he did not know much about them because Morrison had not been in the East End very long, having been in Parkhurst serving a sentence of seven years penal servitude. He was wanted by the police for failing to report to the police: he was a convict on licence. Morrison was a burglar and a contact man, born in Russia or Poland.

The evidence went to prove that Morrison and Behren were very friendly. Morrison was told that the gang had a large haul of stolen jewellery to dispose of, but it was highly dangerous to do any business in the usual place, because of police activity, so the meeting place was made for Clapham Common, because Morrison was well acquainted with the locality, having lived there. Morrison met Behren in the Warsaw restaurant, told him of the deal: time 31 December 1910 at about 6 p.m. From that minute, Morrison never left Behren in case he should inform the police of the meeting place; these precautions are always taken when a would-be fence is told of a meeting place.

The two men left the 'Warsaw' together and some time after midnight they travelled to the meeting place at Clapham

Common. When they arrived at the meeting place, Morrison left Behren with his executioners, not knowing the fate that awaited his former friend. After leaving him Morrison then went to a house he knew and burgled it for some jewellery, which he afterwards disposed of.

The next morning, he went into 'Cockie Flatnose's' place – a spieler off the Commercial Road – and heard the news. He shouted excitedly, 'So that's what they got me to "lumber" him for,' and hurried out. Morrison was next seen in the 'Warsaw' restaurant, looking for a friend; then, not seeing the person he was looking for, he went to Whitechapel railway station and left a gun in the left luggage office. By this time, the news had already become known and the papers had a full account of the murder.

It must be clearly understood that Steinie Morrison had not left Whitechapel nor his lodgings, and even after the murder he continued to use the same restaurant for his meals, where he was arrested. These were not the actions of a man on the run.

Morrison was arrested and charged with the murder of Leon Behren. My old enemies Det. Sgts Brogden and Dessent, supported by a number of CID officers including my old friend, Sgt Jack Stevens, made the arrest on the orders of DDI Wensley.

Steinie Morrison was put on trial at the Central Criminal Court before Mr Justice Darling. There was a strong circumstantial case against Morrison; and he was handicapped by lack of funds to brief a good criminal lawyer, he had to be satisfied with a good trier and that is all that could be said of the lawyer, Mr Edward Abinger. But his greatest misfortune was the state of public opinion, which was inflamed against foreign Jews.

Morrison had been seen leaving the Warsaw restaurant about 11.45 p.m., carrying a heavy parcel. The police made out it was a bar of iron to kill Behren. Morrison's real story that came out after his conviction was that it was a gemmy used for breaking in houses, and that he had broken into a house at Clapham Common that night and stolen jewellery. But he didn't put that forward at the trial because he was scared he'd get a long term of penal servitude.

Morrison didn't stand a chance. Instead of putting forward a true alibi, he claimed that he had spent the evening with two girls at the 'Olympia' theatre, Shoreditch. And he made matters worse by attacking one of the witnesses – a Jewish woman who said she had seen him go away with Behren in a cab. He called her a 'stinking, dirty culiver' (brothel-keeper). She said, 'I'm not a culiver, you're a gonnoff' (thief). Under cross-examination he became worse in his manner, because Jewish people the more you torment them, the more violent they become. From the jury's point of view here was a man, 6 foot tall, who looked a desperate man, who spoke violently in the dock, who had just come out from serving seven years for burglary and who was a foreigner. The memory of Sidney Street, and of the Houndsditch murders, was fresh in people's minds, when they'd had to call the army out to deal with just such desperate men. The jury didn't need corroboration – they'd have found him bloody guilty without any evidence against him. His looks were enough to put the noose around his neck. The judge summed up in his favour, but after the jury's verdict, he sentenced him to death.

Morrison was reprieved by the Home Secretary, Winston Churchill, and sentenced to life imprisonment instead. He died at Parkhurst prison in 1921, strangled by a warder who was helping to artificially feed him because he was on hunger strike.

I will write more of Morrison and tell what prison had done to him when I saw him last in 1920.

12 Vendettas

The only mob that I knew when I was a youngster was One-eyed Charlie's lot who hung out at Clark's coffee house. They weren't skilled thieves, only van-draggers. Later I discovered there was another gang nearby in Turin Street, but I never knew them.

The Titanic mob belonged to the Nile,[1] by Moorfield's Eye Hospital. That's where the Chandlers were born. Pat O'Keefe kept the pub on the corner – he had been a champion boxer.[2] He was a pal of Steve Donoghue,[3] the great jockey who won the Derby. Afterwards he became manager of the 'Olympia' music hall[4] (that was the old Standard theatre) in Norton Folgate. The first time I saw the Titanics was when I was on remand in Holloway prison in February 1902. They were all very well dressed fellows. I think they were named after the liner because they were so well dressed. The Chandlers were part of them. They had plenty of money and they used to straighten everybody up. They were a good proposition from a police point of view. Very specialist. They used to rob men only. A crowd of six of them went up – at the theatre or the railway stations or going away to the races.[5] They were whizzers (pickpockets) but they would also take part in burglaries.

The Hoxton mob came from round Hoxton Street – they used to use the 'Spread Eagle'.[6] They weren't such good-class thieves as the Titanics. They were more hooligans than thieves. Spencer became a part of them in later years, when things were getting bad and he was getting old – after I was married. They worked ten- or twelve-handed; Friday night was their night when the dockers were paid. They all finished up on the Poor Law, or cadging. Their leader died a pauper, whereas the leader of the Titanics ended up owning a dog-track.

The only time the Hoxton mob came into Brick Lane was Sunday morning for the market. But I got involved in a quarrel with one of them – Greeny. I belted the life out of him. It was about 1910. Greeny was interfering with Sunshine's, a spieler in Shoreditch High Street.[7] It was a Jewish club used by people like Betsy, the comedian, and the bookmakers coming home from the races. Benny Hall asked me to go up and sort him out. I got pinched while I was setting about him. A couple of policemen came along while I was doing it. One of them said, 'You'll have to go down,' so I said, 'That's all right.' I wasn't afraid. The police took him in; he was already half-unconscious, but what I didn't like is that when they got him into Commercial Street police station they kicked the bloody life out of him. He was twelve months in hospital. The police hated him. He'd only been out of jail six months for setting about a CID chap in Bishopsgate. When I came before the court at Old Street, Clark-Hall, the magistrate let me off. The police said there had been a scuffle going on. The magistrate had it in for him too.

Greeny was a scoundrel. The kind who would stick a knife into your back without warning. He terrorised Hoxton. His uncle was a terror and all. The police in 'G' Division hated the sight of him, because he was always knocking coppers about. Greeny couldn't thieve for toffee. He was a no-gooder, a scrounger. But he ran off with a shopkeeper's wife, Mrs Webster – they had a fish shop which took more money than any other shop in Bethnal Green. Lovely woman she was, with beautiful blond hair. Well she went for an outing to Southend and she met this bleeding tike in a pub, and she left her family, her home, her husband and everything for him. Forsaking everything, lovely house, lovely business, to live with this bloody tike, who never earned a bleeding penny in his life. He used to knock her about terrible and in the end he divorced her. It was a real tragedy. He wasn't even goodlooking – wasn't tall – nothing attractive about him.

Vendettas could start up almost by accident. Someone would get into trouble and they would come to me for help. If it was a friend, you had to help out. One time – about 1908 we had a quarrel with the Titanics. We got involved with them because of a man named Pencil. He used to go with some of the brides down Brick Lane. Me and some others set about him one night at the coffee stall in Shoreditch High Street, top of Bethnal Green Road. They were taking liberties with the chap who had the stall and I knew him so we belted him and that led to a bit of gang warfare between us and them. Stevie Cooper was in it. The next night they come down from Hoxton. But what they done was crafty. They set a trap for us. They was well in with the police and directly the fight started the police were there. They got hold of us – including Cooper, who had a loaded gun on him. It wasn't an offence to carry a gun, but we got a week's remand for causing an affray. I always had it in for them afterwards. I thought, 'You twisters – you always have the bogies on your side.'

Pencil's wife came out of the Ratcliffe Highway. She was a fighter – I once fought her outside a pub in Brick Lane. Millie – she was a real prostitute and a thief. Later he took a young woman for his partner and bed-mate and that changed him and made him an honest man. She was handicapped – a sort of mental defective – but she looked after him and supplied his need for home comfort and he treated her with kindness and consideration. He took up work as a messenger in the City, and earned a good living. I once saw the two of them together – he was holding her tightly because she was very weak and I wondered what had changed him so: his devotion and care for this poor handicapped young woman was the outward sign of his loneliness and need for companionship. He used to come to my shop to buy clothing for her and he was very happy. When he died he left £500. Millie tried to get his money, though she hadn't lived with him for years, but the court ordered that it should go to his common-law wife.

Another quarrel we had was with Simpsons.* The Simpsons were a very tough mob. They come out of the Nichol. They wasn't thieves, though one of them turned burglar and done a lot of time for screwing. They was a vicious family. Alf Simpson,* the father, was always getting into fights. His son Bert* was a leader of the Mosley crowd in Bethnal Green. About 1900 the Simpsons were involved in a murder case

*Fictitious names.

when a chap was stabbed to death in Kingsland Road. Alf Simpson was the type to do it. He wasn't a thief but a hooligan – stabbing people and all that sort of thing. He didn't make any money at it – it was just terrorism, the instinct of the savage. In later years I was on speaking terms with him. He belonged to Mosley's party and I used to meet him when I went up to the meetings up at Ridley Road. He used to speak to me of 'the Good Old Times'. I said, 'You tried to make 'em bad old times for me.'

In 1908 they got a man five years in prison – Dodger Mullins. I was a witness for him. At that time the Simpsons were involved in a war with One-eyed Charlie's gang. The two brothers came down Brick Lane on a Sunday and there was a skirmish at the corner of Bacon Street. A policeman came up, Nobby Clark, the champion wrestler of the Metropolitan police force. Somebody stabbed Bert Simpson – there was blood pouring from him, it could have been a hanging job. Nobby said, 'Who done it?' The fellow who done it was Bob Wheeler but for some reason Alf Simpson pointed at Dodger Mullins and said he had done it. He was a thief but not a violent type. He was completely innocent but he got five years. I went up as a witness for him.

Another man, Charlie Callaghan, tried to shoot Alf Simpson. He was one of those put away with me in the Vendetta case. Callaghan[8] belonged to a Bethnal Green gang – he was old enough to be my father. The Simpsons picked him out one night. They saw him outside the 'White Hart' in Shoreditch and hit him on the head with a hammer. They split his head open. That night Charlie came back and shot Alf Simpson outside his home in Duval Street. He was a good marksman and he caught him in the groin. Callaghan went on the run. The Simpson family had it in for me. They were dead enemies. One of the brothers accused me of having done it – he didn't know my name but he called me 'Callaghan' and said, ''Ere's that man.' When we got to the station the Inspector said, 'You made a mistake, his name isn't Callaghan, it's a different name entirely.' Eventually they caught Callaghan, but he only got six months. I think the magistrate knew what was going on. I gave evidence that he couldn't possibly have known who shot him because he accused me of it.

Callaghan was a pal of Jack Parr that got hanged. He was a cabinet-maker and he had been a straight fellow; but after Parr got hanged he started knocking people about. A lot of hooliganism started in Bethnal Green after Parr's hanging. People were upset.

Another feud was with George King.[9] A real right scoundrel he was; a villain; he lived in Bacon Street. He was much older than me, old enough to be my father. He used to be my pal years before, but when he come out from doing five years we were rivals.

Once he took me down Dossett Street because he wanted to do a fellow. About 1907, something like that – when I was in my prime. He wanted to do a fellow named Billy Maguire. He was also a terror. I fired at him but Kingie got the blame of it, not me. I knew he'd got the blame of it, but I was bleeding reckless. I didn't know what I was doing.

Burglars as a rule are not terrors – some people don't realise that – and Kingie was a crack screwsman, the leader of a gang. But he was also a villain. He'd think nothing of sticking a knife into you. Everybody was frightened of him. After a raid, if there was £500 in the Peter he used to say it was only £250 – he would knock them for the other.

There was a couple of good people working with him. They didn't belong to Bethnal Green, they belonged round Walthamstow way because a lot of screwsmen came from Walthamstow. And there were also some from Bethnal Green.

Eventually it got talked about. They done a jeweller's shop somewhere over Deptford way. And when the report of it got in the local paper it stated how much money was in the safe and how much jewellery had been stolen – much more than Kingie had shared out. He said that it was only to get the insurance money that the papers gave such a big sum. But people didn't believe him.

Screwsmen, they keep to themselves as a rule. But chaps like me used to get in – they'd tell us all about what was going on, what had happened. So I talked to one of them and he said that Georgie King had done them and they weren't going to stand much more of it. So I thought to myself, 'I could get a few quid out of this.' I said, 'Well come down and accuse him.

Don't be frightened. I'll be there.' I went down there with them and that started it.

After we became enemies, he got away from our end, and started collecting rent from the stall-keepers at Walthamstow. But he still lived in Bacon Street – he lived there till he was married.

Kingie was a very dangerous chap. After the row at Walthamstow he was determined to do me in. He signed up with Darky the Coon's mob, and he and Phil Shonck and some others came round to pay me a visit. There were six of them. They wanted to kill me, no doubt about it. They thought, 'If we do him, we'll do the lot.' I just about began to realise that the whole thing ought to be settled with and done with. I thought to myself, 'Bugger, I'm going to get out of this business, this is getting a bit too serious,' a couple had already got shot, another one had his head split open.

On this particular night, it was about 1 o'clock in the morning. Taylor and Spencer, who were living with me at the time, down the Gardens, hadn't come home. I thought, 'Cor blimey, I wonder what's happened to them.' I couldn't go to bed. I was waiting for them. Suddenly 'Bang Bang'. I run up the court – I saw Phil Shonck laying out and I saw Spencer (we used to call him Emsey), holding his face. Taylor was standing there with one of the gleaming revolvers in his hand; he said to me, 'I'm down here, Arthur, run down here.'

I wasn't scared. In my pocket I had an Irish Constabulary revolver, fired bullets as big as that, it would have knocked holes in a brick, never mind a body. I never intended to shoot anybody with it, it was for my own protection. So I run down there, that was the turning opposite and who should be coming up but two uniformed policemen. They never done anything. Very wise of 'em, probably had their orders – don't interfere with them, let them kill each other. They knew me, they weren't friends of mine, but they never said one word.

Tommy Taylor and another chap had broken into the gunsmith's somewhere and they'd got about six guns, all brand new ones, the ammunition an' all. I got up the top and I said to Taylor and Spencer, 'Come on down the court, give me them guns.' So, I got the guns off 'em, put 'em in a bag and my mother took 'em right round to Prince's Court and left 'em with a woman round there, in case the police come round. They took Shonck to the London Hospital where he was admitted, a bullet went right through him.

This brawl led to a series of affrays in which guns were used and men shot. It got so bad they had to call the police out from all over the East End. Detective Inspector Wensley took charge of the case, and in the end we were arrested and charged with several wounding offences. After prolonged court hearings, eight of my friends including myself were committed for trial at the Central Criminal Court. Eventually all of us were convicted and sentenced to terms of penal servitude. My share was nearly five years, twenty-one months for being armed in a court of law.

We were already involved in a feud with the Coons. They were the biggest villains that the East End had; they were all foreigners, living on the girls, and all 'shundicknicks' – ponces. Darky the Coon lived round Commercial Road. His real name was Ikey Bogard.[10] Usually the man who lives on a woman is a coward, they're not usually fighting men. But Darky was a big man and a fighter – he'd think nothing of giving someone a rip, and he could be very vicious. He was gaffer over all the Jewish chaps up Whitechapel and Aldgate.

Darky was a Jewish chap, but as far as religion was concerned, he wasn't the type to keep up his religion. He'd have been the same if he was a Roman Catholic. He was very flamboyant. He dressed like a cowboy. It was before the cowboys on the pictures y'know. He used to wear a big open shirt, like a woman's blouse, and a flash belt with something stuck in a case. It wasn't illegal to carry a gun at that time; he had a big weapon stuck down his belt; a big panama hat on – he was quite a character in his way.

Darky the Coon had some brilliant girl friends, lovely girls – he used to meet them off the trams at Gardiner's Corner. I can never understand why beautiful girls go wrong. I think if a man's got a bad name and all that it appeals to them. In 1911 he was living with a beautiful English girl. She come out of the Broadway, by Hackney Road and used to go up the West End. Being a good-looker she would draw a lot of money. She'd have been a good film-star today, but he had her on the streets.

The other chaps in Darky's gang were similar. A couple of them were boxers with cauliflower ears. They all come out of Commercial Road, a gang of about six or eight of 'em. I know Phil Shonck 'cos he was shot. He was also what they called 'shundicknick' – a Yiddish word for a man who lives off girls.

What the newspapers called the Vendetta affair started over a quarrel about a girl. It was just after we'd been holding up the spielers in Whitechapel High Street. A lot of people in trouble used to come to me to see if I could help out. Tommy Taylor was one of them. He had been knocking about down the other end with some of the brides. And Darky the Coon set about him. Taylor came and told me about it and I said, 'Come on we'll give them a belting.' Taylor was as bad as the Coon. They both lived on women. But he was one of our lot. I said, 'Where do they hang out?' He said, 'The Blue Coat Boy', in Bishopsgate. So I got a few chaps up and we went up there.

On a Sunday night, it was August or something like that. There were seven or eight of us, and a mob of about twelve of them. I said to Tommy Taylor and the others, 'Come on let's go in there, the more the merrier, if you miss one you hit another.'

Well, we go in the pub and they're all in this bar. They gave us the eye and then the Coon said to me, 'What you having Arthur?' (he used to talk in an American accent). Everyone's nerves were tense, and when he handed me a drink I threw it over him. We smashed some glasses and started hitting out. There was about eight or ten of them, but they didn't have a chance with us because we were all adept, except Taylor, at fighting, brawling, that kind of business. I didn't even have a scratch. It was a wonder no one got killed, the judge said, and he was right: We had seven guns between us. I had this Irish Constabulary revolver with bullets as big as a nigger. As it was, we did a lot of damage. The Coon had a face like the map of England. He was knocked about terrible. I hit him with a broken glass, made a terrible mess of his face. I knew I'd hurt him a lot, but not anything that could be serious.

When it was over, the whistles were blowing, the police arrived and an ambulance came up – all that kind of thing. We had come out of the 'Blue Coat'. I said, 'Where's Taylor?' I went back in to find him and as I did he came out. I saw him put something in his outside pocket. I said, 'What 'ave you got in your pocket there?' He said, 'Nothing.' I said, 'Come 'ere' – put my hand in and pulled out a blood-stained knife. I said, 'Bleedin' villain, tell me what you done?' 'Cos you know I was a bit scared, if he'd killed anybody, we'd have had it. He said, 'I just give him a slash.' 'Where?' 'Round the neck.' I said to the others, 'You better clear out of it.' I was scared.

On the Sunday morning I went down the Lane to Clark's. There was plenty of gangsters down there then, and they all wanted to be in it. We were getting plenty of support. I suppose it's part of East End life, if there's trouble, then people want to be in it. They were all against the Coon.

On the Monday, we heard that the Coons were going to the Old Street police court to ask for protection. This was Wensley's doing right enough, it must have been. They went up to the court and so did we. The police said there was twenty of us, but there wasn't; anyway we went up there to the court, to catch 'em coming out. Inside, there was a big police escort round the two principal ones, that was the Coon and Georgie King, none of the others were there, only them two. They were up there to swear information warrants.

And then suddenly van-loads of police come up. I don't know where Wensley was, he must have been in a van. At my trial he said that he'd seen me put a gun in my pocket. Now that's a very serious offence, to be armed in a Court of Law. I got a sentence for that. I gave my gun to another chap, I said, ''Ere mind that, I think they're after pinching me.' When it started, I got seized, and then found the gun dropped. It was mine, but I didn't drop it, it was the chap I gave it to, he dropped it. Me and this other chap, who gave the Coon a punch, got arrested. That was Bill Andrews.

The police caught four more of our chaps in Brick Lane. They had been having a fight amongst themselves, and each had a gun in his hands. Spencer said that the others saw me being taken in and hadn't done anything about it. He was frightened of going home, in case my mother and my sister started on him for not getting me away. That's what the row was over. When they come up in court, they all had their heads in bandages, a bloody sight. When I saw them in the corridor, I said, 'What's happened?' They said, 'We were fighting with each other.' Some of them said Spencer had let me down.

When the case came up in the Old Bailey – we was fourteen weeks in remand – the papers made a great case of it. They called the eight of us 'the Vendetta gang'. They had a special van to take us back and forwards. They played us some tricks in Brixton. One day we go into chapel and who should be sitting there but one of the other mob, Jackie Berman, who was in for being a suspected person. I got up and set about him, in the prison chapel. I bloody nearly strangled him.

Eight of us stood in the dock at the Old Bailey. Tommy Taylor, Bill Andrews, Charlie Callaghan, Bob Wheeler, Bill Newman, Spencer and Stevie Cooper. We all had convictions except Tommy Taylor, he'd never been in prison and they never had anything against him at all. All the others had convictions, so if you attacked a witness's character they could read out a list of your convictions. I said to Tommy Taylor, 'Say to Shearman' – that was his counsel – 'don't be frightened, attack their character, never mind what they can prove against us.' The judge said to his counsel, 'You're taking a great risk, Mr Shearman.' He said, 'I'm sorry, these are the explicit instructions of my client.' So they had to read out a list of the other gang's character. Darky the Coon had a terrible record: eighteen months and a flogging for living on immoral earnings; and some of the others had been convicted for immoral earnings.

With the Phil Shonck shooting I got acquitted. It was a separate indictment. The two policemen said they saw me with a gun in my hand but it wasn't a crime to have a gun, and they couldn't find any other evidence against me. Phil Shonck said I wasn't there when he was shot. Well, I wasn't there; he said Spencer and Taylor was there and started the firing. Muir,[11] who was prosecuting for the Crown, said that after due consideration they couldn't prove who was the people who started it, because both sides of the roadway windows were broken, proving that two gangs were firing at each other. So I got acquitted and Spencer and Taylor got acquitted 'cos they said they were attacked first and you're justified in protecting yourself. And Phil Shonck he was helping them. He said he wasn't sure who it was who shot. The landlord of the 'King's Head' gave evidence for me and Bill Smith. He proved that that night we had been drinking quietly in the pub.

On the 'Blue Coat Boy' affair the landlord of the pub wouldn't give evidence against us. He was so terrified he ran away and gave up the pub. He lost £100 on his forfeit, as a witness. I came across him years later, he'd opened a big club in Southend. He was still frightened of me and that was years afterwards. I said: 'What did you run away for?' He said, 'I didn't want to be involved in it, I'd never get me licence back.' He said, 'I'm glad I got away, its all right here, I wasn't cut out for that place; it was too tough!'

Jackie Berman was the one who got me my time. He was a ponce. Without his evidence it would just have seemed a drunken brawl. He told a pack of lies. He said that I had stopped him in Shoreditch and asked, 'Where can I find the Coon?' and that he had said, 'You'll find him in the "Bluecoat Boy"', I've just left him.'[12] He said four of us were there. That proved we were out to prove grievous bodily harm.

He straightened me up afterwards, he gave me a gold watch and chain and some money, when I come out of prison. He said he was made to do it, or they were going to pinch him on immoral earnings, and a man don't want a charge like that against him. They brought him up from prison to give evidence against us at the Old Bailey, he had prison uniform on and all. He's the one who got us convicted. I could have got out of it only for him. When I came out of prison he was in the racing lark with the Raddies – the Italians.

If Taylor hadn't have used that knife, none of us would have had a weapon. I always said in any fight: 'If they find anything in your pocket you've had it. If you pick up a bottle or a glass in anger, they can't pin anything on you.' You couldn't get hung if you didn't have a weapon. So I'd asked each of them whether they had a chiv. I said, you can use anything you can when you get in there – bottles, glasses – but no weapons. As an Englishman, I would never use a knife.

I've never told a lie in the witness box, and when I went in there for the Vendetta case I admitted the whole affair. I got twenty-one months in Wormwood Scrubs for possessing fire-arms in a court of law and then three years in Portland for causing a dangerous affray. Why we got lenient sentences was that not one policeman had been interfered with – the only damage we'd done was to ourselves and to the Coons. Spencer and I got the longest sentences because we were convicted thieves.

Cooper was charged separately from us for shooting an unknown person. There were no witnesses except two policemen who had caught him with a gun in his hands. As a matter of fact he was firing at Emsy (Spencer) because Spencer had hit him in a pub the night I got pinched at the police court. Cooper was the unluckiest fellow in the world. He'd had so many bashings that it turned his head. He was given three years and he cut his throat in prison. Wandsworth. It was a pitiful thing. They sent him to Broadmoor. In 1915 I went down there with Posh Reed to see him. He was completely gone. He died a couple of weeks after.

Bob Wheeler got fifteen months which he spent in Wormwood Scrubs. Afterwards he worked as a look-out man for Posh Reed, the bookmaker. He lived till he was eighty or eighty-five.

Billy Newman got fifteen months. When he came out from doing time he went into the army. At the time of the Vendetta he was a bit of a salesman or a porter, at Spitalfields market. It was he who caused the police to pinch us. Most of the men at Commercial Street station were on our side, but Billy Newman went in there and started bawling them out, and after that they had it in for us. When he came out of the army he became a big East End bookmaker, up Mare Street, Hackney. He was one of the Old Nichol mob – they were a crooked family.

Bill Andrews, 'The Lube', got fifteen months. He had no convictions against him, but they claimed that I had given him the gun at the police court. He'd never been in prison in his life, and was really an innocent fellow, but I had that influence over him. He was a glass-blower by trade. He had a nice mother, very respectable, who lived down Roman Road. He wasn't a thief, but he liked to be with us. He used to come down to the 'King's Arms' in Sclater Street where we drank, and when the feud was on, he wanted to be in it. After he came out he went into the army and was killed.

Callaghan got two years. He had been a cabinet-maker and a family man but one of the Simpsons hit him on the head with a hammer and that turned him crooked. In all bad districts where there are thieves you get tappers who live off the others. Callaghan was one. How he came to be involved was that Darky the Coon found him in the 'Horns' opposite Shoreditch Church and hit him on the head. So he had already had trouble from him. In later years he worked for Billy Newman when he was a bookmaker.

Tommy Taylor had no record so he received two years imprisonment. We were separated at Wormwood Scrubs, he was released some time in September 1913. When he was released he went back to Brick Lane, where he soon got into trouble making counterfeit coins. For this offence he received four years; this was his second conviction, so he was sent to Portland to join up with me. Some time at the end of 1914 – just after coming out of jail – I met up with him again. I had a shock, he looked ill, so I told him to go sick and see the MO. When the MO examined him he admitted him to hospital at once. After some weeks he was released and sent back to Bethnal Green Hospital; his case was hopeless. He had been ravaged by VD. I saw the MO, Dr French, and he allowed me to see him before they took him away. He died in 1915 in Bethnal Green Hospital. He was the third one to die of the eight men who stood together in the dock at the Old Bailey on that day in December 1911.

Life had been unkind to him. Orphaned at an early age, he was sent to an orphanage to be cared for. After leaving the home, he hung about Brick Lane and we became friends. He was always by my side when there was any trouble. In some unknown grave he lies and a verse from *Gray's Elegy* might be a fitting epitaph:

> Here rests his head upon the lap of Earth
> A youth to Fortune and to Fame unknown
> Fair Science frowned not on his humble birth
> And melancholy marked him for her own.

Darky the Coon joined up when the war started and was decorated with the Military Medal. Then he become 'governor' of the stalls back of Petticoat Lane and Golston Street. He looked after the stall-keepers, stopped them from interfering with each other, and they paid him 'rent'. He was the guv'nor. All round the fish shops and the stalls, he was in charge. On his own behalf; they had to pay unofficially.

Darky wasn't a bad fellow at heart. I remember when I came out of jail – five years doing time – I met him near Aldgate. He still had the scars on his face: but he said, 'Come and have a drink,' and, do you know, it was genuine: he meant it. He didn't have any evil in him. He said, 'Hello Arthur,' and put his hand out. He never talked about what we had done to him. I've never seen him since.

I think in later years he worked for Nutty Sharp. Sharp was a noted character in Whitechapel. He had been head of the Flying Squad and then became a bookmaker in Wandsworth after the Bow Cinema murder. Nutty was very friendly with Darky the Coon – he told me that he had shown brilliant conduct in the war. I never regarded the Coon as an enemy, he'd never done me any harm. It was Taylor who caused all the trouble.

I spent most of the next ten years in prison.

Wormwood Scrubs, where I spent the first year and a half of my sentence for the Vendetta affair, had not changed since my first term there in 1902. Hard fare, hard boards, hard work were still the rule.

In May 1913 we were sent to Portland, where the rest of my sentence was spent. Some twelve other men went with me. We travelled from Waterloo in a special compartment that had been reserved for our party. Three warders made up our escort. We were all chained together by a long chain. The warder in charge of my landing was an old officer from Borstal, who was surprised to see me back.

Portland is a very healthy prison,[1] the climate is ideal. It is built on a headland 500 feet over sea level. Very bracing and on a clear day it is said you can see the Isle of Wight some 85 miles away. The prison had been established under the Penal Servitude Act of 1857 as a convict prison for the construction work in the dockyard. Portland Harbour was built entirely by convicts, the stone being quarried from the local quarries where the convicts worked. My cell was on the seaward side of the prison, so I had a good view of the harbour where the Home Fleet lay at anchor.

Discipline was very strict, the governor believed in punishment; he was an ex-army officer, one named Captain Schuyler.[2] The question of reformation never caused him the slightest anxiety, he never considered it a part of his duty. The separate cells were a block of cells for the most dangerous and troublesome men. Those who had committed assaults on prison officers were flogged and had to wear chains rivetted round their legs for a period of six months.

The carpenter's shop where I worked was located outside the back gate of the prison wall. There were some twenty men working in the shop. One warder was in charge and he stood by the door which was always open. The warder was armed with a truncheon which he carried in his hand attached to his wrist by a leather thong. Most of the men in the shop were long-sentence men; the strange thing about these men was that none belonged to gangs or were criminal types. Most were serving sentences for violence. I was completely out of place among them, they did not even speak the same language as myself. All the men in the shop were practically first offenders; none of the men could be classed as embryo habitual criminals conforming to Lombroso's definition of a born criminal.[3]

When I first went into the shop I noticed one man specially; he was wearing a parti-coloured dress of yellow patches and brown on his convict suit. He was also wearing long chains on each leg rivetted round his ankles, which seemed to be fastened around his waist. This was the first time I had ever seen or heard of convicts in England having to wear chains, so we have not advanced very far along the road to Utopia. The man had attempted to escape from the carpenter's shop by jumping over a wall, but the other side of the wall was some fifteen to twenty feet deep and he nearly killed himself. After coming from hospital he was punished for his attempt to escape.

Four of the men in the shop were serving life sentences for murder. They had all been in the death cell and reprieved. In 1912 a life sentence was at least twenty years.

These lifers were well behaved men, three of them had served ten years of their sentence, they had reached a higher grade which entitled them to have a blue uniform and more privileges; on the completion of seven years a small sum of money was credited to them to buy sweets and other little comforts, but no tobacco.

Number one was a Londoner from the East End, he had served some ten years. He was the shop orderly and looked after the small garden outside the shop; he took great pride in it. One could understand the keen interest he took in it; that garden representing everything to him, the wife he had loved and lost, the care he gave to the garden was for her, what he would have given her, 'a thing of beauty is a joy for ever'. When the governor and other officials made their daily rounds each and every one would show interest in the garden. You see, they understood it gave the lifer a joy of living.

Lifer number two, a fine powerful man standing nearly six feet, some fifty years of age. Very good carpenter, what the garden was to number one the carpentry was to number two. He made staircases for the new houses and he would always have some example of his work in the shop, so that visitors could see his work was first-class and much admired by the many visitors. He was Yorkshire, I believe, and was the longest term man in the shop, having served twelve years. Wife strangler, no intention to kill. Mental deterioration was apparent, would become worse if not released soon. For some reason he was very friendly with me, maybe he recognised a kindred spirit in me. He liked joking with me. Warder warned me to be careful not to upset him.

Number three, a child killer, had done some ten years, spoke like an educated man, could have been about forty years of age, same type as homosexuals. He was very far gone along the road to mental deterioration. Would ask me every morning if I had heard the crowds around the prison demanding his release. Always believed that MPs were demanding his release. He was a native of Birmingham, harmless, should have been in a mental hospital.

Number four was my bench mate, sane, strong, no pity for anyone. No illusions about the inmates of HM prisons. No sympathy for others, would have made an ideal warder at Dartmoor. I heard from him the sordid story of a drunken wife and a baby left all alone in the house for hours, sometimes all day. He was a Yorkshire miner and on coming home from work found the house deserted, the baby crying on the bed with none to care for it; he ended the brief existence of the unwanted child and was sentenced to die, reprieved to serve a life sentence. He was young, strong and cheerful; he had served some two years or more. He did not seem to have suffered himself from the ordeal he had passed through.

At Portland I could always get a favour. I got on very well with the top people – the governor, the medical officer and the rest. The reason I got in with them is that I was a very good carpenter. I used to go and do little jobs for the top people – any doors or windows that needed doing. I had on my record 'Can be trusted', the womenfolk and children; they knew that I'd make no attempt to escape or nothing like that. Both at

Portland and Parkhurst I used to go out, they didn't have no trouble. They used to give me a drink. 'Tea or drink?' they used to ask, and sometimes there would be cakes.

I was very friendly with the medical officer at Portland: French.[4] He had been a naval surgeon before. He had a lovely wife, many a meal I've had in his house, he liked me. And when my friend Cossor came there, he was his friend too. When Cossor got into trouble he told me, 'You gotta be very careful with him, 'cos if anything happens like that again I'll have to send him to Broadmoor.' The doctor always thought a lot of me. I was in a position that I could talk to him freely. I remember one day when there'd been a fight between one of our heavyweight champions and some foreign champion, I think it was Carpentier, y'know the French champion. Carpentier won; he got him to turn his head and knocked him out. I said to him, the MO, 'What did you think of it, sir?' He said, 'I could do better myself.' I said, 'I haven't the slightest doubt you could have done.' He was a fine, big, athletic man.

For my own opinion of Portland I think I gained more in health, wisdom and learning in the two years I was there than I could possibly have gained anywhere else; looking back, I do not regret my stay although it was enforced. I wish the same could be said of Wormwood Scrubs.

September 1915 duly arrived and I was taken to the railway station, and given a ticket for Waterloo. I was served with documents stating I was to report to the police at Scotland Yard immediately I arrived in London. I was in the pink of condition, healthy and strong, twenty-nine years old, with the best riches in the world – health and intelligence.

My home had become more prosperous while I had been away. Business had been very brisk and we all had comfortable beds to sleep on. I arrived back to find that my family occupied three of the seven cottages in Gibraltar Gardens. My brother George was married and lived in No. 6. My mother lived in No. 5 and in No. 4 lived a family with several young daughters. One daughter aged thirteen years was at school; she was very friendly with my mother, always doing her shopping for the family, and as the years passed and I had gone on my long travels again, the child grew to womanhood, still doing the odd jobs for my mother and sisters. She was like one of the family; to me she was still a stranger, I hardly knew of her existence. Later she became my wife.

At this time, November 1915, the War Office was raising a local battalion, Royal Fusiliers, City of London. They never had rifles to train with. I went to Columbia Road Market in Brick Lane to watch them march away to Waterloo station to entrain for Aldershot; the best part of them had been drinking. This battalion was composed of Bethnal Green men and boys. They had lived all their lives in slums not fit for human habitation, some were illiterate, they never had the stamina to learn at school, they had been too hungry. Some, like myself, had slept on the bare floor. They had never had a chance.

Your King and Country needs you. Yes, they were needed all right, needed to rot in the trenches, needed to make up the 60,000 casualties on the first day of the Battle of the Somme. This was the only time in their short lives that the country needed them.

Many of these boys did not return. We remembered them by having plaques fixed in the streets where they lived – 'lest we forget'. Little wayside shrines. Then the Second World War came and the bombs fell and the mean streets disappeared. So we who lived had nothing to remind us of those who gave their all for King and Country.

It is a sobering thought to realise that if I had not been taken in by 'Jew Boy' Stevens in March 1902, I too might have been one of these dead heroes who died in the war to end all wars.

When I left Portland that morning free at last after four years of prison, I was determined never to go back to prison. I thought I was too clever to make a mistake again, but my return ticket was already issued.

I got involved in a big swindle on the railway.[5] Bert Simpson was in it and my brother George. The two of them knocked off a van-load of whisky and went off to a pub to sell it. It was the 'Black Dog' in Mount Street – the governor was a Jewish man. Two CID men went after them. My brother got away but they caught Bert Simpson. My brother came home crying his eyes out. They were just two young boys at work. My brother had got involved because he was a bit jealous of Bert

Simpson who was making money from the tea he thieved at work, and so he asked to join in.

Bert Simpson turned King's evidence and accused me of having forged the papers they had taken to the docks when getting the van-load of whisky. I was also accused of writing out the bills for loads of tea.

My old enemy 'Jew Boy' Stevens took me in. He called round at my house in Gibraltar Gardens and not finding me in left a message for me to meet him at a pub on the corner of Commercial Street. He left it to be understood that this was just a routine check. When I left Portland, I had become a ticket-of-leave man for the unexpired part of my sentence of three years. That was a nine months' licence, and during this period the ex-convict was at the mercy of the police. They can at all times arrest him at their discretion. So I went to keep the appointment under duress, knowing that Det. Sgt J. Stevens would avail himself of the first opportunity to send me back to prison. 'Jew Boy' told me the 'governor' wished to see me about a little matter. I knew that it was no social visit. When we reached Leman Street police station I was on the verge of running away, but 'Jew Boy' said to the PC on the door, 'Tell Inspector Wensley he has a visitor.' So I was invited into the spider's web. 'Come in Arthur,' he said, 'It's a very cold night.' He said, 'I'm on the phone to Scotland Yard.' Then he told me about the charge.

It will be noticed the difference in the way I am treated. No more the illegal entry into my bedroom. The arrest without warrant or evidence of a charge, the detention in a cell for many hours. No, this treatment would not be right for a pupil who has graduated with honours from Portland. Now I am politely asked to meet the CID outside the police station, where the police apologise for the inconvenience caused. A statement is read out to me to justify my detention, then I am placed in a detention room. The usual business of a cup of tea and a cigarette to soften you up for the kill. Kind words and a couple of cigarettes work wonders, police are your friends and only wish to help you.

I was remanded in custody for a week, and they tried to trick me into talking by putting me in the same cell as Bert Simpson. Then they stuck me up for an identity parade. But no one picked me out. The following week I appeared at the court, charged with conspiracy to rob the railways. I was to have been legally defended, but the solicitor was held up at the Marlborough Street court and phoned to ask for the case to be put back till he arrived. The magistrate, Mr Wilberforce[6] said, 'Mr Harding do you want the case adjourned or can you go on without him?' I said, 'I can go without him, sir.' He said, 'I thought you could.' That was Wilberforce. I was on the point of saying to him, 'Sir, you bear a very honoured name!' He said, 'Very well we'll go on without him, I don't think you'll lose anything.' At the end he committed the other fellow to trial and said, 'There's no case against you Harding.' And just then the solicitor came into the court, he said, 'You're too late, he's done quite well without you.' Just like that. I'll always remember it.

Soon afterwards they took Wilberforce away from that court and put in a new magistrate, Sir Chartres Biron – he was a bloody villain, he'd have sent his own mother to prison, in my opinion, if it was to get him an advantage.[7] I told him straight: 'You're just a man who's been paid to carry out other people's wishes.' He said, 'I can sentence you for contempt of court.' I said, 'You can do what you like about that, but that's my opinion of you.' That was Old Street, later they sent him to Bow Street, as the chief magistrate. He became the bloody terror of the Metropolitan police courts. They made him a Sir, 'cos he done everything the government wanted, they brought all these Crown cases in front of him and all that. A dead villain was Biron: I heard he died at sea, on a cruise he went on.

The railway conspiracy case was heard in March 1916. Two months later, in May 1916, I was back in jail, sentenced to five years penal servitude for receiving. This time it was over something I hadn't done. It was Spencer who had got me into trouble. I had done nothing at all. Spencer was serving in the army. He had joined up in the RASC but he had frequent leaves and when he come home for the weekend he lodged at our house in the Gardens. Spencer was a confirmed thief, or rather a clever pickpocket. So when I went home and saw him in army uniform I knew that it was not patriotism that had influenced him. In 1916 there were a number of known pickpockets in the Hoxton and Shoreditch districts, and most of them were in khaki. By bribing the responsible NCO they would get weekend passes and carry on their professional operations under the cloak of their army uniforms. Spencer was one of this gang of pickpockets who numbered some ten men, and they were doing remarkably well. One weekend, they robbed a man of some £350 at King's Cross railway station, this money was all in Bank of England notes. Spencer's share of the loot was £35, one £20 note and three £5 notes. These notes were left with my mother to look after. It must be remembered that in 1916 the public could not change Bank of England notes in any place unless they were known. Spencer could have sold his notes to a fence for £30 but he wanted the full value.

At that time my sister was running a Christmas Club at home. They used to pay out half-a-crown on every share. Anyone who wanted to borrow from the club could take out money, but they had to pay out interest on it. Spencer had about £80 of shares in the club. When Spencer paid this £35 to my mother he never said a word to me about it, never said a word about where it come from. I thought at the time he must have done a job – stolen some jewellery or something. I never thought that the notes themselves might have been stolen. But I said to mother, 'Don't take that money up the bank, I'll change it for you.' I was courting at the time and perhaps I thought I would be a wee bit flash, changing a £20 note. Anyway I changed the money. I gave £20 to a bookmaker, Albert Rod down Brick Lane, still there, he was a friend of mine and this is how fate paid me out for being a daft idiot.[8] I gave my tailor a £5 note, he's still there, Bernard's, a lovely tailor, corner of Brick Lane, I know the father and son, they think a lot of our family. I gave £5 in the pub at the corner – the 'Blade Bone' – and £5 to I forget who. They was all friends of mine, and I wouldn't have implicated them if I'd have thought the money was stolen, I'd never have changed 'em like that, I'd have sold 'em. I could have got £30.

The trouble began when the notes got into the bank. Albert Rod was all right 'cos he was a bookmaker and could say he got it off a punter. Bernard was all right. It was the bloody pub that was the trouble. Somebody put their money in the bank –

the brewers' money – and it went to the Bank of England, and one of these notes was amongst them. The chaps from King's Cross police station came down, Inspector Butt, they knew the numbers of all of 'em. They laid a trap for me and I fell in it. If I'd had anything to do with the robbery I'd have been better prepared.

I was coming home one afternoon and I saw two detectives standing at the top of the Gardens talking to the governor of the pub. I'd already got the squeak that they were making enquiries about the notes from Bernard, the tailor. Seeing the publican talking to the CID man I thought that he'd told 'em that I was the one who gave him the note. Whoever had the brains to put him there talking to Bernard was very clever; he hadn't told 'em nothing, but I did not know. It was very neatly done. The CID man from King's Cross asked me to go along with him. I didn't know him or anything. If I'd have known him, I'd have been all right, I'd have known what type of man he was. We got into the Commercial Street police station. All the way along I was puzzling my head about how much they knew. If I said I'd given Bernard the £5 note they would say, 'Did you give anybody else one?' and if I then said, 'No,' and they do know, then I'm proving I know they was stolen by not telling 'em the truth. So I decided that I should tell them the lot – all the people who I changed them with – and that would go in my favour. They couldn't come back at me in a cross-examination. I was faced with the problem of where, how, did I get the notes. I said, 'You probably know that we lend money to people, I had a chap borrowed from my young brother, borrowed £40 for the races, he was a racing chap, he hadn't paid him back and I'd been round to where he belongs asking for him and on the Sunday I met him and he paid me £40 – £5 interest on the money y'see.' They said: 'What's his name?' I told 'em some fancy, bloody name, anything that came into me mind. 'I changed the notes afterwards,' I said. I don't know whether he was a cleverer man than I thought he was, but the Inspector read the statement out and said to me, 'Look I don't want to trick you, shall I tear it up?' I thought, 'It must be a good statement else he wouldn't want to tear it up,' so I said, 'No,' though I was rather uncertain about what I had said. He said, 'You want to keep to the statement, very good, but don't forget, I asked you.' So he signed it. We had a taxi and went up to King's Cross station, where I was charged with receiving the notes. Arthur Phale was my solicitor. He was a crooked solicitor, that is you could trust him. Any villainery, he'd do it for you. He came from Marlborough Street, had an office there, all the pickpockets had him for a solicitor. He says to me, 'Why didn't you let them tear that statement up?' I said, 'Well, I thought it would go in me favour.' He said, 'Well, we've got a lot of explaining to do, but it's credible as long as you don't retract it now.' I'm worried. I was in a nasty state, mentally. I had a beautiful girl, lovely girl, but when fate's against you, you've got nothing in the world, don't matter if they're angels, they won't wait. I said, 'I'll go on trial with my story.' Then the solicitor committed suicide. Just my luck, he put himself under the bleeding electric train, during the trial. I was very much upset by it. I don't know whether Spencer had anything to do with it. Anyway he was killed on the station. He died and they had an inquest – Phale his name was. I think he was a Spanish Jew. We come up for trial and I come up in front of the worst possible man I could have come up against, the recorder, Sir Forest Fulton.[9] He was a dirty tike, he was a bully and everything else, he was the man who sentenced Adolph Beck, the greatest case in British criminal history, when they convicted a Norwegian of being another man, and this bloody judge abused the man, called him filthy names; he should never have been a judge.

I come up in front of him. The man who was robbed, a Rumanian gentleman, told the court, 'This man isn't one of the gang that robbed me, they were all in khaki as soldiers, he's not one, I would have recognised him at once if he'd have been one.' So the jury found me 'not guilty' of taking part in the robbery, but guilty of knowing that the notes were stolen. If Phale hadn't committed suicide I would have objected to the judge. If there was any justice, I should never have been done. The indictment charged me with stealing the money and secondly of being knowingly in possession of stolen property. This is how he done it. My mother came up as witness to say that the notes were given to her not to me, she didn't say who gave them to her. I couldn't possibly have been convicted for knowing them to be stolen if I got them from my mother. First indictment to the jury, 'Do you find him guilty or not guilty of stealing the money?' 'Not guilty.' On the second indictment the judge said, 'Of course if you find him guilty, when you hear his character you will know' – he near enough told them I was a convicted man. He twisted it very quick. Curtis-Bennet, who was defending me, jumped and said, 'My Lord . . . .' He said: 'You sit down, you've said all you had to say.' The judge had it in for me, but when we appealed he said the shorthand clerk must have made a mistake. A detective officer went into the witness box to tell my record. The judge said to him: 'You've known him for some time?' 'Yes.' 'He goes with the gang a bit?' 'No my Lord.' So he said, 'He's a professional buyer of stolen property?' 'Well', he said, 'I wouldn't say that.' Then the judge said, 'Stand down.' Being a lawyer he probably thought I'd straightened him up, but I hadn't. He knew I wasn't a buyer of stolen property, and he wanted to tell him. But you can't argue with a judge.

All through the trial I made the biggest mistake of my life: I went dressed up with a nice new suit of clothes, posh. The judge must have weighed me up and thought 'he's been getting a good living at it'. If I hadn't been so loyal to Spencer – if I had implicated him – I could have got off easy. As it was I got a five-year sentence for something I hadn't done. The thought of it made me ill. I wrote to the Home Office. From the hospital at Wandsworth prison I wrote to the Home Secretary, told him the truth about it. They sent a team to interview me, but it included the biggest enemy I had in the police force – Wensley, he passed an adverse verdict on it. He hated the bloody sight of me and I hated him. He was glad to put me away.

The case came up in the Appeal Court. I was asking for a reduced sentence. Rufus Isaacs, that was Lord Reading, one of the finest Lord Chief Justices, I come in front of him and he said it was a very severe sentence for such a crime. Avery who formed one of the members said that I'd got a record for violence. 'But', Lord Reading said, 'violence is a different thing to felony.' But they overruled him.

So the friendship begun in 1903 when I was released from Wormwood Scrubs had brought misfortune to both of us. Spencer was led into the Vendetta case by me and got four and a half years. And I got five years through his carelessness. My family closed the doors on him and he had to find another lodging. The £80 that he had saved and put into the club was confiscated by my sister and put in War Loan for the day I finished my sentence.

So I served the time, and had the experience of every prison in GB, even up in Scotland they sent me. But looking back on it now, I'm not sorry. Because I should have probably got killed in the First World War if I hadn't been inside. I would have joined the Veterinary Corps. A lot of the 'heads' was in it. They was getting horses and selling them to the Belgians, it was a racket all the way round. They was making a lot of money in there and they wanted me to join them. They said I could become a sergeant. I said, 'Look, I'm not fighting, I'm not going in the army at all, because when I had a war of me own, I got sent to prison for fighting meself and I'm certainly not going to fight for me country and I'm not going to do anything to injure it either.' All the same I probably should have finished up in the army because I was just potty enough to do it and be one of the first to crawl over the bloody top, 'Come on boys' sort of thing, would have finished up with a gun-load of bloody machine-gun bullets. Being in prison saved me from that.

During the years 1916–20 I passed through Dartmoor, Parkhurst and Peterhead in Scotland. I became acquainted with most of the notorious criminals in this period. What impressed me most was the conceit and vanity of their characters. First and foremost, everyone wanted to be regarded as belonging to the highest ranks of the criminal fraternity. They told stories of their criminal activities involving thousands of pounds. I enjoyed their confidence because I was a good listener, and they relied on my reputation as a tough guy to protect them from any enemy they made. In a convict prison, the inmates have a tendency to only associate and talk to men of their own standards of professional behaviour. Men from London and Brum seem to dominate the prisons.

After my sentence at the Old Bailey I was first sent to Dartmoor, and then after about six months I was transferred to Parkhurst. I served most of my time there, but they had suspicions I was trafficking with the warders, and so they sent me to Peterhead. This was a Scottish convict prison. I got on lovely there – working on the new sea-plane station for the Admiralty. We worked with civilians there – no warders.

It was in Parkhurst that I got to know Steinie Morrison. He was located on the BIs, that's the punishment cells, not that he'd done anything, but he preferred it that way, he didn't want to mix with the others, he was secluded. Didn't want to talk to anybody. I was the orderly on his landing and he used to speak to me. He couldn't avoid talking to me, he was a wee bit scared. We both come from Brick Lane, I knew him when he come home, I knew him when he got his first lagging.

Steinie was against everybody, 'cos he thought all the world was against him.[10] When he was being taken to prison he made a great disturbance on the railway station. 'I'm Steinie Morrison, I am an innocent man, convicted for a crime I never committed.' And he used to rave on about it in prison. The other prisoners didn't want anything to do with him, 'cos he kept carrying on about his case. He didn't want to know 'em. I said to him, 'Hang on, you're bound to be released 'cos public opinion is in your favour.' That's how I used to talk to him, to give him hope. When I left, his last remaining contact with the people he knew was gone.

Steinie was sent to Parkhurst mainly 'cos he was a Jew – it was the only prison where they'd got a synagogue and a rabbi. There's always about twenty or thirty Jewish people serving their sentence there. If he had have been a clever man, he would have played the rabbi up, and through the rabbi he would have got a tremendous amount of Jewish influence. But he wasn't a clever chap; he only knew how to break into houses. And he wouldn't hide his opinions. He said he didn't believe in religion, that he was an atheist. He wouldn't even talk to the rabbi.

And he turned good people against him as a communist. His political opinions was the cause really of him being in the position he was in. He was always talking to me about politics in prison. Morrison was a communist by nature, because he believed in communism. I wasn't very well up in communism, I knew what anarchism meant, but not communism. Communism wasn't a common name then. It was anarchist, people used to talk about that. I think people dropped the word anarchist, 'cos it sounded too much of the bomb-throwing and the shooting. Myself, I think that the left-wing people who were half and half decided that the best thing was to wash out 'anarchist' 'cos it frightened people, and adopt the word 'communist'. They say 'Christ was the first communist', he was undoubtedly. Sometimes Steinie would talk about communism – that things would never be no good till we wiped them all out. It didn't appeal to me. I didn't have any political opinions at all. For me it was too much to scheme to live.

The officers belonging to Parkhurst prison sympathised with Morrison; none of them would have gone out of their way to report him. As far as I know it was many years before he was reported for any offence, only refusing food. But the prison officers were afraid to go out of their way to show him any extra kindness in case he resented it. He'd go off in a rage for no reason at all. They didn't want him at Broadmoor, they said he wasn't insane. He wasn't, he was just a man who was suffering under a false charge, being in prison for something he hadn't done. If he'd have done it, I don't think he would have carried on like that – he didn't when he was doing his seven years, he got his remission.

People began to say at that time he was innocent. There was always people willing to take up a lost case. I think Conan Doyle was one. Several people engaged in the campaign, big people. So there was always the possibility that he'd be let out.

Steinie died in 1921. He'd gone on hunger strike again, and as the prison authorities didn't want him to die from starvation, they had to forcibly feed him, as they'd done many a time before. They sat you in a chair, your arms were strapped to the chair, your head was pulled back so that the gullet would be wide open. He was a strange man, Stirling the warder, bit on the tough side when anybody was breaking up the cell, bit rough, bit strong, bit of a go-er. Whether he put on any extra pressure I don't know. Anyway poor old Steinie was strangled. In my opinion it should have been handed over to the civil authorities, like the hospital who'd have probably made a better job of it, keeping him alive. But when you consider Morrison's case – he'd been in prison some eleven years, he'd had no hope given that he wouldn't have to do another eleven years and finish there. He'd given up hope of ever getting out.

14 Gambling

I always had a good knowledge of gambling. It ran in the family. My father used to go with the racing gangs. Uncle Peter, who was the friend of my aunt Liza, and who had that pub on Bethnal Green Road,[1] all the racing men went to his pub. In the Nichol we used to play at 'pieman'. It was a proper game of chance. One boy would spin two halfpennies in the air and then you'd call. The thrower had a little slip of wood to hold the coins, so that he couldn't manipulate them with his fingers. If the children hadn't got any money they would play with bits of paper or buttons. That was common. Buttons were a scarce article because boys were always needing them.

Some of the first pennies I earned was holding up the boards for 'Crown and Anchor'. That was a game like the three-card trick no one could win, except the people who had the board. I used to go with them, when I was quite a child, about twelve or thirteen. Our job was to keep a look-out for the police. Immediately they said 'turn it over' we used to slide the board over.[2] It was made on hinges. We had to take out the jinny – the spinning jinny that goes round and round – and make it invisible. It was a swindling game and you could be sent to prison for it.[3]

There was a big mob used to go down to the races with the 'Crown and Anchor'. One was Billy Walker's uncle. Uncle Tanty they used to call him. He belonged to the old Didicai lot. Then there was Dicky Atten and White Knob, Tommy Renobles, oh there was a crowd of them. White Knob was a real good player. They played it, I just held the board. Years later I used to paint the boards for them, but not at that time.

One place we went to was Grove Park, down Lewisham way. It was a military race course, steeplechasing over the sticks. Years later they closed it up and transferred it to Sandown Park.[4] It was an open course – if it was 2s to get in then we'd slip in without paying. You had to give the police a little something, not much – half-a-crown – they wasn't out for pounds. We used to get a good bit of money there and the police never used to interfere. I used to be the one to go and see the police was all right – if there was an inspector coming along I went up to him. The police wouldn't arrest kids, especially the kind of police you used to get down there. We used to get ten bob – all according to how long they played. To us it was a fortune. Tommy Taylor was one of those who came with me.

In later years I used to be in charge of the whole operation. We used to get a couple of lads to hold the wooden boards – one each end – just as we'd done ourselves when we were boys. Then the sheet with the colours painted on it was put over and then you started performing. You soon got a big crowd coming round. We played it on Sundays at the market, mostly up on Hurst Street – what is Cheshire Street today. And also in Sygnet Street, which is just off Sclater Street – Club Row. You'd get forty or fifty people round a board. And you'd have six people playing – including a couple of your own people. The rest were in prominent positions, as look-outs, in case any of the CID chaps were coming through, or plain-clothes men. It was a swindle but there wasn't a great deal of harm in it: a man wouldn't lose more than ten or fifteen shillings.

Sometimes you had to give the man on point duties ten bob. If they were greedy, then a pound which was a lot of money at that time. And then they'd let you be, just gradually stroll by without seeing you. Of course it became a racket amongst them. Those that never ought to have been there came round for the money. You changed your position according to the type of policeman who was on. If there was a good policeman on point duty at Sclater Street, you played there.

The police didn't want to stop the 'Crown and Anchor', because they knew they would get more crime if we went back to snide-pitching, shoot-flying and the rest of it. With the 'Crown and Anchor' they knew where they were. The man on point duty was paid his rent, and I was well in with the inspectors, because I knew exactly what the bookmakers paid them. The governor – Inspector Budd – had a great respect

for me. He was always very civil. At that time they didn't have
that superfluity of superintendents they've got today. A superintendent was the head policeman of the whole division and
there was nobody to challenge him – no 'chief' superintendent or anything like that. Today they've got five or six
superintendents for every division.

One Sunday there was a disaster. We were playing in Sclater
Street, just next to a jellied ell stall. Benny Hall was there, my
brother George and a chap called Mick Loftus, a nicely-spoken
chap who was always with me at the 'Crown and Anchor'.
Just as we started, one of our look-out chaps pushed through
the crowd to tell us there was a plain-clothes chap coming
through. He must have pushed against a couple of chaps in the
crowd, and a fight started. Well all along Sygnet Street there
were stalls dealing with auxiliaries for bikes and motor bikes.
Some of the barrows had bottles of petrol and when the
fighting spread they got knocked over. 'Bang! Bang! Bang!'
people thought they were guns. The cry went up, 'They're
shooting', and that started a stampede. It was 1911, the time of
Sydney Street, and everyone thought it was the anarchists and
the police.[5]

There was a terrific rush to get away. Nearby in Club Row
was the great bird market and thousands of birds were
trampled underfoot. The stampede spread out like a wheel,
with people running in all directions to get away. A couple of
people got killed. A policeman is said to have put a stop to it.
He was on point duty at the top of the Wheeler Street Arch,
just where Club Row starts, and when the panic reached him it
is said to have stopped. He got a reputation for it, the great big
London policeman who put a stop to the stampede. Everyone
wanted to give him a pint on the strength of it. But he no more
stopped it than he could fly. It just weakened at the edges. I
knew that policeman well. He was absolutely bloody useless
as a policeman – he would never trouble to arrest anybody for
fear of endangering himself.

There was a tremendous amount of damage – shop windows broken, birds killed, stalls overturned. People lost a lot
of money and the Commissioner of Police was sued for damages. The people in Club Row put in for a terrific sum of
money – so many valuable birds being killed, parrots and all

the rest of it. To tell you the truth, we didn't know it had happened. We were in Sygnet Street and the stampede had gone away from us. We just stopped where we were. We didn't know what was happening in the outer circle. The chaps who started the fight, they got knocked about a bit, but when they went away, we started playing the 'Crown and Anchor' again.

The police straightened us up. In the afternoon a CID chap comes down to my house in Gibraltar Gardens – 'Jew Boy' Stevens – and says, 'The guv'nor wants to see you, Arthur,' he says, 'see if you can help him. He's in a terrible state.' I went to Commercial Street and saw Inspector Budd. 'Look here,' he says, 'I've been pretty lenient with you chaps.' I said, 'That's true.' He said, 'I've allowed you to get a living, knowing how hard it was for you to get a job.' 'Couldn't you help me?' he said. So I said, 'How can I help you?' He said, 'Well find me a couple of witnesses.' One of the shopkeepers had said the stampede was caused by the people playing at 'Crown and Anchor' and he was frightened the police would have the blame for allowing it. He wanted witnesses to say that it was an ordinary crowd, and the stampede had started by people pushing against each other and losing their tempers. Well I got a couple of witnesses. They said it was caused by two people starting a quarrel after they had pushed against each other which led to blows and then to the quarrel spreading out. Nothing about the 'Crown and Anchor'. One of the witnesses was Mick Loftus; he told the inquest that the police had acted very bravely, and come out of it with flying colours. Anyway it all blowed over. We gave it a rest for a while, went to play somewhere else, but after a few weeks, things went back to normal.

There was a lot of spielers round the Commercial Road and Whitechapel – the police used to allow them, 'cos they could keep their eye on the anarchists. And other people used to keep contact there, to see if there was anything crooked to buy. These spielers were ideal places for the disposal of stolen jewellery. One of the most important was 'Cocky Flat-nose's' off the Commercial Road. Here one could buy any jewellery that was for disposal. All these gambling houses were permitted to open by the police because they were the channel from which much information reached the CID, also the Special Branch.[6]

Moey Levy started off as a chucker-out at the spielers. He married an English girl, Polly Cash. He was a terrible gambler – he once won £20,000 on a horse called Brackett. He died two or three years ago. There were several brothers of them, Jewish chaps who come out of Aldgate really,[7] but they went down to the other end of Brick Lane, the English End; they got mixed up with the English girls there and married them. Nicky Levy, the brother, was a tall smart boy – you'd say they couldn't possibly come from the same mother and father. He joined the army, became a sergeant major, and ended up in the mad-house. A smart kid, intelligent. We beat up Moey in 1922. He had got involved with one of the racing mobs.

Bobby Nark was another big racing man down White-chapel.[8] He had a little gang of racecourse touts, all Jewish. The City police were dead scared of them – they used to stand about at the top of Petticoat Lane, at the Aldgate end. One night I came along there with another chap, Winey, and there was about ten of 'em all standin' there, all men of bad character. So I started on 'em, kicking at their ankles and one thing and another, and they walked away. A couple of policemen were standing on the corner of Mansell Street and they was bloody thunderstruck. They thought I was due for a belting and instead it was the others who had gone away. So they come over and said, 'You done us a turn there', and one of them called a cab, put me in it and away we went. That's how I came to be a favourite with the city police.

When I was a teenager Albert Rod was the biggest book-maker around – he had thousands when he died. He lived in the same turning as us, in Bacon Street. I was a great favourite with his family. They kept a big cat's meat shop, but his real money came from street bookmaking. His partners were Albert and Goff Gold, Jewish chaps whose father kept a tailor's shop.[9] One day they was in a pub and there was a big race on – the Derby or something – and I said: 'Put ten bob on for me,' that was half a sovereign. I was quite young, must have been about sixteen, seventeen. 'I wouldn't do it,' Albert said, 'you'll only lose.' Well, being young, it made me all the more determined. When my horse lost, he gave me my ten bob back. He said, 'Don't ever back a horse again,' and I didn't.

The only thing I ever did in regard to the bookmakers then was to 'put up' for them when the police wanted to have an arrest. Now under the law if a bookmaker got convicted two or three times they could send him to prison. So consequently every bookmaker at that period had to go in at least twice a year. It was what they called 'taking a turn'. In some divisions it was three times a year, to show the authorities at Scotland Yard, when they made up their statistics, that the police were doing their job. In every division the police had two men whose job it was to take the bookmakers in. They didn't have to hide in a cart or anything like that, they'd come round quite polite and say, 'Albert, stick a man up tomorrow, we're having a raid.' Well, all he had to do was to find a man who was hard up – any Tom, Dick or Harry – and say, 'Here's a chance to earn yourself a couple of quid,' and they'd say, 'Oh blimey, yes.' They'd stand in the street, and then the plain-clothes men would take them in, and charge them with illegal betting. That way the bookmaker wouldn't have a record against him. It was all part of the game. The magistrates knew all about it. The top people at the yard knew about it.[10] But they couldn't put a stop to it. I went in once myself and got fined £8 at Thames police court – and got a fiver out of it. Another time I was going to do it but a chap at a lodging house offered to do it for me. So I gave him the £10 for the fine and the £2 I was being paid and he went off. Well, when the magistrate said '£10' he said, 'I'm not paying the £10.' So he was sent to prison for a month and came out with £12 – £3 a week, that was a lot of money in those days. He did well out of it.

Jimmy Smith was the man who straightened up the police.[11] The street bookies gave him the money to share out among the different sergeants and inspectors, and they relied on him to keep out strangers. He had a good team against anybody who caused trouble. He was the paymaster – the police trusted him and the bookies trusted him. He was a generous man, always good for a pound when anybody was hard up. He was the governor about Brick Lane.

When I was quite a child Jimmy was the head of the street

gambling business, the places where people used to go of a
night to play 'Sovereigns' and all that. I knew Jimmy Smith's
mother – a very nice, intelligent woman. She used to keep a
provision shop in Bacon Street.[12] Jimmy used to live over the
shop. Later he went to live with Benny Hall's mother in
Flower and Dean Street, after she left her husband. Jimmy
loved her more than anything, he left her £60,000 when he
died and she married a Brighton bookmaker. He spent all her
money and then done himself in. That's what comes of ill-
gotten gains.

Jimmy made the best part of his money by selling coals
around Flower and Dean Street. He had a coal-shed there and
by selling small quantities of coal and that, running round with
the coal when the customers come who couldn't carry it
back, he made a tidy bit of money. He earned a packet by
selling coal at double the price. That's how he bought the
furnished rooms and the kip-house down Flower and Dean
Street. Like Johnny McCarty down in Dossett Street. He was
an old-clothes dealer and then he went in for furnished rooms.
Those Irish blokes who came over here set up little businesses
like that, they got it out of swindling the poor people out of
small sums.

Jimmy Smith was paralysed all over – come home drunk
one night, fell in the bloody fire, burnt all the sinews of his arm
and he became paralysed. Billy Newman's brother used to
lead him about. His name was Joe. It was his week's work and
Jimmy used to pay him good wages. He used to walk about
holding his arm, and he did it so constantly that in the end his
arm went stiff – I often thought I ought to have written to the
Lancet about it. Joe lived in Bacon Street until he got married.
A right bride she was – he died shortly afterwards.

As a bookmaker Jimmy's beat was all around Brick Lane.
He had a big pitch in Prince's Court. He used to settle up with
the police every month, on behalf of all the bookies, and all the
police in Commercial Street station. A police constable got a
shilling a day, sergeants and inspectors got more and at Christmas time they all got a bonus, sometimes a crate of whisky
(that didn't cost much, you could buy whisky at about half-a-
crown a bottle). Every month they settled it up – all the
different wages according to their positions.

Jimmy Smith died sometime in the 1920s; for a time he had been living near to me, in a turning opposite Gibraltar Gardens. After Jimmy Smith died, Posh Reed took over the job of paying the police – you know, the 'banker'. He was a bookmaker down in Hare Street. A decent fellow. He died about 1923 and left a lot of money. I was at the funeral.

Edward Emmanuel was a great gambler. He was the guv'nor down Spitalfields and Aldgate way, the top man of the Jews. He started off as a market porter in Spitalfields. Then he got into the spieling business,[13] and through that into racing. Tommy Dido, one of our mob, used to work for him – he used to pay out the local policemen. Edward Emmanuel was associated with some big racing scandals. In the 1920s he was in with the Darby Sabini mob, but they fell out. He also went in for boxing. There used to be some big fights at the Wonderland, Whitechapel, where they were mainly Jewish boxers. Emmanuel put up a lot of money for them. And he also used terrorism. One fight led to a stabbing about 1910. It was a match between Cockney Cohen and Joseph Ashel of Aldgate. Emmanuel wanted Ashel to win and they paid Cohen, the other man, to lie down. It was a big fight, two Jewish chaps fighting and all the Jewish people betting. They stood to pick up a lot of money. Cockney Cohen was regarded as the top man of the two. When he refused to lie down somebody stuck a knife in him. That was about 1910. I'm not sure if the fight ever took place, but if it did, Cockney Cohen won.

Most of the racing people were south London, a few from Islington, Billy Kimber their gaffer, was a big Birmingham bookmaker. About 1910 Billy Kimber used to have control of all the racecourses down south – Newbury, Epsom and all the Park meetings belonging to London – Alexandra Park, Earls Park, Kempton Park. His gang were known as the Birmingham mob, but most of them came from the Elephant and Castle. They were generous to us, and plumped down some money for us in the Vendetta affair. They wanted us to join their gang, if we got acquitted. We was so much talked about that all the big gangsters wanted to get hold of us. But we were put away.

The Darby Sabini gang started up about 1910. They used a

famous pub in Clerkenwell, the 'Yorkshire Grey'.[14] They were an Italian mob. There wasn't an Englishman among them. They didn't come down to the East End, but they joined up with the Jews on the racecourses to go against the Birmingham mob. When the Italian mob started getting on the race tracks there was fighting with the Birmingham mob. The Jewish boys had to mix in because if they hadn't they would have lost their pitches. The Sabini mob were after pinching all the bookies' pitches, because there was a lot of money in that kind of business. So the Jewish chaps joined up with the Darby Sabini. The Birmingham mob were all English chaps, all 'rough house'. They weren't as clever as the Darby Sabini lot. Darby Sabini got in with the Flying Squad, which had been formed about 1908 or 1909; they got in with the race-course police, the special police, and so they had the police on their side, protecting them. Directly there was any fighting, it was always the Birmingham mob who got pinched. They was always getting time, five-year sentences and that. In the end Billy Kimber decided they'd have to go back to Birmingham. That's how it ended up. Darby died about 1916 or 1918, but Harry Boy Sabini took over, and the gang still did a lot of harm. They used to import young gangsters from Sicily, give them a couple of knives. Many of the street bookies paid them rent, and on the racecourse they were dominant.[15]

The first I got to know about the Italian mob was 1910 or 1911, just before I was put away for the Vendetta case. I had a chap, a friend – he wasn't a pal of mine, but he entered my life in various ways – Charlie Callaghan. A real vicious chap. He was a bad 'un when under the influence of drink which he quite often was. He was one of those convicted with me in the Vendetta case. Well it seems that he was sitting in a pub in Brick Lane when four of the Darby Sabinis came in. One of them pulled a gun and threatened to shoot him. It nearly come off but there was too many people in the bar. It seems they'd come there because Callaghan had taken a liberty with a chap named Danny Curtis, and Curtis must have primed them to frighten him – I don't know whether they really meant to shoot him.

Curtis was a very clever crooked man. He came from Hox-

ton. He 'had to tweedle' as we used to say – that is, he acted as
a go-between for diamond stealers and their customers. By
mixing with all different classes of people he got to know if
someone wanted to buy a nice diamond ring for his wife or
fiancée or the woman he kept. Say a certain rich Jewish man
wanted a good diamond ring, well Danny put it round so that
any screwsman who had done a place and come across a good
ring would take it him. People would come to him and say,
'Look Danny I've got a man who's got plenty of money; he's
got nice property and he wants a good ring for his wife.' And
Danny would say, 'What's the size? Find out what kind of ring
he wants' – three stone, four stone and all that – and he would
make sure he got it.

Another time I brushed with the Darby Sabini gang was
about 1920. There was a gang of bookmakers from Hackney
who were in the protection racket. They had all the police
straightened up but they were having trouble from the Italian
mob. They asked us to go down to Dick and Bella Burge's
place in Blackfriars Road[16] – the big boxing arena – to impress on them what would happen if they tried to start any
nonsense.

We went over there to protect Georgie Saul,[17] a boxer who
had been knocked about by the Italians. I took a couple of
tearaways, and we sat in the front row seats. But nothing
happened.

The racecourse business was a profitable one. When a gang
went to a race course like Brighton they could clear £4,000 or
£5,000 easy. At Epsom, on Derby Day, it could be £15,000 to
£20,000.

Hymie Davis, the big Aldgate bookmaker, had trouble with
the Darby Sabini gang and he paid me to look after him. They
said they were going to do him at Kempton Park and he asked
us to come. So we got together a team and went down to
Brighton. Altogether there must have been about sixty of us. I
went with the top men in a car, driven by a chap named Foster,
a dead reckless chap. There were about eight of us in it, one of
these old towing cars. The only chaps I took were two from
Hackney and by ginger they were two goers. One was Charlie
Barwick, a boy who was in the office lark, stealing wallets.
When we got to Brighton the Italians were already in the top

ring. Harry Boy Sabini was keeping a book outside. Our mob were all in a booth, sixty-handed. Then the police came in and started battering them about with their truncheons. Not me, I was too wise for that. I was watching the performance from afar. Several of them were pinched and they were given twelve-month sentences for stealing glasses from a pub. I got a gold watch and a chain from Hymie Davis as a reward, but I couldn't help him. By that time Darby Sabini lived in Brighton and he had the local police all tied up.[18]

Another brush with the Sabinis led to murder, though no one knew who did it. What happened was that Harry Boy Sabini set about a market porter in Smithfield market. Somebody asked me to help and we went up to the 'Yorkshire Grey' in Theobalds Road to sort it out. I was a married man by then, but I still had a name. Dodger Mullins, one of the biggest terrors in London at the time, roped me in. He told me about it one night at the 'Blade Bone' in Bethnal Green Road. I went up there to see what was going on. Harry Boy Sabini came over and I 'ready eyed' him. There were two smart-looking fellows at the bar and I pretended they were Yard men so he left me alone. At the end of it all there was a barney in one of the clubs up there and an Italian got stabbed to death.[19] Nobody was got for it, but Greenow, who was head of the Flying Squad at the time, claimed that I did it. When he retired he had some articles in the Sunday papers. He didn't name me but he said that 'one from Bethnal Green . . . committed a cold-blooded murder when he stabbed one of the gang'. All that fanny. Greenow came from Aldgate – he ended up as a racing man.

Buck Emden got killed about this time – I think it was 1925 or 1926. He was a Jewish chap, a lovely fellow. Buck was a bit of a fighter and he got in with the Darby Sabinis. By this time the Jews and the Italians were working together on the race-course. One night Buck Emden was stabbed to death in the West End. The man who did the murder was another Jew. It was a deliberate murder, it was intended to kill him, but they made out it was an accident. By law, if you are attacked first then you use a weapon it's manslaughter, even to the point of 'diminished responsibility' and you get out of it. Buck Emden was supposed to have called this man a name which would justify him in attacking him, and after that a quarrel ensued.

The knife was supposed to be on the table; it wasn't, but they got witnesses to say it was. I don't say that they planned to kill him, but they certainly meant to get him. There was a great big funeral for Buck Emden, on a Sunday. Everybody was there. Someone was said to have paid the police £16,000 to straighten them up.

15   Dealings with the police

Early on I taught myself the law so when I came up I could defend myself in court. Between 1901 and 1922 I had twenty-seven acquittals. But I also served time, ending up with five years in Parkhurst (1911–16) and five years in Dartmoor (1917–22).

The police were very zealous in carrying out their duties where I was concerned. They put me away for things I didn't do as well as for what I did. Here is a list of my early indictments.[1]

10 April 1901	Suspected person; 100 yards from my home; this case was dismissed. Age 14 years.
4 March 1902	Larceny simple; 12 months hard labour; attempt to steal bag of rags from a van. Age 15.
10 March 1903	Larceny to the person; discharged. Age 16.
21 April 1903	Larceny to the person; 20 months and hard labourt; taking a metal watch from another lad I knew. Age 16.
17 January 1905	Larceny to the person; discharged. Age 18.
28 May 1905	Larceny to the person; discharged. Age 18.
6 April 1906	Shooting with intent; acquitted. Age 19.
13 April 1906	Assault; £5 or 1 month. Age 19.
24 July 1906	Robbery; discharged. Age 19.
26 September 1906	Assault; discharged.

Once you had served time the police had their eye on you, and if you had served twice you were very vulnerable. Under the Prevention of Crimes Act of that period, it was only necesssary to prove that a defendant had been convicted twice on indictment for him to be put away automatically if he was convicted, a third time, as a suspected person. If a defendant was found in a public place without lawful excuse the court had no alternative but to sentence him to twelve months under the Act. This is what happened to me about 1909.[2]

It happened like this. One Saturday morning I was doing business with a firm in Finsbury, when I saw Det. Sgt 'Jew Boy' Stevens, taking notes outside the firm's premises. I lost my temper and told him I would apply for a summons against him for molestation. The next day, Sunday, I went out at 10 a.m. to meet my friends at Clark's coffee shop in Brick Lane. On leaving my home in Gibraltar Gardens, I noticed my old friend Det. Sgt Stevens and another CID aide; they were standing in a doorway. I did not take any notice of them because on a Sunday morning it was usual to see a large number of plain-clothes police mixing with the crowds in the markets, looking for pickpockets. After leaving my home, I walked down the lane to Clark's coffee shop, a distance of some 300 yards; when I reached the corner of Hare Street, opposite Clark's, there was a sudden rush and I was seized by a complete stranger. I was on the point of throwing him to the ground when he said, 'Don't start anything you'll be sorry for, I'm a police officer. I'm arresting you as a suspected person attempting to pick pockets.' I then noticed 'Jew Boy' Stevens in the crowd and several other plain-clothes men. Some of my friends had run across from Clark's and were waiting for me to have a go. I looked at the man who had arrested me, he was fairly big, but he did not look too good in regard to his health and I decided to go quietly to the station without any trouble.

I was charged as a suspected person, attempting to pick pockets. The man was a police officer from Leman Street and was always in the company of DDI Fred Wensley.

Now one of the most difficult charges to refute is that of suspected person, even if the person charged is of good character. Every known thief is a suspected person and every policeman knows that a convicted person is easy target for a suspected person charge.

I appeared at Old Street police court, was remanded for a week, no bail. The following week I was charged under the Prevention of Crimes Act, and sentenced to twelve months hard labour, the penalty under 'the Act'.

The years have passed and the utter falsity of the charge has been proved. The authors of the plan have long since passed away, but no person can be guilty of a crime to send another to prison on a perjured charge without his own conscience accusing him. The perjurer has to live with the knowledge of how evil he is, he cannot escape from himself.

This charge was utterly fabricated. Every Sunday morning for years I had walked through the Lane to Clark's coffee shop to meet my friends; the police knew this, so did DDI Wensley. If I had been guilty of such foolish behaviour as to pick pockets in this way I should have been sent to a mental asylum not prison. Let me repeat a quotation from the *Detective Days* by Wensley thirty years after: 'I resolved to teach him a *lesson*.'[3]

This Act has now become obsolete.[4]

The police officer involved in this case was promoted to the rank of detective inspector. A short time after this, he fell dead outside Leman Street station.

Another time I was framed up – this time unsuccessfully – was just after my release from Borstal. In February 1906 I was charged at Commercial Street police station with shooting a young girl and causing her grievous bodily harm.[5] The police evidence was that I was seen running away from the scene of the shooting. That was sufficient evidence to obtain a committal to the Central Criminal Court on this very serious charge. When it is realised that this charge can carry a penalty of life imprisonment, that I was refused legal aid, also that my family were still so poor that we could not afford a dock brief, which cost a guinea, one wonders how England became famous for justice and human rights. I was nineteen years of age; I had to wait trial at Brixton prison for some six weeks. The cell was an observation cell and I was under constant supervision. The reason for supervision was to see if I was mental; if I had been guilty of this offence I would have been in need of a psychiatrist.

On the 4 April 1906 I was put on trial at the Old Bailey. I had no legal assistance but I had a good judge.[6] The scene of the shooting was in the Whitechapel area, a few hundred yards from Sidney Street, where the siege took place a few years later. There had been fighting between two rival gangs of Jews – and a girl nearby had been struck by a stray bullet. These street affrays were quite common at that time, and she was not seriously injured. The only evidence against me was that of a policeman who had seen me running away. The policeman had said, 'What are you running for?' So I says to him, 'There's a fight going on down there. I don't want to become involved. There's shooting and all.' He said, 'I think you'd better come to the station.' Fortunately for me two people came forward and told the court that they wanted to give evidence as they'd seen it all happen. They were quite respectable people, a man and his wife, and after hearing them the judge stopped the case. The police had found no gun on me, and no witnesses against me except the policeman and all he said was that I was running away.

The strange thing is that afterwards this policeman and I became firm friends. His name was Phillips.[7] When he retired he became Mayor somewhere Surrey way. When any of the crowd from Bethnal Green used to go around hawking old clothes, he'd say: 'How's Arthur going on?' His wife was a cripple, an exact copy of my mother. He was a very, very nice chap. 'Y'know,' he said to me, 'if I'd have said what the CID wanted me to say it would have been a different ending.' He reckoned it stopped his promotion. They wanted him to say that I'd said: 'I didn't mean to hurt her.' Never seen the girl in me life and never seen her afterwards. But those few words would have been just enough to turn it against me.

As I grew up I got wiser. I bought law books second-hand in Shoreditch High Street – 3d or 6d a time – and learnt the finer points of the law. I got so that I could defend myself in court – and help others prepare their defence. I taught myself the art of cross-examining. In all I got no fewer than twenty-seven acquittals for myself in court cases between 1901 and 1922 the last time I was put away.[8]

In 1906 I was able to turn the tables on the police, and expose a frame-up which one of them was attempting. At that time a Police and Public Relations Commission, set up by the House of Commons, was taking evidence, and the Police and Public

Vigilance Society got in touch with me to see if I could help. I got the case of Ashford brought up before them – a real villain.[9] He was caught out in several lies before the Commission and later he was brought before the courts.

Ashford – PC 207 – lived in Nuneaton Buildings, just by Gibraltar Gardens,[10] where my house was. He lived in the same block as 'Jew Boy' Stevens. He had a nice wife but he was always after the women. He wasn't intelligent enough to catch a thief, but he was good at perjury and he could do a man an injury by strength. One night, in August 1906, he was walking by the Victorian lodging house in Old Montague Street. It was one o'clock in the morning and he was coming off duty. A young man called Gamble, living in a lodging house, was walking in the street. Quite a respectable chap, he came from the country and was working in a factory.[11] He met one of the brides there[12] – a girl he knew – and she suggested they went to one of the 'doubles' in Flower and Dean Street. While they were talking, PC Ashford came up. He wanted the girl to himself and he told Gamble to clear off. Gamble walked away because he didn't want to be involved with the police. But the girl didn't want Ashford and he lost his temper and took it out on Gamble. He knocked him down and kicked him so terribly between the legs that he ruptured his urethra. When they got him to hospital he was on the point of death.[13] A police sergeant came up and said to Gamble, 'Get up and fight like a man,' but he was finished. When the sergeant saw how badly the man had been beaten, he turned to Ashford and told him to come away. 'Leave him alone,' he said, 'You've done enough.'[14]

Well it happened that there had been two people who had seen what had happened – a newsboy and an elderly person.[15] They didn't have their kip money and they were spending the night on the pavement. I found that out by what you might call the underground. I said to the newsboy, 'Could you identify this policeman again? Would you recognise him?' and he thought he would. I said, 'I tell you what, listen, I know where I can find him, come with me.' And when he saw Ashford he said, 'That's him.' So that I got the Police Commission investigator, a former Scotland Yard man named Norman, to go into the lodging house and get the statements about the assault.[16] Then we found a Jewish woman who lived in Spelman Street[17] – Cossor Gilbert found her. She had heard a man scream, 'Leave me alone.' She heard it again and she thought to herself, 'Somebody's being knocked about,' and she lifted the window up. By a wonderful coincidence there was a street lamp there and she not only saw the policeman but was able to spot his number – she was a very intelligent woman. As a matter of fact she was our best witness at the trial. We got a very good statement off her and she told a straightforward story at the tribunal. She was able to put the sergeant in it and all.

When the police found I was on their trail, they tried to have me put away. A couple of days later they sent two CID chaps round to take me to the station. They kept me there all day and brought in about twenty different persons who had been robbed or mauled in the Commercial Street area to try to get me identified.[18] They failed on every occasion. So there we was in the Charge Room at Commercial Street police station. I had a packet of cigarettes that one of the policemen had given me in the cells, and I pulled one out and lit it off a gas lamp. Divisional Inspector Wensley – my enemy – who was there, said, 'Put it out.' I said, 'Be your age, everybody's looking at you.' He went wild, but the superintendant in charge of the station didn't like the CID butting in and he said to Wensley, 'That's enough.' Wensley said, 'I'll have you, if I don't get you for this I'll get you for something.' But the superintendant said, 'That's enough of it. Arthur, you can go.' He said, 'You can smoke a cigarette outside but don't smoke in here.'

Four days later a policeman came to the door and gave me a summons. 'That'll surprise you,' he said, 'laugh that one off.' It was a summons for assaulting a policeman. I knew it was a get-up. The assault was supposed to have taken place just off Brick Lane and there were six police officers who claimed to have been present. What had happened was that I was having a drink in a pub, and when I came out the police were kicking a man. Nothing unusual about that – a drunk putting up a bit of a fight, the police knocking him about, and the crowd gathering round and hooting at them. I gave them a bit of a rising, like the others, but I never assaulted anybody, I mean you would be potty to assault a policeman. Well that night was a very hot one – everyone was sitting outside because of the bugs, they couldn't sleep – the place was flooded with people. Some of them went to the police station to complain of the brutality of the police. And among them were four Jews. The Jews were the best people in the world to get as witnesses against the police for this reason: that they remembered the brutality of the Russian and Polish authorities – they were only too glad of a chance to hit back at them. Well anyway I got this summons. But they made a mistake of sticking PC Ashford on it. I defended myself.

The policeman who summoned me – PC 47, McCann – made a mess of it. He didn't know what he was doing, and when he came to court he was all confused. The next policeman to give evidence against me was a villain, a young one out to get promotion. He swore that he had seen me do this, that and the other. Then came Ashford. I said to him, 'How long have you known me?' 'Six Years.' I says, 'Are you sure?' That was a trick of the trade to get him thinking so that he would forget what he was going to say next which he'd learnt off by heart. He says, 'Yes.' I says, 'How long have you been in the force?' He says, 'Six years come this month.' 'Ah. . . . So immediately you joined the force you knew me?' He said, 'You were pointed out to me.' Then I said, 'By the way, what duties were you doing when the assault took place?' He said, 'I wasn't on duty.' I'd known that, it was why I'd asked the question. I said, 'You must have been tired after a long day's duties, patrolling the streets.' 'Yes, yes,' he said. He'd forgotten himself now. I said, 'So after you got home from the station you went to bed.' 'Yes,' he said, 'I did go to bed, I was tired.' 'Well how did you come to be outside the pub with the other police officers when the assault took place?' 'I heard the police whistle.' 'You heard the police whistle in Nuneaton Buildings; all that way from Brick Lane?' 'Yes.' 'What did you do then?' 'I put my clothes on and run down to see if I could render any assistance.' I said, 'You left your wife in bed, you run downstairs and suddenly you were there. You must have dressed yourself very quickly. Did you take your truncheon?' I was kidding him now. But the magistrate looked at me and said, 'That's enough.' When the next witness was called he got a bit windy. 'I didn't see much of it at all,' he said. 'I saw

Harding there, but I didn't see him assault anybody. He shouted something like "don't murder that man".' Then came another policeman and the magistrate said, 'I don't think we'd better call anybody else.' He said, 'I've listened to this case very carefully. The police evidence leaves me no alternative but to say that perjury has been committed and therefore the case is dismissed.'[19]

That's when it was brought out about all the times I'd been arrested. The magistrate whose name was Cluer, said, 'Always remember your safeguard is a magistrate sitting in this court. Don't lose your temper. Come up to this court about it.'[20] Next day the papers had whole columns about it – 'Man complains of Police Persecutions' – but they didn't know the crux of the business, which was that the police wanted to get me convicted to discredit me for the other business at the Tribunal.[21]

The Tribunal found that Ashford was guilty of assault and that police sergeant Sheedy was guilty of dereliction of duty in allowing the assault to take place, and hiding a criminal offence that had taken place.[22] Ashford was brought up in the Court at Old Street and committed to trial at the Old Bailey. They gave him nine months and both he and the sergeant were dismissed from the force.[23]

I had quite a good understanding with some of the CID men at Commercial Street police station. Tommy Smart – the one who got me my time in Borstal – used to tell the stallkeepers to keep an eye on me. 'Why don't you turn it up?' he used to say to me. Brogden was also quite friendly. Many times he stopped my mother and said, 'How's Arthur going on?' and she'd say, 'Well,' and he would say, 'Well keep on trying to get him to work.' But he didn't expect me to change. Brogden was the son of the Chief Constable of Yarmouth. He was a big powerful fellow, six foot tall and broad with it. He looked very imposing. He was in some of the most famous murder cases of the time, and he pinched Steinie Morrison after the Clapham Common murder. When I last saw him – about 1922 – he was looking after taxi cabs at Bella Burge's boxing ring in Blackfriars Road, a sort of doorman: he had been chucked out of Commercial Street during the war. It might have been drink or women – these were his two weaknesses.

Once Brogden had me arrested as a joke – or I think it was a joke, though with policeman you could never be sure. It happened like this. One morning, early in 1907, I was talking to a friend in the High Street, Shoreditch, when I noticed my old friends, Sergeants Brogden and Dessent, coming towards me from the police court. On seeing me they stopped and Sergeant Brogden said to me, 'I am arresting you on suspicion of house-breaking in Chilton Street, Bethnal Green.' This street was opposite Gibraltar Gardens and just as poor. It is no exaggeration to say I was known to every person in the street. Not a house had anything worth stealing, so I was alerted to the possibility of a fabricated charge.

On arrival at the station, the time was 11 a.m., the two CID men had a talk with the inspector in charge of the station. I heard the inspector say to them, 'Well, get your witness here at once. I'm not having him detained here all day. This case must be settled today.' At about noon the identity parade was held and a witness from Chilton Street came into the room, walked up to me and touched me on the shoulder, so according to the rule book I had been identified. The parade was dismissed and I was taken into the charge room to be charged with the offence. Realising the need to act quickly before the witness made a statement, I said to the station inspector, 'Ask him what he has identified me for. What did I do?' The station inspector then questioned the witness. The witness then stated, 'This is not the man who broke into the house. The 'tec told me to touch anyone I knew, so I touched Harding because I know him.' The inspector looked at the two CID men who at once said, 'Let him go.' So ended that episode. These two CID men could not resist the chance of taking me in, although they knew perfectly well that I was not a house-breaker. A few hours' detention in the station was their idea of a good joke.

Another CID man at the Commercial Street station was 'Jew Boy' Stevens. He started off as a constable, later he was made a sergeant and he was still a sergeant in the 'cap mob' in 1910. About 1911–12 he was promoted: he wasn't a very clever man, but he'd been in the force fourteen years so they promoted him. 'Jew Boy' Stevens ought to have been transferred when he was promoted but he stayed at Commercial Street all his life. When he left the force he bought a big hotel in

Harlow, about 1920. He lived in Nuneaton Buildings, like PC Ashford.

'Jew Boy' Stevens sometimes helped me with information. Once I promised him some money for some business we done with him, but I never gave it. Another time he had me put away for pickpocketing in Brick Lane.[24] It was a complete set-up, and I always had that grudge against him though when he retired he said he was sorry about it. One night I had him in the pub and said, 'What do you think I'm doing?' 'Counterfeit coins,' he replied, 'You're snide-making.' He said a couple of men were watching the chimney pots (when they suspect anyone of coining they put a couple of men on the glasses to watch the chimneys at night). I didn't know they knew about it and it gave me a turn, so I packed it up (coiners always worked by night so as not to be disturbed, but they forgot about the sparks in the chimney). Another time Stevens helped me was much later, in 1916. We were in a cab being taken to Old Street magistrate's court for the Dock case – stealing loads of tea. He said, 'Don't open your mouth.' He knew that if I got into conversation I would get myself into trouble.[25]

'Jew Boy' Stevens didn't like me, and I didn't like him, but he must have had a change of heart, because at the end of the bank notes trial in 1916, when he had to give evidence on my record, he said that I didn't take in stolen property.

I had one real pal at Commercial Street station, a man named Rutter.[26] He was a detective sergeant and he saved me from being done several times. Once we had stolen a load of cloth from the back of a van and I sold it to one of my Jewish friends – Harry Simons, who had a tailor's shop in Jamiaca Road, Tower Bridge.[27] He was a boyhood friend of mine and in the tailoring business it would come in handy. He gave me a few pounds. Well I happened to go up to Worship Street police court, to listen to a case where somebody I knew had been pinched, and I saw Rutter there. 'Good morning, Arthur,' he says. So I says, 'Good morning.' And we got talking. 'Do you know anybody over Jamaica Road?' he says. So I said, 'What d'you say that for?' He said, 'Anybody named Simons?' That's all he said but I got over there as quickly as I could. I said, 'Harry, what did you do with the stuff?' He said,

'It's in the back there. . . .' So I told him, 'Get rid of it.' Then I said, 'Look, I'll tell you what to do. Go up to Tower Bridge police station at once and say a fellow left this stuff in your shop yesterday and said he'd call today, and he ain't called, and would they come and take it away.' Well of course the police tumbled to what had happened, but they couldn't do anything. Afterwards Harry said to me, 'Thanks, but don't bring me nothing more. This lot has cost me a lot of money.' I said, 'Listen 'Arry, I'm not going to tell you the policeman's name, but you'll have to give him something. He took a chance.' He said, 'Half a sovereign?' I said, 'Cor blimey, you can't give him that.' He said, 'You dropped me in it.' So anyway I got a pound out of him. But when I offered it to Rutter he wouldn't take it. 'No, it's all right,' he said. He didn't have to say that twice, I can tell you: I put it in my pocket.

Rutter wasn't what you would call a crooked policeman. The reason he was so friendly with me was that I gave him protection. The first time I knew him he was getting a terrible bashing. It was a holiday Monday and he was new to the division. Well, he came along under the Brick Lane Arch where they were playing 'Crown and Anchor'. And like a bleeding idiot he considered it his duty to try to arrest the men who were playing. They battered him about terribly, broke his nose. Now these chaps had no business to be there, it wasn't their manor, and when I heard about it I set about the fellows who did it. I said to them, 'You caused a lot of trouble for nothing, 'cos this policeman was new to the Division, he didn't really understand what it was all about.' I gave them a belting. Well, Rutter got to know about it and he came and thanked me. I think the belting frightened him – a real good belting does. Because he said to me, 'See that nothing happens.' Afterwards I got quite friendly with him. He was a nice chap, rough sort of man, more like a docker than a policeman.

Another policeman I was friendly with was PC Gussett. One night he was beaten up by some fellows from Hackney Road, and I found him lying in the street unconscious. It was about midnight one Sunday night, I was walking through Boundary Street, Bethnal Green. My companion was a well-known funeral undertaker who had a business in Bethnal Green, by name Joe Barker.[28] At first I thought it was a drunken man, but a closer look revealed that the man was a policeman. He was bleeding from a severe wound in the head, he was unconscious, his helmet had fallen off and was lying close by.

I had a choice of remaining by him and rendering him help or, for all I knew he might have been dead, of leaving him and very likely getting convicted of murder. I had a white raincoat on and lifting his head to stop the flow of blood, me coat all got blood on it. My friend was rather frightened and near panic, wanting to leave the PC lying there, not through any dislike of the police but the possibility of being involved in a court case. For myself, I had quickly realised the dangers of the case; if I panicked someone may have come along and seen me leave the unconscious man. He could have died, then we would indeed have been in trouble. My clothing stained with his blood – do you believe the police would have accepted my story that we left an unconscious man bleeding from a wound in the head, because we were afraid? No jury would accept such a story. So I blew the whistle of the PC and helped him as much as possible. Soon a number of police arrived and the unconscious PC was taken to hospital where he regained consciousness and was able to give a description of his assailants whom he knew. Those men were afterwards convicted and sentenced to long terms. For myself, I was arrested and detained until the PC was able to clear me of any connection with the attack.

Afterwards I became friendly with this policeman. They put him in plain clothes on the bookies' round. He didn't have to do much work on that job because the arrests were all arranged. But he was always ill with the terrible blow he got, and in the end he left the force and finished up as a security man at Hackney dog-track.

The only policeman at Commercial Street who gave us a lot of trouble was Detective Sergeant Redman. He was a big bully. The other policemen hated him and they were glad when he was shifted.

One night in 1907, shortly after midnight, we were standing on the corner of Sclater Street, and Brick Lane. There were four of us there – me, Tommy Hoy, Stevie Cooper and Bob Wheeler. About 1 o'clock Redman came by. We told him to go to hell. In a flash he had his truncheon out and started attacking us. We knocked him to the ground and made off. But Redman got to his feet and ran after Stevie Cooper, the man who had struck him. He caught him on the corner of Bacon Street, and, using his truncheon freely, beat him unconscious. Then he blowed his whistle for assistance. According to the officers, Redman was in a terrible rage, and they had considerable difficulty in restraining him from beating Cooper up some more. They took Cooper to the cell, bleeding from cuts, and kept him there till the next morning, when he was charged with assaulting Redman.

The magistrate sitting at Old Street police court that morning was a former Liberal Member of Parliament, named Mr Pickersgill,[29] who had represented Bethnal Green in Parliament. When Cooper appeared in the dock he was in a piteous condition, his two eyes had been blackened, his head cut, and he bore the signs of other injuries, mostly relating to the beating-up he had received. The magistrate was horrified, and when he was charged with assaulting the policeman (who was in no way marked), the magistrate asked, 'Who was charged with assaulting the prisoner?' He dismissed the case with the words, 'If you do this to defendants I will not convict.'

I was keenly interested in this young policeman, and I learned from the others at Commercial Street that he was the same with them, knocking them about in the canteen. I was determined to have him. Well, a few weeks later I was standing by the lavatory at the bottom of Bethnal Green Road – near where my aunt used to have her shop – when I saw Redman, talking to a policeman. He was in plain clothes and looked a right villain. I was with a man named Griffin, who had just come out of prison after doing a three-year stretch. I said to him, 'Go and spit at the man in plain clothes.' He did so and Redman lost his temper, violently attacking Griffin and knocking him to the ground. The uniformed man walked away, not wanting to get mixed up with it. But a crowd collected and I seized hold of Redman, called on the police constable to come back, and asked him to arrest Redman for assault. The uniformed man said, 'I can't arrest him, he is a policeman,' so I demanded his name and address. He refused, then the uniformed policeman realised the seriousness of what was happening, a crowd of witnesses to the assault and the possibility of becoming involved himself. So he said to the plain clothes PC, 'Give your name and address or I will have to take you in. I'm not taking the can back for you.' The young PC then gave his name and address, which was as follows: Peter Redman, Section House, Commercial Road, E.1.

The next morning we applied to the magistrate at Old Street for a summons. This was the beginning of a week of intense activity. The summons was returnable the following week, so if the police wanted to avoid publicity the matter had to be settled before the case was due to be heard. The police didn't like Redman, but they weren't going to have one of their men convicted for assault. They threatened the bookmakers that if Redman was convicted, they would put a stop to street betting. Jimmy Smith, the leading man of the bookies, promised to straighten me up. He offered me £35 if I would let the prosecution drop. I said I would, provided that they made Redman leave the district. The police agreed. Redman was transferred to Epsom, and I had £20 for Griffin, and the rest for myself.

The CID chaps at Commercial Street were good policemen. They were brutal, but they were proper policemen. At Leman Street – the headquarters of 'H' Division of the CID – they were villains. There was more money about and the police got their cut. There were the spielers; there were the brides; and in Black Lion Yard and other places a lot of stolen property changed hands. The top men of the Jews, like Ruby Michaels and Edward Emmanuel, did a lot of business with the police at Leman Street.

The man who presided at Leman Street was my great enemy, DDI Wensley – 'the Weasel'. He had started off in 'M' Division in the Borough. Then he came to Arbour Square, as an ordinary constable in 'H' Division (the newspapers called it 'Thames Division'). He got a reputation for a so-called 'Gallant Fight' on a roof. Someone had been trying to burgle a house and murdered someone; it appeared in the newspapers that this brave PC had climbed on to the roof and fought with the murderer until help arrived. That was all fiction. What happened was that the Assistant Commissioner of Police – Macnaghten – came down from Scotland Yard while the affair was going on. He arrived in a hansom cab, and the first

on the scene was Wensley who said, 'I'll escort you, sir.' Well,
the Assistant Commissioner took notice of him after that.[30]
They became friends and he helped him to get promoted. First
of all he was put in what they called the 'Cap' mob – that is,
CID aides. You had to be very careful of those people –
they were all eager young men noted for their perjury and
anxious to get on. Wensley went in for promotion. But the
head man at Arbour Square – Divall,[31] the DDI – wouldn't
pass him. Wensley went to Scotland Yard and Macnaghten
promoted him to sergeant in the CID. Then he had him
transferred to Leman Street. When a man is promoted
from constable to sergeant he gets moved and so Wensley got
away from Arbour Square. Later he got promoted to detective
inspector, about 1903. In the 1920s they took him to Scotland
Yard and made him a chief constable. Only time they had
that post. They did it to get him away from the East End.[32]

Wensley disliked me intensely and I reciprocated his feel-
ings. I considered him a vain, bullying type of detective. Some
thirty years after the events I am about to relate, in his book,
Detective Days, Wensley wrote of me:

He was a young man of great cunning and astuteness who
had picked up a considerable knowledge of loopholes in the
law, that had on more than one occasion been of service to
him. I resolved to teach him a lesson. He had some years
before made a complaint of police persecution and had even
appeared before a Royal Commission on the Metropolitan
Police.[33]

My first brush with Wensley[34] was when Brogden and
Dessent arrested me and took me to Commercial Street police
station. When he came in they said, 'It's the guv'nor.' It was
the first time I'd ever seen him. I lit a cigarette from one of the
gaslights while I was waiting for the identification parade and
we exchanged words. He said, 'Put that out,' and I said, 'Piss
off.'[35] I brought Wensley before the Royal Commission on the
Metropolitan Police for trying to fix me in an identity parade.[36] And he hated me always after.

In 1916, when I came out of Parkhurst where I'd been
serving five years for the Vendetta case, Wensley tried to get

me over a racket in the London docks. One night a detective called at my house in Gibraltar Gardens and said to my mother, 'Where's Arthur?' She said, 'I don't know.' 'Well tell him I want to see him, I'll be waiting opposite the pub.' I went up to meet him about 8 o'clock. I said, 'What do you want to see me for?' 'The governor wants to see you.' As a matter of fact I had a girlfriend to meet, and I didn't see why I should miss an appointment. I said, 'Tell him I'll see him another time.' I was on the point of skipping off the side, I could have easily beat him running, he wouldn't have had any right to chase me. But in the end, I decided to go and we took the tram down to Leman Street. It was a cold night, dark, wintertime. The detective – Stephens – told the chap on the door, 'Tell Inspector Wensley that he'd got a visitor.' Wensley was waiting for me. He said, 'Come inside Arthur,' 'Talk about the spider in the web,' I thought. He said, 'Cold night, do you think we'll have a raid tonight?' It was during the First World War. I said, 'I never give it a thought, I'm not that scared.' He said, 'Well, I'll tell you what I wanted to see you about. There's a chap in custody who says that you gave them these papers so that they could go down the docks and get a load of tea and a load of whisky. I'm in communication with Scotland Yard and if they decided that you should be put, I shall have to detain you.'

When the case came before the Old Street magistrate's court, the chief witness against me was Bert Simpson, who said that I'd told him to pinch the stuff, and then sold it for him. The magistrate, a man named Wilberforce – I always remember his name because of Wilberforce who liberated the slaves – said, 'Have you any questions?' So I said to Simpson, 'You come up in this court for stealing the van-load of whisky.' He said, 'Yes.' 'Did you plead guilty or not guilty?' 'Not guilty.' 'Did you go into the witness box and tell the Magistrate that you didn't do it?' 'Yes I did.' I said, 'And then you went to North London Sessions and you said the same, that you didn't do it, you picked the Bible up and took the oath?' 'Yes.' So the magistrate said, 'I think I've heard enough. You committed perjury in court and you may be committing perjury today, so on that evidence I close the case.' The daughter of the pub landlord identified me – the police must have put the frighteners on her. But magistrate Wilberforce wouldn't accept her evidence, and he wouldn't commit me. Wensley had thought it was a certainty. He went potty.

In the underworld, you had to be well in with the police if you wanted to make a living. You'd do them favours, and they would look after you. But you had to make a good bit of money before they'd look at you. The Titanic mob were well in with the police. They had an inside man at the Tottenham Court Road police station – a constable named Paine. When they worked the railway stations he got the railway police straightened up. He was a scoundrel.

All the spieler owners paid the police a cut. They had to in order to keep open. I used to go with Tommy Taylor who did the paying out for Ruby Michaels. He used to give the police their wages every month, at a pub on the corner of Commercial Road.

I also knew the man who paid the police out for Jimmy Watts – Bob Wheeler. Jimmy Watts was well in with the police. You had to be very careful what you did with him. He was a sly, cunning person, and he could always have a man put away if he wanted to. I wish I knew how many people he had put away in penal servitude. He was a real villain, a very dangerous 'agent provocateur'. He had the cunningness of an illiterate person: he couldn't even reckon.

Jimmy Watts belonged to Walthamstow. There were two or three brothers. One had a big pub – never ought to have had a licence, he was a convicted man. The other brother was a screwman, a burglar. But the police over at Walthamstow were famous for being bent. I once went up to Walthamstow to settle up with them when there was a case on at the County of London Sessions. I went there with Jimmy Watts, to help him get two burglars off. It was very easy. The two chaps both had convictions behind them and they got caught with this van. The DDI there – Georgie Pride, the sub-divisional inspector – got them off. They called him 'uncle' George. His son had a garage and he took the van for a drop. When they came up before the court all that happened was that they were bound over.

Georgie Pride helped me a tremendous lot. In 1926 I was up in court with two others for an affair in Whitechapel Road –

shooting Long Gardiner, one of the Titanic mob, and slashing Moey Levy's face. Pride done me the favour of leaving me out of the charge – it was nearly a murder; another eighth of an inch and they would have had Moey Levy by the jugular vein. The other man I was with – Charlie Horrickey – got three years for it. I was acquitted. It was a big favour.

The police made a lot of money from stolen property. Say, for instance, a publican bought a load of something that got knocked off, if the police got a tip-off they would turn the place over and then get their cut. They used to work like this: they didn't give 'em time, they got a few quid off of them. Course it wasn't done on the scale it's done today, £20 was a lot of money to give, they deal in thousands today. On this particular occasion I am thinking of it was cloth that had been stolen. A woman who kept a pub in Bacon Street bought the stuff. She was Ikey Wakeman's sister – a burglar who used to live down our court, Gibraltar Gardens. Somebody gave 'em the information and they went and turned the place over and they found this silk and they had a case. Well, she got acquitted.

The biggest buyers of stolen property in London at that time were the Johnsons★ of Walthamstow. Johnny Johnson, the father (he had one leg), was a bookmaker. Crooks would come over from America to sell him stuff. Young Johnny, his son, was born in the Nile, Hoxton, and went with the Titanic mob. Johnny's father died about 1905 and he came into the kingdom. He bought up two big houses, the Manor House in Harringay. Two houses. One for himself and the other for Wensley. Johnson was quick to sum a man up. He knew that Wensley was in with the top men at Scotland Yard, that he was coming in. Later he had a greyhound track.

Edward Emmanuel was another man who had the police buttoned up. He could be seen drinking in the 'Three Tuns' with the top detectives from the Yard – the 'Three Tuns' in Aldgate. He knew all the top men. My friend Tommy Taylor was employed by him – he used to give the police their weekly cut. In the 1920s he was in charge of the whole East End underworld – or at least the Jewish part of it. He got

★ Fictitious name.

himself into everything. In London and all the big cities you've got to have a go–between, a man who can make deals between the police and the criminal world because he's trusted. Every community needs a man like that, the Jews the same as the rest. People go to a man like that with their troubles. For instance a man buys some stolen property and then the police come round after it. Perhaps he'd been given away by the man who sold it to him but he doesn't know. The go–between says – speaking Yiddish to convince him that no one else will know – 'Well look here, you're in very bad trouble Mr Lazarus, but if I can help you I will.' The old man who's been arrested is in a terrible state and he says, 'What can you do?' 'Well,' comes the reply, 'I done this detective sergeant a favour once. I helped him out of a little bit of trouble. I'll go and see if he can help me out. But you know, the police won't do favours for nothing. He's going to risk his job if he's found out, so you'll have to make it worth his while.' Well the money changes hands and when the case comes up the detective lets a little doubt creep in, and the man gets off.

Before the First World War the top Jewish man for getting people out of trouble was a newsagent who had a shop at the corner of Brick Lane and Hanbury Street. His name was Abbie something. Afterwards it was Edward Emmanuel. You'd go to him and he'd say, 'I'll do the best I can but it'll cost you a good bit.' Well, he might get the sentence down to six months, instead of a man having to serve six years.

The only policeman I ever gave money to was years later, after the Second World War. He was in the Flying Squad. One of them had done one of my friends a good turn, and I met him at the 'Baker's Arms', Leyton. I said to him, 'Come out the back,' and gave him £100 in the urinal. He said, 'Is it all right?' and I said 'Of course it is Ted.' I was doing it for a woman, for someone in the CID she had got out of trouble.

The Greens★ used to get money from the police. Every bent raid, every hijack they knew who done it and where it was going. And if they didn't like the mob they would pick up the phone to the Squad office at the yard and tell them where the stuff had gone. They'd get £100 out of the police fund for in-

★ Fictitious name.

formation. And then when the Squad took the stolen stuff away from the buyer they got 10 per cent of the value from the insurance people.

The time I got to know the police best was when I worked with the 'ghost' squad. It was during the Second World War. I worked then for some of the top men in Scotland Yard and my estimation of the police fell a tremendous amount: I found they were crooked from top to bottom.

The 'ghost' squad were an undercover branch of the specials, who had been set up to deal with wartime rackets. Everything they did was dead secret. They was not supposed to be known to anybody. They had no radios; they wasn't allowed any form of communication whatever, only a telephone. If they were going out on a raid they would never tell anyone else in the police, otherwise someone might pick it up. They never gave evidence in the courts. They didn't have a centre, but used to meet in different places. They first got in touch with me about 1942 or 1943. They came to me, I didn't go to them. They would pick me up at home. I used to go out with them several nights, sometimes drinking, sometimes working. We done very well.[37]

16 Marriage

When I came out of prison in September 1920 I'd determined that that was the lot. I only got one sentence after that – four months for hitting a policeman, though I never touched him.[1] But I found it difficult to keep out of trouble. Even after I got married I would still get mixed up. I was in a big fight in 1926, two years after I was married, and it was potentially a hanging job, when we beat up Moey Levy. All over London, in all the criminal fraternities everybody had heard of me. So whenever anyone got into trouble with anyone they would call on me for help. Dodger Mullins, he would be round at my house at 1 or 2 o'clock in the morning, and say, 'Come on.' All the terrors knew me. Sometimes they wanted help to smash a club up, or to protect some bookies. Inspector Greeno said that I killed the Italian in that pub.[2] People were frightened of me. In a way I liked it, it was all excitement.

On my release from Parkhurst I resolved henceforth only to associate with working people. I fitted up a workshop at No. 3 Gibraltar Gardens, bought myself a set of tools, and began to work, to make work that I could sell, such as food safes, kitchen tables, dressers, etc. The wood didn't hardly cost me anything because my step-brother had sons that was out buying big cases – packing cases – in the West End. His son Dick, he worked for the Council over at St Luke's – he used to go and buy the packing cases. They used to buy them for next to nothing and he said, 'Uncle Arthur, I can fetch you some.' I used to buy the timber off them and it didn't need much cleaning-up, especially for wooden safes. They used to have a tarpaulin so the water would run off. I used oil cloth – they sold them in rolls outside the oil shop, 7s 6d a roll. They looked quite all right and they kept the water off. These food safes were very, very saleable, and I had plenty of orders for kitchen tables. People who knew me would say, 'Can you make us a

food safe to put outside, or a good strong kitchen table like you
made so and so?' They only used to pay a shilling a week, so
that's why I got a lot of trade off it. My brother-in-law – as he
was after – he bought all of his things off me when he got
married.

All you needed for a kitchen table was six-inch batons and
they glued them together. You could buy a pair of legs from
the turning shops for next to nothing – about 2s 6d. Drawers
you could make out of anything. You planed them up – glued
them – and put a bit of shine in them. Not much work–any
carpenter could do it. I used to sell them for about 10s.

I got quite a good living making meat safes for about six
months, then I got into trouble again – 1922 it was, or 1921,
I'm not sure. Anyway, we went out on the Saturday night up
to the West End drinking. And we left it too late for a No. 8
bus, it had gone. So we had to walk home. There was me,
Berry and a couple of other chaps – hawkers. One of them
was Benny Hall. So, we're walking through Holborn, where
the Prudential whats-its-name is, and then comes Gamages.[3]
Well outside Gamages was a taxi-cab, not a soul about, so I
said, 'Perhaps he's gone down the toilet.' There's a toilet in the
middle of the road, but it was shut up. So I said, 'Where the
bloody hell could 'e have gone?' We thought of pinching the
taxi 'cos we wanted to get home. Anyway this young Benny
Hall was a chap that no sooner said than done. He'd hit
anybody, and he could punch bloody hard. Quite a nice fella,
about my strength, but much younger than me, and the other
two were much younger than me, I was the oldest one there.
They wasn't thieves nor nothin', they wasn't men of bad
character, they was quite respectable working boys. So, one of
'em got in the taxi to see if he could make it go. You know,
when you're drunk you do all the silliest bloody things in the
world. And I didn't say nothing at all. Now the funny thing is I
only had a raincoat on. And this was the cause of all the
trouble: I had this raincoat on, I always carry a raincoat with
me when there's any possibility of rain. It was a light coat. A
fella came across the road in plain clothes, he said, 'What are
you interfering with the taxi for?' So I said, 'Are you the
driver?' So he said, 'Never mind what I am.' Now if he'd said,
'I'm a police officer,' it would have been all right. But this

young Benny Hall said to him, 'What's it to you?' So he said to young Benny Hall, 'Shut your mouth.' And he hit him, Benny Hall hit him, down he went. Well, Leather Lane is just aside of there, and he run down Leather Lane. Like a bloody idiot I took my raincoat off and gave it to him, so he shouldn't be recognised as the one who hit him.

Unfortunately for me, a blinking Jewish man, out for trouble, was walking across and saw me take my coat off and give it to the other bloke and he come to the conclusion that it was me that hit him, and that was why I took me coat off. His name was Silverman. He lived in Victoria Park Road.

Well, we heard the police whistles going. I looked about, saw the other two and said to one of them – nice boy, never done anything in his life – 'Where's. . . .' He says, 'He's got locked up, a policeman came and took him.' So, we walk down towards the Old Bailey where the police station is: the City police station. Snowhill. I go in the police station with the other chap with me. So, the other boy who's got arrested is in the police station. There was a bit of an argument going on there. I can't see the man who got hit. So I said, 'I've come to bail my friend out – what's he been charged with – drunk?' So the inspector says, 'Look here come back in half an hour, we don't know what he's going to be charged with yet.' He said, 'A man's been assaulted and we want to know who's done it.' Quite nice, he spoke to me quite nice, didn't bully or anything like that.

I wanted to bail him out, but I thought 'bugger it' and started to go towards home. We were walking by the Old Bailey when two police officers came up and one of them said. 'Are you the two gentlemen who've just been at Snowhill?' I said, 'Yer, that's right.' So he said, 'The inspector said will you come back, he wants you.' So we had to walk all the way back. When we got there, this bloody Jewish bloke was waiting. He said, 'That's the one,' pointing to me. I was thunderstruck. So the three of us was charged with assaulting a plain-clothes police officer – he was in the hospital, a jaw broken or something like that. We were kept in there all Sunday and the Monday we came up in court – and the three of us got re-manded.

We came up the following week at the Guildhall.[4] By that

time the two boys had told who Benny Hall was and they took him in. But the Jewish man who was the witness said I was the one who hit the policeman. I thought, 'Oh blimey.' But the policeman himself said, 'No, not him [that was me]. He didn't do it.' He said, 'He done it,' pointing at one of the others – straight kid, never done a day, never been locked up, never been in a police station in his life before. Three months they give him, and I get four, the other two were discharged.

Well, I was on ticket-of-leave – I'd got a licence of sixteen months and it had not yet expired. So, I thought to meself, 'I'm not safe.' And I said to the magistrate, 'Y'know, sir, you're putting me under a terrific strain', I said. 'It's not only four months in prison – I deserve that for being drunk and being there, I should have known better. But I can assure you, that I didn't raise my hand to the police constable, that's a thing I wouldn't do. And I've got a licence, so it's a serious matter.' He said, 'We don't believe you'll be made to serve that.' So I said, 'Would you allow me bail? I'm going to appeal against your decision.' So, he said, 'Yes. You're fined two sureties of £100 each.' So I got the sureties and was given four months bail.

During the four months what I had to prepare the case before the Appeal Court sat, I went and found young Benny Hall. He was a rough sort of chap, but he didn't have no time against him. 'Now look here,' I said, 'the other chap got three months. You know if I lose the appeal I'll get, I'll have to do nearly eighteen months in prison.' I said, 'Don't you think you ought to?' He said, 'That's what I'm going to do, I'll come up and tell 'em I done it.' So I came up in the Appeal Court, and Benny Hall gave his evidence. So I said to the Court, 'You've listened, he's come up and he's voluntarily told you that he hit the police officer.' I said, 'What would make him come up here and tell the truth, *only* when he knows what the dire penalty stands me in the face.'

Well the Crown had Muir to prosecute me. I don't know why, every time I came up before the courts I had Muir to face – the greatest criminal lawyer in the country. Even on a tuppeny ha'penny bleeding business like that – he's there. It was the fourth time I'd faced him. The judge said to Muir, 'What have you got to say to that?' So, this is what he said,

'The police officer says that Harding didn't do it, and now Hall says that he done it. But Silverman [that's the Jewish man] said he saw him take a kick at him.' 'It's never been suggested,' Muir said, 'and I'm not suggesting for one minute, that Harding was the one who struck the police officer. But, he did attempt to kick him. Because you have a prominent witness: Mr Silverman who says he saw him take an attempt to kick him.' Bloody pack of lies that was, he deliberately come up there and swore to a pack of lies that Jewish man. Anyway that finished me, and I had to do my four months, and I had to do my ticket. They sent me to Dartmoor.

When I came home from Dartmoor, I fitted up a little workshop again and started making boards and easels. The firm's still in existence what supplied me with the wood – Cartwrights – they're still in Vallance Road and they've got a place down the High Street, Walthamstow. I'd buy 'em and have them grooved down the middle and the board would fit right into the grove. I used to get the board from wood which came from Austria. It was very good three-ply and cheap and all I had to do was stain 'em and use some black stuff on 'em. I bought three inches for the price of two inches. Then I made inch and a half legs for them to stand on. It wasn't really hard work because I used to get all my timber planed. It was just a matter of sawing the top and making the frames. I used to make about five gross a day.

It was poorly paid work but I was pretty swift – towards the end of the week I used to work all day and night and I had a couple of chaps working for me. I made them different sizes. I sold them for 7s 6d a dozen. Sometimes I stopped up all night getting them dry. Getting near Christmas all the wardrobe dealers that wasn't doing anything, I had them all coming round to take them out selling them – I gave them 6d on each one they sold. In Houndsditch they'd buy grosses off me, big warehouses. They'd worry the bloody life out of me at this time of year, preparing for the Christmas trade. Jack Taylor took some out for me, but I couldn't allow him to take too many because I had my own brother-in-law, who married my sister, he used to come down. David Jones. He used to take them out on his day out (he was a bus driver) to earn money.

I kept it on when I was married because I used to get my wife to do a bit of staining the boards.

Milly Worby, the girl I married, was fifteen years younger than me. In fact by a strange coincidence the date of her birth corresponds with that of my arrest in February 1902.[5] She and her family lived next door to us at No. 4 Gibraltar Gardens. She was twenty-two when I married her, sixty-six when she died in 1968. It was the family who put me up to it. I had never spoken to her before. But I knew her better than her sister because she used to come in and help my sister and my mother. Clean up for them. Four weeks before we were married I had never spoken to her, or noticed how she had changed from a child to being a woman. Then one day as she was coming home from work for lunch my brother said to my sister, 'That's the one *I* would marry.' My brother and sister looked at me. So I said to them, 'Why not?' I knew she wanted to get married. All the family slept in one room – grown ups and all. There were about ten of them. They wanted her off their hands. She was rather shy. So was I. I simply said to her, 'It's no good hanging about, let's get it over.' Both the families wanted it.

We got married on 21 April 1924, an Easter Monday. It was a church wedding and immediately after the service we all went to Brighton. There were about fifty guests, travelling in coach and car. The reception was at the Imperial Hotel, which is where my sister took coach parties of her customers in the summer months. After the reception lunch we spent the afternoon on the beach and then had high tea back at the hotel. Looking back one wonders how they could supply us with a splendid lunch and a high tea all for 12s 6d. My wedding was unusual for the East End at that time. By custom and tradition weddings were a local affair, with the reception in the local pub. Most weddings finished up in a fight or disturbance. By going to Brighton we avoided trouble.

When I first got in with the Worbys they lived next door to us. My mother was great friends with 'em. We never used to go in the pubs with 'em. As my wife told me many years after, 'We always thought of the Hardings as somebody right up the top, yer know, with plenty of money.' So, of course we didn't have that personal contact. My sister did 'cos she had to keep in with all the customers, that family used to pay my sister pounds on a Saturday. My sister had a great deal of trust in Mrs Worby. Milly, the daughter who I married, had very nice clothes – most of them she bought through Mighty. Mr Worby was a railwayman in regular work. But the family was quite poor and very overcrowded. There were thirteen of them, and they all slept together in the one top room. Even at holiday time, or when it was a special time, like at Christmas time, when you got all the sons-in-law down there, they only had the top room. It was always a great mystery to us where they all went. When they come home from work to get their dinner as a lot of 'em did, they'd go right through the passage into the small kitchen at the back. Even the sons-in-laws, when they got married, they'd come to their dinner there. It all helped the old girl to make up the weekly money.

Milly had worked at de la Rue's, the printers in Chiswell Street,[6] ever since leaving school. But after the wedding she stayed at home. She thought she should go on working as she was but I said, 'Oh no, you're not going out to work,' and she never worked again in her married life, except indoors. I had to do something regular for a living now. And after I was married I got a job as a carpenter in Bethnal Green. I tried to make myself look like a regular workman but the money was no good to me, so I turned to my own workshop, making boards and easels. I worked night and day and made thousands of them. I got a good bit of money at Christmas. We talked the matter over and decided to make as much money as we could. To save. To get out of Bethnal Green and have a house in the suburbs. My wife was obsessed with it. Every penny we could save, we saved.

In the following year 1925 our first child was born (a boy) in the Marie Celeste ward of the London Hospital.

After our wedding we settled down to live at No. 3 Gibraltar Gardens.[7] This was a house which my sister had been using for business purposes. Before I had lived at No. 5 with my mother. We kept the house until 1932, when we moved out to Leyton.

I was still getting into trouble. Immediately I went into a pub I couldn't help mixing with my old pals. One Sunday we went up to 'Dirty Dicks' in the afternoon and there's three or four of us and there's a bit of a barney outside where the lavatory is, and somebody give the top man in Petticoat Lane – him and another man – they give 'em a bit of a bashing. No weapons. I hadn't done it, but he went in and swore blind I asked him for £2, that was the usual business. So the next day they swore out a warrant for me, or a summons, in the Guildhall.

The next day the CID chap there, the governor, must 'ave said, 'Well, who's going to take the summons down to him?' So, there was a chap, a CID chap, a very nice-looking chap, named Dicky Bird, and another one Bishop, he got a pub in Oxford when he retired. Well, they sent Dicky Bird down. Now, it was like sending a lamb to the slaughter. He never knew nothin' about it, he was a City man, he lived at Peckham Way, quite a nice fellow. The older ones frightened him up a bit. I can always see the humour of the thing. So he comes down the Gardens, where I lived. It was summertime, about 6 o'clock, I should think, or 5 o'clock. He sees me in the garden – we had a big garden in front of the house – and I'm looking at him and he said to me (he must have lost his courage), 'Could you tell me where Mr Harding lives?' So I said, 'Right round the corner,' pointing to where my mother lived in the next house but one, No. 5. She heard what was going on and she said, 'What do you want, Sir?' He told her, so she's hollering out to me, 'He wants you Arthur.' So, I was laughing. He comes back and said, 'I knew it was you.' So I said, 'Well, what's it all about?' He said, 'They gave me the summons to fetch down to you.' So I read it and said, 'Is that all it is?' So he said, 'It ain't nothin'.' So, I said, 'Wait a minute, I'll go an' put me hat on, we'll go and 'ave a drink.' So I take him down to the 'Blade Bone', that was the pub in the turning opposite,[8] and I got him boozed. I got meself boozed an' all. People were coming up to him and saying, 'What you having, Sir?' He didn't like to say no. Years after he told me, 'You ought to know I was paralysed with bleedin' fear, I thought I'd 'ave a bleedin' glass in me face any minute.' So I sees him on the bus, No. 8 bus. He said they was worried up there, at the City police, they was sending out patrols to try and find him. You can imagine the bloody man, I mean, it's laughable but I could understand.

1 Arthur Harding as a Barnardo boy, 1896 (aged 9)

2 'Flash Harry', Arthur's father, in his debonair days as a racing man

3 'Flash Harry' as an old man

4 Mary Anne Harding,
Arthur's mother, with Arthur's
son Lennie, in Gibraltar
Gardens, *c.* 1928

5 Mary Anne Harding,
Arthur's mother, in Gibraltar
Gardens in the 1930s

6 Sister 'Mighty' (Harriet),
c. 1900

The Park Photo Co's Studios

18
BISHOPS' ROAD
CAMBRIDGE HEATH

7 Harriet in her 40s with niece
Maudie

8 (*above*) The 'Jago' or 'Nichol' (Boundary Street, Bethnal Green), *c.* 1890, shortly before it was demolished

9 (*below*) A 'Jago' court *c.* 1890

10 Gibraltar Gardens outing, 1920. *Left to right: bottom* Mr Worby (future father in law); Mrs
sister Harriet; Ada Davis; unknown; —Davis; brother George and youngest son; *top* Alice
(George's wife); half-brother Dick Rich's wife; Mrs Freeman ('married a Jewish chap but al
come down the garden for outings'); unknown; unknown; Mrs Barclay ('the one who had th
visitors down'); unknown; unknown; Mrs Taylor ('Jack Taylor's wife, the French polisher');
Webb ('died in a refuge in Spitalfields . . . husband a totter'); Jimmy Davis's wife ('he was a b
unknown; unknown; Mrs Johnson; Maudie, sister Mary's daughter; *inside the coach* unknow
mother; sister Mary; unknown; unknown; future wife's sister Annie; future wife'
Lil; unknown

11 A Brighton trip *c.* 1923. *Left to right: front* Benny Hall (convicted for assault on City police
Holborn, *c.* 1922); brother George; Arthur (with trilby hat); *back* unknown; 'Edgy' ('used to
buying and selling old clothes'); Jack Lincoln ('a carman, worked on the railway'); Tom All
sister Harriet's husband ('son of a Kent farmer . . . met him when hopping'); Dave Jones, sis
Mary's husband

Arthur with his two [niec]es, both called Maudie, [brot]her George's daughter [on t]he left, sister Mary's on [the r]ight, Ramsgate, c. 1923 [('At t]hat time I wore a gold [watc]h and sovereign – you [can] see it. When I got [mar]ried I left it off')

[A]n outing from [Gibr]altar Gardens c. 1935. [Left to right] Mrs Milton ('her [husb]and was a wardrobe [deal]er'); sister Harriet; Mary [Har]ding (brother George's [2nd] wife); Frances Harding [('she] lived in Hoxton, her [husb]and was my step-[brot]her – my father's son by [his f]irst marriage'); Grace [Har]ding; unknown; ['Mi]mie' ('she used to sell [hat]s made of old [wa]rdowns at Hoxton and [Brick]man Road Markets'); [Fran]ces Harding ('uncle [Bill]'s daughter – lived in [Lu]mbord Street, back of [the "]Gardens"')

14 Arthur *(second from left)* with the 'Hackney Hookers' football team, 1946

15 A drinking party with the Kray brothers, Bow, *c.* 1960. *Far left* brother George, *fourth from right* sister-in-law Alice

Anyway, I made a pal of the chief CID man there. Bryant[9] his name was – it was his uncle that got killed in with the gangsters in Exchange Buildings, when the five policemen got shot. He said to me, 'I don't care what they say about you, the Metropolitan police – you're a gentleman. And I was very pleased that you treated our man like you did.' Made a dead pal of him and the summons was never brought.

The last time I got taken in was over an affair in Aldgate. Believe me I've never been so scared in my life. I had one child, it was 1926. I was straight then, working for my living. But one night Charlie Horrickey came up the Gardens, and asked me to give him a hand. He wanted to sort out Moey Levy – some affair about bookmaking, I forget the details. But Charlie was a sort of friend of mine and they'd knocked him about. Charlie was a small chap, not a man who could stand up in a rough house. So when he told me that they'd knocked him about, I said, 'Come on,' if it wasn't for the drink I wouldn't have gone up – I was half-winey.

Moey Levy was the 'terror of Aldgate', a very, very famous man – he had about forty convictions for violence. He and a chap called Gardiner had a club there.[10] I knew where Moey lived, and where he got off the tram, and we waited up there. By a stroke of fate the two of them got off of the tram, it was pouring with rain and they went into a doorway and I said, 'There they are.' So I walked up to 'em with Charlie Horrickey, and said, 'What are you interfering with Horrickey for? Couldn't you pick somebody better than him?' A few words, just a few words was said. Before I knew what had happened Charlie whipped out a razor from his sleeve or his coat pocket and slashed Levy across the face. And Levy ran right up to Bethnal Green Hospital, I found out afterwards, the other chap Gardiner, he'd got about fifty convictions, he ran for the police station, where the old station is now, that's where it was, on the corner. And as he ran Horrickey pulled a bloody gun from out of his pocket and fired I think two shots at Gardiner.

And that bleedin' swine he said it was me that done it. He was on the danger list, Levy, from the razor. The shot missed so that was no proof that a revolver had been fired. No bullets found. They sent an SOS round, the CID men came round early in the morning, took me out of bed. I came down, didn't say nothing to the wife, so they said to me, 'This is nothing to do with us,' they meant to say they didn't care which way it went: 'Gardiner said that you fired a revolver at him, that you tried to murder him.' They kept emphasising it was nothing to do with them. So I went peacefully to the police station and when I got out in the Gardens I saw the place was bloody surrounded with police – they must have expected trouble. It was about 4 o'clock in the morning. The governor came about 9 or 10 o'clock in the morning and said, 'You've got yourself into a nice bit of business here. Listen they've told you it's nothing to do with us, you don't have to be afraid of nothing from us – if I can help I'll help you. I know you're going straight, that you've got a wife and a child.'

They'd taken Horrickey out of his bed, searched his place, but couldn't find nothing – he must have dumped the gun. We was remanded, no bail as usual. I was terribly upset. I'd been in worse charges than that. But, I'd married a young girl and she was a lovely young girl, she was straightforward, didn't know anything wrong. I'd got a boy. I could see the end of my life staring me in the face. I was getting to such a state that they put me under observation in Brixton.

Horrickey was charged with nearly killing Levy – it would have been murder if he'd died – he was charged with inflicting grievous bodily harm and I was charged with feloniously firing a revolver at Gardiner. My people got me to the cleverest lawyers they could.

Anyway I come up for trial. I had Cassels to defend me.[11] He came down to see me, I didn't have my hair cut, it had grown long, he said, 'Good gracious me,' he said to Garcia, my lawyer, 'get a brush and comb, you can't go in front of the jury like that.' He said, 'You know if the learned judge thinks it advisable he can send you to penal servitude for life.' That just about put paid to me.

I had some very good witnesses. A young Jewish lad from Brick Lane, he said he was up there and saw it happen. Polish Mick we used to call him, a lovely boy, he was, his mother was very poor, and sometimes I used to say, 'There you are, take ten bob home to your mother.' The father was consumptive. He used to hold the gamblers' boards up for 'em. I used to see that they paid him well, he came up for a witness: 'I saw it all, that man there [that was Horrickey] he's the one that fired the gun.' And he got a pal of his, who was with him, to come up, and there was two other chaps come up, who'd been under Bethnal Green railway arch. The judge said to Cassels, 'It was nearly 1 o'clock in the morning, I expect you've noticed it was pouring with rain, there was nobody about according to what you said to the jury. But what appears to me to be the truth, is that there must have been half of Bethnal Green under this railway arch. . . .' The judge was dead against me. He must have looked at my record – three times acquitted at the Old Bailey for the same kind of thing. Cassels cross-examined Gardiner and Levy and they had no evidence about my having a gun or the razor. I was acquitted – Horrickey got three years.

What put an end to my fighting days was a row I had with Dodger Mullins. It was about 1930 – I already had three children and I was still going straight. Dodger had been in Park-hurst with me. He lived on terror and he was always getting me involved in his affairs. It was Dodger who lumbered me with the Italian affair – when I was lured to the 'Yorkshire Grey' to meet the Darby Sabinis.

While business had been prosperous I had often been asked to give money to certain gangsters who, when in need of funds, would visit the local bookmakers and certain publicans, also any old timers like myself who had been in jail. When I had been asked to give I casually contributed my danegeld towards peace and tranquility, it was a sort of insurance against disturbance. Being a father of four children with a wife to keep, I had to be careful of every shilling. I was not eager to pacify these parasites who were no better than the bullies and pimps who lived on women, so I decided to stop giving money to these cadgers. Most of these cadgers will build up a reputation by using violence against men who have previous records. Three or more of these characters will attack and scar a victim with impunity because the victim is afraid to prose-cute. Dodger was one of these men. When he couldn't get me out fighting any more, he would come round for a little 'loan'.

One night there was a knock on the street door, I looked out of the window and saw Dodger and another notorious gangster at the door. I looked at my wife and told her to look after the children and not to worry. She went to the children's room. I went downstairs opened the door and asked the two villains what they wanted. When they asked for two quid I simply said no and shut the door. My wife opened the window and told them to clear off. They then started banging on the door. My wife opened the upstairs window and told them. 'You won't get anything here.' They foully abused her, using the most filthy language that I had ever heard even from the prostitutes of Dorset Street. I used to keep an automatic pistol in the wardrobe and when they came for me I rushed after them with the loaded pistol. I took aim but the pistol jammed and they got away. I chased them up the Gardens – they managed to escape in a car or cab, they never had the courage to face me. My wife had followed me to the top of the Gardens, she had no fear of them only a burning desire to make them pay for the foul abuse they had used against her. She looked at me and said, 'No more fighting, you're done with that. Come on up the police station. We'll settle this in the courts.' And that's what I did.

The CID were only too willing to apply for warrants for their arrests; some time after one was arrested on Doncaster racecourse, the other man was arrested in the West End. We had a strong case against the two men and they were committed to the Old Bailey for trial. What was going to happen was anybody's guess. The various interested parties began to be very friendly and if it had not been for the outrageous names that they had shouted at my wife, I might have been more friendly disposed towards them. It is surprising the amount of money that is collected for the defence of well-known gangsters when they have been arrested for demanding money, especially when someone like myself has the moral courage to prosecute them. Every would-be gangster resents one of our own turning to the law; they say it gives the mugs encouragement to prosecute. The underworld which includes all the idiotic fringe which thinks it is policy to associate with gangsters to further their own dubious schemes – all these mixed up characters rally round the gangsters. They collect large funds to brief the best lawyers and find witnesses who for a few pounds will be willing to swear anything. The suggestion is always made to would-be givers that certain top men, i.e. police, wanted a large sum to hush the case up. The clever idea behind this innuendo is that high-ranking police officers are behind the gang.

I was offered large sums of money to alter my evidence, also my witnesses from the Gardens, but although they alternated between bribes and threats, I was determined to put a stop to demanding money from people in their own homes, and from people like myself who were trying to live decent lives and break away from their past associates. I knew that if these men were convicted, I should have to be on my guard against a frame-up – I have known it to happen. A parcel of stolen property is made up and left at the victim's house when they know he is out or away from home. An anonymous call is made to police that a certain address has a quantity of stolen property. The man accused has a very hard job to convince a court that it is a frame-up. May I add that this trick was actually used on this occasion when I was visited by Detective Inspector Chapman. The plot miscarried when the inspector told me of the reason of his visit.

The day of the trial duly arrived. There were a large number of the gang at the court: several crooked bookmakers and their hangers-on, even in the corridor some friends of the accused tried to arouse my sympathy but all to no purpose.

Both men were defended by expensive counsel. I believe it was the original intention to put my character at issue but wiser counsel prevailed. The accused were found guilty of demanding money with menaces, heavy sentences were passed. The judge took the unprecedented step of warning that if any person interfered with any witness in the case they would be brought there to be dealt with, even if they interfered or molested any relative or friends of the witnesses. This warning put a stop to any possible trouble.

Mullins got six years for demanding money with menaces. The other chap got less. His people straightened me up – they gave my wife £50 or £60 so I was lenient in my evidence. It was the best thing I ever done when I put Dodger Mullins where he belonged. I should have been at everybody's beck and call when there was a fight on if I hadn't done so.

I started in the old–clothes business by accident. There was a wardrobe dealer at the top of Brick Lane, English chap. I think his shop may have been a 'blind' for another business because I never knew anybody to buy a suit out of there, although he had good clothes in the window. One day, he saw me in the street and said, 'Will you do me a favour, a woman called in the shop to ask me if I'd buy some clothes off of her, she'd just lost her husband, that's the address, would you like to go there for me? I'll give you a few bob; I didn't like to turn her down, but I don't want to go down and buy 'em.' I said, 'All right.' It was in Bethnal Green Road, it was in the Buildings there, right at the back of the police station. I went there expecting to see a lot of old tripe, 'cor blimey I had the surprise of me life – beautiful suits! He was a printer, in the printing business, he had wonderful clothes. I reckoned them up, I thought, 'There's a good few quid here.' She said, 'Are they any good to you?' 'Well, they're very difficult to sell,' I said, 'especially if they know they've come off anybody who has died, you know how people are.' She said, 'I realise that, that's why I didn't try to sell them to anybody. Will £3 be too much?' 'Well,' I said, 'I know you're up against it,' and I paid her the £3.

I never let him know, when he said, 'How did you get on?' I said, 'I earned a few bob.' I told my brother about it, he said, 'Whatever you do, don't let him know about that.' If he'd have only known. They was beautiful, West End suits, Hector· Powe suits.

Bethnal Green was noted for the large number of second-hand clothes dealers, they were called 'hawkers' because they hawked plants, ferns and china around the estates on the outskirts of London. They exchanged their plants and china cups and saucers for old clothes which they sold in the Exchange in Cutlers Street, Houndsditch (Exchange Buildings) –

scene of the shooting of five policemen 1910. On Sundays the hawkers put up stalls and sold their clothes in the northern part of Brick Lane. It was called 'Turk' Street when I was a boy.[1] This market was only on Sunday morning up to 1 p.m., when all the stalls had to be cleared away. Poor people came to it from all over east London.

These old hawkers were descendants of the gypsies who were living a more settled life in Walthamstow and Leyton in the last years of the nineteenth century. They had large families who all became hawkers and horse-dealers, many of the hawkers belonged to Bethnal Green and Hackney. The Smiths, Berrys, Krays, Kellys, Harpers, were all families engaged in hawking. These hawkers were called the 'guinea getters' because they were supposed to earn more than the average working man whose wages at the turn of the century was less than a pound a week.

A hawker is not a pedlar. The pedlar is a person who sells to the lady at the door. A hawker is one who buys from the lady at the door. And he is the only caller who gives the householder money for something the householder no longer wants.

Hawking ran in families. My mother tried her hand at it, even though she was a cripple. She used to sell the clothes they pinched from the church sales. She used to sell in the Lane. And she and her cronies would visit the Old Clothes Exchange in Cutler Street when they had trousers to sell – 5s a pair she could get. My uncle Bill, his wife was a wardrobe dealer, she had a stall in Brick Lane. She was a very shrewd woman and her sons were wonderful swimmers – all got prizes and medals at it. She lived to be eighty-five. I became a wardrobe dealer and my brother was a wardrobe dealer. Strange. You know why it is? I'll tell you. The reason is this, you can't submit to discipline, you have to be your own master. So, you pick something where you have to depend on your wits. It's a precarious sort of living, but you are not under a foreman. There's nobody to say, 'Do this and do that,' don't y'know what I mean. I think that's why most Romany peoples pick it. The Krays come from a Romany family.[2] None of them went into a job. None of 'em, from the oldest to the youngest.

The Berry's were a big hawking family. They come from

the Mount,[3] which was a part as bad as the Nichol, and close to it. The Berrys was all totters and hawkers. They'd always been at it, even the uncles and aunts. They had a stall Sunday morning, at the top end of Brick Lane. The mother was a wardrobe dealer – she went out with the basket and bag. She was a very shrewd woman. And her sons all became wardrobe dealers, and her sister, Mrs Thornton, her sons and daughters was all at it – they moved to Southend.

The Harpers were another mob from the Nichol. I knew them all. As a matter of fact my wife's aunt married one of them – Sammy Harper. She died young, left a big family. And that's how I knew them personally. They was hawkers, all hawkers, going round with a little pony and cart, and barrow. They all used to live in Brick Lane, round Gibraltar Walk at the bottom; they had a stable. Old Sammy Harper, his father, used to drive an old hansom cab, sometimes a brougham, sometimes hansom cabs. He used to swag a lot of crooked stuff and crockery, so if two or three chaps were going to do a job, they'd make an arrangement with him, say, 'Come along Chiltern Street about 5 o'clock tomorrow morning and make sure you'll be coming by.' They timed themselves after doing a place; they'd have it all packed up and he'd come along in his brougham and take it off. Then they'd walk home. The police wouldn't challenge a bloke with a hansom cab.

They caught him once, with the stolen property in his cab, hansom cab I think it was. Anyway he got committed to the North London Sessions and he got out on bail. So, in order to impress the jury, he went to work as usual on that morning, drove his brougham outside the Sessions and left it there, while he went in, thinking that the case would go his way. But it didn't. The jury found him guilty and the judge said to him, 'You told the jury that you were so sure you'd be acquitted, 'cos you knew you were innocent, that you'd left your horse and brougham outside the Court – is that true?' So the jailer said, 'Yes, my lord, they've been in and complained about it, it's been there, standing all day long outside the court.' He gave him twelve months, he said because, 'You never paid any attention to the poor horse who's been waiting there all this time and never been fed.'

Sam Harper's brother left £12,000, when £12,000 was a lot of money. He was a rag-and-bone man.

The Smiths were another well-known family, well-known in Bethnal Green, all of them wardrobe dealers even the children, all the daughters and all. Proper cockneys, one's still got a shop in Bethnal Green next to the 'Green Gate',[4] still selling old clothes like his grandfather and his father did before him – been in the family for donkey's years. They still go round: round Golders Green and round Sutton. There was a lot of brothers of 'em. Now today of course they're dying out. They had a shop down in Chiltern Street before the war.[5] They been at it when I was a baby. I can remember them in Bacon Street. The old grandfather – when I was a child of twelve – used to live in Bacon Street, right opposite. He had one leg. He'd lost a leg in an accident or something. As I look back, he was the Didicai all over. Fresh-coloured, as if he'd been in the open air all his life. With a real cockney twang in a very coarse voice. Same as the father – Alf Smith who brought up the big family. Old Alf Smith lived in Bethnal Green. When he died he left a packet of money. One of his two sons married one of the Mundays – they was a Didicai family. He had this family of about eight sons. One, Jimmy Smith, just died. He owned one of them big seaside places down on Clapton coast.

I knew that family as part of Bethnal Green. But I only took notice of them when I went into the business. They had a stall down Turk Street of a Sunday, same as me.

The Morgans had a shop in Brick Lane, next to the 'Duke of York'.[6] You could buy clothes in there for about five bob. The sons went out hawking. Old Mother Morgan used to be a hawker. Then she made a pile and she opened a big shop. Used to get some good clobber in there. Where they had the advantage was this: the ladies who used to come slumming down the Nichol used to leave parcels of clothing and what the people used to do, as soon as the ladies had gone, they used to run the clothes round to Mrs Morgan and she'd buy it off 'em. The Morgans had a shop when my father was a baby. The sons and all. They finished up in Hoxton with furnished rooms. Mother Morgan – she was a very rich woman – had loads of rings on her fingers you know because they all believed in gold you know. That's the first time I ever took an interest in second-hand shops, when I see their shop, because I once went in to try and buy a second-hand suit.

The Krays come from a great hawking family, one of the biggest in London. Old Jim Kray, he had the next door to me in Brick Lane, next to the 'Prince's Head',[7] so I knew him quite well. He was a wardrobe dealer, but more a rag-and-bone bloke years ago – they used to call 'em 'totters'. He dated back to the Nichol. They had a way of going to the tailoring shops, where they'd be a lot of cuttings, small cuttings, and they're only too glad to get someone to take 'em. The dustmen wouldn't take 'em away unless they paid, so they were glad when the old totters came round. Then they'd take them down Radgies – they bought all rags and that. A totter understands the value of different clothes and different wool. They used to sort the rags which saved Radgies employing girls – it was a terrible wage for girls, rag-sorting. Bones they didn't give any money for, though there was always a sale for them, but certain medicine bottles they would pay for. Any metals what they got, usually the housewife never knew a bit of brass from a bit of lead, or a bit of lead from a bit of iron. She'd say, 'Can you take them away for me?' an old gaspipe or something, course it was all money in your pocket. They kept them till they had a nice pile, it was so much a pound – it was a living, they knew where to go. Dirty old trade, but there was a good living at it.

Before 1914 you were a 'totter', but not after. You was a dealer after. It looks more posh. Don't look so bad on the crime sheet does it? You know, 'Prisoner was a totter' – the magistrate would think he was a bloody villain, whereas calling yourself a dealer put you on the business scale. There was an old totter down Gibraltar Gardens, Weston his name was.[8] I never used to speak to him, he was an old chap there. God knows how long he'd been at it but he had his own buyers and all.

Before the First World War the hawkers never used to buy and sell old clothes, they used to *trade* them – swap them for china or ferns. They hadn't got to the stage where they went out with money. Most women fall for the fern if it looks nice. They got them from Spitalfields market, in pots. Crockery was very, very cheap. You could buy a tea-service in Houndsditch, nicely made up. The cups and saucers were 1s 3d for half a dozen, down Bell Lane, and there was a place in White's Row where you could buy 'em. All big wholesale places down there. They'd have a great big basket to show what was carried – some went about in donkey carts you know; you'd be surprised the amount of crockery they'd carry. When you got to the door you would say to the lady, 'What do you want with them old trousers? I'll give you three cups and saucers.' And then, when she had done, 'Look I tell you what. Find me some decent old shirts what you don't wear no longer. Or if you got any good children's things . . . I'll give you the other three. 'Ave a nice 'alf a dozen.' She'd say, 'Wait a minute – I'll go and 'ave a look round.' And she'd find some of the kid's clothes which were as saleable as old gold.

After 1920 the hawkers began to use money. Instead of plants and crockery, they paid for the goods in cash. They also began to select more classy districts where the city people lived. Surbiton, Purley, Orpington, and other suburban places. These residential districts offered more scope for buying good second-hand clothes. Before the war they didn't call them wardrobe dealers. They was hawkers and not at all respectable. When a woman fetches something to the door, and you are going to give her next to nothing for what she's got, you have to inspire a bit of fear in her. You're not the gentleman. You had to look like a man who wouldn't take no for an answer. After the war it was different. The hawkers had risen to a higher position in the world, and they were buying off a different class of people. The whole thing's changed now – from the horse and cart to the bag. Because the clothes they're going to buy now are not rags. They're clothes that you're going to earn a pound out of a suit. They could travel out by train and dress nicely.

The hawkers would go out to the Asylum where the quarters were – the quarters of the warders belonging to the Asylum – where you got a uniform crowd. They all wore a uniform. Well all those uniforms were saleable. The Berrys would go out anywhere and so would the Krays. Because uniform people have a pride in their clothing, and they all want to be smarter than each other. That was the line of argument. The police uniform, you could sell every part of a police uniform. The tunics and all. The trousers were very, very saleable. All dark clothes were. And you got the boots. You can't let the policeman walk down the streets with his heels down. See what I mean? They got to issue them regularly to keep them smart. So if you got a bag full of trousers you had a good day's work. All over Brixton they used to go – where the City police used to live. And to Victoria – there was a tremendous great police barracks at the back of the Army and Navy Stores. And then there was Wormwood Scrubs, where the prison warders lived. They did all these people in their quarters. They reckoned like this: that they weren't too high up in the intelligence. Old Jim Kray always kept to the LCC estates, where he could fiddle with a few bob. Didn't have to lay out much. He'd say, 'Would you like 'alf a dozen cups and saucers mum?' There were a lot of LCC estates going up after the First World War – places like St Helier's. They were good places for the hawkers to work if they weren't too greedy.

I got into wardrobe dealing when the cabinet-making began to get bad. After the General Strike people didn't seem to have so much money to buy toys for the children. And then in 1929 came the depression. I knew I'd have to find something where the bad times would be in my favour. Second-hand clothes seemed the answer. If times are bad people can't afford to buy new suits, but they will buy a second-hand suit at a quarter of the price. My old dad used to say, 'When one door shuts another one opens.' So I decided to branch out into another line of business, and enter the second-hand clothes trade.

I used to be pally with the hawkers. I knew they got a good living but most of them spent what they earned in the pubs, gambling and horse racing. So I made a few enquiries and I began to look about for someone who would teach me the trade. I was a wee bit shy of approaching people but there was one chap – Bill Berry – who helped me. He come from a real hawker's family and lived just round the corner from Gibraltar Gardens in Furrell Square. He used to drink with my brother – he was one of the gang. I says, 'Would you take me out Bill and show me how you do it?' He says, 'It wouldn't suit you.' But I persuaded him. Berry was a good sort, a typical cockney, always ready to share his luck and help out anyone in trouble.

I always remember the first time I went out with him. It was a Saturday and he took me to West Acton. We started near the tube, about 10 o'clock in the morning. I'd never been there before and he knew all the best streets and places so he said, 'Now you knock on that side and I'll knock on this side.' I was not too sure of myself and passed several houses before I plucked up the courage to knock at the door. But I could see Berry on the other side of the street, going in and coming out of the houses, talking to people, so I started to knock myself. Soon the shyness wore off and I began to speak freely to the people when they opened the door. My first day earned me a £1 in not more than three hours' work. It must be remembered that in 1929 a pound was equal to three or more pounds of the present time, 1976. Believe me that day's work made me very happy, so that my wife and I went out to celebrate. My wife was very proud to know that she was helping in my rehabilitation to a better life. My family had increased to three, two boys and a girl, so it had become vitally necessary to work harder.

One day we went to Feltham in Middlesex. We collected a lot of clothes from the married quarters of the officers belonging to the Borstal Institution. We were able to buy a good load of uniform clothes which were saleable. Some time after a while we were carrying two large bags we were stopped by a squad-car load of CID men. One big ginger-haired man, obviously in charge, said to me, 'What's in the bags?' I told him, 'Old clothes.' I had seen this man before and recognised him as the famous Detective Inspector Selby[9] of the first Flying Squad. One of the CID men took a casual look in one of the bags and said, 'OK Selby,' then he said to me, 'All right, carry on but I don't want any nonsense round here, understand, I know who you are.' He mentioned my name. I said to him, 'And you are Mr. Selby.' He replied, 'Well, now we understand each other, let's carry on.' They all got into their car and drove away, so we carried on to the station. That was my first and last encounter with the famous Detective Inspector Selby. The police had been told of what I was doing for a living and told to leave me alone.

Berry wasn't ambitious, and although he had a family he used to spend what he earned in the pub. He was like his father. His father never got nowhere except a pub. Bill was a boozer.

The reason why he learned me – and why he stayed with me afterwards – was because I could get any amount of capital where he couldn't – he never had the ready money. If he had a pound he would spend it. When he was skint, he'd meet me at Liverpool Street and say, 'Which way are you going?' I'd say, 'Well I'm going so and so.' He'd say 'I don't want to go there – I've got to get 'ome quick. Could you lend us thirty bob? It's stock money.'

After Berry learnt me the trade, I realised that I wasn't going to get rich by following his estate lark. He'd go out perhaps with ten shillings from one block of flats. Arthur Howard was another one who never seemed to do much good. So I started to go out on my own. I went to the posh places 'cause I could talk to people at the door. The Berry's never had the gift of the gab. All they knew was policemen's trousers.

After some months tuition I decided to work on my own, I had cards printed with my name and address as a wardrobe dealer.

I was now working the better class residential suburbs of Surrey, Kent, Middlesex and Herts. This work was hard, by this I mean the districts were hilly, like Purley with long drives leading to the front doors, but the work suited me. I made it a rule not to work after 2 p.m. because the lady of the house usually likes to rest in the afternoon or go up to town. Another factor is the police regard hawkers with suspicion if they see them knocking after 2 p.m.

One afternoon at Coulsdon on the Brighton Road, near Purley, I was looking at some adverts in a newsagents when I noticed a man busily engaged in writing in a notebook some addresses from the adverts. I looked him over and thought he might be an afternoon prowler, so I paid him more attention. You see, if an afternoon prowler has a number of addresses in his notebook, he can call upon the lady of the advert without arousing any suspicion. If she is out and no one at home, he has every opportunity of getting in and having a look round for money or jewellery. If he is stopped and asked his business he has the names and addresses of a person in the district who he is calling upon.

So knowing this I paid him more attention. I was surprised to see he was writing in a Metropolitan police notebook. I said to him, 'How you going chum?' He said to me, 'Any luck?' He asked me if I knew him. I said, 'No, never seen you before.' He replied, 'I have seen you before on the manor.' I then told him how I was able to recognise him, he was surprised he had never given it a thought.

This was my first meeting with Detective Constable Ted Collier of Kenley police. He was a very fine policeman, an expert at catching burglars and house-breakers, also a very brave man. Some years before he had encountered a suspect near Wallington late at night. When about to arrest him the suspect produced a gun and threatened to shoot. Collier told the man to be sensible and throw away the gun. Collier walked towards the man who fired point blank at him – the bullet hit him in the thigh. The suspect was arrested and sentenced to a very long term of penal servitude. No promotion had come his way, he was still only a detective constable doing his duty, always by himself, riding a bicycle along the roads of Kenley, Purley and Wallington looking for burglars and house-breakers.

By regular calling at houses, and by fair dealing, I became known to the residents of these exclusive residential districts and by courtesy and civility I was able to become the regular wardrobe dealer to many persons who had never before sold anything at the door. I found that the people were very nice people to talk to, and soon the shyness wore off. What surprised me more than anything was that people you'd never seen before in your life, they trusted you: they'd say, 'Come inside for a minute and I'll have a look round.' Sometimes people would say, 'Have a cup of coffee?' It's a funny thing when I look back on it, nobody ever asked me to have a cup of tea, always a cup of coffee. These were totally different people than the people I had been used to in the underworld, whom you had to watch and mistrust, to be always on your guard. These people had no suspicion. They'd say, 'I got an old suit upstairs but I don't think it would be of any use to you.' So you say, 'How much shall I give you for it madam?' and she'd say, 'Well, is it worth anything to you?' and I'd say, 'It's worth five shillings' – 'Worth as much as that is it, thanks,' and then she'd say, 'Wait a minute, I think I've got some old shirts that might be of use to you.'

It was to be expected that the police in the districts where I was calling soon began to take an interest in me. There were many house-breakings in the area where I was calling and I would be stopped and the bag examined by the police. I always insisted on the police making a record of the stop-and-search business for future reference. On these occasions I always gave the police my business card. Scotland Yard must have given me the all-clear signal, because the stop-and-search ceased after a few months.

Saturday was the best day out for hawkers, you didn't sell any clothes on a Saturday, you went out to get them then – it was our best day. You get out to say Purley, well there's two railway stations at Purley, people used to work on Saturday morning then. Well, you pal 'em up, as they come out of the station, a lot of the ladies would say, 'He'll be home about lunchtime, he's got two or three suits upstairs, give us a call back.' I've worked till 5 o'clock on a Saturday. It was the best day of the week, you could earn more on a Saturday because it was far better to deal with the man, than the woman, 'cos she'd say, 'I know he's got a couple of suits up there, but whether he wants to part with them I can't say.' You'd get the man and he'd put the money in his kit, what he's sold his clothes for. Now, if she sells 'em, she puts the money in her housekeeping.

The hawkers used to meet at the top of Devonshire Street, that's opposite Liverpool Street station. We used to meet outside in the street, or sometimes the night before in the pub. All the hawkers, so we wouldn't crowd each other's manors. They'd say, 'Here, are you working tomorrow?' I used to take Charlie Kray. He'd say to me, 'Arthur, can I come out with you? Will you stand me?' He was a good hawker, but he was often short of stock money. He would say, 'Give me a few bob to start' – that was to pay for at the door. You could always bank on him. A lot of 'em would take him out 'cos you could earn out of him. He'd buy a suit worth £1 for 5s. He'd come home and say, 'I give her a dollar for it, how much is it worth, Arthur?' I'd say, 'How much do you want for it?' He'd say, 'That suit would fetch £1 in the Lane, give me 15s.' I used to pay him out like that, because sometimes he was lucky. And when I was at the gold-dropping lark, I used to take him out. Another man I went out with was Benny Hall. He was a greedy bugger, and mean. He had £2,000 hidden away in the piano where he lived but he never told us.

Men's clothing was a better line than women's. A suit I would give 10s for at the door – it might be worth 15s or even £1. Of course, you would try to get it cheaper.

There were a lot of what we called 'auction' suits around – part-worn City suits. The chaps who went to serve for their king and country had all been – the majority of them – the people who worked in the City. They all wore a uniform although they didn't know it. Striped trousers and a black jacket, waistcoat and bowler. And it was just getting a wee bit tedious to them. Then they joined up and they were put into an army uniform. Tom, Dick and Harry was all the same – no better or worse than anybody else. When the end of the war came, they were sick and tired of being in the uniform, and they bought themselves lounge suits to go to work in. That was a harvest to the wardrobe dealers. It may have been them that put them up to it. Anyway they were determined they weren't going back in uniform. Another thing. Saturday morning business was done away with. And those that did have to work on a Saturday morning, they went up in plus fours and a sports jacket.

There was a good sale for the black jackets and waistcoats – what the city people were getting rid of – but the striped trousers were a drag on the market, because a workman would look silly if he went to work in them, perhaps in a factory or a timber yard. You couldn't sell 'em. So when the lady brought them out you'd say, 'Sorry, madam, but that's just the kind of thing we can't sell. But if you've got any undertakers in the neighbourhood they'll buy 'em at once.'

Most wardrobe dealers didn't have a shop. They would go out buying in the week, and then on Sunday they would have a stall down the Lane. Many of their clothes were sold to the dealers.

The dealers' market was in Exchange Buildings, Houndsditch. It was the place where the hawkers sold second-hand clothes to the dealers. You could sell anything there. They'd take them any day of the week. From Monday to Friday. Not Saturday or Sunday. Sunday morning you could sell 'em yourself if you'd got your stall down there in the market. If you were lucky you would make very likely a pound or more on your clothes.

The Jewish people started the Exchange, 'cos a large number of them were noted for going round collecting old clothes. They had to have a place where they could exchange their clothes for money so they fixed upon round there, it was the back of Port of London Authority, where Dillinger Street comes down. The turning that led out into Houndsditch, that was where the original Exchange was: that was only a small house really, several rooms in it, they was the Exchange Buildings. It was an oldish place, but in about 1920 they had another place that the Port of London loaned to them, at least to Sid Mendoza and his brother.[10] It was a proper enclosed place, there was a gate where the hawkers came in with their bags and paid their 2d at the gate to a man who collected it. They usually had an old-time policeman there.

You went in there, you put your bag of clothes down and you took 'em out, your suits you put there. Everything that wasn't a man's suit was called 'rubbish' – shirts, pyjamas, ladies clothes – everything made of linen, you might say, was what they called 'rubbish'. It wasn't rubbish in the literal sense, it was the name for it. Each parcel of goods had its own buyers. The people who bought shoes had no rights whatever to buy anything else – they couldn't go and buy the suits. The man who bought the suits, he wasn't entitled to go and buy the 'rubbish'. There was the 'rubbish' buyers, they bought all the ladies' stuff – frocks and blouses; and gentlemen's shirts and pyjamas; and children's clothes. All these goods were bought by special buyers who sold again to dealers in the poorer districts of London and country markets. A couple of Jewish chaps were 'rubbish' buyers, but it was mostly English women brought the 'women'.

Sid Mendoza used to buy only auction suits, they were called that 'cos they were auctioneered in the country towns. They could sell as many as 100, 150 suits on a Saturday. Norfolk was one of Sid Mendoza's places, he used to go to Norwich and he'd knock out a load of suits, him and the man who was in partnership with him, on a Saturday. The dealers bought the auction suits off of the hawkers, it was a recognised thing. When you got in the Exchange the auction suit buyers would stand around and look at what you'd got. They wouldn't bid against each other. One of them would say, 'I'll give you £3 for the lot,' six suits. If he left them, once he walked away, he was finished. He couldn't come back, the others would step in, the one who was next. But they never outbid anybody, they just said, 'You finished Sid? – £3 the lot, I won't bid you a penny more.' That's the signal that he's finished. The other dealers are standing round there – you could get five or six – and they would take it in turns. The whole business was conducted like that.

At the old clothes exchange you got to know who the best dealers was. Jolly fine lot of people they were – men like Sid Mendoza, Joey Lyons, Lewis Tenerman[11] and others. Most of them were Jewish people – some had moved out to Brighton. All these dealers bought gents' suits. It was a very profitable business, and people made fortunes out of it. The dealers would pay you, say, 15s for the suit. It cost them 3s 6d to have the suit mended and pressed – there were Polish Jews with little shops they could send them to. They would do them for next to nothing. What with cartage, and the expense of taking them down to Norwich, they might pay out another 1s 6d – that's £1 the suit costs them. Well, they auctioneered them suits at as low as 25s. They only earned a dollar a suit, but if you're selling 100 suits in a day, it's a week's work isn't it? The whole business was conducted like that.

When they were auctioning the suits in these country places they would shout out, 'Try the jacket on,' because the jackets were all right. The trouble was trousers, but the country people didn't know that. If the seams were fraying they used to rip the sides out and sew them up again. It was odds on the trousers wouldn't fit the chap when he put them on; round the waist it might be all right, but directly you put 'em on the crutch they would be too tight.

Another set of buyers who earned a good living at Exchange Buildings were the 'shippers'. They bought all sound men's clothing, women's coats, uniforms irrespective of fashion or condition so long as the goods were sound. These goods were bought for shipping to the African and Asiatic ports for sale to the natives.

In the latter part of my career, I used to save all my clothes for Sunday mornings. In Brick Lane, never in Petticoat Lane. I had a stall at the top end – what had been Turk Street before the war. These stalls were all licensed by the local council at a small fee of two shillings weekly. It was very difficult to obtain a license of the limited number of stalls so I would take a chance to sell without a licence which meant continuous interference by the police who would move me on. The MP for Bethnal Green was Mr Percy Harris. I went to see him so I could tell him of my position. The result was that I was granted a licence to have a stall, also the police informed me that the Commissioner of Police had ordered I was to be given one free. I was very thankful for their help, because if you have a Pedlar's licence, the policeman don't stop you, you have a licence, he doesn't interfere with you. All this I owed to the influence of Sir Percy Harris. He was a good man for Bethnal Green.

I got a wonderful name among the Jewish people. One of them, a crippled chap, he'd been very unlucky. I helped to put him on his feet. Now he's got a big place and he always tells everybody, 'Arthur, he made me.' What happened was that I had a 'dead 'un' (that's someone who has died) and I bought a load of suits off of 'em around Bromley, and I got a chap to help me carry them home, I gave him £2, I bought them for next to nothing, let her make the running and she asked £2, for about £50 of stuff. I was a bit generous to this cripple. I'll always remember it, I'd seen him down there buying, but he didn't have much money to lay out. So I said, 'Here,' I said, 'There's a load of clothes there, you can earn out of them.' He says to me, 'I'd love to buy 'em, but I haven't got all that cash.' 'I tell you what,' I said, 'I'll lend it to you.' I'd had a good deal and you get in that way, that when you see anybody decent, and y'know they're up against it, you give 'em a chance. He said he built his fortune on it.

This was the testing time in my life. I was already the father of four children, I had broken off all contact with the criminal fraternity. I was now working six days a week to collect the clothes and Sunday, to sell them to the dealers who came to my stall. For some eight years I had been free from prison life. The police knew I was living an honest life, I no longer had any cause to complain about police persecution. My old enemy PC

381[12] had left the force and all my hostility had gone with him. The fight with Dodger Mullins finally and irrevocably cut me adrift from the criminal world of East London. I was no longer regarded as one of them.'

18 Domestic life and social change

The First World War had made a great change in Bethnal
Green. Before then it was practically impossible to find work.
But with the war every firm was getting busy and the people
they said was 'unemployable' became the people to fill the
jobs. Even the people round the corner in Gibraltar Buildings
got jobs. People who'd been scroungers all their bloody lives.
They got to Aldershot, building the army huts, and on
Hounslow Heath. I was asked to go down there in 1916 when I
come out of my five-year term. I said, 'Oh blimey, I can think of
something better than that to do.' The Hollys out of Gibraltar
Gardens – four of them went to Aldershot, building huts.
And Arthur Gardiner, he lived round the corner in Gibraltar
Walk. And the two Halls. But you couldn't go there if you
were of military age – not unless a doctor certified that you
were unfit. At Lebuses,[1] the great furniture place, instead of
cabinets they were turning out ammunition boxes and cases to
put the shells in. Many people went to work there. They got a
good living. As long as you could use a saw and a hammer you
were all right. Making packing cases. They got much more
money out of ammunition boxes than out of furniture. They
didn't get conscripted. It paid the top people at Lebuses to say
that a man was a good workman and couldn't be spared.

There were increased wages for those who went out to
work and the widows and mothers were getting large sums of
money as allowances for their boys and husbands.

Before the war a mother might have had a couple of sons
that never fetched a bloody penny in. Now in the army they
got regular wages. The same with wives. Terrible things
happened over that. When a husband deserted the wife would
sometimes give him away because immediately any solider
failed to return to his unit they stopped his money. Well when
a woman's been drawing three or four quid every week, she's
not going to stand for that. The allowance was like Klondike

to 'em, fur coats and pianos and beds to lay on. The money turned the women's heads. They had all these wristlet watches – nine-carat wristlets which the shops said were twenty-two. I found out all about those swindles perpetrated on working people during the war later on when I went to buy up old gold. Fur coats became the ambition of all the young girls. There were people buying fur coats who never had a bed to lay on. One man, Mr Easton, he was getting his bloody legs blown off in Flanders and his kids were sleeping on the floor but his wife had a fur coat which cost about seventy guineas.

Everybody had plenty of money coming in and they were spending it recklessly. They all wanted a piano. Pianos was eighty guineas, half-a-crown a week or five shillings a week. In my opinion that was the cause of a tremendous amount of unrest. It caused a lot of trouble. People bought pianos and couldn't pay for 'em. You didn't have to pay a shilling a week on 'em but five shillings. We had a Brookes' piano.[2] That was a big furniture place in Bethnal Green Road. They opened about 1910 but it was in the war that the money started coming in. The first piano we had was an eighty-guinea one and I gave £10 for it to a man who had bought it on the hire system and couldn't pay for it. That was 1930 – the first piano we had. But my mother-in-law had one before that. It was a nice piano and they bought it for 2s 6d a week. One of the girls, Ivy, was a wonderful piano player. They didn't have no one to teach her: she learnt herself.

My sister Mighty did very well in the war, when people started buying more expensive things. She was well established down the Gardens as a money-lender and credit clothier, and now that people were getting regular money they came to her more often. All the neighbours came to her and people from the other turnings nearby.

After the war she started organising outings for the people she done business with. The people from the Gardens came and people from all over Bethnal Green. They went to Brighton, Southend, Hastings and Eastbourne. Sometimes they had two coaches.

The first outing she organised was after I came home. My younger sister lived at Old Ford – Mary. Her best friends and some neighbours down there, they came to the outing as well.

So it was a mix-up – they set out from the Gardens but they didn't just come from there. It was about 1923 or 1924.

Saturday night was the big night for parties down the Gardens. When we were in the Nichol the only place had a piano out there was the Mission Hall, that had a harmonium. The pubs used to have a penny-in-the-slot one – but homes no. The first one I ever see in a home was my mother-in-law. They had a piano. They had a piano and nowhere to sleep. In their cottage there was one small room in front and a kitchen behind with a small scullery to wash the clothes up in. And upstairs was the big room, that covered the whole area of the house, it covered the passage and everything. Well, upstairs they all slept. And there was, as far as I know, now about thirteen in the family. Well, of a Saturday night they'd have a party, mostly every Saturday night they had a party. A gallon or two of beer, they all had dancing and the piano. And of course Ivy used to play and Albert Smart, a chap married to one of the daughters, he was able to play it, to knock it out. Mrs Worby, the mother, she was a very poor old dear. Her life ended at seventy, like the doctor said she was worn out. A tragedy. All them women of the working-class areas, they was worn out: the good ones. But that Saturday night was her only picture of heaven that she had a chance of enjoying. An' she'd sit down there, she'd be up in the 'Blade Bone' – the pub on the corner – and she'd sit with a glass of beer. And the old man. They were *happy* on a Saturday night. The party would start when they came back from the pub. They wouldn't sing nor nothing in the pub.

The parties were held in the parlour. That was the old front room. It wasn't very big. To me the greatest mystery of it was they was all able to dance in it, round and round, holding each other. If the daughters was married they were down there with their husbands and when the sons got married they came down there with their wives and family.

The piano took up the best part of the room. It was one of Brookes' pianos – they got that out of Bethnal Green Road or Green Street, they had a big shop in Bethnal Green and a big shop in Green Street (what is Roman Road now). They bought everything from there, the wringer, everything. The price flabbergasted me – it cost something like £70. My wife paid the best part of it 'cos she says to me, many years after we married, she says, one day when I was talking about the piano, 'I paid for most of that.' She badly wanted a piano, she was a wee bit more refined than the rest of 'em. They could afford it because the girls were all at work. There was Milly, my wife – I'm talking about when she was a young girl – her sister Anne, that was two. The next one was Jenny and then Nell. That was four at work. They all put in about a shilling each I suppose. It was the only piano down the Gardens. I don't think the old man put much in, the mother might have put something in out of the living money.

The unfortunate thing about the East End of London and all slum districts is the one-bedroomed house. And no separate accommodation for the girls and boys. In a good many cases the girl and the boy as they grow up together become intimate. So you had to be very, very careful. If it could harm anybody you had to shut your eyes to it. Like down the Gardens there was a brother and sister living together, I said, 'She's nice-looking, the sister, isn't she?' My wife said, 'There you go, about nice-looking, that excuses it I suppose.' They was there from about 1924 up to the time I moved away from there. I'd never noticed them before, but I noticed them because she was rather good-looking in a continental way, a gypsy girl. You couldn't help noticing that the kids were a wee bit daft, barmy, they went to a special school. He wasn't nobody's fancy, however the sister loved him I suppose.

Our family, the Hardings, were better off than the other families in the Gardens. We had much more space. We didn't only live in Gibraltar Gardens, you could say we more or less owned it. There was no traffic, and no strangers coming through. By the time I left the Gardens in 1932 we owned four or five houses. My mother had one, my sister had one, my younger brother George had one, and one of his daughters had one. She married a boxer, Davis. He's a taxi driver now. Then there was the Worbys, my in-laws, they had a house. We didn't exactly own the houses, but as the people moved out we took them over. The landlord let us have them. My sister was running a good business, and she helped the whole family. 'Cos my brother wasn't earning a lot of money, and he had ten children to bring up. He lived at No. 6.

Gibraltar Gardens was always called Mrs Casey's Court after the Irish woman who did the laundry there. She came from the other end of Brick Lane where the ladies of the town lived and God knows what her early life was like, but there was nothing evil about her. She was illiterate and knew very little of the cruel world she lived in, but this I am sure of, she had nothing to fear from death and the hereafter.

Mrs Casey was the mother of two children, a boy and a girl. The daughter wed an American soldier in the First World War. She went to the USA in 1918, had a large family. The son got married 1920, had a family, left Bethnal Green, and left the children with his mother to struggle for existence alone. Mrs Casey earned a living by taking in washing and doing charing for the Jewish people in the Lane. Her struggle for existence had soured her to such an extent that every lodger she took in left within a few days. Policemen coming down the Gardens to deliver a summons to somebody would have to pass through a verbal barrier of obscenity that made them run by her door. My house was opposite her door and so I had a good view of the comedies that took place daily. Having described her worst habits let me tell you of what a wonderful old lady she was. She slaved from morn till night at the wash tub. She refused charity from anyone. She loaned money from my sisters and never missed paying back. I have never seen her with a coat on; winter or summer, she went out with only a skirt and white apron and an old woollen cardigan or jumper on. During the last war, although she was about seventy years, she never left her home for shelter from the bombing. She neither asked for or received gifts from Father Jones or any other charity. Another remarkable thing, I had never seen her in a pub or taking beer to her home. Everybody called her Mother Casey and the children in the Walk called the Gardens 'Casey's Court'.[3]

We had several pubs quite near the top of the Gardens. There was one a few yards away from the top of the Gardens[4] and they used to go in there and get winey and if anybody was dead they'd get well boozed. They'd always leave it till it was closing-up time – pack a few bottles, and have a wake. To me it's a horrible bloody business, the people at that time thought it was the natural thing to do. I think my mother said to me,

'Anyway it's better than crying.' I said, 'But you were laughing.' She said, 'Well ain't it better than crying?' All that sort of
thing. Of course that type of people were very ignorant. It was
the state's fault.

In all, there were sixteen cottages in the Gardens, seven on
one side, nine on the other. At one end of the Gardens were
Gibraltar Buildings – three tenement houses each with twelve
rooms. Most of them were let to separate families. They were
the same as Keeve's Buildings in the Nichol where I was born.
The sixteen cottages were owned by two different landlords[5] – the seven on the right being owned by one and the
nine on the left by the other, who also owned Gibraltar Buildings.

The whole court was about 100 years old. It was surrounded
by the backs of two timber-yards, and a large block of workshops. The Gardens were a complete cul-de-sac except for an
alley leading into Bethnal Green Road. The 'Gibraltar' – a pub
in Gibraltar Walk known as the 'Gib' – had made a small
passage into the Gardens, for people to come to fetch their
beer.

At No. 1 lived Mrs Morton and her husband.[6] She was a
timid little woman who had been born in the Gardens. She and
her brothers were orphans. She married a man who must have
been twice her age and who weighed 18 stone. They kept
themselves to themselves. He had a regular job and every year
they went away to a week's holiday in Southend. They had no
children. About 1926 the husband died suddenly. The wife
shut herself away and a few weeks after she was found dead
'from neglect and starvation'. My niece and her husband
moved into the cottage and remained there up to the bombing
of 1940.

At No. 2 lived Mr and Mrs Gardiner[7] and their family of
two lovely children. They had come from Hoxton and were
very pleased to live down the Gardens in a nice little house all
to themselves. The husband was a racing man and lived a
hazardous life, but they were a happy family and proved good
neighbours.

At No. 7 lived the family of Mr and Mrs Mason.[8] The
mother was a large woman weighing 16 stone or more. She
was a regular customer at the 'Blade Bone' which was only a

few yards from the Gardens. She could be seen going up and down the Gardens with a jug for her 'medicine'. The children were well behaved and went to church on Sundays.

Mrs Worby[9] who lived in No. 4 had ten children, seven daughters and three sons, so with the mother and father there were, at one time, twelve people living and sleeping in this one small cottage.

On the left-hand side at No. 8 lived Mr and Mrs Davis[10] with a family of four sons and two daughters. Mr Davis was out of work. He was a one-time athlete who had broken many records and was a fine-built man. But he was not too fond of work and the wife, a very pretty woman, did her best for the family with the little money she received. The house had a rat-run from the former burial grounds and was plagued by the large rats which infested that side of the court. Life was hard for the family and many times I saw the boys running barefoot up and down the court even in cold weather. But by some strange fate these boys grew up to be fine physical young men, though the youngest was placed in a home for mental defectives. But Jimmy Davis became a great boxer and could have gone far if he had had financial backing.

No. 9 was rented by Mr and Mrs Daniels.[11] Mr Daniels was the owner of a small roundabout with which he visited many parts of London. Children paid a small fee to ride on it. The roundabout had six or more chairs and was drawn by a donkey whose stable was in the yard of No. 9. Mr Daniels was a Romany and a fine figure of a showman – 6 foot tall, well-built and with a splendid head of hair. He was fond of his beer and tobacco, and was never without a pipe or a cigarette in his mouth. He left the Gardens in the morning early and never returned till late at night. Mrs Daniels was a different type of person. She was suffering from partial blindness and the children suffered accordingly. There was one boy called Charlie who was eventually placed in an institution for care.

At No. 10 lived a widow Mrs Gibbs[12] with her family of two boys and four girls. Her husband was killed during the First World War. He was the brother of Mrs Alice Harding, my brother George's wife. She remarried and had more children who were of school age when the Second World War started. One was killed in the bombing at Liverpool Street, another was evacuated to the United States.

At No. 11 lived Mrs Casey.

At No. 12 lived Mrs Asher[13] the wife of a disabled ex-serviceman with her family. No. 13 – the woman here went to school with me at Nichol Street and had a photograph of me taken when I was there.[14] At No. 14 lived Mr Whitehead who was an old 'totter' who lived alone with his daughter, a very peculiar young woman who kept house for him.[15] At No. 15 the family were a highly religious clan who attended the Red Church[16] – not Father Jones's – at St Paul's. They were very reserved and did not mix, I don't know why they stayed there. The father liked his beer but only patronised the bottle and jug bar so he did not mix with the herd. He always filled the jug for his wife. They had two very nice daughters who went dutifully to church and belonged to the Girl Guides.

The house next to this was the Rectory where the Vicar of St Matthews lived in a twelve-roomed residence. He had his wife and one child. They never came down the Gardens. The Rectory fronted on to Bethnal Green Road: the planners demolished it instead of converting it and now it is an open-air garage for the sale of second-hand cars.

No. 3 was where I lived. When I moved in 1932 we let the house to a Mr and Mrs Johnson who were the daughter and son-in-law of Mrs B who lived in Gibraltar Buildings.[17] They were ordinary Bethnal Green folk and attended Father Jones's church on Sunday. Their two children left when they married.

In No. 4 lived my mother-in-law, Mr and Mrs Worby and her family of five daughters and one son.[18] Two daughters and two sons had married and lived elsewhere. My father-in-law had been a railwayman since leaving school. After having several accidents he was nearing the end of his service and had been working in a farrier's shop. During the war one of his daughters and her husband were killed at 'the Bank' shelter on 11 January 1941. A bomb destroyed the Worbys' house during a daylight raid but fortunately they were in a shelter. Before the end of the war both of them had died through ill health.

The old vicar, Father Jones, had all the children of an age that they could be trusted to go away to a Holiday Camp. He had all of them of a Sunday morning singing in the choir, they'd be all washed, cleaned up, clean hair, brushed right back, and they'd go to church round Glossop Street. And then on a Sunday afternoon they'd come down: Father Jones would fetch the choir lads and all the people would be out and he'd conduct a service round there, that was the usual thing, in the open air. I'm not talking about the winter – that was the summer.

Father Jones had a terrific influence for this reason. When he started his appeal in the *Daily Telegraph* the money come rolling in and somebody must have donated a big cheque. Because he bought a bit of ground out in the country, I think it was at Littlehampton, I'm not sure. And they had a home there, for the country holiday, and all the children used to go there. They had to be on their best behaviour – going to church. The mothers went on the Monday. Really and truly it was a very praiseworthy business.

There was some characters down the Gardens that really the room only saw them of a night, when they come home, or of a morning. Mrs Howard had a bloody scandal of a husband. My wife knew the inner history of both of them, 'cos they would go to my wife to discuss. My wife used to say, 'What happened?' She'd say, 'The bloody tike come home drunk last night.' The wife and children were all scared. She's telling my wife, and then she'd tell me, and then perhaps next night I'd say, 'Don't you think you ought to be bloody ashamed of yourself appearing like that before your children?' He'd say, 'Sorry Arthur, she aggravated me.' I'd say, 'Well you bloody well stop it, 'cos if you don't stop it I'll have you chucked out of that blinkin' place, I tell you.' They knew, I put the fear in 'em. But they used to go to my wife first.[19]

Even in a little community like that – I don't suppose there were more than 250 down the court – you had this class business. It was a tightly-knit community but people in the blocks – Gibraltar Buildings – were different. They were very rough and crowded. In 1930 I counted that there were over 100 people living there in 36 rooms. There were some right characters.

The people at the end house was very religious people, used to go to church and all the rest of it. So that they tried to keep themselves a step – a wee bit higher – than the kids round the

corner, there was the class business. My wife used to keep my
children away from the children round the corner. She was no
different to anybody else but she had just that wee bit – what
shall I say – she thought she was better than anyone round
there. But it wasn't only her. My brother had ten children and
those children didn't associate with those round the corner. It
was a community together, but separated by class. I used to
laugh about it because to me the whole thing was ridiculous.
The ones in the terraces thought themselves better than the
ones in the Buildings for this reason: they lived in one room
and we had a house.

When I first went down there we had two rooms at the top
of the first house, I was fresh from Borstal and I had my own
ideas of what was right and wrong. So, I was willing to be
friendly with everybody. But it was only very rare occasions
that the children would go knocking at other people's doors
saying, 'Is . . . coming out?' 'What do you want him for?'
would be the reply. The people in the Buildings were very
poor. None of them had any kind of a home where you could
invite anyone in, there was only one room. They didn't want
any of the others to know anything about their indoors life –
they was poor.

Directly I got married I said to the wife, 'We won't be here
very long,' 'cos I wanted to get out. But the wife had a child
every two years, 'cos she didn't believe in abortion or taking
contraceptives, and it didn't seem as though we would ever
have sufficient money for a house. Then the 'gold rush' came.
It was an absolute God-send. The children were growing up,
and we wanted to get out so we stinted ourselves, we
never went away on holidays or anything like that. From
the day Dodger Mullins came down and called my wife
those filthy names, it became like a craze with us to get away.
My wife was the same. What kept me down there longer than
I should have done was that me mother, me sister and me
brothers were there. They told me afterwards that they cried
their eyes out the day we moved away, it was like somebody
dying.

First, in 1932, we took a flat in Leyton, and then, in 1934,
we bought a house in Canterbury Road, Leyton. It was a
nearly new house – seven years old – one of those which had

been built with a subsidy from the government. It cost us
£675. The interest was only 4½ per cent. I had one boy born
there, David, the last born, 1936. We lived there for twenty-
two years. I paid right through.

All my family was brought up there. They changed from
Bethnal Green kids to something a wee bit selecter. They'd
forgotten all about Bethnal Green, and even today they don't
want to know anything about it. They changed. They went to
school and they began to speak better. Another thing was they
was all clannish to their mother. They was always at home,
they didn't associate with anybody at all hardly, until after
some time they got in with the children round there. As they
grew older they grew more selective, more clannish. It's unfortunate in my opinion.

Down in the Gardens my children were in some ways
fortunate. My mother lived next door and they had aunts and
uncles down the court. And they had playmates – my
brother, he had ten children all growing up, all down the
Gardens. When we got to Leyton they never made friends.
Only time they made friends was when I sent 'em to college
and they made friends there. Pitman's or Clark's College, they
made friends for life there, some of them, my girls did. Today
they're still the same, they're very clannish.

We moved away to Leyton but my brother's family stayed
put. My children didn't mix with 'em, from the time when we
moved away to Leyton they never associated with any of their
cousins any more.

One of these cousins – he was named after me, 'Arthur',
but we used to call him 'Boy Boy' – started to get into trouble.
When he got to the age when he should be leaving school and
starting a job he was out with a crowd who was thieving; he
gets in trouble for stealing a watch in a café, something like
that, that was his first lot. So their uncle has to be the one who
has to be the benefactor, they phone me up about it. Him and
another couple of arabs, they're all at the juvenile court. I get
him out of it, I knew a lot of the police, it was quite easy; that
boy was often in trouble and I had to be the one to get him out
of it. I said the only thing we can do with him now – 'he's got
to get married'. Anyway he's all right now. I've read the Riot
Act out to him so often that he says, 'Uncle you'll never see me

do anything wrong again.' He's still a bit of a villain. I've often thought to myself, sooner or later, that's how my children would have gone, if we hadn't got away from Bethnal Green.

In 1932 I gave up wardrobe dealing to take part in the 'gold rush'. This new 'gold rush' started when the government took Britain off the Gold Standard, but instead of having to travel thousands of miles across the seas to find it, the new El Dorado was on our own doorsteps. We had only to travel to the towns, cities and villages of our own land, or even to the poverty-stricken streets of the East End of London, to find we had the precious metal hidden away in old chests of drawers, old jewel boxes in which people had kept their treasures in more prosperous times.

The 'Hungry Thirties' were for most working-class people disastrous times. Unemployment was rife, people were forced to economise by the terrible economic pressure to draw out their savings and to sell their possessions to obtain the wherewithal to live. Gold had doubled in value – it was possible to get as much as £2 for a sovereign in 1933. Soon after this date, the price rose to much more than this so people began to look out their old treasures to raise money for their needs. During this period it was a common sight to see hundreds of hunger marchers on the roads making for London. This being the state of things in the 1930s, I decided that the people did not have the money to buy second-hand clothes so it would be more profitable to buy old gold and silver instead of clothes. I travelled to many towns and villages in Devon and Cornwall. I was a good judge of the value of jewellery. I also carried the necessary scales for weighing old gold and silver.

It was a great surprise to me when I began to realise that nearly every house had broken pieces of jewellery such as rings, watches, chains and brooches; nearly all these old trinkets were worth money.

In the First World War, the workers in the munition factories were earning big wages, they spent large sums of money on jewellery, such as heavy gold bracelets, chains, rings and wrist watches, etc. All this old stuff was laying about in old boxes or drawers considered by the owners to be of little value, because they were not fashionable. So you can understand that when the old gold man called at the door, a little soft persuading and the people were glad to sell their old ornaments. The remarkable thing was that the old Victorian jewellery was far more valuable than the modern stuff of the 1930s. Ladies' watches which hung on a chain round the neck or fastened on the dress were of eighteen carat gold while the modern wrist watches were of nine carat gold.

When canvassing a district for the purpose of buying old jewellery, I always employed a man to put circulars in the letter-box of a house telling the householder I was calling to buy any old jewellery they wanted to sell. The circulars had my name, telephone number and business address. The man I employed was of good character, never been convicted of any offence and today, forty years after, he can still say the same.

The Gold Rush lasted a jolly good time. I reckon myself that we saved this country millions and that we helped them to pull 'em back. Gold was very precious. The government didn't know how to get it, but we did. I was getting a marvellous living. That's when I went out and bought a house. I was praying night after night that I was going to have a lucky touch, so that I could get my kids away from the East End. I didn't fancy my children growing up down there. That was the chief thing. My wife used to say, 'I'm not putting up with this much longer.' I used to say, 'We'll get out of it.'

I'd have been nearly a millionaire now, with the price it's gone up to. Half the people up in the Midlands and round there didn't know the value of what they had. I remember one particular instance in Northamptonshire. Sunday we used to go down there, me and my brother, had lodgings in Rushton.[1] On this particular occasion, Saturday morning came, we'd been away from home since the Monday morning. I said to my brother: 'We'll work up to 12 o'clock and we'll get home in time to go and see the jewellers in Clerkenwell – we've only got £5 left, be careful how you buy.' Anyway I knocked at this door, I had about £2 left and I meant to sell it dearly. A man come, first of all he sold me one of those bracelets, they had 'em from the First World War, came from the munitions factory times, nice and heavy; I gave him about 5s, they were worth £5. I says to him, 'Have you got anything that *looks* like gold, it doesn't matter if it isn't real gold.' I wanted him to fetch out anything. 'Even if I don't buy it, I'll tell you if it's worth anything.' That's what I used to say. He said, 'The children were playing with an old chain, we've had it for years, must have belonged to my father.' He went over to the coal cupboard and brought me out a man's double chain from a double breaster, about a two-ounce chain.

He was a policeman and I found them the best customers out, they're more daft; he was such an idiot that he didn't know it was gold, though it was stamped on every link. So I said, 'It ain't much good, you can have a couple of bob for it.' Something like that. He stood for it. He said, 'It's no good to me, have it.' That's the way you bought gold, you had to be shrewd.

I had a windfall with a police inspector once. It was in Reading. You would expect him to be a bit clever seeing he was an inspector, but this man wasn't. I called on him at his home, and after seeing a few things, I said, 'I've got to call back to see the Doctor to pick up some old stuff.' I went back there later, 'cos the longer you give 'em the more they can find. In the front room he had it all laid out on a round table. He said, 'I've got those coins there.' I could see one or two was sovereigns. When I looked at the silver coins, he had an ordinary 5s piece amongst 'em, I thought, 'Blimey, he's more daft than I expected.' He kept his wife's wedding ring and a few other things but the rest were all for sale. I bought 'em at his price, I give him what he asked.

Another time I was working round Lavender Hill, me and another chap, quite a respectable chap, never been in trouble in his life. I bought a bracelet off a woman, a gold chain bracelet. I weighed it and it was worth a few bob, and I said to her, 'How much?' She said, 'What can you give me for it?' That was the 'Hungry Thirties' – everybody was hard up, everybody was wanting money. And I said to her, 'Look here, madam, I know it's hard times.' She said, 'My husband's up the Labour Exchange.' So I said, 'I'll give you 30s for it.' She rushed at it and I thought to meself, 'She'd have took £1 for it.' 'Cos 30s was a lot of money, it was a week's wages. So I said, 'Do you have anything else laying about?' So she said, 'I'll tell you something, my husband picked up a brooch at Battersea Rise, could you tell me if it's worth anything?' So I said to her, 'Certainly, madam.' I expected to see a Woolworth's brooch. She brought it down, I looked at it and I nearly had a fit. It was solid silver, but by kidding her that it was no good – just imitation – I got it for ten bob.

I used to sell the stuff to a wholesale jewellers – Golding Brothers, two brothers up in the jewellery quarter in Clerkenwell.[2] Sold them regularly of a Friday afternoon or a Saturday morning. I think I sold that brooch to them. They used to pay me a good price. Jewish, lived round Golders Green way. I used to collect all my jewellery for the week, used to come home of a Friday, and used to take it up there, to sell out to them. My brother still takes it up to Cohen in Houndsditch there – he's the son of the previous owner.

I had to drop the Gold Rush when I got arrested as a 'suspected person'. It was a trumped-up charge, and they had to drop it. I didn't have nobody to advise me, but I decided that if I went against the police I would be finished because they had my record, and if they brought it out in court, the people I dealt with would find out, and my living as a wardrobe dealer would be finished.

I tell you how it happened. When I went out gold-dropping I always put round circulars to say I would be calling. I had a man who dropped them in the letterboxes. We went away to give people a chance to read them and then came back and worked the houses. On this particular occasion we were out Woodford way. They was all well-to-do people. At one of the houses, a lady said to me, 'Well come in, I've got some old stuff I don't want, I was thinking about disposing of it.' I bought some sovereigns off of her, some half-sovereigns and a chain and a bracelet. I laid out a few pounds, gave her a good price, as much as what she would have got in a shop for 'em. Then I went on with my round. It was August – burning hot; and about 1.30–2.00. The other chap says to me, 'Shall we call it a day?' So I said, 'Right.' There was a lovely big lawn there. So he said, 'I'm going to have a lay-down here.' A few minutes later he got up for some reason and said to me, 'Oy, something's happened over there, where we've just come from, look at the police.' I said, 'I bet somebody's screwed the gaff.'

At that moment a police sergeant came along on a bike. He spotted us and said, 'Did you see anybody with a sports coat and flannel trousers come this way?' So I said, 'No.' 'How long you been here?' he said. 'About half an hour – nobody passed this way.' Then he said, 'By the way, what are you doing here?' Tidily dressed we were, didn't look like labourers or nothing. So I give him my card and explained we were buying old jewellery. I opened my case to show him what we had bought. He was perfectly satisfied and he told us that somebody had tried to break into one of the houses. Then he went away on his bike. I said to my mate, 'We'd better clear off from here, otherwise we might be in trouble.' We got on a No. 9b bus on Eastern Avenue.

At one of the stops I see a fellow with flannel trousers and sports coat get on. I weighed him up and said to my mate, 'Look.' And he said, 'Cor blimey, that's the geezer they're looking for.' The bus stopped at the 'George' hotel and this fellow with the sports coat come upstairs and said to me, 'I'm a police officer, would you mind getting off the bus.' We got off. There was a squad car waiting on the corner. So I said, 'Who's in charge here?' A fellow said, 'I am.' And so I explained it to him same as before, and showed him the jewellery. He said, 'I'm not satisfied, you answer the description of two men.' I said, 'Very well.' We jump into the police car and we go to Barkingside police station. That's where he's made his first mistake, 'cos not a 100 yards away was another police station – Wanstead. I thought to myself, 'Why hasn't he brought us to Wanstead, why Barkingside, that's about five miles away?' We got there, an old police sergeant was in charge there. He said, 'Turn your pockets out.' I put all my jewellery out there and I had £40 in money; the other chap had some as well. I could see him looking at my money. This geezer says, 'Well, y'can put your money back in your pocket.' After about ten minutes he said to me, 'Come for a drive.' I didn't put this up in court, I didn't have a chance to speak to tell you the truth. But the obvious question should have been, 'Why did you go for a ride?' Anyway, he took me back to the place where there had been a break-in. There was a couple of women talking out there just by the house that was supposed to have been broken into. He got out, went to speak to these two women. One of them come over and looked at me in the car. She said, 'No, certainly not, that's not the man, he had a sports coat and flannel trousers.' Now, I knew what had happened – the police had been screwing the place themselves. I looked at the police officer and said, 'It's getting a bit naughty isn't it?' He said, 'What do y'mean?' I said, 'Y'know what I mean, she described the other man, the man who's with you.' He said, 'I don't want none of that.' We go back to the station. He thought I was going to give him my £40. But I knew that I'd got him 'cos of the police sergeant and why he hadn't took me to Wanstead. Well, we go back to Barkingside and he got on to the Criminal Record Office, learnt who I was, and charged us as suspected persons.

My wife's wondering why I've not come home (we were living at Leyton at the time, having moved out of the East End to escape trouble). She was a bit on the frightened side. About 5 or 6 o'clock in the evening, my wife was getting the children to bed when all of a sudden there was a banging at the door; it was pushed violently open and in came two police officers. They said they'd come to search the place. All they found was an old case full of old silver – broken silver, watch-cases, what I saved till I got a large quantity of it, it only fetched 1s an ounce at that time. These weren't the chaps concerned in arresting me, these were CID chaps from Barkingside police station. So, they go back and they say to the head man, 'They've made a mistake, that chap's a dealer.' They realised that they'd done wrong, pushing the door in and frightening my wife like that – they wanted to be on my side now, so I wouldn't make no complaint against them. The head man said to the bloke in charge of the station, 'Let him out at once.' So they let me and the other chap out.

We come up Stratford police court next morning and this chap who was in charge of the car, Gerrard his name was, told the biggest pack of lies. Now police officers can sometimes be villians, but they don't usually tell lies to get a bloke in prison if they know he's innocent. This one did. He said that he'd followed me and watched me trying the doors of the houses, while the other bloke stood guard. I only wish I could have had a chance of cross-examining him.

The whole bloody thing was silly, I knew he was a mug. He told how he heard the glass being broken over the door and the latch being pulled back and how he had gone to get help. Every time he opened his mouth he put himself in it. 'Any questions?' Before I could answer in jumped the inspector from Barkingside and he said to the magistrate, 'Your worship, I ask for fourteen days remand, on their own bail.' He said 'On bail?' He said, 'Yes, your worship, we have a reason for asking that.' The magistrate was amazed.

I would have liked to defend myself but I thought it advisable to get a lawyer so I went up to Bloomsbury and I engaged a firm of solicitors. I had a Jewish lawyer that I knew very, very well, Gershon his name was, he was a good man. Been in my house a lot. Used to have a man who worked for him – I helped him to get clients, without engaging a solicitor's firm, 'cos half the barrister's money that they get for the case goes to the solicitors.

On the morning when the case came up I was up the solicitor's office, they had the appeal papers, in case the magistrates convicted us as suspected persons – they give you three months.

You really aren't a normal person when you've got a charge hanging over you, especially when I was a wee bit frightened 'cos of my wife and children. I thought to myself, 'It would be terrible, ruin me blinkin' life.' We go up to the court. And the police from Barkingside are there and they're giving this police officer and the other bloke that was with him such a terrible look. 'It looks like I'm going to be off here,' I thought, 'they've got it well in for 'em.'

The police was represented by police lawyers. They don't know – no one in that court knew – that I'd been up to see the Commissioner of Police and told him the full story. They had a consultation and this is how they worked it out. 'If he goes into the box and tells his story, there will be hell to pay. Here is a man who's had everything the law can do to him, and now he's been going straight for ten years.' It would show that they were deliberately trying to put him in prison. This is how they got themselves out of it. Up jumped the police solicitor, 'I beg leave to withdraw this case,' he said to the magistrate. The detective had entered the witness box thinking that the case was going on and he had the bag with the jewellery and my money in. Now the fear entered into him, he realised he was in it.

I could have started an action for damages but I thought like this: the police done all they could to remedy it. If I started an action, everything would have to come out in the public. So, I let it drop.

I received all the jewellery and money back after the case was finished. I read in the local paper, the *Leytonstone Independent* a brief report of the case which ended with the words: 'This man had a number of convictions recorded against him in the past.' The past was some twelve years ago.[3]

The result of this was notice to quit from our flat. It was now vitally necessary to find a house where we could let the family grow up without the knowledge of the past becoming known to them, a place outside the vicious circle of the East End. We found just the place, transport very convenient, school quite close to the house. So I paid the deposit and obtained a mortgage from the Essex Building Society without any trouble. I was forty-nine years old without any regular employment with a wife and five children to support. No health service, no social security, no unemployment pay. So I had to work, I could not afford to be ill and have days off. Believe me when I looked around at our own home and at my lovely wife and children, I knew that all our worries were nothing compared with the blessings of our healthy children, a wonderful wife and mother, a merciful providence that had given me good health and strength to be able to work for them. So I knew our ship had reached port safely after a very tempestuous voyage; 1935 would be the beginning of a new life. Of one thing we were determined, the children were to have a good education so that they could have a good chance of better conditions and careers.

The house had a good garden, back and front, so I would have plenty to do when I was at home. It was 1936. My family had increased to six by the addition of another boy so we had the honour of being the largest family in the road. The eldest boy was eleven years. My wife was thirty-four years old and I would be fifty in November.

The great Gold Rush had petered out, the hungry people had sold their valuables, even the fur coats and pianos they had bought in the luxury days of the munitions factory of the First World War.

20 A shop in Brick Lane

The year 1938 saw me back as a wardrobe dealer. I had started looking up all my old customers and also canvassing new districts. Some wardrobe dealers give notice by putting cards and circulars through the letter boxes – these give notice of calling and give the householder time to sort things out. This is what I now did.

In 1938 another attempt was made to frame me, on a felony charge. One day an ex-policeman of 'H' Division who had known me in the old days before 1908 called at my address in Bethnal Green. He said he had an interesting proposition to make to me, so I listened to him. The following was his story. He was friendly with some people who had a large amount of stolen postal orders, all that was needed to change them was a date stamp. He could get the postal orders cheap. I had known the man for years, when he was a CID aide back in the early years of the century, and I did not trust him. He had been dismissed for conduct prejudicial to the force. He was known to be associating with men and women who were known to the police. So I had no doubt that some villainy was planned; in all probability it was intended to sell me the postal orders and then inform the police.

You must understand that professional thieves know where to take and sell stolen £5 notes, postal orders, jewellery, without any risk to themselves, so why come to me, who was known to have sent two well-known gangsters to prison? I pretended to go along with him and asked when he would bring the postal orders. I consulted the Yard and prepared for the showdown. About a week later I received a message late at night that I should meet the former PC at the rendezvous in the East End. The ex-PC and myself travelled down to the meet. A woman joined us at the bus stop, we walked a little way down the road, the Yard men took them both in. They were in possession of hundreds of pounds of stolen orders from a burglary at Wood Lane, W.1. So another silly scheme to get me sent to prison failed. The lady involved in the plot was the wife of a good screwsman, who told me afterwards that he knew nothing about it. I believed him. Believe everybody, but trust nobody.

On the outbreak of war I put on the warden's helmet and joined the ARP. The wages were £3 weekly but the government had declared a moratorium so the anxiety about mortage repayment, etc. was allayed by these measures. Being a full-time warden with only £3 weekly, I fell behind with my mortgage repayments and rates so as nothing was happening, and press, also public, were talking of 'this phony war', I left the full-time warden's job and became a voluntary part-time ARP warden of a night. In a few weeks I had soon recovered my losses and things seemed to become normal again in the early months of 1940. Second-hand clothing coupons were saleable because clothing coupons were required for new clothing.

The surprising thing about wartime was that the second-hand clothes trade, despite the scarcity of coupons, was very brisk. I was buying more suits than I had ever bought before in one day, good quality suits, complete wardrobes. Trade being good I suddenly made enough money to pay my mortgage dues and also the rates. Christmas came and went, and when the children came back home the war was r.early forgotten. I found that people were willing to sell their clothes more readily than before the war, especially those with men who were prisoners of war or missing.

A lady at Coulsdon called me into her large house. She knew I came from the East End, and gave me a large quantity of beautiful children's clothes on my promising to sell them cheaply to the poor of Bethnal Green. Then she sold me all her husband's clothes. He was a major in the army and had been missing since Dunkirk. Among the things she sold me was a silver cocktail set, wedding gifts, gold watches. Such tragedies were to be found everywhere in middle-class districts.

At Shirley near East Croydon I called on a Mrs Smith. This lady always had clothing for me and she would tell me of her family affairs. Her eldest son was a fighter pilot in the RAF and he held a good rank. Her youngest son was in the army and his name was Norman. On this occasion when I called upon her she was beside herself with grief for he had been reported missing at Dunkirk. She said to me, 'If Norman is dead I shall die.' She had a letter from his colonel saying that the last he saw of him was he was fighting a rearguard action to stop the Germans getting to Dunkirk. A couple of months later I called on her but the maid told me she was dead and buried and the house and its contents was up for sale.

About 1942 I bought a shop at No. 250 Brick Lane, and kept it till they served me with an eviction order in 1956.[1] My sister lived upstairs, and downstairs were the old clothes. I still went out to the suburbs, collecting old clothes, shutting up the shop while I was away. Sunday was my best day – same as for the people in the market.

It was the war that made me get the shop. My mother was bombed out, down the Gardens. They moved round the corner and in 1942 she died. My sister said, 'I can't live in this house anymore.' Lots of shops were empty in Brick Lane, so I said I would go and get a shop to put the clothes in, and my sister could live upstairs. I'd never had a shop before. Otherwise I just had a stall on a Sunday.

There was a lot of rackets with clothing during the war, and it was through them that I became involved with Scotland Yard's 'ghost' squad. The 'ghost' squad were interested in anything that was detrimental to the war – possessing coupons, or Black Market business. There were people who were making fortunes for themselves out of rationing. Vast quantities of forged coupons were put on the market. In one case they were selling coupons at a shilling a time and when the people who bought them came to undo them, all they found were bits of paper. The crooks in the West End were raiding the town halls to find out where the coupons were stored, and pinching the whole lot. They would sell the coupons at 4d or 6d each, according to the value of the coupon. The forging was done in the West End – all round Shaftesbury Avenue but they were sold in the East End. I knew some bleeding villains that was at it.

I knew a lot about the Black Market because of the old-clothes business, so I could help the 'ghost' squad a lot. People came in to sell clothing coupons, I used to give £3 for a book, but I never sold them for money, only exchanged them for second-hand clothes. Mind you I made a great bargain out of it, for £3 I might get £20 of clothing back. I could never understand why wealthy people risked their reputation and character in order to get something the rest of the community wasn't getting. The poorer people used to sell the coupons, because they couldn't afford to buy new clothes, so I exchanged them for old clothing. It was the better-off people who bought them – magistrates and all, one was a man sitting on the local bench somewhere down Epsom way.

During 1942 another incident happened caused me to make a protest to the Commissioner of Police. In the course of my business as a wardrobe dealer, I often received a postcard or letter from a customer who had clothes to dispose of. On the day in question I had received a postcard from a lady who lived at Hendon, north London.

So on this day I travelled to Hendon by tube from Liverpool Street. I bought the clothes and returned by tube to Old Street, that being my best station for my shop in Brick Lane. Passing Old Street police station, a policeman stepped out of the entrance and stopped me. He said, 'What have you got in the bag?' I told him but he said he wasn't satisfied and asked me to turn out the contents. Words passed between us and he arrested me.

We walked into the station and he had a talk with the station sergeant who said to me, 'Take your hat off.' When I refused to do so he knocked it off. I told him he would be sorry. He again threatened me, so I took a card from my pocket and told him to get in touch with the phone number written on it. Immediately he saw the number, he realised his mistake – it was a number of one of the top men at the Yard – and phoned the CID for advice. After a phone call to my home and to the lady at Hendon who had sold me the clothes, the sergeant apologised for what had happened and allowed me to leave.

The question of stop, search and detain, is a serious matter. The police have powers to do this under the Metropolitan Police Act. They use these powers on the slightest pretext. They are supposed to have some justification for acting and detaining a suspect. In this case I had given a true and correct account of my home and shop, yet I was seized as if I had committed a serious crime.

I sent a full account of what happened to the Commissioner of Police for inquiry into all the facts. A short time afterwards I received a visit from a police officer I knew. He explained that he had been asked to visit me to see if I would accept an apology from the chief inspector at Old Street police station.

I left the shop because they pulled it down. They give me £50 – if they'd known I was an old age pensioner I wouldn't have got nothing. They were pulling the bleeding places down each side of me so I had to get out. That was about 1956. But I still went on wardrobe dealing. I used to wait to get letters. A lot of people had my address and they used to send to me, all good people and when they sent to me I knew I was on a week's work. People in the outskirts they got very lonely and they wanted someone to talk to. I didn't go out, only when I got letters and my David – that's my youngest boy – he used to take me in his taxi to pick up what I was offered and up in Dalston I had a couple of chaps who had stalls, they used to buy it off me. Saturday by the Waste,[2] I didn't go out too often. I was getting old – over seventy – I was getting a pension for me and the missus, so I had to be very careful that I didn't get done for working.

A man's got to have something in his life. When he's growing old, he can't walk about, expecting pity off of people 'cos he's getting old. He's got to stop being old. But after the wife died in 1967 there didn't seem so much point in it. Also I was afraid that they might start making enquiries that I'd been copping the Old Age Pension. So I gave it up. My brother is still doing it now, though he is turned eighty. He has an old-clothes stall down Cheshire Street market.

21 Politics and philosophy of life

My father was a Conservative. He couldn't even write his own name, so I don't know how he could vote for anybody, but he was a Conservative. Perhaps he got someone else to vote for him. He was definitely Conservative. And his brothers, they were all Conservative. And all the children that are alive now, they're Conservative. But we used to get a Liberal paper. When we moved to Gibraltar Gardens we had *Lloyd's* newspaper on a Sunday – my mother liked a good murder story and I used to read them to her. And I bought the *Star*[1] – that was a racing man's paper, which came out every night. It was dead Liberal.

In the 1906 election my father was all for Major White. White was the Conservative MP for South-West Bethnal Green. He was a major in the army of some sort – Major White. He was a flamboyant type.[2] He didn't hide his colours. And he used to bring the toffs down here, posh people. The Liberals were a different type of person. They were more human. In those days all the costermongers were Conservatives. They used to have all their stalls decorated with the colours on election day. Major White was the head of the costermongers' union,[3] that's how he got in, because the costermongers were the chief people with influence. The Conservatives used to take them out on holiday runs.

The Conservative Party stood for Tariff Reform, that was, taxing all the goods that came into the country, like German mouldings. So all the people whose living was in jeopardy – like my father – was on their side. My father was a carver and gilder, and all the brothers were cabinet-makers of one sort or another. The cabinet-maker was told by his governor that he had to vote Conservative, because if they voted Liberal they would be out of work because of Free Trade. The market would be flooded with cheap furniture from abroad and the cabinet-makers would end up in the workhouse.

You've got to realise the people had a different mentality at that time. When Queen Victoria died in 1901, we had to wear black bands on our arms, and every place had the shutters up. People done it because they genuinely believed all the nonsense that had been printed about royalty. The people were definitely for the King and Queen. When I saw a royal procession, I used to take my hat off as they went by. I wouldn't do that today. But the whole thing was that we wasn't educated enough. If we'd had more good schools, more good learning, people would have thought different. The Conservatives had a powerful party just before 1900 and for a few years after. They stood for law and order. They were powerful enough to send a vast army to South Africa, and protected the rights of the landowners and the diamond dealers. Britain ruled the waves. The other side, the Liberals, were more for the foreigner – Free Trade – the foreigners were as good as us, etc., etc. Well the British people didn't like that because they had all been brought up on 'Rule Britannia'. I mean, even when they looted the West End in 1886, when the unemployed smashed up the jeweller's shops, trying to impress the people up West with their condition, they marched back to the East End singing 'Rule Britannia'. Now what more patriotic, more conservative song can you have than that? But at that time every band played patriotic songs.

Major White was the costermongers' champion. If they had a grievance against anybody he would take it up in parliament.[4] Also, the Conservative party stood for the publicans. In every pub you would see a Conservative picture at election times. In the pubs you couldn't argue politics. The landlord would say, 'Here, none of that 'ere.' He was the governor of all he surveyed, he was the policeman. You always saluted the publican. The only way men knew of having a friendly conversation was going into the pub, but if they knew the publican was against it, they stopped it.

The Conservatives weren't interested in education. And they were determined that the working men wouldn't have any clubs, where intellectual people got up to tell them that there was a better life in store if they'd only change their politics. Immediately the Liberals got in in 1906 they started having working men's clubs,[5] about 1906, when the politics in

Bethnal Green changed from Conservative to Liberal. At the working men's club, when you went in of a Sunday morning, you would have a good speaker, who would talk about politics, and explain what was going on. So the working man began to learn how he could better himself. He learnt how to argue, how to raise himself up. The chief Liberal club was in Pollard's Row, next to the Red Church. It's still there now.

The clubs were more extreme than the Liberal party in those days. In Bethnal Green they had speakers who were barred at other places – the out-and-outers. The official Liberals were educated people, who had been to Oxford and Cambridge and all the rest of it. But in Bethnal Green they were ordinary people who kept little businesses. They nearly all had businesses. That's how they were so well known. They were all local people who had been known all their life. There was Tom Brooks,[6] one of the finest men I've come across. A right agitator. He was a chimney sweep and lived by Brick Lane. He was Mayor of Bethnal Green, three times, for the Liberals. He wanted more for the working people. Father Jones was the same. He married me. He was Vicar of St Paul's in Gossett Street. And there was Miss Maloney, she was another Liberal. She sat on the Council. She lived in Bethnal Green Road. Her brother was a doctor. She was on the council. She was a nice woman, Irish, a practical young woman. There were several other Liberals like them. There was a chap who kept a coffee shop in Virginia Road, he was prominent. Ordinary people turned to them. They knew – or thought they knew – that as long as they had a Liberal government there wouldn't be another war. I knew Brooks for years. He was friendly with me. But he always had that wee bit of fear. Bethnal Green thought the world of him. I used to see him sitting outside his house, at the top of Gossett Street, by Brick Lane. He was a very respected man. If he'd been less respected he would have had his place smashed up, because he got rid of the top part of Brick Lane as a Sunday morning market. Father Jones helped him – Father Jones's church was just round the corner.[7]

The Liberals were against the pubs. That's why so many of the working men's wives were for them. Before the 1909 election there were pubs everywhere. Drinking was dominant. There were more pubs than paper shops. But the election led to the closing of the pubs. Beer was causing most of the misery in the country. It didn't matter how much they gave the worker, so much of his weekly wages went in the pub, and that was money wasted. The working man liked to enjoy himself with other men in the pub. But the women realised that every penny spent in the pub meant less for them to spend at home amongst the children. So they were dead against it. Lloyd George knew that fewer pubs would mean more money in the working man's pocket. He closed pubs all over the country. He closed the 'Red Cross' in Hare Street – they turned that into a Jewish synagogue. And the 'White Horse' and the 'Crown'. They closed four pubs in the space of a hundred yards. All of them in 1911.[8]

Lloyd George wanted to tax the land, because he said that the land belonged to the people, it didn't belong to the select few. That drew hundreds of thousands of people. 'God gave the land to the people,' he said. Could you have a better voting sign than that? I was all for it, and so were the crowds in the West End. That was about 1910 or 1911, when they closed all the pubs. They done what no Conservatives would have done. The Conservatives stood for beer.

It was about that time we started to hear about the new ideas. Down in Whitechapel, in the Commercial Road area, there were these old Jewish people who used to sit and talk politics. And they were putting forward something the ordinary working man had never heard before – equality, every man was entitled to this, that and the other. There were men like Rocker,[9] the German anarchist. People wanted to learn more about it. The anarchists had a place just off Hanbury Street. And in the Warsaw café they used to talk politics.

Those Russians were more anarchists than communists, in fact you never heard the word communist – I think they only started to call themselves that when they wanted to be a bit more respectable, many years later. The reason they were called anarchists is that they were against the Tsar, the system of politics in Russia, what they called 'the autocracy'. I knew some of them Russian chaps. They were on the run from the Tsarist secret police. If there had been a socialist party at that time they would have been regarded as heroes. But they were treated as criminals. They got mixed up in the Houndsditch murders and in the Siege of Sidney Street, and in the murder on Clapham Common, because they were dead against the police. When they saw a man in uniform they thought they were the same as the Cossacks, and they shot it out with them. That was how the Houndsditch murders happened. That was really at the bottom of it.

I knew Gardstein's mob. The mere fact that they were on the run from the police made them friendly with us. So we were friendly with them. When I look back I feel sorry for them. If only someone could have spoken to them in their own language and explained the difference between English police and Russian police they might have all settled down and gone to work. I admired them for this reason. Out of all the millions of people they were the ones who had the guts to fight oppression. I was always against the police, for the brutal way they knocked people about. That's why I hid Milly in my house, when she was on the run. These two Russian chaps they killed in Sidney Street was innocent. The only thing they had against them was that they had Luger pistols. They didn't take part in the murder of the police officers. That was a daft thing, caused by a fellow called Max who opened fire on them. He was the fellow that shot Gardstein too, and he got away to France. When the Russian revolution came my sympathy was all with the revolutionaries. I knew about the autocracy and how they governed. I knew a lot about the Russian business. It was a cruel country. Today there are some people who believe we would have been better off if we'd done the same as they did in Russia. But I don't think the Russian people are better off. They put guards and dogs to stop them getting out.

About 1922 I helped the Liberals in St George's in the East, protecting them against the Labour. Jimmy Watts got us the job of bodyguard for the Liberal candidate, Major Nathan.[10] They didn't call it being a bodyguard, just 'looking after him', to see that nobody attacked him or knocked him about. Major Nathan was a Jewish man, but he didn't look too much the Jew, he had a good war record. Gosling was the Labour man – he'd been a docker all his life and St George's was a dockers' constituency. We used to stop them breaking up his meetings. The Irish mob from Watney Street supported us – they was all for the Liberals, and the dockers seemed to be coming round. There was a big meeting in Stepney and hundreds of dockers were there and they all cheered him, not for anything he said but for his absolute courage in coming down there and facing them. Gosling won, but Major Nathan won somewhere else. They gave him a peerage in the final.

Before the war most of the working people were Liberal. Education had increased. There had been all those big demonstrations in the West End – 'the land for the people'. At the working men's clubs they would listen to talks from people who had thought more.

The Liberals were against war. They proved the connection between the Conservatives and the armament firms. But they got us into the First World War and gave us all those bad generals.

To me it was always a mystery why there wasn't a revolution against that war, same as they had in Russia. But you couldn't get at the upper people in England. No one would catch them napping. They shot a boy of sixteen in the Connaught Rangers – instant court martial. They knew how to put down trouble, how to stop it spreading.

People had different ideas after the war. They wouldn't work on Saturdays. Clerks rebelled against uniform. They appeared at work with flannel trousers and sports jackets instead of black jacket and striped trousers. They were done with the tradition. I knew that, because when I was wardrobe dealing I was always being offered striped trousers, and you couldn't sell them for love nor money.

I made a lot of money being a bodyguard in the General Strike. I had these fellows I employed as terrorists, to frighten the dockers. They were mostly Irish chaps from down Watney Street. They'd do anything for money.

There was a colonel at the Guildhall who was employing tough guys to stop the strikers from interfering with the food convoys. The rougher, the more hooligan they was, the better. Well I knew plenty of tough guys, and I went up to see the colonel. He was very pleased with what I had to offer, and agreed to pay me whatever I needed. He paid good wages – a pound a day. That was a lot of money then. I got a good whack out of it, in fact most of the money which the colonel paid out ended up in our pockets.

The art of terrorism is not to hurt anybody, just frighten them. With someone like Dodger Mullins – he was one of the men I recruited – the name was enough to inspire fear: he could walk into a pub and terrify anybody. Every docker knew Dodger Mullins or had heard of him. All our escorts had to do when a load of strikers got round, was to frighten them off, that was better than fighting. They used to have the convoys in the middle with the foodstuffs. They would sit in the van and if anyone came up they would jump out and say, 'What do you want?' It was a matter of frightening them.

It wasn't the colonel but someone lower down who did the drafting. He'd say, 'How many men have you got today . . .it looks like being a rough house,' and I'd say, 'I've got twenty men, will that be enough?' 'No.' 'Well we'll get another ten. . . . They'll want about a pound a day.' He'd say, 'That's reasonable . . . now Mr Harding, here you are, here's five pounds, is that enough for you? Do the best you can and if you want more, spend it and tell me.' I didn't do the paying or the recruiting – I put that into somebody else's hands.

I didn't take much interest in the General Strike. In our language these strikers were what we called mugs. But we weren't against them, except when they got in the way of the convoys. We didn't mind which side we helped so long as it brought us in money. So when I got the chance of being sole agent in the City of London for the strike paper – the *British Worker* – I was only too pleased to give a hand. With my licence I could get as many copies as I wanted. I handed it over to my brother, and he made his money at that, while I spent my time on the convoys.

Two of the men I employed on the convoys were the most prominent hooligans in the East End of London, a couple of real tearaways, blackmailers – Dodger Mullins, who I've already spoken about, and Timmy Hayes, one of the terrors of Aldgate. Two years after they were indicted at the Old Bailey for demanding money off of a billiard hall, and there was a further indictment against them for being habitual criminals. Both got convicted. The judge gave one nine years under the Habitual Criminals Act and the other four years.

The case went to appeal, and I agreed to give a hand by citing their services to the government during the General

Strike. Now if you could prove that you went to a Labour Exchange, or that you'd had a job, it was a defence in law against being convicted as a habitual criminal. A friend said to me, 'Could you give evidence on their behalf?' So when the appeal came up, I told them about the colonel at Guildhall: here was the nation in industrial strife, and everybody was against law and order, and yet this man, who had a bad character, had volunteered to help the authorities safeguard the food convoys. Mr Justice Avery tried the case at the Central Court and he got Dodger Mullins off. He said to me, 'And you paid these men £1 a day?' I said, 'Sometimes less, sometimes more, according to the reputation they had for terrorism.' I said the mere face value of them was enough to frighten off the dockers. And I said, 'I was working for a good cause,' and he agreed. He said, 'You were,' and he said that if Timmy Hayes had been paid 25s for a good day's work he hadn't any need to demand £3 off anybody. He said to the other members of the appeal court, 'Here we have a man who hasn't been long released from prison, and according to the witness, Mr Harding, he was trying to get an honest living. He had money in his pocket, so he had no need to go up that night to demand two pounds from a club. He was working for a good cause and he deserved credit for that.' But the other judge said, 'We can't give him credit for being paid for a decent job – probably the most honest piece of work he's done for years – because obviously he must have spent that money in a pub.' The court dismissed his appeal but let Dodger Mullins off. Timmy Hayes done the whole sentence. He was sentenced to eight years imprisonment, and served all of it.

In South-West Bethnal Green the MP for many years was a Liberal. Sir Percy Harris.[11] They only got him out in 1945. He was a Jewish man but a gentleman – you would put him in the same class as the Rothschilds. I voted for him only once – when he first got in, about 1920. He beat the Conservative – Labour hadn't yet really entered the arena. He had an office at the corner of Carbela Street, opposite Gibraltar Gardens. There was an agent there who would put you on to anything. A very smart chap – the West End type – he knew how to look after you. He helped to set me up in the Lane. At that time – it must have been 1927 or 1928 – I was selling old clothes and fighting to get a licence. I didn't have a regular stall and so they kept shifting me down the Lane. So I went to see Percy Harris's man and he got me a licence. He had so much influence at the Home Office that the Home Secretary gave the Commissioner of Police orders that I should be supplied with a licence that would enable me to trade in any part of London. I didn't ever have to pay for it. The superintendent said to me, 'Look here, Arthur, you've got everything your own way now.'

Percy Harris done me a lot of services. A boy I knew, he was only a boy, Johnny McKenzie, he was doing three years for an offence that the judge sentenced him to twenty months for. He said to the judge, 'Give me three years instead of twenty months.' And the judge said, 'Do you really mean it? Well all right,' and he gave him three years. He said, 'What do you want it for?' He said, 'I want to go to Dartmoor.' So he said, 'You shall go to Dartmoor.' Anyway, he went there and found it wasn't up to what he had expected. So he assaulted a warder, one of the worst warders at Dartmoor, dead villain he was. And he got a flogging, had to wear the chain. The doctor ordered that he should be sent to Parkhurst on the Isle of Wight, and he attacked another warder there. The Home Office was right up against it. They couldn't very well order him another flogging. So he was ordered to be tried by the assizes at Winchester. Well, his mother come round to me, they used to all bring all their legal troubles to me. And I said, 'Well, I'll go and see Sir Percy Harris.' Went down and had a conversation with him. He said, 'I'll see what I can do, but it's a very difficult case.' But he went and saw the Home Secretary and he sent for me, he said, 'Listen you've got to be very careful how you go, because they're considering whether they shouldn't send him to Broadmoor – that's what the Home Secretary told me.' He said, 'He's told me to tell you to be very, very careful how you go about this, 'cos if there's any public outcry, they may be forced to certify him.' So I went to see his parents and I said, 'Look, we've got to be very careful here, but I'll promise that they're going to give him every attention, because of him having his sentence increased to three years.' 'The judge has got into trouble about it, there's been a lot of fuss.' So, I thought to myself, the best thing I can do is go to Winchester Assizes. First of all I had to get somebody who was on the Western Circuit, a barrister. So, I go round to Sir Percy Harris and he said, 'Well I don't know anybody at the Western Circuit, but go up to Lincoln's Inn and find out.'

Blake-Odgers was the man he sent me to, later he became magistrate for North London. He was a gentleman, the head of the firm. I told them the story of Johnny McKenzie, I said, 'This is the truth, I'm telling you. When he was quite a lad, one night he was going home, he was attacked by a gang, they ripped his face right down,' I said, 'He's got an awful scar and the doctors, or the hospital didn't make a very good job of it, it's a very vivid scar right down his face and it's affected his mental outlook, 'e thinks that everybody is against 'im.' He called his partner in and they were spellbound, honest, they all but cried. I got 'em right at it, and they said, 'We'll take the case.' And another thing they said, 'Mr Harding we won't ask a penny, we've got the right man for the job.'

Anyway, I got up there, I took my wife there and I got into the court in Winchester and somebody – I don't know who it was, must have been a policeman – told me who the warder was. So, I was in the corridor of the court and I see this fellow come out, and like a bloody idiot I said to him, ''ere just a minute you,' and I frightened him and he went up and got the police. A police officer came up to me with the principal warder of the prison and said, 'Look here, you've got no right whatever to interfere with a witness.' I said, 'I didn't know he was a witness.' Then the barrister came out, and he said, 'For God's sake, don't start interfering with witnesses.' Then he said, 'The Lord Chief Justice is going to take the case, and he won't listen to any sentimental defence.' He said, 'I really don't know what to do about it, I've told him if he pleads guilty he's got a possibility of getting a lenient sentence.' Lord Hewitt was the Lord Chief Justice, and I knew he was a man that was all for giving the juvenile offender a chance. So I said to him, 'Can't you plead to the court what I've written out.' He said, 'He won't stand for that, it's too much sentiment.' He was bleeding wrong he was, the barrister, but I let him have his way, he's the lawyer, I thought to myself, 'Oh, cor blimey, if this goes against him I'm going to tell you off.'

Well the case comes up. Lord Hewitt was weighing him up,

and you could see the scar right down his face. Three warders to guard him. It appeared that one morning he struck this warder with a chamber pot, hit him on the head with it. So the Lord Chief Justice said to him, 'Did you in any way cause him to lose his temper?' He said, 'All I did was I kicked the chamber pot inside.' So he said, 'Well, you had no right to do it.' He said, 'It was his chamber, he emptied it and put it down and you kicked it in, and he lost his temper.' Then he called the prison governor and said to him, 'Have you got the punishment sheet?' When he produced the punishment sheet the judge said, 'I see you gave him two days number 1, what's number 1?' 'Bread and Water.' 'I thought so, two days bread and water for the terrible offence of talking. Who was he talking to?' 'He was talking while he was working.' 'Who gave you authority to give a man like him two days bread and water in a punishment cell? I notice he's been punished several times for small offences. Did you ever study the fact that he'd been flogged at Dartmoor, and that he'd been sent to you for a different treatment?'

That's how the judge went on. He rollocked them all, and at the end he said to Johnny McKenzie, 'You've pleaded guilty to causing grievous bodily harm – it's my duty to punish you.' He said, 'I don't want to advise you, your lawyer should not have advised you to plead guilty, and I could have dealt with it in a different manner. As it is, you'll be sentenced to six months hard labour.'

I only voted Labour once. That was in 1945 when I was at Leyton. A bloke with a Norwegian name got in, Sorensen. It was the only time I ever voted Labour and I never heard the end of it from my family. The war was finished and Churchill was the great hero. But not in the East End of London. Everybody wanted their sons and brothers and fathers out of the army. And they started to whisper the word that Churchill, instead of demobbing them, was going to keep them. And that he was saving the German prisoners for the same reason – he wanted a war on Russia. So people began to get frightened at the very name of Churchill. The trouble started in Walthamstow when they pelted him with eggs. A big crowd of them marched from Walthamstow right through to Hackney. They wanted their sons and brothers and fathers out of the army. They didn't want no more of the bloody war. They thought he wanted to have a go at Russia.

When I'm looking at the television I sometimes says to myself that my sympathies are with the Conservatives, that I'm a Conservative at heart. But I don't vote for the Conservatives. I've never voted for the Conservatives. They usually win anyway. The Conservative party is not made out of ordinary people. It's made up of people from the top. It always has been and it always will be. They're the leaders of this country, the people who've got most influence. And they are helped by the same class of people in other countries. The same breed. They stick to each other like glue. Look at what they did to Enoch Powell. A brilliant man but they chucked him out. Heath will go the same way. They've got that brilliant intelligence, but they had the Conservative party to contend with. That's what has brought the Socialists down too, money and wealth. They know what they're doing but they always fight short of going for the top people in the Conservative party. People you very rarely hear about, but doing all the underwork. Even in this day and age they've still got thousands and thousands of acres for one man while in London we have people homeless, standing outside the Savoy to keep warm. In 1911 millions of people were singing 'God gave the land to the people', but they still haven't got it and I don't think they ever will. There are more millionaires now in this country than ever before in history.

I remember the governors of the prisons. They looked at you as though you didn't exist – you were just a number or a nuisance. They had you crop your head to look inhuman. Some of the judges are the same. Look at this case there's just been in the papers. A man from Eton – some sort of major in the army – batters a bank clerk round the head, steals £17,000 and he's let off by the judge. Probably one was fag to the other. Or they come from the same families. Or they was in the same regiment. That's a glaring example of what Conservatism means. They stick together. Tyranny can reign supreme behind a veil of silence.

They say the nation has become lazy, and it's the truth. Without the labourers from Ireland we would not have any roadways. Ireland has the greatest and most valuable export in the world: human labour, which could be making their country a paradise. They've driven them out because there's no work for them and now they've driven them here. Every turning you go where there's drains being put in, it's the Irishman doing it. I was talking to one yesterday. Freezing cold it was. He said, 'I'm trying to find a pipe.' So I told him a little story. Couple of weeks back I was walking down that turning when I saw an old lady – totally blind. I was talking to her and said, 'Be careful how you go.' She told me she had had a nasty fall and said, 'I was lying there, and those lovely coloured people rushed over, and they were so kind and helpful to me, and took me right home.' And I looked at her, and I thought to myself shall I disillusion her? Because there's no coloured people round there: they were Irishmen, she thought they were coloured people by their talk.

The people I feel sorry for are the West Indians. We sold their children into slavery. That's how these big estates got into being, and where they got their money. I read a lot of books about the Slave Trade. To me, it's one of the most ghastly stories in the history of mankind. It was worse than the cannibals. The clever ones said, 'Don't eat them, make them work.'

The ideas I got of politics came not from other people's opinions but my own. The ordinary working man wasn't much interested in politics. He just knocked his half-pints back and stood it. He wouldn't fight for his rights.

Dickens made a great impression on me. I read him first in 1902 when I was doing my time. The first one was *Oliver Twist*, and the one with Sydney Carton, *Tale of Two Cities*. and *Dombey* – his great pride was that his son should be a somebody in the City.

The book which influenced me more than any other was Gibbon's *Decline and Fall of the Roman Empire*. I read that when I was doing time in Dartmoor. It turned me against all religion. It's such a varied book – seven or eleven volumes. Once I saw a woman in a wheelchair and she said she was bored, she had nothing to do. And I said to her, 'I'll tell you what you should do, you should read Gibbon's *Decline and Fall of the Roman Empire*.' And she told me that she'd already read it three times, it was her favourite book.

Another book which made a big impression on me was *Les Miserables* by Victor Hugo. The two chief characters in the story are Jean Valjean, the ex-convict, who tried to become a worthy citizen, and police inspector Javert, who considered it to be his duty to send Jean Valjean back to prison and in pursuit of this object used every trick however illegal and wicked to accomplish this purpose.

My brother joined the Blackshirts. And his children belonged to it, they wore black shirts, dark glasses and all. They classed the Jews and Reds as one. But his condemnation of the Jews didn't reach into business: he was a wardrobe dealer and he used to sell his clothes in the Jewish market at Petticoat Lane. He treated the Jewish buyers as if he'd known them all his life. The Blackshirts had a strong mob in Hoxton. They had women and all belonging to it, lots of women and girls used to march with the band. I wasn't interested in it then. I had to get my living, I didn't want to get involved. And at that time I was mixing with the people out of Aldgate, who were Jews. I had Jewish friends. I was involved in their quarrels: them and their tailors were at loggerheads. In the racing business I went with the Jews, protecting them against the Darby Sabini mob. Hymie Davis paid me to take a mob down to Kemp Town – he was frightened the Italians were going to take his pitch. They thought a lot of me down in Aldgate. My brother-in-law was dead against the Blackshirts. He was an ordinary working chap, a bus driver, and he was dead against it – my sister Harriet's husband, Tommy.

I would never have belonged to the Mosley people. I mean its daft to set about somebody for nothing. But I did give them a hand after the war, when they were holding their meetings in Dalston, at Ridley Road Market. I think the reason was this. I was a married man with a family growing up, and I didn't want to get mixed up with crooked people. But I wanted to get out of myself. There was that urge of excitement – I couldn't sit at home all the time, and so I used to go down there. To me that part of my life was taking the part of criminal activities. I was born to be involved in something.

The people in the special branch couldn't understand it. One of them – he was next to the top governor of the local special branch – he took me for a drink one day and said, 'I can't place you, why do you mix with them? Are you getting wages?' I said, 'No, I come here for a bit of excitement.' He said, 'You know what could happen.' I said, 'All them short-hand writers, why do you keep them writing down everything, all the tripe they keep shouting out. It makes them feel they're important.' He said, 'It gives them practice. But do you know during the war, we had the greatest difficulty in stopping policemen joining the fascists. We had to threaten to dismiss them if they were seen talking to them.' I said, 'I'm not surprised because if they've not the experience you and I have had, you might stand there and think they were the saviours of the country.'

The Mosley crowd made a sort of hero of me. They used to call me 'uncle'. There was a sort of nucleus in Bethnal Green. They used to meet at the 'Salmon and Ball'. They were fervent admirers of Mosley. They'd sell the Union movement papers of a Sunday, go all round the stalls. It was like a church to them. I had three nephews, my brother's boys, George's boys, who were members of it. They used to call me 'uncle' and the result was I was 'uncle' to everybody. Mosley himself finished by calling me 'uncle'. I walked along the other day to a butcher's shop and the butcher said, 'Hallo, uncle.' He was a Mosley man. It was a sort of password. Mosley was an intelligent man, but he was very aloof, you could see it was just a part of his trying to get further on. Intelligent, very intelligent. Enoch Powell will finish off like him, he's also a very brilliant man. Last time I saw Mosley I had a drink with him in the Bethnal Green Road.

Flockhart, Alf Flockhart,[12] he was the chap in charge of the London area. Don't know where he come from, but he was a pretty shrewd customer. But like everybody he'd got a weak spot, and that was he was a homosexual. He got time for it, two years, and Mosley turned him out of the movement. He used to enlist all these young boys for the band. At the same time I suppose he had them for his own purposes. He wouldn't have anything to do with me, he was a bit scared of me. He knew I was a dangerous chap from his point of view, that if I spotted him he would have been for it. He was the organiser. He had an office in Vauxhall Bridge Road, where they used to print the paper. Jeffrey Hamm was a good speaker.[13] He was the best educated bloke of the lot of them in regard to speaking. He was a select sort of chap, tall, he could speak all right, none of this shouting and raving. The others used to march up and down with this cry: 'The Yids, the Yids, we've got to get rid of the Yids.' Or sometimes it was the Reds.

One Sunday night there was a big smash-up and I got arrested. I saw the leaders of the Reds and the Jewish chaps, all the real tearaways, and I heard 'em say what they were going to do up at Ridley Road. So I went to one of the inspectors of the Special Branch. I said, 'You'd better get some more men up, you know they'll smash the meeting up.' They had plenty of police there but a fight broke out and one young fellow came up behind me and hit me in the face. I turned round quick and booted him, but a couple of young policemen got hold of me and put me in the van. Good tally of lads they took in that night on both sides, but mostly they were the Jewish chaps, the opposition. Dalston Lane police station was full of chaps they'd taken in. Southwaite, the superintendent in charge of the division, came in and I said, 'Excuse me, can I have a word with you?' I wanted to tell him who I was, that I was working with the Special Branch. But he said, 'You in custody?' I said, 'Yes.' 'Well, I can't talk to you. It's a police regulation.' Afterwards he said he was sorry. 'I wish you had told me,' he said, 'you've made me look a bloody idiot.' The police did what they could. The young policeman who arrested me, they told him to go back to the station, he wasn't wanted, and in court a police officer said, 'Mr Harding was trying to help the forces.' But the magistrate said, 'You've pleaded guilty, you'll have to pay the fine, 40s.'

I can see now, that if things go right, there will never be another war. Because as Mosley used to say at his meetings – nobody used to understand what he was talking about, but he was right – we must join Europe. And now we've got 400 million people, the most intelligent intellectual people in the world, against Russia. They're the only country in the world that could start a war. They say now we're in the Common Market the price of potatoes and turnips and all the rest will go up. I say, 'I don't care if I have to pay a pound for a potato if my grandchildren are going to grow up in a world that'll be free from the nuclear bomb. As long as I know that we are protected, that Germany is our friend, there will never be another war.' We shouldn't fight Russia. Let them be what they want to be. But today they are spending thousands of millions of pounds to increase the deadly power of nuclear warfare. It's a pity the scientist who first discovered the possibilities of nuclear power didn't blow himself to smithereens. I once saw a picture of the dropping of the atomic bomb. It's always been on my mind, there were those Japanese children, at 12 o'clock noon, just like our children, going to school in their blue overalls. And they tell me that today there's still people who die from the effects of it. If I'd been the man that dropped the bomb I would have blown my brains out. Innocent children, what were they brought into the world for, to be murdered like that? Years ago they weren't as wicked as that. I think we've grown wickeder. I've seen some brutal things done by ordinary people. I've seen people battered to death with an axe. I've seen prison warders stripping a man and kicking him about and I've thought to myself, 'Cor blimey, they're not human.'

I was talking to some people at the door the other day, religious people, terribly well educated people. 'Never be discouraged,' I said, 'because go to any of the great teaching hospitals in London and you'll see the nurses there: they don't walk, they're always running, to do the job. They are always lovely and they are the future mothers of England.' Not the bloody people you see on television with their breasts all showing. My Lenny he turns it off, he says, 'You don't want to look at that.' None of the nurses smoke and none of them drink. My eldest grandchild, she's sixteen. She wants to be a nurse and my mind goes back to when she was in hospital, about five or six years ago. There were coloured nurses in there and they gave her something. I said, 'Who gave you that Diane?' She said, 'The nurse with the pink frock.' Not the coloured nurse, the nurse with the pink frock. Now to her – people really can't understand it – she wasn't coloured, she was a nurse, a lovely nurse. To her, Jews, Germans don't exist. They're just ordinary human beings. And we are. I don't care if a man's Irish or Scotch, he's just an ordinary person. That's my idea of politics. To me they're all just ordinary people only they speak a different language. Nobody has any say about where they were going to be born. Why should anybody, Americans, English or German, pat themselves on the back and think they are more super than anybody else. They had nothing to do with it did they?

About religion I think this: that we've still got a great deal to learn about ourselves and the world we live in. When you think of those Jewish rabbis thousands of years ago, studying the Bible and giving their idea of how the world came into existence, well they're still guessing, like they did thousands of years ago, the meaning of it all. If you go into any Jewish restaurant in the East End of London you'll see them talking about it, like they did in the Warsaw Restaurant when Steinie Morrison was there. Maybe in thousands of years to come we will have some idea, but who knows. Here we have vast planets and we don't know whether they're populated or not. We don't know whether there are other forms of life. I don't believe Darwin's theory at all. The other day I bought some chicken for the dog – they've got all those things, the entrails and that, and they're the same as those of a human being but they're not the same. But then you think of the ants. They've got intelligence. They can build cities and yet they're no bigger than a pin's head. However did nature pack all the different things which constitute a living cell into a small body like that? If you study them so much you say, how are we going to fathom the mystery of life, what's going to be the end of it? Who's got any bloody idea? Only guesswork. Darwin's theory of evolution is just a bloody load of tripe. A bit of protoplasm was washed up on the sea, a little bit of jelly, and by constantly running he made himself legs. Darwin must have looked at cows and the horned animals and said, 'They must have got their horns by bashing their head against a wall.' Who knows? Do you think we'll ever know? I don't. Although a hundred years ago if anyone told you that you'd be able to press a button and you would hear marvellous music from the Royal Albert Hall in your own room, just by having a piece of wire, we wouldn't have believed it, would we? So anything is possible.

Now the world when I was a child when I lived in the East End of London was a much happier world than it is today, do you know that? The people who come here, they all say the same thing. I say to them, 'But you're better off today than you were. No fear of starvation.' They say, 'We miss the friendship of the East End, of streets where everybody was neighbourly.' There was always someone knocking at the door to help you. Today your neighbours don't want to know you.

The people round here are just ordinary working-class people who have got on. But they act as if they were lords of the land. They'll never let on that they came from Bethnal Green or Hoxton. Next door from here there are some people who have bought a house. I asked the man, 'What part of the world do you come from?' He said, 'Walthamstow.' I looked at him and I thought, 'You don't sound like Walthamstow to me.' His wife told me the other day she comes from Hoxton. Now why is she afraid to say he comes from Hoxton? He's got a house and a nice big garden now but he would possibly have been like I was once, with one room for the family to sleep in. But now he's made a step up in the world he doesn't want to know.

A glossary of underworld talk

Bag-snatcher	Thief who specialised in ladies handbags.
Barney	Fight.
Beak	Magistrate. A book-learning word, used by news-papermen. 'The old boy on the bench.' Mostly they are for the police, but not always.
Blag	To seize. Another word for snatch.
Bogy	Plain-clothes policeman. Detective.
Brass nail	Prostitute. The girls had the cheek of the devil. The better bred they were the worse the language. I knew a lot of the girls down Spitalfields. I used to treat them with respect.
Bride	Prostitute.
Broad mob	The three-card mob.
Broad-player	Card-shaper
Broads	The three-card trick.
Cane	Jemmy. 'Have you got your cane?' 'Have you got your stick?'
Carpet	A sentence of three months. 'You'll get a carpet for it.'
Case	Brothel. 'I went case last night.' If a chap turned up late you would say, 'What, were you case last night?'
Caser	5 shillings – 25 new pence.
Chiv	Knife. They call it a needle now. Covers the lot up to a carving. I detested having anyone with me having a knife in his pocket. The Darby Sabini gang had these long, thin, daggers. They cut people about but it was more to frighten them. They never done much damage.
Croaker	Doctor.
'Crown and Anchor'	A kind of roulette played with a board and counters. Not a cheating game, but a real game of chance.
Cosh	Iron bar, a loaded stick with lead poured into it.

Not a very dangerous weapon. It takes a lot to kill a man with a cosh. Umbrellas are more dangerous. You can kill a man with an umbrella quite easy. You don't get many murder cases with a cosh. It had a flat surface. A razor blade or a sharp little knife do more damage. The only thing a cosh is any good for is in your own home, to defend yourself.

Dabble	Stolen property.
Deaner	Shilling – 5 new pence.
A doubler	A bent policeman who will cop your money and do you at the same time.
The drag	The Black Maria. Prison van. 'The bleeding drag's a long time coming,' you might say when you were waiting in the cells to be taken to prison.
Dropsy	Money.
Flute	Policeman's whistle. A wonderful thing for them. Better than any telephone. They would get assistance in no time when they blew it. They used to sell police whistles at the corner of Artillery Lane, I don't know where they got them.
Gonnoff	Jewish term for a thief. As with Moishe the Gonnoff, who specialised in watch-snatching. Moishe was a nice fellow. He didn't believe in violence. When the Jews saw him they would say 'Mein Zage' – my watch.
Grass	A police informer.
Groin	Ring.
Iron hoof	Pouf = homosexual.
Jacks alive	Fiver.
Joe	Prison. We say 'Done any Joe?' The police use the same word.
Jug	Prison. They used it in Bill Sykes's time. We still use it today.
Kettle	Pocket watch.
Lagging	A sentence of three years and over, penal servitude.
The law	Police. Cockney, not underworld talk. Used by straight fellows.
Lifer	Life sentence. 'If you're not careful they'll throw away the key' – i.e. you are in jail for ever.
Mugs	Straight fellows.
Nick	Police station.
Nicker	Pound – 100 new pence.
Palled-in	Living with a woman.

Peter	Safe. Cell.
Pieman	Pitch and Toss. All of One-eyed Charlie's lot played that. It was a crooked game. You could skin a man at that. You toss up two halfpennies – but they used to slip in a double-headed halfpenny. Soldered it on. Surprising thing how much money you had on the ground. And when there was a lot down they would slip in a double-headed coin.
Pinched	Arrested.
Pit	Wallet. 'There's more money in the pit, who wants to be a miner.'
Poge	Lady's purse.
Ponce	English name for a man who lived off immoral earnings.
Potty house	Madhouse. There were a lot of them at Epsom which had more mental hospitals than any other town in England.
Razor	The old cut-throat, open razor.
Ready eye	To plan.
Rent	Protection money.
Rozzer	Ordinary policeman. Copper.
Runner	Bookie's runner. The chap that fetches the prices up.
Screwsman	Burglar.
The Scrubs	Wormwood Scrubs prison
Shooter	Gun. You could buy them up in Wardour Street or down the Highway. It was very hard to get hold of a gun, but not illegal. I liked guns myself. I've been three times committed at the Old Bailey for shooting with them though never sentenced.
Shoot-flier	A snatcher. The one who grabs a man's watch and chain. Or his wallet.
Shundicknick	Jewish name for a man who lived off immoral earnings.
Sixer	A six-months sentence.
Smoke	A cigarette.
Sneak thief	They went out in pairs, robbing tills, gas-meters. Today they are pretty skilled – they do the supermarkets. Then there was only a few bob in it. Wally Shepherd from the Nichol was one.
Snide	Counterfeit.
Spinning Jinny	Roulette table, also known as 'the Tables'. They had them in the spielers, fitted underneath and raised so it could be stopped. No punter could win

	with this. The mobs had a way of fixing it so that they could stop the board.
Spieler	A place where they gamble. Had to be a quiet place off the main road. In the 1900s there were a lot of them off the Commercial Road where the Russian Jews were. They were mostly off Commercial Road and Aldgate because that's where the money was. The Jews were natural gamblers. The only crooked spielers was where Faro was played.
Squirter	An ordinary pistol. 'Be careful, he's got a squirter.'
Steamer	Mug, fool.
Stick	Policeman's truncheon.
Stir	Prison. 'Done much stir?'
Stook/stuke	A silk handkerchief.
Straight bogy	A crooked policeman (i.e. one who works with crooks).
Straighten up	To bribe. 'You've got to pay the police their wages' – you have to give them a bit of dropsy.
Stretch	A sentence of twelve months.
Tackle	Watch–chain.
Tapper	A cadger.
Tea-leaf	Thief. Different from a snatcher who is a bloody hooligan. A tea–leaf treats his victim very kindly. Doesn't let him know he's been robbed. Wherever a tea–leaf goes he finds something to take.
Top man	Police superintendent. Underworld king.
Topped	Hanged.
Twirl	Warder.
Under the Act	A sentence of twelve months under the Habitual Criminal Act. My own first conviction was under this Act. They didn't have to prove anything against you – only that you were a suspected person who was acting suspiciously. Obsolete in law though it still goes on.
Using the glass	Using broken glass in a fight. It was a much more sensible way to fight than carrying a weapon because you could make out it wasn't planned.
Van-dragger	A man or boy that steals from vans. Only railway vans had guards behind. But in the City van-draggers had to be smart because they had plain-clothes police specially looking out for them.
The Ville	Pentonville prison. 'Have you been away?' (i.e. to a big convict establishment). 'No, I've only been to the Ville.'

Whizzer	A pickpocket, pure and simple. He wouldn't take anything else.
'Working with the bogies'	Grassing.

Notes

Throughout the Notes, place of publication of works cited is London unless otherwise stated.

Chapter 1   Inside the Jago

1 According to an estimate made by the London County Council in 1896, the population of the 'Nichol' was 5,700. This referred to the area cleared and redeveloped by the LCC. It was bounded on the north by Virginia Road, on the east by Mount Street, to the south by Old Nichol Street, and to the west by Boundary Street. It did not take account of Church Street (formerly Red Church Street), commonly regarded as the high street of the Nichol. Greater London Record Office, *A Description of the Boundary Street Scheme. . .*, 1896.

2 *Ibid.*, p. 5. 'In Old Nichol Street alone, there dwelt at one time no fewer than sixty-four ticket-of-leave men.' The 'evil reputation' of the Nichol owed a great deal to Arthur Morrison's fictionalised account of it in *A Child of the Jago*, and to the sensational articles and appeals of Father Jay, the slum priest from whom Morrison drew his information. The figure of 'sixty-four ticket-of-leave men', for instance, quoted with such confidence in the LCC report, seems to have been taken from Father Jay (cf. 'The English Barbarian, his Haunts, his Homes, his Habits,' *New Budget*, 22 August 1895). Later writing on the East End has amplified such claims. For typical statements, cf. Walter Besant, *East London*, 1903, p. 329. ('the place consisting of a dozen miserable streets, was of the vilest kind'); Chaim Bermant, *Point of Arrival*, 1975, p. 177 ('the Old Nichol, home of a notorious pack of cut-throats known as the Old Nichol gang'). For some earlier examples of the vilification of the Nichol, cf. Raphael Samuel, *East End Underworld*, vol. I, forthcoming.

3 The Nichol Street Ragged School was opened in Turville Street in 1836 by Jonathan Duthoit, a silk merchant of Huguenot descent. It actually preceded – along with eleven other London schools – the formation of Lord Shaftesbury's Ragged School

Union in 1844. The present buildings, untouched by the Boundary Street clearance, were opened in 1866. The school's activities were later absorbed by the London School Board, but it continued as a Sunday school and mission centre until 1939 when a Dangerous Structures Order closed it. The building is now used as a youth club. Details of the school will be found in the Ragged Schools Union *Annual Reports*, 1845–60 and Ragged Schools Union, *Quarterly Record*, 1887, pp. 24–9. For the closure, Shaftesbury Society Minute Book, 17 February 1939. For some accounts of the Ragged School Movement (designed 'to convert incipient criminals to Christianity'), C. J. Montague, *Sixty Years in Waifdom*, 1904; Kathleen Heasman, *Evangelicals in Action*, 1962, ch. 5. Henry Mayhew, an early critic of the Ragged Schools, produced figures to suggest that the schools *increased* the incidence of juvenile crime. The controversy this produced is discussed in Eileen Yeo and E. P. Thompson, *The Unknown Mayhew*, London, 1971, pp. 32–4.

4 Established by two deaconesses of the Church of England who came to Bethnal Green during the cholera epidemic of 1866. A home was opened in 1871 and in 1871 the Mildmay Trust was established to run it. In 1877 a warehouse in Turville Street was converted into a thirty-bed hospital. This was replaced by a purpose-built hospital – the present Mildmay – in 1892. For an account of it, see Phyllis Thompson, *No Bronze Statue, a Living Documentary of the Mildmay Mission Hospital in the East End of London*, 1972. A vivid, if moralistic, account of the Mildmay's educational and medical work is given by the Countess of Tankerville in her pamphlet *A Bright Spot in Outcast London*, 1884. Medical work was organised around home visiting which was seen as a way of getting the deaconesses into the people's homes to instil habits of cleanliness and godliness at the same time as distributing tickets for beef tea, groceries, milk, bandages and dressings. The mission's school had difficulties in coping with the 'Ishmaelite nature' of the boys attending it: 'When the teacher knelt for prayer they would make unearthly groans, or repeat sentences which they had heard at the penny theatre, or perhaps the low rhymes of some infidel author', *A Bright Spot*, p. 4.

5 Originally Nichol Street School, opened by the London School Board in 1875. It later became part of Rochelle Street Schools after the London School Board added a mixed Junior department to the north in 1899. It was known as Rochelle Street Council School from 1904. More recently it has been a depot for Tower Hamlets Social Service Department.

6   According to Arthur Harding, the police station was too close to the Nichol for comfort and had to be moved to Bethnal Green Road.

7   Rev. A. Osborne Jay (1857?–1945), vicar of Holy Trinity 1886–1921. Father Jay, an Anglican, began his ministry in the Nichol with a chapel in a loft over a row of stables. This was followed by a purpose-built club room, gymnasium, lodging house and (on the first floor of the premises) a small church. Jay was a great publicist for his activities, accompanying his appeals with lurid cameos of slum life, and he is credited with great influence in helping to promote the Boundary Street clearance. He cultivated friendly relations with his parishioners while at the same time giving them a bad reputation with the outside world: in 1896 he was propounding a 'new scheme' for sending the submerged class to penal settlements (cf. *London*, 12 March 1896). Arthur Morrison's *Child of the Jago*, dedicated to Father Jay, gives a fictionalised (and heroic) portrait of him as Father Sturt. For another account of him at this time, Arthur Mee, 'A Transformation in Slumland, the remarkable story of a London clergyman', *Temple Magazine*, vol. 21, no. 181, 1898, pp. 449–54. Father Jay's own writings on the Nichol are *Life in Darkest London, a Hint to General Booth*, 1891, and *The Social Problem, its Possible Solution*, 1893. There is a short essay on Jay together with an account of his father, in Hall Caine, *Father and Son: a Study in Heredity*, 1914?.

8   For an account of Macpherson's dispensary, see Annie Macpherson, *The Little Matchbox-Makers*, 1870

9   Newcastle Street Board School, built 1875. It became Virginia Road Board School in 1899 and Virginia Road Council School in 1904.

10 The seat of Sir Frederick Graham, two miles outside Longtown near Carlisle. The robbery occurred in 1885 when four men were disturbed making off with diamonds belonging to Lady Graham. In their attempt to escape they shot and killed one police officer, inflicted gun-shot wounds on two others, and knocked a fourth unconscious. John Martin, a bookie's runner – already wanted for the murder of a police inspector at Romford – and Anthony Rudge, a dog trainer, were later arrested at Carlisle by a gang of twenty railwaymen armed with sticks. James Baker, a greengrocer with a shop at No. 126 Montague Street, Bethnal Green, escaped but was picked up at Lancaster trying to board a London express, and returned to Carlisle where police had difficulty controlling a crowd out for his blood. All three were subsequently hanged. Later a fourth man, James Francis Baker,

was arrested and charged (*The Times* 7 and 8 May 1886) but police witnesses failed to identify him and he was released. See *Illustrated Police News*, 7, 14, 21 and 28 November 1885. Soon after the crime was committed, William Baker was picked up by the police in Manchester (*The Times*, 3 November 1885). This Baker, who had stolen the Duchess of Montrose's jewels at Newcastle some five of six years previously, was discharged when police witnesses failed to identify him.

11 Most of it was blacked out by the back of Jeremiah Rotherham's warehouses. Strictly speaking mention should be made of a public house, the 'Ship and Blue Ball', at No. 13 and a fluctuating number of other small businesses. In 1890 there was another pub, the 'Old Ship,' at No. 51 and a cowkeeper at No. 41 on the west side of the street. In 1905 a chandlers' shop is listed. In 1890 a saw-mill is listed at No. 24 on the Nichol side of the street; a beer retailer at No. 26; a baker at No. 28; another beer retailer at No. 46; the tinplate works of James Keeve & Son at No. 52; and a timber-merchant at No. 80. Source: *Post Office Directories*, 1890 and 1905.

12 There is no record of Aunt Liza's shop in the street directories or in the working papers of the Boundary Street clearance scheme at the Greater London Record Office. No rating books survive for the years 1878 and 1900 so it is not possible to check its putative address.

13 This may have been the 'Portobello' pub.

14 Turk Street was the upper part of Brick Lane. Its name was changed to Brick Lane in 1884. There is an autobiographical recollection of it in George Acorn, *One of the Multitude*, 1911.

15 Mrs Susan Morgan is listed as a wardrobe dealer at No. 223 in *Kelly's London Directory* from 1909 to 1924. A Henry Morgan appears for the years 1905–8.

16 The directories list James Julier as fried fish shop at No. 19 from 1890 to 1896. No. 19 is not listed as a business before 1890.

17 Strictly speaking four doors up at No. 27 – White Bros, lath and timber yard, who traded at this address until 1911 when they were replaced by a moulding manufacturer and then a number of Jewish timber-merchants. The firm can be traced back to 1831 in the London directories.

18 The *Star* (1888–1960), a London evening paper founded by T. P. O'Connor. Together with the *Sun* (1893–1906) it capitalised on the success of W. T. Stead's sensational *Pall Mall Gazette*, which had been started five years before, setting the seal of success on the 'new journalism'. See E. A. Smith, *A History of the Press*, 1970, p. 55 and A. J. Lee, *The Origins of the Popular Press in*

England 1855–1914, 1976, chs 5 and 6. The *Star* kept up a tradition of liberal—radical journalism through the inter-war period, lasting till 1960, when, together with its sister paper the *News Chronicle*, it was bought by the *Daily Mail* and suppressed. It is no accident that the halfpenny evening papers (*Star*, *Evening News*, *Sun* and *Echo*) were also sporting newspapers. Their success was closely connected with the rise of street betting.

19 Not listed in *Kelly's London Directory*.

20 Listed for the years 1897–1907 under the name of Mrs Sarah Burdett – probably because the husband was in gaol.

21 Listed in *Kelly's London Directories* as George Clamtree, dining rooms. The business ran in Clamtree's name from around 1856 until 1906.

22 In *Kelly's* this does not appear as the Salvation Army but as the 'League of Charity Mission House'. It occupied Nos 31 and 37 from 1902 to 1914.

23 The market in Shoreditch High Street was overtaken by growing traffic problems and the increased popularity of Hoxton Street market. The tramlines ran close to the stalls. A fierce rearguard action by way of test cases and public meetings was fought by the Costermongers' Union, a body about which little is known but which was active on a local basis in Bethnal Green and perhaps other metropolitan boroughs. For example when in 1902 the council tried to enforce traffic regulations seventy members of the union attended the North London Public Court to demonstrate solidarity and opposition to the prosecution (*Hackney Gazette* 5 February p. 3 and 19 February, p. 3, 1902). In a later incident after the council had attempted to ban Sunday trading after 12.30, 200 costers threatened to seek simultaneous entry to the workhouse, if their forty-year-old privilege was taken away. The Costermongers' Union warned the police there would be trouble if they tried to enforce the ban (*Hackney Gazette*, 11 September 1905, p. 3).

24 London Music Hall (1856–1934), known as Griffin Music Hall and Public House to 1896 and the London Music Hall 1896–1916. This name persisted even when it became the Shoreditch Empire. Reconstructed in 1894 to seat 1,000, it was bought by Jeremiah Rotherham in 1934 and demolished in the next year. For a fuller chronology see Diana Howard, *London Theatres and Music Halls 1850–1950*, 1970, pp. 221–2. According to A. E. Wilson (*East End Entertainment*, 1954, pp. 219–20) it was customary for the stars of the various pantomimes in London to come together for a programme at the 'London'. The theatre styled itself as 'the model music hall'.

25 There is no mention of this pub in the London directories of the
     period.
26 There is no record of the billiard saloon in the directories.
27 Bonnet Box Court was a local name for Hare Alley. There is an
     alley of the same name in roughly the same position on a map of
     1745 in Hackney local archives.
28 Jane Shore (d. 1527?), beautiful and vivacious mistress of
     Edward IV and wife of William Shore, goldsmith in the City of
     London. According to the *Dictionary of National Biography* it
     seems she was involved in one of the conspiracies against Richard
     III who imprisoned her on charges of sorcery. She was then tried
     as a harlot before the Bishop of London. However she was
     pardoned after Richard's solicitor fell in love with her. Later she
     died in poverty. There is no evidence to show that she starved to
     death, or – as the mosaics in the pub suggested – was murdered
     and her body dumped in a ditch. The name Shoreditch ante-
     dates this 'incident', (it never actually occurred) by at least 250
     years.
29 Royal Standard Theatre (1837–1926). Began as the Royal Stan-
     dard Public House and Pleasure Gardens and became in turn the
     'Royal', 'New' and 'National Standard' theatres – with a gap in
     between when it was simply the 'Standard' – before ending up as
     the 'Shoreditch Olympia'. It was burnt down and rebuilt 1866–7
     and remodelled nine years later in 1876. It was not demolished
     until 1940 (Howard, *London Theatres and Music Halls*, pp. 222–4).
     According to Wilson (chs 10 and 11) it went through various
     phases. The first was as a Shakespearean temple also putting on
     Schiller, Beaumont, Fletcher, etc. The second, its great days,
     when it combined sensational melodrama with ambitious light-
     ing effects and mechanical contrivances, e.g. hot-air balloons
     rising from the stage, huge aquatic tanks and realistic life-
     boat rescues. Finally about 1900 it turned to melodramas in
     which 'women of the wickedest type figure . . . [and] attract-
     ing vast local patronage' (Wilson, *East End Entertainment*,
     p. 134).
30 Strictly speaking only two pubs; the 'White Swan' at No. 196 and
     the 'White Hart' at No. 197. The 1900 *Post Office Directory* lists a
     wholesale hat shop at No. 198; a beer retailer at No. 199; a
     scale-makers and rate collector at No. 200; a tobacco manu-
     facturer at No. 201; the 'New National Standard Theatre' at No.
     204; a dining rooms at No. 205; a fruiterer at No. 206; with the
     'George' at No. 207. Contemporary photographs show how
     close to one another these buildings huddled.
31 More likely Italian. *Kelly's* records his name as Hugo Karamelli.

He traded here from 1881 until 1924 when the shop became known as the 'Standard Hat Shop'.
32 Official name, 'Jerusalem Tavern'.

Chapter 2   Relatives

1 To give its full title, Shoreditch Parish Workhouse. Now St Leonard's Hospital.
2 Wilmer Gardens was the single most common address at local police hearings in the years before 1914. A report in which a young man was stabbed in the face with scissors speaks of the 'notorious Wilmer Gardens, where a constable was recently murdered' (*Hackney Gazette*, 22 February 1905, p. 3). If this is a reference to the crime witnessed by Arthur Harding's aunt, the date given needs revising. So bad was its reputation that in 1907 the council wanted to change the name of the gardens (*Gazette*, 24 May 1907, p. 3). A police court case three years earlier (*Gazette*, 13 April 1904, p. 3) illustrates something of its character. In this instance, plain-clothes detectives trailed two women and a man who had been observed shoplifting in Stoke Newington High Street. They were arrested just past the canal bridge at Shoreditch on the return journey. However, as they passed Wilmer Gardens, one of the arrested, Mary Wells, 'called out, and in an instant a rush of 18 or 20 thieves took place, and the officers were mobbed'. Two of the suspects escaped. At the police court hearings Mary Wells claimed police harassment. Later she was discharged although her companions got two to three months (*Gazette*, 22 April 1907, p. 4). James Shuttleworth, known as 'Old Jim the dosshouse king', set up lodging houses and cheap restaurants for down-and-outs at Wilmer House, Wilmer Gardens. On his death in 1908 he left £1,011 (*Hackney Gazette*, 24 June 1908). The chief sanitary inspector to the council reported in 1907 that in one lodging house in Wilmer Gardens 141 men lived in 34 rooms. The rest of the Gardens at this time contained 800 men, women and children in 600 rooms (*Gazette*, 24 May 1907). According to local tradition, a police constable was hanged in Wilmer Gardens when a rope was lowered over his head from one of the houses and the noose pulled tight (Stanley Tongue, Hackney Archivist, recalling a story told to him by his father, November 1977).
3 It has not been possible to identify the date or circumstances of this murder.
4 Known as Waterloo Buildings and built and owned by the Im-

proved Industrial Dwellings Co., 1883 (*Kelly's Post Office Directory*, 1884).

5 Cambridge Music Hall (1864–1936). Also known as the Royal Cambridge Music Hall. Destroyed by fire in 1896 and rebuilt over the next two years in an oriental style. One of its managers, E. V. Page, wrote songs for Nelly Power, James Fawn and Jenny Hill, 'the first queen of the halls' (A. E. Wilson, *East End Entertainment*, 1954, p. 219). Charles Coburn and George Robey played here, and Vesta Victoria and Charlie Chaplin made early appearances there. It was demolished to extend Phillips's tobacco factory (Diana Howard, *London Theatres and Music Halls 1850–1950*, 1970, p. 201).

6 Approach Road is close to Victoria Park in the northerly and more respectable part of Bethnal Green.

7 I can find no reference to this case nor to the drink shop mentioned by Arthur Harding in Chapter 1.

8 Mead Street did not join Mount Street. Instead it joined Christopher Place which led into Mount Street via Fournier Street. The shop was probably at the junction of Fournier and Mount Streets where the narrow strip of development created by Christopher Place would have allowed criminals to escape into the Nichol.

9 This is not the correct name.

10 At the Cambridge Heath Road end of Bethnal Green Road.

11 Marie Lloyd (1870–1922), best known and best loved figure in the history of English music hall. Born in Plumber Street, Hoxton, daughter of an artificial flower-maker and eldest of nine children, she began her meteoric rise in a small theatre attached to a pub in Commercial Road, where her father worked as a part-time waiter. A defiant cockney, she maintained her back-streets irreverence and contempt for respectability in face of commercial success. For some attractive accounts of her life and character, see Naomi Jacobs, *Our Marie*, 1936; Daniel Farson, *Marie Lloyd and Music Hall*, 1972.

12 Alec Hurley (1870–1913) married Marie Lloyd in 1907. He was a cockney coster singer in the tradition of Gus Elen and Albert Chevalier. He was popular but, unlike his wife, never quite top of the bill. Universally liked, he was remembered as a homely, self-effacing, humorous and kindly man who shared his wife's passion for horse-racing (Farson, *Marie Lloyd*, pp. 80–1). Though the marriage – Marie's second – collapsed within five years, Hurley is quoted as saying, 'It was a real love-match. I idolized her' (Farson, p. 85). He died three years later of double pneumonia exacerbated by drink and the grind of working in

provincial towns, whilst his ex-wife, about to enter into a third and disastrous marriage to an Irish jockey, Bernard Leech, was on an American tour. A sympathetic account of Marie Lloyd and Hurley is found in Leslie Bell, *Bella of Blackfrairs*, 1961, pp. 102–4 and pp. 113–15.

13 Real name the 'Sugar Loaf'. Arthur does not mention that Jack Harding, who mixed with Marie Lloyd and Alec Hurley, was president of the West Ham Football club the year the team took part in the first Cup Final.

14 The 'Paragon,' Mile End Road (1848–1933). Started out as the 'Eagle' public house and became in succession 'Lusby's Summer and Winter Gardens', 'Lusby's Music Hall', 'Paragon Music Hall' and the 'Mile End Empire'. It was rebuilt in 1885 and demolished in the 1930s to make way for a cinema (Howard, *London Theatres and Music Halls*, pp. 151–2). Charlie Chaplin appeared here in Fred Karno's Mumming Birds (Wilson, *East End Entertainment*, p. 219).

15 Pavilion Theatre, Whitechapel Road (1828–1934), known at the height of its fame in the 1870s as 'The Drury Lane of the East'. Its seating capacity after its reconstruction due to a fire in 1856 was larger than that of Covent Garden Opera House (Wilson, *East End Entertainment*, p. 80) and its 70-foot stage was only exceeded by La Scala in Milan (Farson, *Marie Lloyd*, p. 58). Joe Lyons sold sketches and song sheets at the entrance before opening a small tea shop close by. Later he fell in love with the daughter of the general manager of the theatre who disapproved of the match because Lyons had no prospects. Until 1900 the theatre was one of the most cosmopolitan in London. After 1900 its fortunes dropped, but they were later revived when it became East London's leading Yiddish theatre. Among the actors and actresses from Poland and America who appeared there in this phase of its existence were Paul Muni, Jacob and Celia Adler, Joseph Kessler and Maurice Moscovitch.

16 Marie Courtenay (188?–1967), stage name Marie Lloyd Jr – Marie's only daughter by her first husband Percy Courtenay, a work-shy punter with an addiction to drink, other women and his wife's money (Farson, *Marie Lloyd*, pp. 41–2). Her life on the stage was spent mostly doing imitations of her mother. Farson, whose account is sympathetic, comments that this may have deprived her of the chance to achieve fame in her own right (p. 168).

Chapter 3   Home life

1 Matches were manufactured by Bryant and May in their factory at Bow Common. Matchbox-making, however, was a home industry, in which there were more people employed than at the factory itself. For an autobiographical recollection of the home matchbox makers in the 1860s, cf. Mrs Layton in Margaret Llewellyn Davies, ed., *Life as We Have Known It*, Virago reprint, 1977. For an instance of the misery of many of the home workers cf. *Hackney Gazette*, 5 February 1904, p. 3: inquest into the death of Sarah Ann Young of New Inn Broadway, Shoreditch High Street – a matchbox maker who worked with her daughter, the mother of three children aged 7, 10 and 12. 'We earned 1s 3¾d when we had made seven gross of match boxes – (Sensation). We both worked at home. We occupy two rooms, the rent of which is 4s 6d per week. For some work we received 2¼d per gross and for other boxes we got only 2d per gross, having to find our own paste etc.' The witness could make one gross of boxes in an hour. The total earnings of herself and mother were about 6s 6d per week. 'But what did you live on? – About 2s altogether. You and your mother and three children could not live on 2s per week? – We had to.' Cause of death was recorded as exhaustion resulting from disease and lack of food. The coroner gave the witness 10s from the poor box and promised to forward any other sums received. Often when cases like this appeared in the local press members of the public would send money to the coroner's office or magistrate's court.

2 There is a reference in the *Post Office Directories* to Richard and John Agambar, matchbox makers, at 49 Bacon Street for the years 1892 to 1912. The firm surfaces again as chip-basket makers from 1915 until 1957. Agambar (also Agombor) is an old Bethnal Green name – still current.

3 I.e. the Shaftesbury Society's Ragged School Mission.

4 It is difficult to convey the amount of philanthropic attention and anxiety focused, over a long period, on the Nichol. *The Ragged School Union Quarterly Record*, 1887, p. 72, gives some indication of the scale of relief: 'Nichol Street gave a Tea and Entertainment to 1,675 children at a cost of about £42, Free Breakfasts were supplied for four months on four mornings a week to 180 children, at a cost of 16s per morning. Twice weekly about 100 or more quarts of soup were distributed at a cost of £3 7s 6d per month, the recipients being supplied at about half the cost.' A later example, from the bad winter of 1895, appears in the Managers' Yearly Report for the Rochelle Street schools, a refer-

ence kindly suggested by Mr A. R. Neate, the keeper of the records at GLRO: 'During the winter there have been ample opportunities for feeding the children. Free breakfasts by the Ragged School Union, free soup by Lady Jeune and the School Dinners' Association, and halfpenny dinners by the Rev. Osborne Jay and the Mildmay Deaconess have been supplied.' In addition to this 25-30 boys were taken weekly to Mansford Street baths, Fr Jay organised a flower show for the children, there were summer holidays for 160-200, something called a 'Happy Evenings Association' and a 'well-used' library with a stock of books described as 'good'.

5 The ticket system seems to have been used almost everywhere to relate numbers to the gallons of soup available. See *Hackney Gazette*, 11 January 1905, p. 3. In this instance a Kingland tradesman gave out 25 gallons of free soup and 50 loaves. Various tradesmen and a publican were involved, a ticket system was used and the work co-ordinated by 'sisters of various religious denominations'.

6 There is no mention of Hughes in the *Post Office Directories*.

7 George Jackson, fishmonger, is listed in *Kelly's Post Office Directory* for the years 1892-1943. The name Hare Street was changed to Cheshire Street just before the Second World War.

8 Probably Hugo Karamelli's next to the Standard Theatre.

9 Listed as the Shaftesbury Memorial Hall, built in 1889. It stood on the corner of Gibraltar Walk and was swept away in the 1950s to make way for the local authority housing.

Chapter 4   Out and about

1 See Rose Lowe, *Daddy Burtt's for Dinner: Growing Up in Hoxton between the Wars*, 1976. Although this deals with a later period there is a brief mention of Superintendent Burtt and evocative photographs from the earlier period.

2 Kingsland Road police station – torn down and incorporated in the new Old Street magistrates' court together with old Worship Street police court. Opened 1906. The new building was the subject of witty and sarcastic attacks by one of the magistrates, A. R. Cluer (*Hackney Gazette*, 30 May 1906, p. 3).

3 A photograph of Fr Jay's boxing ring beneath Holy Trinity Church appears in the *New Budget*, 22 August 1895.

4 For a history see Charles Poulsen, *Victoria Park – a Study in the History of East London*, 1976.

5 The Britannia Theatre, High Street, Hoxton (1841-1923) or

'Brit', probably the most theatrically varied and most warmly regarded of the popular theatres in East London. It was founded by Samuel Lane at the back of the Britannia Saloon, which remained its name for nineteen years. The theatre was closed and Lane fined when he put on an unauthorised performance of *Black Ey'd Susan* (A. E. Wilson, *East End Entertainment*, 1954, p. 164). The agitation surrounding the case marked the start of the campaign to abolish the monopoly of the licensed houses. Lane began with variety turns, moving on to plays written by resident dramatists. *Sweeney Todd, or the Demon Barber of Fleet Street* was first performed here in 1847 and Wilson (p. 168) says the first 'real Shakespeare Festival' lasting several months took place at the Britannia during the tercentenary of 1864. Lane's success must have been considerable because he was able to rebuild the theatre in 1858 to seat 3,200. He died in 1871 when his widow, Sara, took over replacing home-made plays with melodramas adapted from West End successes. Often these would be mixed with Shakespeare, variety acts and sketches. However, Mrs Lane is best remembered for her pantomimes. Although these contained significant spectacle and technical effects they also preserved the earlier tradition of harlequinade. Later on, they became integrated with music hall and G. H. Macdermott (previously resident playright and adaptor of *The Mystery of Edwin Drood*), Marie Lloyd, Ada Reeve, Marie Kendall, etc. together with the Lupinos – connections of Mrs Lane by marriage – starred. Wilson mentions Marie Lloyd playing Princess Kristina who 'had the lamp which represented her modesty stolen, and . . . suddenly became a bold and forward-going thing. It can be imagined how well Marie Lloyd expressed that change' (p. 187). On Sarah's death in 1898 the theatre passed to her nephew and his brother, A. C. and W. J. Crauford, respectively. However, its days were over. The decline of melodrama, demands by the LCC for extensive repairs, competition from the cinema and newer halls, and the conservative taste of its Hoxton public multiplied its difficulties. It was one of the first places to show films in London (1899) and during the First World War was bought up by Gaumont. See Diana Howard, *London Theatres and Music Halls 1850–1950*, 1970, pp. 32–3; Wilson, *East End Entertainment*, chs 14 and 15, and the brief sketch by Stanley Tongue in the *Shoreditch Newsletter*, December 1963. There is an excellent biography of the Lanes in Alfred C. Crauford, *Sam and Sallie*, 1933.

6 G. R. Sims. (1847–1922), journalist playwright and author. Sims is best remembered as author of *How the Poor Live* (1898) and *Christmas Day at the Workhouse*.

7 The Melville brothers, Walter and Frederick, sons of Andrew
   Melville, the Birmingham theatre-owner, who took over the
   Standard Theatre when the Douglass regime came to an end in
   1889. They were both playwrights and Walter's melodramas in
   particular were a mainstay in this last popular phase of East End
   theatre. Wilson, *East End Entertainment*, pp. 135–9.

8 There may be a confusion with the Standard Theatre in Shore-
   ditch High Street. Wilson (*East End Entertainment*, p. 134) lists a
   number of Walter Melville's lurid melodramas, e.g. *The Worst
   Woman in London*, *The Female Swindler*, *That Wretch of a Woman*,
   A Disgrace to Her Sex, *The Girl Who Lost Her Character*, *The Girl
   Who Took the Wrong Turning*, *The Girl Who Wrecked his Home*.

9 Wilson, (*East End Entertainment*, p. 179) agrees, 'The Brit, in fact,
   offered a liberal education to the playgoer which the West End
   could never have provided.'

10 Possibly Algernon Syms, who, according to Wilson (*East End
   Entertainment*, p. 177), later became a West End star. He is described as 'always breezy and handsome'. He starred with George
   Bigwood, J. B. Howe, Walter Steadman, Topsy Sinden and Lily
   Elsie in Mrs Lane's historic last Festival in 1898 which marked the
   seventy-six-year-old proprietress's farewell after fifty-five years
   at the Brit (Wilson, pp. 198–9).

11 'One particular idol was Jenny Granger, who had so many fans
   in the East End that when she left the theatre she would be
   escorted down the Mile End Road by a party of Bryant and
   May's match girls' (Wilson, *East End Entertainment*, p. 84).

12 The Variety Theatre, Pitfield Street (1870–1910) was known by a
   number of titles but always reverted to the 'Variety Theatre'.
   According to Diana Howard (*London Theatres and Music Halls*, p.
   247) it 'adjoined and communicated with the public house. The
   back parts of the boxes and gallery were formerly the 1st and 2nd
   floor of the public house, and were added after the original
   construction'. Set up to compete with the Britannia, it achieved
   success under its second owner, George Harwood, who invented
   the 'twice nightly system' known in the musical hall profession
   as 'Trial House' because of the rough treatment meted out to
   artists by the audience. Dan Leno, Jenny Hill and G. H. Macdermott made some of their earliest appearances here. Harwood
   sold the theatre to Gus Leach who some time previously had been
   owner of the Forester's Music Hall, Mile End. After him G. H.
   Macdermott took over, and later Leonard Mortimer who con-
   founded critics by turning social topics of the day such as immigration into drama and drawing packed houses. In the same
   spirit he set up a fund to send local children on holiday and followed

this up by putting on special performances to provide free dinners. The response enabled 5,000 children to be given meals for
one season. After 1910 the 'Variety' became a cinema. It still
stands in Pitfield Street but has been closed up since 1923.
(Undated cutting 'The Varieties Theatre' and information from
a sketch written by Stanley Tongue and available in Hackney
Archives Department.)

13 The Forester's Music Hall, Cambridge Heath Road (1825–1917).
In turn 'Artichoke Public House', 'Forester's Music Hall', 'Royal
Foresters Music Hall', 'New Lyric Music Hall' and 'New Lyric
Theatre'. Both Dan Leno and Little Tich made their first London
appearances here. In accounts of the music hall it is remembered
chiefly for the boisterous and emphatic verdicts of the audience.
Often 'the curtain was rung down on the hapless performer',
(Wilson, *East End Entertainment*, p. 215).

Chapter 5   Totting and busking

1 James Hughes, oil man, traded at No. 60 Church Street from
1895 until 1911. Before that the business belonged to a Thomas
Williams, also oil man, who developed it out of a tallow chandler's. After the first World War its name changes in the directories
to 'oil and colourman's'.

2 Cf. *Hackney Gazette*, 18 July 1904, p. 3: 'One of the lads was
actually on the back of the van, and the others were waiting to
catch the tub [of margarine] when it rolled off. Hillery [the
driver] said that these robberies were frequent and he had not yet
done paying for his last loss.' In other words goods stolen in this
way had to be paid for by the driver. This particular theft
occurred in Kingsland Road. On 30 October 1905 the *Gazette*
reported (p. 3) a Great Eastern Railway van theft case: 'This was
one of the numerous cases of robbery from vans passing through
the warehouse district of St. Luke's and Shoreditch.' Whilst the
carman was making the deliveries, the attention of the van boy
left in charge was distracted by unbuckling the reins. See also
Hackney Gazette, 12 November 1906, p. 4 when a parcel of
jewellery was stolen from a moving brougham by a french
polisher who dashed into Prince's Court, Gibraltar Walk, threw
the parcel into a doorway and escaped into model dwellings
where he was captured. The case could have been taken from
Arthur Morrison's *A Child of the Jago*.

3 There is no reference to this business in the directories.

4 *Royal Commission upon the Duties of the Metropolitan Police*. The

complaints by shopkeepers appear in the verbatim evidence of the Commission, P.P. 1908 (4260) L, p. 479, e.g. Q.21217: 'I have also seen Harding and his gang rob vans, take the goods into doorways, and send small boys to fetch them with barrows.' Q.21243: 'Since Harding and his gang have used Sclater Street they have ruined the street.' Q.21250: 'I have continually seen Harding and his clique molest and rob people of their watches and handbags.' In view of the damage done to Arthur's case by these attacks and the use made of them by Richard Muir, Treasury Counsel, it is not surprising that they should still rankle. Q.21257: '(Muir) Several people, if these statements are true, in your neighbourhood, seem to have a very bad opinion of you? – (Arthur) Each one of them says there have been several robberies, and yet I have been free from prison for nearly three and a half years, and there are honest, straight people yet. I have never been convicted for one offence, and yet they saw me commit so many. That is a very funny thing.'

5 Norfolk Gardens was renamed Dereham Place in 1907. It lies to the north of Bateman's Row.

6 The theatre which was built in 1576 was an octagonal-shaped structure lying just north of what is now New Inn Yard (see W. H. C. Moreton, 'Shakespeare came to Shoreditch', Hackney Local History Library, 1976). It was once the precinct of St John the Baptist, Holywell, and is commemorated by a plaque in Curtain Road. There is also a memorial in St Leonard's Parish Church to actors associated with the theatre as well as to some who were not.

7 Traded in Brick Lane between 1881 and 1919, first close to John Street and later between Hare Street and Bacon Street.

8 I can find no mention of a shop of this description in the street directories of the time.

Chapter 6   Bacon Street and Queen's Buildings

1 For a history of the LCC Boundary Street scheme, see R. Vladimir Steffel, 'Housing for the Working Classes in the East End of London, 1890–1907', Dissertation for Ohio State University Graduate School (copy at Tower Hamlets Local History Library), and R. Vladimir Steffel, 'The Boundary Street Estate, an Example of Urban Development by the London County Council, 1889–1914', *Town Planning Review*, 1976. There is a very full collection of the working papers generated by the various phases of the clearance in the Greater London Record

Office. A contemporary account of the evolution and execution of the scheme is to be found in the LCC's own publication, *The Housing Question in London*, 1900, pp. 190–213 which describes the various housing schemes of the Metropolitan Board of Works and of the LCC from 1855 to 1900 and summarises the acts under which they were carried out.

2 Probably the 'Red Cow'.

3 The timber-yard, Marshalls, was at No. 11. The firm has been listed from 1879 to the present day as saw-mills and timber-merchants. Between 1874 and 1878 it appears as cabinet-maker in Edward Street which occupied roughly the same site as Drysdale Street. In 1895 Drysdale Street, numbering 32 houses, had 21 businesses, 14 to do with wood-working and 10 of these squeezed into Edward Terrace which recalled its previous name.

4 Between Bethnal Green Road and Sclater Street and cutting across Brick Lane almost halfway up its total length, close to Shoreditch tube station.

5 Bacon Street appears in the Booth MSS (drawing on school board, clergy and police records of the 1890s) as being 'all very poor people of casual class & possibly semi-criminal – the houses are closely packed mostly with families unknown – this street is used as a refuge for pickpockets, who, if they get a start of their pursuers, can never be found in these houses.' London School of Economics, Booth MSS, B.47. Emanuel Litvinoff, who was brought up round the corner, describes Bacon Street as being 'squalid even by our standards' (Emanuel Litvinoff, *Journey Through a Small Planet*, 1972, p. 25). Mark Gertler, the painter, was brought up in Bacon Street. His biographer records that No. 8, where he lived, the property of a Mr Skurmick, was, 'not a pleasant place to live. It was one of a terraced row of cheaply built dwellings, mostly of four storeys, with crabbed arched doorways opening on to the street. Above the sullen, badly proportioned windows, projecting courses of brick formed a meaningless decoration. From a narrow frontage the house rambled interminably back for eighty feet – a long thin strip of gloomy rooms – almost entirely surrounded at the sides and back by other houses built directly on to it. The one at the rear was a sawmill, and its noise mingled with that from the twenty-three-track railway only 160 feet away. . . . The people of Bacon Street were put in the category "very poor, chronic want" by a contemporary survey. This applied more to the north side; on the other, where the Gertlers lived, there was in fact a certain rough variety. It was occupied mainly by cabinet-makers, but a fried-fish shop at No. 20, and a rag-and-bone yard at 30, added

their smells to the sharp reek of timber. Between them and No. 8 was the inevitable pub (there were very few blocks in the district without at least one, open twenty hours a day and much frequented). Next door on the other side, at Nos. 4 and 6, a tin-plate worker plied his noisy trade, and next to him on the corner was a workers' coffee room. The street itself lay just to the north of the Great Eastern Railway, which marked the limits of the area occupied by the Jewish community, so that English was heard as well as Yiddish; people with names such as Evans, Meadows, Houghton and Webb lived alongside the Shifferblatts, Lebofskys and Moses' (John Woodeson, *Mark Gertler*, 1972, pp. 34–5).

6 These businesses do not seem to have been listed in the street directories.

7 Charrington, Sells and Dale & Co., enormous coal and coke merchants and importers, established in 1731, who had two head offices, one in Broad Street dealing with sea-borne trade, and another in Gray's Inn Road for coal brought to London by rail. They also had depots at all major city and suburban stations.

8 This is a reference to the notorious Finchley baby-farmer who took in unwanted children for small weekly payments, murdered them and continued to draw the money as if they were alive. She was hanged in 1896.

9 Liptons opened in City Road, on the corner of Cayton Street, in 1896; it was bombed 1940. There was an unsuccessful attempt to unionise the firm before the war, and a successful one in 1917 (Richard Hyman, *The Workers Union*, Oxford, 1971, p. 109).

10 John Clarke, greengrocer, traded on the corner of Roman and Libra Roads from 1896 until around 1930. The business opposite was a corn dealer's belonging to a family called Farnham who are listed here from 1872 to around 1930.

11 Official title 'National Incorporated Association for the Reclamation of Destitute Waif Children', sometimes abbreviated to 'National Waif's Association'. Stepney Causeway lay off Commercial Road to the west of Regent's Canal dock and the entrance to the Grand Union Canal. At this time Barnardo's had about 8,000 children in their care. Stepney Causeway contained the original home opened under the patronage of Lord Shaftesbury in 1870, Her Majesty's Hospital for Sick Children opened in Victoria's Jubilee year and a school called the City Messenger Brigade or Boy Commissionaire Corps. About 400 boys were accommodated in the school (A. E. Williams, *Barnardo of Stepney*, 1953, p. 22). On Dr T. J. Barnardo (1845–1905) see Janet Hitchman, *They Carried the Sword* (1966).

12 Known as the Burdett Dormitory (*Kelly's Post Office Directory*,

1900). It contained about 400 boys. (Williams, *Barnardo of Stepney*, p. 39.)

13 On the north side of Gossett Street between Princes Place and Chambord Street. The pub opposite at No. 18 was the 'Queen's Head'.

Chapter 7   Criminal apprenticeship

1 Pharmaceutical and manufacturing chemists, and wholesale and retail druggists. Their head office was in Lombard Street and they had, and still have, laboratories and a large warehouse in Three Colts Lane off Cambridge Heath Road, close by the Bethnal Green Station of the old Eastern Counties railway.

2 Probably John Burtt and Henry Lewis's horse clothing manufactory – beside the Mission Room and Ragged School in Boot Street. The factory appears in the *Post Office Directory* in 1899 and disappears in 1905. Boot Street lies directly behind Hoxton market.

3 Edwin Atkins, chair manufacturer at 47–55 Church Row, who in 1905 absorbed No. 45 and in 1915 No. 22. Listed for the years 1893 to 1934. By the time they closed they were occupying only one building in Church Row at No. 20. Church Row is now St Matthew's Row.

4 There appears to be no newspaper record of this first court appearance of Arthur Harding.

5 Edwin Woodham, Standard Glass Works, listed as bottle manufacturer at 169 Hanbury Street from 1885 to 1928 or 1929. Previously the firm had been located in Buxton Street, within a stone's throw of Hanbury Street, and at Underwood Street in Mile End.

6 Samuel William Butler, cabinet-maker at this address from 1890 to 1901. Previously the business had been carried on in Charles Street off Curtain Road.

7 Coffee rooms, one door up from Sclater Street at No. 121 and later at No. 119, listed from 1885 to 1945 under the name of Walter Mark and from the middle 1920s Mrs Nancy Ellen Clark (London *Post Office Directories*).

8 W. R. McConnell (1837–1906) a contemporary of Herschell and Russell on the northern circuit and then counsel to the Board of Trade and later Board of Customs. McConnell, who was counsel at the Goncourt Turf Frauds and in the Maybrick case, was a criminal lawyer of great ability and for this reason was regarded as an ideal choice for the County of London Sessions where he

was chairman for the last ten years of his life. His kindheartedness was well known and he was especially lenient towards youthful offenders. He would ask prisoners to tell him 'all the good of yourself' (obituary, *The Times*, 22 December 1906). It is interesting to ask, what would have become of young Arthur Harding had he appeared in court number 1 and not in court number 2 before Loveland Loveland. *The Times* obituary is a striking confirmation of Arthur's memory.

9　Richard Loveland Loveland KC (1841–1923), deputy chairman of the County of London Sessions 1896–1911 and author of various legal treatises.

10　The famous or infamous public house in Limehouse bought by Barnardo in 1873 and converted to a mission hall and coffee palace, the centre of his evangelistic work in the East End. See A. E. Williams, *Barnardo of Stepney*, 1953.

11　A game in which two halfpennies are thrown up on the end of a board and bets taken on the assumption that the coins will not come down the same side together. If this does happen the banker wins. The trick was to palm one of the halfpennies whilst it was being placed on the board by a double-head-coin –increasing the odds in favour of the bank. According to Arthur, a lucrative game and one which is still being played.

12　I have been unable to find any references to Edward Spencer in the local press except for the Vendetta affair for which he served 4½ years. However, he did appear before the 1906 Royal Commission on the Metropolitan Police alleging police brutality in Brick Lane, under the name of Emms. (Emms's and Norrey's cases, pp. 570–647 and pp. 682–98, as well as the main body of the report pp. 357–79.) Spencer gave his address to the Royal Commission as 10 Gibraltar Gardens. After serving out time for his part in the Vendetta Case Spencer joined the Royal Army Service Corps. After discharge he joined the Titanic mob, before falling into petty thieving.

13　Sir Ralph Littler (1885–1908), Chairman of Middlesex Sessions from 1889 to his death, and also from the same year chairman of Middlesex County Council. He is remembered for two achievements. The first is his part in securing and administering Alexandra Park for public use (see Ron Carrington, *Alexandra Park and Palace – a history*, 1975). This is overshadowed by his harsh record as a judge. Frequently criticised in the press, at the time of his death he was involved in libel actions with *Reynolds' Newspaper* and *Vanity Fair*. Old Street prisoners would often ask for their cases to be dealt with in the lower court rather than go before Littler. See exchange in *Hackney Gazette* 21 December

1904, p. 3: 'Elliott caused a smile by asking the Magistrate to send all the charges to the Old Bailey, and not single out the Tottenham case for trial at the Middlesex Sessions. Mr Dickinson (Magistrate): Yes, I quite appreciate your point. You don't want to go before Sir Ralph Littler. Elliott: That's it. (Laughter).' See also *The Times*, 26 October 1908, where Littler refers to criticism in the Commons and in the press of his sentence of three years penal servitude on a young man called Freeman for stealing apples.

14 Brogden and Dessent seemed to have worked as a very successful team and their names crop up in police court cases as if they were twins. William Brogden seems to have been the more interesting of the two and his comments in the courts often show a sociological awareness. He joined the Metropolitan police in 1877, resigned in 1897, but rejoined in the following year. In the twenty-three years he had served up to 1911 he had been guilty of one breach of discipline (making a bet with a bookmaker on behalf of someone else) for which he was reduced to the ranks, and had been commended on 135 occasions (*Report of the Inquiry held by Mr George Cave Esq. E.C.M.P. into the Evidence given by the Police at the Trial of Steinie Morrison*, P.P. 1911 (5627), XXXVIII, p. 6). After the First World War he was thrown out of the police and Arthur remembers him looking after the cabs and spectators' cars outside the Blackfriars' boxing ring run by Bella and Dick Burge. 'Brogden came through to go to the lavatories and looked at me. I was sorry to see him come down to that and said nothing. I never took the rise.' Arthur remembers Harry Dessent as 'a thin man who walked with head cocked over to one side, a Sexton Blake . . . the detective all over.' The two men lived close by Wensley and were with him when Steinie Morrison was arrested in Fieldgate Street in January 1911. (F. P. Wensley, *Detective Days*, 1931, p. 116). They may be regarded as the best detectives under Wensley's command and appear in the more important police cases. For example, in the case of the men with the bolt-cutter who stole 1,806 boots (*Hackney Gazette*, 5 August 1907, p. 3), they were commended along with Wensley, then Detective Inspector, Detective Sergeant Hodgson, and Detective Constables Smart and Rutter. According to Arthur, Dessent and Rutter hated Wensley and from time to time provided him with information about police activities.

15 A year later the *Hackney Gazette* (14 September 1908, p. 3) reported the suicide of Simms's wife, by drowning in Regent's Park Canal after being made the victim of gossip about her husband in the box factory where she worked. Alice, who was

twenty-five and left two children, is described as 'bright and cheerful'. Pointing to her difficult position after her husband's sentence, the coroner commented, 'The separation from her husband gave rise to all sorts of injurious suspicions, and she had apparently ended her life rather than bear it.' Recalling Simms's arrest and trial the paper said that police had watched Simms's workshop from a house behind it. When they closed in Simms jumped from an upper window and climbing over a fence, fell into the arms of one of fourteen policemen surrounding the house. The coins were described by experts from the Royal Mint as 'simply marvellous specimens', they 'defied the bending test'.

16 See *Hackney Gazette*, 10 April 1908, p. 4: 'At the Sunday Bird Fair.' Arthur is described as 'a tall, slim, young man, who obtained considerable notoriety by his accusations against the police at the Royal Commission.' Together with another man he was observed by two detectives: 'The officers felt justified in arresting both men and as Harding tried to wrench himself free a purse was seen to fall from his side.' No owner was identified. Nevertheless a remand was ordered. The *Gazette* did not report subsequent trial proceedings. Arthur's version is that the case was got up fraudulently by the police. His recollection is that he had gone down to Brick Lane, on this Sunday as on every other, to meet friends. 'Jew Boy' Stevens and another police officer who had been brought in by Wensley were standing at the corner of Church Row where there was a clear view of the entrance to Gibraltar Gardens. 'A few people came out and said "Jew Boy" is watching from Church Row but I didn't take much notice. When I got to Clark's coffee house there was a rush and I remember seeing "Jew Boy" and something fall on the floor. The detective sergeant got hold of me and said, "I am arresting you for being a suspected person."' Arthur's confederates gathered round but were warned off by a nod of the head. 'The policeman didn't look too well. I was going to put him over but it wouldn't do me any good.' The case came up before Cluer. 'All he said was, "Why did you go down Brick Lane on Sunday morning?" "I went down as I have done for years and years to meet my friends." "I have got no choice in the matter. The law says that if you go down a public place without a good reason you are a suspected person. The only penalty is twelve months."'

17 The Habitual Criminals Act, 1869 (32 and 33 Vict., ch. 23). The act, which replaced earlier penal servitude legislation, enabled police to arrest without warrant ticket-of-leave men, i.e. convicts let out on licence under police supervision prior to the

ending of their sentence, or those with two convictions or more, and allowed magistrates to try and convict on suspicion. The grounds for arrest were wide. The accused had to satisfy magistrates that he was earning his living honestly, that he was not about to commit a crime or waiting for an opportunity to do so, and to explain satisfactorily his presence on any premises or in any grounds. The penalty was up to twelve months with or without hard labour. Two years later the act was amended and stiffened by the Prevention of Crimes Act (34 and 35 Vict., ch. 112) or, more simply, 'Crimes Act'. Section 7 extended police powers to arrest anyone with a record and extended the time for which ex-criminals could be supervised to up to seven years after release. It forbade anyone arrested in this way to withhold their address from the police. It may be significant that Arthur was arrested once and once only in this way, i.e. within two years of appearing before the Royal Commission, and close to the time when its report and proceedings were published. In general, the Crimes Act was used to supervise and sometimes harass criminals known to the police. Section 7 was formally repealed in 1967. This kind of legislation plainly runs counter to the tradition of civil liberties. Its passage moved James Greenwood, the writer on 'low life' London subjects, to a rare expression of concern for the fate of the criminal poor. Alwyn Soames (*The English Policeman, 1871–1935*, 1935, p. 171) quotes Greenwood on Lord Kimberley's proposed 'Habitual Criminals Bill' – later Crimes Act, 'No law that could be passed could put the criminal, the burglar, and the house breaker more at the mercy of the dishonest policeman than he now is.'

Chapter 8   Gibraltar Gardens

1 Albert Rowland Cluer (1835–1942), magistrate at Worship Street Metropolitan Police Court from 1896, and, after its disappearance in 1911, at Old Street. After this he was judge at Whitechapel County Court for twenty-three years. The only metropolitan magistrate to bring particular cases to the attention of the Royal Commission on the Metropolitan police of 1906. See evidence pp. 1047–53 where he mentions eight cases against the police. In reply the Commission quoted extensively from the Commissioner of Metropolitan Police, Sir Edward Henry, without judging Cluer's charges as they do the rest, and so implicitly rejecting them. This may have harmed Cluer's career. According to Arthur (discussion November 1977), 'Cluer was

not a lenient man, but he didn't like the police. . . . He didn't like the habit of the CID in talking to the magistrate before cases came up. . . . For example, Cluer was told that, although I was only seventeen, eighteen, nineteen I was an old timer, and stood for it. But as time passed he changed his opinion'.

2   It is not possible clearly to identify this man in the police court reports of the period. A George King is mentioned warehouse-breaking in Curtain Road (*Hackney Gazette*, 7 September 1903) and shopbreaking in Bermondsey (*ibid.*, 10 May 1907). However, it is difficult to know whether this is the same man. The address in the second case is given as Lynddoch Street, Kingsland Road and occupation as flower-seller. See *Hackney Gazette*, 24 April 1911, p. 5 and 19 June 1911, p. 7: King, cabinet-maker, Bacon Street on charge of robbery of sub-post office in Kingsland Road, 'thieves possessed of unlimited bravado'. The jury stopped the trial when witnesses swore that 'King was at home at the time'.

3   Cf. *Hackney Gazette*, 6 January 1902, p. 3, where details are given of the career of a veteran criminal Tommy Cox alias Langton. This excellent account of Langton's gang and method of operation, with its reference to 'latest American equipment' gives an identical story to Arthur Harding's – as indeed does Det. Serg. Hodson five and a half years later (*ibid.*, 5 August 1907, p. 3), in proceedings against three men who stole 1,806 boots from a Pickford's van. 'These men were in possession of a very remarkable tool, which one of them had designed to cut off the steel bolts of revolving shutters.' The same theme, this time concerning a glorified tin-opener designed to cut the backs of safes, comes up in Eric Parr's *Grafters All*, 1964, pp. 59–66.

4   Wickham's began trading in Mile End Road around 1850, branching out first from linen draper, then to drapers and in the 1920s into a department store owned by Barkers. It closed in 1971 after the premises had been used by Great Universal Stores as a warehouse (*Kelly's London Directory*).

5   The 1905 West Ward rating books for 1905 record the landlord as J. Dunn of 25 Princelet Street, Spitalfields. The Hardings are listed at No. 10 Gibraltar Buildings as renting one room on the second floor at 2s 6d a week on the same floor as a family called Revell or Ravell. The other rooms were rented out at 5s or 5s 6d a week – a good indication of the Hardings' real povery.

Chapter 9   Cabinet-making

1 P. G. Hall, *The Industries of London*, 1962, pp. 74–92 and J. L. Oliver, *The Development and Structure of the Furniture Industry*, Oxford, 1966, for a description of the industry. The three great manufacturing industries of Victorian London were clothing, furniture and footwear. Oliver describes how the furniture trades were pushed out of the city along and around Curtain Road, and how its growth and location were determined. The Jago itself had a thick concentration of cabinet-making workshops.

2 Charles and Richard Light, 134–148 Curtain Road, three doors up from Rivington Street. Cabinet- and furniture-makers at this address from 1848 to the end of the First World War when they moved to Old Street and then in 1925 to Great Eastern Street. The firm closed in 1974.

3 'Darling and Son Limited, printers to H.M. Stationery Office, engravers and bond printers'; 34 to 40 Bacon Street first appears as their address in 1898.

4 William Fox & Sons, 109 and 111 Bethnal Green Road, the fourth door along from the 'Black Dog', originally part of Church Street. An old firm which closed in 1970. Another shop further up Bethnal Green Road closed in 1973.

5 See map in Hall, *The Industries of London*, illustrating the dense concentration of cabinet-makers around Boundary Street and Hoxton at this time.

6 Thomas and Robert Hollington, 54 Rivington Street, on the corner of Curtain Road (1895–1972), furniture manufacturers. Eventually expansion absorbed the whole of the site between Charlotte Street and Curtain Road.

7 On Paradise Place which has now disappeared.

8 Mrs Caroline Kemp is listed at 61 Bacon Street (1899–1904) as a dining-table-maker. Kemp was a common London name and it is not possible to trace the movement of various persons who might have been related to Mrs Kemp using the directories.

9 Cooper does not appear in the trade directories. Nor do Jimmy Saunders or Georgie Berner.

10 For an account of the French polishers, see Booth MSS, 'B' series.

Chapter 10   The terrors of Brick Lane

1 Nor it seems the local newspapers, who make no mention of this.

2 Arthur remembers these characters by their nicknames, and it

has not been possible to trace them in the police court reports.

3 For another account of Mother Wolff's cookhouse, see Jerry White, *Rothschild Buildings*, 1980, ch. 3, pp. 115–16.

4 I have found no court cases with anybody resembling Biddy the Chiver. According to Arthur, 'everyone wanted to buy him a drink after the case because of the acquittal'.

5 In March 1909 a Frederick Murphy was charged with violently assaulting a woman off whom he was alleged to be living (*East London Observer*, 13 March 1909, p. 3, col. 4).

6 According to Arthur Harding the murder took place about six months after Singing Rose had been done to death. Spud was given a job as nightwatchman in a shop in Chapel Street and took the woman to a cellar where he killed her.

7 Jack Parr, a cabinet-maker and pickpocket, had been warned off Sarah Willett by her mother, after he had been picked up as a suspected person. A brief account of the shooting appears in *The Times* 29 August 1900. Parr followed Sarah and two other girls to a music hall where he tried to pick a quarrel. Sarah threatened to call a constable and was shot as she was about to go into the police station. The desk sergeant ran out in time to meet Parr coming into the station holding a revolver in his hand and saying, 'I have done it. I have done it.' Sarah was carried in but she died a few minutes later. Arthur remembers Parr as 'a nice lad [but] flash'.

8 Cf. case of Lottie Elliot (*Hackney Gazette*, 10 July 1908, p. 4) aged seventeen, 'a slim well dressed girl' of Drysdale Street who stole a gold watch from Baron von Wachendorf, 'an Oxford under-graduate staying in Jermyn Street'. The Baron had promised Lottie thirty shillings but only gave her ten 'telling her to pick up the watch if she could not trust him'. The court was informed that nothing was known against the girl and she was discharged. Few cases of prostitution appeared in the press and those that do tend – as in this case – to feature robbery or violence. The customary fine for soliciting at this time was twenty shillings (*ibid.*, 5 August 1908).

9 It has not been possible to check this case. Spencer's earlier activities are fully covered in the Royal Commission on the Metropolitan Police.

10 In October 1910, Steve Cooper of Bethnal Green, 'well known to the police', was given a month's hard labour for smashing his landlord's window after he had been evicted. *East London Advertiser*, 29 October 1910, p. 3, col. 7.

11 Old Bailey Sessions papers, December 1911.

12 Royal Commission on the Metropolitan Police, case of Edward Emms (Spencer) and Ginger Norrey, pp. 357–79, 577–82, where Ginger comes across as a secretive and taciturn man.

13 Some other slang terms which appear in police court reports of this time are: 'harvesting snowy' – stealing a wetline of clothes to pledge at the pawn brokers (*Hackney Gazette*, 21 September 1904, p. 3); 'job line' or 'thief's line' – stolen goods (*ibid.*, 20 January 1905, p. 3); a thief referring to his jemmy as his 'toothpick' (*ibid.*, 27 February 1905, p. 4); 'Here comes the German with a red lot', i.e. gold chain, watch, etc. (*ibid.*, 15 September 1905, p. 3).

14 For cases concerning Ruby Michaels, see *East London Observer*, 18 September 1915, p. 8.

15 Warsaw hotel, known as Snelvar's restaurant.

16 At No. 137. The shop was run under the name of Alfred Sutton from 1891 until 1921 and for 1922 under that of Mrs Mary Sutton. It disappears from the directory in 1923.

17 According to Arthur (December 1977), Hyman Eisenberg. Later went to the United States – Arthur says he was active in Chicago in Al Capone's time.

18 Benny Hall managed three of the lodging houses for his stepfather Jimmy Smith, an ex-bookmaker who acted as liaison officer for the street bookies with the police. For another account of Jimmy Smith as lodging house keeper, see Jerry White, *Rothschild Buildings*, 1980, ch. 4.

19 Tommy Hoy twice appeared before the police courts on charges of attempted murder. In the first case, January 1909, he was charged together with two others, with shooting at Robert Francis Russell, landlord of the 'Enterprise' beerhouse in Three Colt Street, Limehouse: 'Prosecutor, the well-known ex-pugilist, deposed that about a quarter past eleven on Wednesday night, he was in bed, and heard a man shouting out, "Shocking tragedy in Limehouse. A publican shot." He got out of bed, and called to his wife to get a paper. His wife returned and said, "It was only a lark." She also told him the prisoners were inside the house, and he told her not to serve them. Witness dressed and went downstairs when he saw prisoners and two other men in the bar. He requested Wendrott to leave, and after arguing he left. Soon after Wendrott returned, and asked to be served. Witness refused, when that prisoner pulled out a revolver and said to his companions, "Look out; I'll shoot his —— brains out." He pointed the revolver at witness's head and pulled the trigger, but it missed fire. Witness closed with him, and got the revolver. While handing the weapon to his wife it was knocked out of his

hand, but he had another tussle and regained possession of the weapon. He gave the revolver to his wife, when all the men set on him, and he struck everyone in the bar as fast as he could. They then wanted to run away, and Wendrott got through the door before he could lock it. Mrs Russell gave corroborative evidence, and added that after Wendrott went away her husband gave the other two prisoners a good hiding. – Detective Sergt. Lee stated that when he arrested Wendrott that prisoner said, "All right. I know I'll make up my own defence tomorrow." Hoy said, "Has Mr Russell done this? I shall say I was drunk and don't remember what happened." Hoy afterwards claimed a cap which was found in the house, and said, "I admit I was there, but we didn't intend to murder him. There was no shot fired." The revolver contained three undischarged ball cartridges, but one went off accidentally at the station – Mr Dickinson remanded the prisoners' (*East London Observer*, 9 January 1909, p. 8, col. 4). In a second case (*East London Observer*, 11 February 1911, p. 3, col. 4) they were charged with attempting to murder William McLaughlan, a Poplar labourer, after he and some companions had set out from Bow Common 'armed with revolvers and bars of iron'. An earlier account of the case summarises the affair as follows (*ibid.*, 28 January 1911, p. 6, col. 6): 'In outlining the case, Mr Graham Campbell said prisoner was one of a riotous gang, who, on the 26th October last, went out armed with revolvers and other dangerous implements, looking for persons against whom they had a grievance, and the evidence would show it was the accused who fired the shot that wounded McLaughlan. Hoy and his companions went to the "Prince of Wales" public house, outside which Smith was standing. Prisoner's brother hit Smith with a bar of iron, inflicting two nasty wounds, and immediately after four revolver shots were fired. Hoy was seen with a revolver in his hand, and he was heard to say, "We will give some pills to Williamson tonight." Soon after other shots were fired. They went into Latham Street, and when McLaughlan came out of his house to watch the crowd he was wounded in the back, close to the spinal column, and it was not deemed advisable to extract the bullet. Prisoner had been identified as being in possession of a revolver, and one of his companions called out, "Don't run, Tommy; let us shoot all the coppers that come down our way." After that Hoy disappeared and was not arrested until the 15th inst., when he was taken into custody in Stepney by Constable Sandford. Prisoner struck the officer and tried to set a bull terrier on him. When charged he said, "I daresay I was there, but I shall have to defend myself the best way I can when before the magistrate." Firing revolvers in the public streets was a serious matter.'

20 A Jewish game at which – so it was claimed – it was impossible to cheat. It was a card game based on casting four letters and trying to ensure that a certain combination of cards came up. According to Arthur, Tommy Hoy was the only man in London able to cheat at it.

21 The 'Darby Sabini mob' are the best-remembered of the old-time London gangs. A fuller note on them will be found in Samuel, *East End Underworld*, vol. I, forthcoming.

22 Crase or Craze's fishmongers, Walthamstow. Apparently still the best fishmonger in Walthamstow.

Chapter 11   Jews and half-Jews

1 Slang or dialect term for gypsy or Romany. Many spellings, e.g. didikai, diddicoy, didakers, etc. The word seems to refer especially to Irish tinkers and nomads who outnumber true Romanies in and around London.

2 See Lloyd P. Gartner, *The Jewish Immigrant in England 1870–1914*, 1960. About 120,000 Jews came to England in these forty-four years (p. 30). The successive influxes of refugees coincided with pogroms and persecutions in Tsarist Russia. After the 1906 Aliens Act the flow was restricted.

3 This is a reference to the LCC estate built on the site of the Jago. The log books for Rochelle Street school confirm that in the 1900s there were numbers of Jewish families living on the estate, though English names predominate.

4 Ted 'Kid' Lewis (born 1896). Lewis, a Jewish boy whose real name was Solomon Mendeloff, started his boxing career at the 'Wonderland' at the age of fifteen. He was a brilliant adaptor of old prize ring fighting to modern boxing techniques, and his active-spirited and committed style made him one of the most popular British fighters ever seen in North America. When he retired at the age of thirty-five he had won three British (feather-, welter- and middle-weight), two Empire, three European and the world welter-weight titles. See M. Golesworthy, *Encyclopedia of Boxing*, 1975. Kid Lewis became the licensee of the 'Stag's Head,' Hawley Road, Kentish Town in 1922 (*East End News*, 7 July 1922, p. 5, col. 6). In 1931 he was associated with Sir Oswald Mosley's 'New Party', and stood as a fascist candidate in East London.

5 'Gannof' or 'gonnoff' is the Yiddish word for thief. Interestingly enough (as evidence for the early participation of Jews in the London underworld) it had been incorporated into London criminal slang in 1850 (it occurs in one of the autobiographical narratives in Henry Mayhew's *London Labour and the London Poor*, 1851); it also occurs – as a curse – in Charles Hindley, *Life of a Cheap Jack*, 1875? p. 145; and is given an entry in John Camden Hotten's *Slang Dictionary*, 1885 edn. 'Moishe the Gonnoff' is untraceable in the police court records, since he is only remembered by his nickname.

6 The Pavillion seems to have started putting on Yiddish operas and plays in 1906 (*East London Observer*, 14 April 1906, p. 8, col. 3); in spring 1908 its season was made up of English plays (*ibid.*, 28 March 1908, p. 8, col. 1); in 1911 it is referred to as the Yiddish theatre (*ibid.*, 24 June 1911, p. 5, col. 5). Isaac Cohen, the man who had made the theatre the 'Drury Lane of the East', had begun his career as an actor at the Coburg, and had later migrated to the East End theatres, playing under the auspices of a fellow-Jew, Morris Abrahams, at the 'Effingham' and then at the 'Pavillion'. In middle age he turned from acting to production, and was also manager of the Pavillion under Abrahams's regime. One of his daughters married Joseph Lyons 'the prince of caterers', who had early business associations with the Abrahams–Cohen enterprise, though according to one tradition, Cohen disapproved of the marriage (Charles Drage, *Two Gun Cohen*, 1954, pp. 14–15). 'In private life' (according to a local obituarist) 'he was a wit and humourist, and his fund of anecdotes was as large and various as that of his old friend and colleague, Morris Abrahams' (*East London Observer*, 8 October 1910, p. 7, col. 5). For a description of the theatre at this time, cf. 'The East End Jew at his Playhouse', *Pall Mall Magazine*, 1908, p. 174: 'Swart and bearded, the signs of excessive labour under unwholesome conditions written in their pallid lips and hollow eyes, these alien-born sons of Israel cast care behind them when the theatre is entered. . . . With them come the daughters of Israel, beautiful sometimes in the flower of their youth, but too often gross and coarse of feature and of figure when once that flower has faded. . . . Capmakers, tailors, glaziers, pedlars, cabinet-makers. . . . What an audience! Babbling, effervescent, undisciplined, it is noisy and excitable after the invariable manner of true Orientals. When the play begins, however, it follows with rapt attention; yielding its emotions with the frankness and simplicity of children. It makes no shamefaced attempt to hide its tears or smother its sobs. And when the comic vein is touched, the "funny man" is rewarded, not with

polite smiles, but with the tribute of unrestrained and boisterous laughter.' The theatre – 'the only Yiddish playhouse in England' – closed down in 1933 (*Star*, 3 February 1933). Most of the actors were foreign-born, coming from Poland or America, but it seems that its earlier traditions as a Victorian playhouse lived on, for instance with the squeezing of a song or two in the interludes of performances (Levy, 'Jewish Theatre', *East London Papers*, 1963, pp. 28–31). In 1937 another Yiddish theatre opened in East London run by the actress-manageress Fanny Waxman. After the war it moved from Adler Street to a theatre in Stoke Newington (Tower Hamlets Ref. library, 'Theatre of the People', newspaper cuttings).

7 The 'Wonderland' started its life as the 'Effingham' theatre saloon. It was later known as the 'East London Theatre' and under various names. For a time, it came under the proprietorship of Morris Abrahams, the East London theatrical impresario. It was rebuilt for the third time in 1880 as the 'Wonderland' and was for a time, according to Diana Howard, a theatre for Yiddish plays (Diana Howard, *London Theatres and Music Halls 1850–1950*, 1979, pp. 75–7). In 1894 it was converted into a boxing arena and became the leading boxing ring in East London and, arguably, the world. As well as staging boxing bouts, it also put on novelties of all kinds – cinema performances, baby shows and benefit evenings for local charities. Both Mr Jacobs its proprietor in the early 1900s, and Mr Woolf, who succeeded him, were Jews, and many Jewish boxers made their debut there. The 'Wonderland' was burnt out in 1911 (*East London Observer*, 19 August 1911, p. 7, col. 5). For some other references, see *Eastern Argus*, 9 October 1907, p. 5, col. 7; *East London Observer*, 7 July 1906, p. 3, col. 3. (Bob Kennedy took part in a boxing night at the 'Wonderland' for an agreed fee of 35s but was only offered 27s 6d.) In later years the 'Wonderland' was replaced, as the East End's principal boxing arena, by the 'Premierland' in Commercial Road (cf. Joe Jacobs, *Out of the Ghetto*, 1978, p. 29).

8 Cf. *East London Observer*, 20 March 1909, p. 6, for a report of this case (Arthur's date of 1912 is wrong).

9 Goodwin appears as a witness when there was a murder among the card-playing fraternity of a neighbouring Jewish restaurant. *East London Observer*, 6 January 1912.

10 For an early case involving Timmy Hayes ('alias Dick Turpin') see *East London Observer*, 14 November 1914, p. 3, col. 14.

11 As a boy of eighteen, Jack Marx appeared before the Thames police court charged with highway robbery in Cable Street – stealing a watch and chain from a passer-by. (*East London*

Observer, 9 November 1889, p. 6). In 1907 he was charged with violently assaulting a local police constable who was too badly wounded to attend court. He was said to be 'well known to the police for similar and more serious offences' (*ibid.*, 22 June 1907, p. 3, col. 3). Two years later he was the victim of violence when a mob of some twenty attacked him in the course of a local vendetta (*ibid.*, 31 July 1909, p. 2, cols 2–3).

12 Ellen ('Dolly') Marks was charged with assaulting Det. Sgt Leeson (in later life the author of *Lost London*) in 1907: 'It appeared that defendant's brother was under remand on a charge of assault. On Wednesday the sergeant was talking to Detective Biggs outside the court when the accused came up and said, "I've done with you, you dirty tyke. We've got him away, you won't find him now.". . . Sergeant Leeson walked away, but defendant followed and spat in his face. She was then taken into custody and was violent all the way to the station' (*East London Observer*, 29 June 1907, p. 3, col. 2). In July she was in dock on a charge of assault, declaring it was not safe for an English woman to walk about the East End streets 'on account of interference from the foreign lads who hung about them'. Barnet Zimmerman, 'a young lad of the Hebrew faith' was one of those who had excited her resentment and she had retaliated, so it was alleged, by hitting him on the head with a bottle (*ibid.*, 31 July 1907).

13 The earliest appearance which I can trace of this successful criminal is in 1904. See *Hackney Gazette*, 28 December, Emmanuel, at that time described as a salesman, was charged with threatening to shoot an Islington street trader called Masters who owed him £22. Emmanuel and a companion called at Master's house and were told by his wife that he had 'done a bunk'. In fact, her husband was hiding under a table and heard Emmanuel threaten to kill him, and pull out a loaded revolver to make his point more forceful. Masters went to the police and Emmanuel was charged with possession of a loaded revolver. Emmanuel's reply was that he acted on impulse. The magistrate, Fordham, commented, 'There was no doubt that he was a dangerous fellow,' and imposed very high sureties of £250 or twelve months prison. In 1908 Emmanuel was the victim of a murder attempt when John McCarthy shot at him outside a public house in Watney Street, St George's (*East London Observer*, 25 July 1908, p. 3, col. 3). Both he and his assailant were described in the charge-sheets as market porters (*East London Observer*, 25 July 1908, p. 3, col. 3; *ibid.*, 8 August 1908, p. 3, cols 1–2). In 1913 he seems to have been mounting a big gaming operation in collusion – or intended collusion – with leading members of the

local police force. See *East End Underworld*, vol. I, forthcoming.

14 See William J. Fishman, *East End Jewish Radicals 1875–1914*, 1975.

15 See Fishman, *East End Jewish Radicals*. The club, originally a Methodist Free Chapel, later a Salvation Army depot, was at No. 165, and was for the most part the achievement of Rudolf Rocker and his entourage. It was opened in 1906, superseding a previous club in Berner Street. Kropotkin came to the ceremony and spoke, although his doctor had warned him not to attend for fear of a heart attack. Afterwards he was a regular visitor. Next door at No. 163 were the editorial offices of *Arbeiter Fraint*, a Yiddish paper which turned anarchist after 1892. At the time of the Houndsditch murders the club attracted extraordinary attention and was widely described as 'a den of thieves and murderers, replete with rituals, secret signs, pass-words, etc., where Peter the Painter had delivered lectures . . . to teach the use of explosives' (Rocker, *The London Years*, quoted in Fishman, p. 289). The club lasted until 1915. During the war the door was closed on immigration and unemployment declined. It seems that with Rocker out of the way the police took the opportunity presented to move and close down the printing press. However, surviving members continued to meet irregularly in premises at Fieldgate Street. (Private information from W. J. Fishman, November 1977.)

16 The atmosphere of desperate exile politics in this period is vividly conjured up in Victor Serge's account of revolutionary extremism in this period in Paris which Rumbelow rightly takes as one of his texts in his history of the Sidney Street affair. 'We had to win our food, lodging and clothing by main force; and after that, to find time to read and think. The problem of the penniless youngster, uprooted or (as we used to say) "foaming at the bit" through irresistible idealism, confronted us in a form that was practically insoluble. Many comrades were soon to slide into what was called "illegalism", a way of life not so much on the fringe of society as on the fringe of morality . . . becoming hunted men. When they knew that the game was up they chose to kill themselves rather than go to jail.

'One of them, who never went without his Browning revolver, told me, "Prison isn't worth living for! Six bullets for the sleuth-hounds and the seventh for me!"' (Victor Serge, *Memoirs of a Revolutionary*, Oxford, 1963, p. 20).

17 Nina Vassileva – Gardstein's mistress. According to Rumbelow, whose account is based on police papers which are never unfortunately listed or described, Nina was watched for eight

weeks after the siege of Sidney Street and then picked up (Donald A. Rumbelow, *The Houndsditch Murders and the Siege of Sidney Street*, 1973, p. 137). She was found guilty of conspiracy to break and enter, and sentenced at the trial of Gardstein's remaining associates to two years in prison – as Fishman notes, 'a heavy penalty' for having an affair with Gardstein. However, five weeks later the Court of Appeal quashed the conviction on the grounds of a misdirection by the judge to the jury. Rumbelow came across her in the early 1960s living alone in a room by herself not far from the site of the murders. By then she would have been over seventy. Arthur refers to her as Milly. This may or may not be a corruption of her nickname, 'Minna'. The refugees from the horrifying Russian persecutions of this time who were involved at Houndsditch and in the Tottenham outrage, an earlier wages snatch in which four people died and twenty-one were wounded, used so many aliases and had such a confusing mixture of foreign and half-anglicised christian names, or nicknames that it is difficult to decide whether he is right or wrong. For example, Rumbelow refers to Gardstein as George.

When Nina was released from prison she was shunned by her friends and taken in by Millie and Rudolf Rocker (Fishman, *East End Jewish Radicals*, p. 293).

18 There is no mention of a van or any plans of this sort in Rumbelow. However, Arthur discounts much of the conventional account of Wensley's part in the siege. He strongly emphasises his opinion that 'it was a lot of bravado about him climbing over this and that . . . a lot of tripe. He ran for his life to get out. [Moreover] he was fond of using furniture vans because he had found them useful for raids.'

19 Rumbelow follows every other account in asserting that Leeson was shot in the house itself. Wensley believed that Leeson was dying, as did the wounded man himself: '"Mr. Wensley, I am dying. They have shot me through the heart. Goodbye. Give my love to the children. Bury me at Putney." Wensley pressed his hand. "We will be with you to the last," he said' (Rumbelow, *The Houndsditch Murders*, p. 113). The problem with this sort of report is to know whether or not it was invented afterwards. Arthur is even more scathing of Leeson than Wensley – if that is possible. He says, 'Leeson was potty. He got scared and went to Australia where he imagined he met Peter the Painter on a train. People laughed at it but it showed what kind of a mind he had. He did well out of Sidney Street – he became an inspector', (interview with Arthur Harding, December 1977). For Leeson's own

account, see Ex-Det. Sgt Leeson, *Lost London*.

20 *The Times*, 13 August 1966. Police Constable Fox, detective Constable Wombwell and Detective Sergeant Head were shot dead whilst questioning three men in Braybrook Street near Wormwood Scrubs. John Edward Witney was arrested in London on 15 August, John Duddy picked up in a Glasgow tenement two days later, and Harry Roberts discovered in a barn at Bishops Stortford on 15 November.

21 Leon Behren. Rumbelow, *The Houndsditch Murders*, p. 180 denies Leon Behren's death had any connection with Sidney Street. He found no evidence to suggest Behren had betrayed Fritz and Joseph to the police.

Chapter 12   Vendettas

1 Nile Street, a market street, branches off Shepherdess Walk. The *Hackney Gazette*, 5 January 1908 ('The Battle of the Nile') reported that 'a portion of Hoxton which is known as "The Nile" was described by the police as a "very rough and dangerous quarter", had been the scene of "a very dangerous disturbance" in which some 500 persons took part.' As a result, three young women were bound over for six months. 'The defence of [Caroline] Strick – a typical coster girl – disclosed the roughness of the neighbourhood. She said that she had been keeping company with a man who turned out to be a thief, and as she had a child by him, she was now constantly called after the jeered-at thief, the design being to make her turn thief and join them. She said that with [Annie] Phillips [another one of the accused], she was attacked by a man and a woman, the man having just come out from seven years' penal servitude. . . . The constable said that Strick had a portion of broken tumbler in her hand. It was a most dangerous weapon, but one much in favour in Hoxton. . . . [Annie] Philips said that if the constables had not removed them to the station, they would have been killed.' Street battles with several hundred taking part were a common feature in Hoxton at this time. Usually, however, they were directed at the police, not at, in this case, local residents.

2 The prize-fighter turned publican seems to have been a feature of Hoxton. Three or four of them turn up in Booth's manuscript notes on the district. As impresarios they seem to have been partly responsible for Hoxton's strong sporting reputation in the late nineteenth century and its numerous pub-based sporting

events (for some advertisements, cf. *Licensed Victuallers Gazette*, 1879).

3 There are several stories of Donoghue in S. Theodore Felstead, *Racing Romance*, 1949.

4 He must have been the *house* manager of the Olympia; his name is not on the list submitted to the Lord Chamberlain. Cf. Diana Howard, *London Theatres and Music Halls, 1850–1950*, 1970, p. 22.

5 For the Titanics, see George Ingram, *Cockney Cavalcade*, n.d., pp. 10–17; S. Theodore Felstead, *London Underworld*, 1930, pp. 40–5.

6 Number 1, Kingsland Road.

7 According to Arthur's subsequent recollection, 'Sunshine's' (which needless to say does not appear in the Directories) was tucked away in a narrow passage off Shoreditch High Street. It was a billiards' hall as well as a meeting place for the card-playing fraternity.

8 Callaghan had some six convictions recorded against him in the years 1904–7. One of them can be found in *Old Bailey Sessions Papers*, 1904–5, pp. 1517–20. Another appears in the *East London Observer* (26 January 1907) when he was charged under the Prevention of Crimes Act with being a 'suspected person': 'Prisoner was seen loitering about shops in the Mile End-Road, and when arrested, a stout wire with a hook at one end was found concealed between his shirt and his waistcoat. This implement, it was explained, was used by thieves for "fishing" things out of shop windows and over counters.' (For a later charge of burglary against Callaghan, see *East London Observer*, 30 November 1912, p. 3, col. 4; cf. also *Tottenham, Edmonton and Wood Green Weekly Herald*, 3 July 1908, p. 4, col. 5 for one of his suburban expeditions.)

9 In July 1903, George King was charged, together with Frederick Smith, a labourer, with breaking and entering a Curtain Road warehouse and stealing £7 10s worth of whisky, cigars, etc. (*Hackney Gazette*, 7 July 1903, p. 3, col. 6). In 1911 when he was described as a cabinet-maker living in Bacon Street, King was charged with a £100 haul from a sub-post office in Kingsland Road. The newspaper reported the theft to be the work of 'thieves . . . possessed with unlimited bravado'. However, the jury stopped the trial when several witnesses swore that 'King was at home at the time' (*Hackney Gazette*, 24 April and 19 June 1911).

10 Isaac Bogard ('Darky the Coon') is still well remembered among old-time residents of Spitalfields as the leading local terror. For

an example of this in oral tradition, see Jerry White, *Rothschild Buildings*, 1980, ch. 3. According to Esther, licensee of the 'Commercial Tavern', he spent his last years as a fishmonger's assistant in Wentworth Street. Arthur says that in the 1920s he was the 'governor' (i.e. unofficial 'protector') of the market stall-holders in Wentworth Street and Petticoat Lane. His earlier exploits as a 'terror' are well documented in the local newspapers. In 1909 he was involved in a triangular vendetta with Jack Marks and John Scales, and was charged with uttering threats to the latter 'whereby he went in fear of his life': 'The prosecutor . . . said that on the day following the assault on John Marks, the prisoner [Bogard] and a man named Millard had called at his home in Cambridge Buildings, Whitechapel, and had asked why he . . . had gone to the police station and . . . "put up" Marks to prosecute Osborne. The other man pulled out a revolver and threatened to blow the witness's brains out. While this man was flourishing his revolver in the witness's face, the prisoner, who had a knife in his hand, tried to edge between the witness and the doorway' (*East London Observer*, 31 July 1909, p. 2, cols. 2–3). In August 1914 Isaac Bogard, 'a fishmonger, of Everard Street, St. George's', was charged with maliciously wounding Reubin Blondin by striking him on the head with a hammer. The victim, however – who failed to appear when the charge was first heard – so modified his story at the second hearing that Bogard was discharged: 'Prosecutor . . . said that . . . on Sunday morning he was walking with some friends in Church-lane when prisoner came up and said, "You are one of the terrors out of Brick-lane, and one of Jerry's pals. I have had you on my book for some time." The accused pulled something which looked like a hammer out of his pocket, and struck him a blow on the head, at the same time shouting, "I am mad; I am mad." He fell to the ground and the prisoner bent over and kissed him (laughter)' (*East London Observer*, 8 August 1914, p. 3, cols. 4–5). Later in the month – when he was recorded as Israel Bongard (*sic*), 'a man of colour' aged twenty-seven – he was sentenced to a month's hard labour for assaulting Constable H 500. 'The constable found Bongard creating a disturbance and requested him to go away, whereupon the accused struck him in the face and also kicked him in the leg. Prisoner then ran through a house in Everard Street, and having got on to the roof of an out-house, he proceeded to pull off a number of tiles which he pelted the police with. Great trouble was experienced in getting prisoner to the station' (*East London Observer*, 29 August 1914, p. 3, col. 4).

11 Richard David Muir KC (1857–1924). Appointed senior counsel to the Treasury in 1901, under which office he looked after the government's interest during the Royal Commission upon the Duties of the Metropolitan Police. From 1908 on he was Senior Treasury Counsel at the Old Bailey which is why Arthur was facing him again. Muir was knighted in 1918. His fame springs from his cross-examination in the Crippen and Steinie Morrison cases. He also sat on a number of commissions including one with Horace Avery – the judge in this trial – on the framing of the Indictment Act 1918. In Arthur's words, 'a great criminal lawyer but a ruthless man'.

12 What was sensational about the Vendetta affair was not the horrific charges, nor the terrible wounds inflicted on Isaac Bogard's face, but the turning of Darky the Coon to police protection and the operation to bring witnesses to court and to arrest Arthur and his colleagues. Instances of gang warfare cutting across legal and judicial institutions in this clear and direct way are rare in Britain. Here is the report on the case which appeared in the *Illustrated Police News* 23 December 1911, p. 6: 'East End Vendetta. Gang of Ruffians Broken Up at Last. The state of lawlessness and terrorism existing in the East End, which has been revealed by the "vendetta" case, was the subject of strong remarks by Mr. Justice Avory at the Old Bailey on Saturday.

'"This riot," he said, in passing sentences on the eight prisoners in the case, "was one of the most serious riots which can be dealt with by law, for it was a riot in which some, at least, of the accused men were armed with revolvers, and it took place within the precincts of a court of justice.

'"I wish to say that the condition of things disclosed by the evidence—that a portion of London should be infested by a number of criminal ruffians armed with loaded revolvers—ought not to be tolerated further, and if the existing law is not strong enough to put a stop to it some remedial legislation is necessary."

'The sentences were as follows:

'Arthur Harding, twenty-one months' hard labour, to be followed by three years' penal servitude.

'Charles Callaghan, two years' hard labour.

'William Spencer, eighteen months' hard labour, to be followed by three years' penal servitude.

'William Andrews, twelve months' hard labour.

'Stephen Cooper, three years' penal servitude.

'William Newman, fifteen months' hard labour.

'Thomas Taylor, two years' hard labour.

'Robert Wheeler, fifteen months' hard labour.

'Among the charges against the different men were:

'Rioting, assault, shooting with intent, causing grievous injury.

'The rioting took place in the street, in a public-house, outside a police court, and even within the walls of the court itself, where witnesses were threatened with revolvers. The weapons used included revolvers, knives, and broken glasses, and several persons were badly hurt.

'"This armed and organised gang," declared counsel, "has terrorised men and women who happened to incur its displeasure.

'Some members of the gang have not been arrested, for their victims were afraid to prosecute them. So great is the reign of terror in the East End that witnesses had to be brought to court on warrants and one of the most important of them vanished during the trial.

'The career of Harding, the leader of the gang, was sketched by Detective Inspector Wensley before sentence was passed. When he was fourteen—he is now only twenty-five—he was bound over for disorderly conduct and being in possession of a revolver.

'At the age of seventeen he became a terror to Bethnal Green, and captained a band of desperadoes. In all, he has been convicted fourteen times, yet he was one of the complaining witnesses before the Police Commission.

'"He has developed into a cunning and plausible criminal of a dangerous type," said the inspector. "I have never known him do any work."

'There were many convictions against Callaghan, one of them being for "shooting with intent." Against Spencer there were nine convictions for dishonesty and three for assault. There were a number of convictions against Andrews and fifteen against Cooper, who had been found in possession of firearms on three occasions.

'Against Newman there were eleven previous convictions, but Mr. Wensley said that for some years he had been a hardworking man. Taylor's character was stated to be "a record of acquittal." There was only one conviction against Taylor and there were convictions for minor offences against Wheeler.'

Chapter 13 Prison years, 1911–22

1 Arthur adds, 'Prison built me up.' Portland was not only health-ier than Bethnal Green, its educational facilities were better, and it was there that Arthur started to study law books. 'I said to myself, "You will always be at the mercy of somebody unless you train yourself."'

2 Captain Edward E. S. Schuyler, governor of Portland Prison, 1911–18.

3 Cesare Lombroso (1836–1909), professor of psychiatry and an-thropology at the University of Turin, who sought first-hand observation and measurement of prison inmates to determine the characteristics of criminal types. His anthromorphic model of the criminal, including skeletal and neurological malfunctions of the 'born criminals', led to the foundation of a whole school of criminal biology, and also laid the basis of criminology as an observational 'science'.

4 Louis Alexander French, deputy medical officer at Portland from 1910–20, medical officer in 1921, appointed medical officer at Dartmoor in 1922.

5 There is no record of this case, or of Arthur's subsequent arrest and conviction, in the local newspapers: court reports peter out soon after the opening of the war.

6 H. Wilberforce was appointed magistrate at Thames Court in 1914 (*East London Observer*, 11 April 1914, p. 3, col. 3).

7 H. Chartres Biron (1863–1940), metropolitan magistrate at Old Street from 1906 until 1920 when he went to Bow Street as Chief Metropolitan Magistrate, a post which carried a knighthood. He was at Bow Street for thirteen years. Biron was a pupil of Horace (later Mr Justice) Avery and he typified well the change-over from the florid advocacy of the Victorian period to a quieter approach with the emphasis on building up a detailed and accu-rate picture. He had none of the quirks, eccentricities or straight-forward faults which bring Plowden, Fordham and Cluer alive in the pages of the police court reports. It seems safe to assume that to challenge this conventional, dour and predictable man would need a lot of courage. For Biron at his worst see *Hackney Gazette*, 3 February 1908, p. 3: 'The whole secret was want of discipline. There was little in school, there was none when the children left – among the class to which these lads belong – and they drifted about the streets, in or out of a "job" – grew up without a trade . . . till they were the unemployed or unemployable.' This was delivered on the remand of five men charged with stealing small articles worth twenty-five shillings. Biron was also the

author of essays in the belles-lettres genre on Dickens, Smollett, Trollope, Fielding, etc. His other hobby was travel. Each year he would save up his holidays and spend all the days owed to him on one trip abroad. This, rightly or wrongly, is the origin of the remark about his death.

8 Albert Rod was a street bookie whose family kept a cat's-meat shop nearby. Arthur seems to have 'looked after' him in return for occasional favours (additional information, November 1977).

9 Sir Forrest Fulton KC (1846–1925), Conservative MP for West Ham North, 1886–92. After he lost his seat he became Common Sergeant (1892–1900) and then Recorder of London (1900–22), legal posts attached to the peculiar administrative structure of the City of London. Fulton's reputation never really recovered from the injustice done to Adolph Beck, who was charged in 1896 with posing as a wealthy foreigner in order to get his hands on money and jewellery belonging to rich women. Beck's counsel claimed that a John Smith, who closely resembled Beck, had carried out the frauds. Fulton ruled this to be irrelevant and Beck went down to seven years penal servitude. In 1904 he was again convicted. When Smith came into the hands of the police, a high-level legal inquiry headed by the Master of the Rolls confirmed that a double miscarriage of justice had occurred. Fulton was singled out for criticism (Horace Avery, prosecuting counsel at the 1896 hearings, escaped censure). The case led to a renewed demand for a separate Court of Criminal Appeal.

10 Morrison was involved in violent conflict with the prison authorities from the start of his incarceration, as the *East End News* reported to its readers on 2 May 1911: 'It now transpires, writes a correspondent, that Steinie Morrison (the reprieved Clapham murderer), after creating the scene at Waterloo station on Wednesday morning, behaved in an even more violent manner in the carriage during the journey to Tavistock. He was accompanied by Principal Warder Saunders and two other officers, and on the way was offered his dinner, which consisted of twelve ounces of bread and five ounces of corned beef. At first he declined to receive it, and changing his mind a moment later he took it and flung it with considerable force full into the face of the principal warder. On arrival at Dartmoor he was taken straightaway to a cell. He immediately became restless, and walking about proceeded to make a football of the movable articles. As he refused to desist he was seized by the warders, and after a lengthy struggle was forced into a straight-jacket. It was evident that he was determined to carry out his threat – that he

does not mean to undergo his sentence of penal servitude. Altogether his conduct was so openly defiant that the visiting committee of justices were notified of the fact, and are to be asked to deal with him for his misbehaviour at Waterloo and during the journey, and for assaulting the principal warder. It has since been reported that Morrison has had to be incarcerated in a padded cell.' For a general account of the Steinie Morrison case, see Eric Linklater, *The Corpse on Clapham Common*, 1971; Kingston, *Dramatic Days at the Old Bailey*, 1911.

Chapter 14   Gambling

1 This was the pub earlier referred to by Arthur as the 'Jack Simmons'. Arthur remembers it as being on the corner of Bethnal Green Road now occupied by a synagogue.
2 'Crown and Anchor' was a racecourse or army game played on a board painted on canvas and covered with crowns and anchors. Dice bought in Houndsditch carried similar marks. If two crowns and one anchor came up, the banker would pay out; but they seldom did. According to Arthur's glossary, however, it could be played fairly as a game of chance.
3 Cf. incident reported in the *Hackney Gazette*, 23 September 1908, p. 4. Two Hoxton labourers were charged at Old Street Court with gambling on a Sunday at Leyton Marshes. A posse of police in plain clothes mixed with a crowd of about 6,000 people. 'Gambling of all descriptions was in progress, and the officers were attracted by the loud cries of the prisoners who had a temporary table. The cover consisted of a piece of canvas on which was painted seven, two O's, two U's, and a blank space. Allen (one of the accused) was shaking dice, and he was urging the crowd to "Back your fancy, come on, lads, cheat or be cheated". Silver and bronze were thrown on the board, but Allen refused to pay out unless the three dice descended alike. The police attempted to close on the men, when Dove (the other prisoner) shouted, "Heads up" and the table was overturned, and the dice etc. thrown in the air. The prisoners were caught, but the surging crowd overturned all other gambling paraphernalia, which was strewn about the Marshes. Eventually the prisoners were got to the Station, where Allen was found to have in his possession a leather case containing three cards (used for the three card trick) and 72 tickets each having three numbers. These tickets, the police suggested, were sold and the person who held the number corresponding to one taken from the hat won the

prize. . . . Mr H. J. Carter (the chairman): We have heard people shout "Heads up" on race courses and know what it means. Allen: I plead guilty, your worship; but there were only two dice. If I used three, I couldn't throw "under" any time. Mr Carter: I don't know; it appears to me that it is about 100 to 1 in your favour. Allen: How is that, Sir; Wouldn't you back 3 to 1 on "overs" every time? Mr Carter: Oh no; not in that system. Allen: It's a quid to a penny you couldn't throw unders with three dice, I only had two, sir. Mr Carter: All right, you will each be fined 10s and 4s costs.'

4 All the 'park' racecourses, e.g. Grove, Kempton, Sandown, were run by the same group. Suburban racecourses were already a feature of London sporting life in the later nineteenth century.

5 There is no mention of this incident in the period 1901–24 for which the local newspapers have been combed for corroboration of Arthur's text.

6 Evidently the spielers could not have existed and flourished without a degree of connivance from the police, but, as with other such tolerated illegalities, they were subject to ritual raids and arrests.

7 According to Arthur the Jewish, or half-Jewish, betting men assembled on the Petticoat Lane side of Aldgate, the gentile bookmakers around the pubs on the opposite side of the road.

8 Arthur remembers Bobby Nark as 'a good fighting man' and one of the 'terrors' of Aldgate. He was a strongman for the Sabini mob, after the Jews joined up with them. In later years he married a 'stone rich' woman (additional information, December 1977).

9 The tailor's shop was at the bottom of Brick Lane on the corner of Sclater Street. Goff Gold made a book and Albert Rod bought it off him. (Additional information from Arthur, December 1977.) The early years of the twentieth century saw a tremendous increase in street betting, provoking a House of Lords inquiry, and an Act to put it down. Attempts to suppress betting as a working-class activity ran up against the difficulty that it was a traditional aristocratic 'right' and that by restricting betting to those with credit there was evidently one law for the rich and another for the poor. The street Betting Act was largely in-operable, because of the multitude of those engaged in a more or less daily conspiracy against the law. As in the case of the 'spielers', the police satisfied the formal requirements of the law by making periodic ritual arrests: according to Arthur, they were liberally rewarded by the street bookmakers for their tolerance.

10 The courts also knew all about it. See *Hackney Gazette*, 29 April 1908, p. 3. Fordham crisply ends the case of a Hoxton book-

maker charged with loitering for betting purposes with the remark, 'You are at the bottom of a regular system. Pay £10.' See
also *ibid.*, 4 August 1905, p. 3. The accused claimed he was taking
slips for a friend who was on holiday. Fined £5. 'The money was
immediately paid by an individual in court.'

11 Jimmy Smith was a tall, likeable man who was a favourite with
everyone. After his accident, falling into the fire, he remained a
bookmaker. According to Arthur, anyone who wanted the
police 'straightened up' went to Jimmy. He would pay the police
according to rank. It may be that his accident and the sympathy it
would attract made his role as a go-between, for which his
diplomatic qualities were suited, acceptable to all parties. It was
difficult to accuse this paralysed and popular man of trading
information with the authorities.

12 No. 31 Mrs Rosetta Smith is listed as keeping a chandler's shop
here from 1898 to 1907 (*Kelly's Post Office Directory*).

13 For Emmanuel's 'spieling' activities, see *East End Underworld*,
vol. I, forthcoming. For his racecourse activities, see Edward
Greeno, *War on the Underworld*, 1961, p. 166. Greeno, a well-
informed source, claims that Emmanuel was also a major sup-
plier of printed lists of runners to bookmakers. These were
printed by him for as little as a farthing each. 'To the bookies they
were half a crown a set.'

14 On the corner of Theobald's and Gray's Inn roads.

15 For the Darby Sabini vendettas in Clerkenwell, cf. Finsbury
Reference Library local history cuttings and numerous references
in the *Islington Gazette*. The Darby Sabinis are very well remembered by older Londoners, and credited with all kinds of
ferocious exploits. According to one, whose father was a
bookie's runner around 1920, when the Sabinis came down
Lambeth New Cut the whole market cleared for fear of them.
The Sabinis lived in the Italian quarter of Clerkenwell. In 1922
they were involved in a shoot-out with a rival Italian family after
Harry Boy Sabini was fired at in the Fratellanza Club, Clerkenwell. The case is reported in the *Daily Express*, 21 November
1922 and the *Star*, 5 December 1922: the various incidents of the
feud are followed in great detail in the *Islington Gazette* between 8
August 1922 and 19 January 1923. (I am grateful to Miss Lewis,
local history librarian at Finsbury, for first drawing my attention
to the library's cuttings on this affair, and to Jerry White for the
references from the *Islington Gazette*.) Cecil Chapman, who began his career as a metropolitan magistrate in Clerkenwell,
writes: 'I had not much experience of the Italian population, but
it was remarkable that all their quarrels were amongst them-

selves . . . that though they lived under English law and appreciated it, their conduct was governed by an Italian code of morals which differed in many respects from our own. It was to them quite natural and reasonable to use a knife . . . when their passions were aroused. . . . They certainly thought that almost anything was excusable to a man who was defending a woman's honour. There was that element in many of their cases, and I liked their picturesqueness as spectators at the back of the Court. They overcrowd their houses, . . . they respect our laws, but maintain their own customs and *festas*. They work to amass sufficient fortune by organ-grinding and ice-cream selling to return to Italy as old age approaches. They keep their distinctions of Frascati, Garibaldians, the Sabini gang etc., and have their own distinctive banners.' Travers Humphreys, in *Criminal Days* (1946, pp. 147–8) recalls an occasion on which Mr Justice Darling addressed one of the Sabinis in Italian. Sabini stared in amazement. Darling, who was proud of his grasp of French and Italian, thereupon lost all interest in the case except for remarking in his summing up that the prosecutors (three of the family were involved) were descended from the Sabines and proceeded to relate the story of the Sabine women.

16 Blackfriars Athletic Club at No. 117 between Union Street and the Railway Arches. Opened 1911. Later the 'Ring' Social Working Men's Club, and then the 'Ring' boxing hall – one of the most famous, in its time, in Britain. It disappears from the directories after 1941. For a full and attractive account of it, see Leslie Bell, *Bella of Blackfriars*, 1961.

17 A boxer who, according to Arthur (additional information, December 1977) set about Harry Sabini after he had tried to pull him off a stand at Brighton racecourse.

18 For the racecourse wars see Graham Greene, *Brighton Rock*; Netley Lucas, *The Flying Squad*, pp. 36–9, and *Britain's Gangland*, pp. 19–27; Berrett, *When I was at Scotland Yard*, pp. 117–20; and T. H. Dey, *Leaves from a Bookmaker's Book*, pp. 231–5.

19 According to Arthur (additional information, December 1977) Alfie Solomons got three years when the charge was reduced to one of manslaughter. The murder, Arthur emphasises, was deliberate.

Chapter 15   Dealings with the police

1 Arthur has taken all but the last of these dates from the *Report of the Royal Commission upon the Duties of the Metropolitan Police*, p. 331.

2 Legislation of this sort put magistrates in a difficult position. Depending on individual attitudes the police might have to work hard to secure a conviction. See *Hackney Gazette*, 4 September 1903, p. 3: 'This prisoner said he was certainly there but was waiting for someone who would give him work. However, he knew no one who would believe that of a man with his character. No one would give him a chance.' In this case the prisoner got twelve months hard labour. See also *ibid.*, 11 December 1903, p. 3: 'A prisoner who failed to report to police got off on the grounds that he might lose a job with a respectable firm if there was a fuss. After pressure by a Christian Mission representative the Commissioner of Police withdrew the warrant.' And 9 October 1903, p. 3: 'Because a man stood at a stable door at midday and ran off when a policeman appeared, was not sufficient to say he was there for an unlawful purpose.' Fordham discharged the prisoner.

3 F. P. Wensley, *Detective Days*, 1931, p. 105. Wensley wrote, 'I resolved to teach *them* a lesson' but there is no doubt that he is singling out Arthur Harding for special attention.

4 Section VII was not repealed until 1967.

5 This is the shooting which occurred in Selby Street described in Chapter 11. One of the two bullets fired by Arthur ricocheted and slightly wounded a young girl, Louisa Fugazza. It seems unusual that no evidence was offered. However, shooting incidents were more common in the East End then than they are today. The police were probably pinning their hopes on a conviction under the first charge – where their case was strong – and thus the two indictments went down together. The couple who testified on Arthur Harding's behalf were the Bodhers (*Old Bailey Proceedings*, April 1906, pp. 305–6). Thomas Edward, the husband, was employed at Waterlows the printers and therefore his testimony would be highly regarded by the court as that of a respectable working man with a good job who had a lot to lose by perjuring himself and his wife. They were members of Harriet's Christmas Club which was a part of her money-lending business. Neither of them was in Selby Street at the time. (Additional information from Arthur Harding. November 1977.)

6 Sir Forest Fulton KC. This does not seem to square with Arthur's remarks about his handling of the stolen pound notes case in 1916. See Chapter 13.

7 Joseph Phillips, at the time PC 363 in 'H' (Whitechapel) Division. He makes a brief appearance before the Royal Commission on the Metropolitan Police in Spencer's case, pp. 697–8.

8 It is probably impossible to trace all of Arthur Harding's convictions and acquittals without access to police records.
9 Royal Commission on the Metropolitan Police, pp. 1906–7. The case is discussed and evaluated by the commissioners pp. 388–410 and the verbatim evidence reproduced on pp. 752–852. Much of the agitation about police methods which led to the Royal Commission began with the case of P.C. Rolls who, it was alleged, had planted a hammer on a cabinet-maker sleeping on a bench at London Fields and then arrested him. The case was thrown out by the North London Police Court Magistrate Edward Snow Fordham (1858–1919) a fat, extrovert man whose exchanges with prisoners were a gift to police court reporters (*Hackney Gazette*, 14 July 1902, p. 3.) As a result Rolls was sentenced to five years penal servitude *ibid.* (22 October 1902, p. 3) and another constable allowed to resign (31 October 1902, p. 3). The case led to the formation of the Public Vigilance Society (24 November, p. 3 and 24 December 1902, p. 3) as well as another committee got up to clear Rolls's name. This second body criticised Fordham who six weeks later was in trouble for a remark about the unemployed ('Any man who wanted work could get it'). A deputation of 200–300 men without work was organised by the Social Democratic Federation on the steps of the court. The *Hackney Gazette*, 13 February 1903, p. 3 reports the discussion between J. Hunter Watts for the SDF and Fordham, and correspondence followed.

For examples of magistrates' criticism of the police at this time see *Hackney Gazette*, 10 August 1903, p. 3. A man and his wife were truncheoned in Bow Road. Cluer threw out the case commenting that it was 'incredible [the police] should have acted as stated'. Generally speaking, where the accused had been truncheoned the courts would require proof that such action had been unavoidable. Betting was an area in which magistrates showed leniency at this time. This may have caused friction in their relations with the police. For example, 29 January 1909, p. 3 – 'people like the defendant were much less to blame than the rich . . . who day after day gambled over bridge' (Cluer). Cluer's evidence to the Royal Commission shows that by 1906 his relations with the police were so bad that his complaints were ignored by the Commissioner as a matter of course. Earl Russell, counsel for the Public Vigilance Society, has this to say about the Royal Commission in *My Life and Adventures* (1923, pp. 304–5): 'I was instructed by a curious body called the Police and Public Vigilance Society run by a fanatic called Timewell. He was prepared always to believe anything he was told against the police and to resent with some indignation the demand for proof which a lawyer always makes. However, we selected about twelve of the likeliest cases, and in spite of the extreme poverty on our side and the whole force of the Treasury and the police against us on the other we succeeded in getting home seven of them, largely on my cross-examination of the police.'

10 It was not possible to identify Nuneaton Buildings.

11 He was a labourer in the painting department of George Trollope & Sons, the builders. Gamble came from a landed estate on which his father worked. When he arrived in London he was unable to find work and was recommended to the firm, by way of a letter from the lady of the house. His foreman testified to his 'sobriety, regularity and capacity in doing his work'. The Commission describe him as 'a working man of diligent habits and good character' (*Royal Commission on the Metropolitan Police*, p. 331).

12 Ethel Griffiths is described by the Royal Commission as a married woman, 'who until recently has been living with her husband at Merthyr Tydvil, but left him owing to his drunken habits, she went to Cardiff, where, to use her own expression, she "went wrong" and then made her way to London. She seems to have tried to obtain some work of an honest kind, but for more than a year she has maintained herself by prostitution. She gave her evidence for the most part well. . . . Her compassionate behaviour to Gamble . . . tells in her favour as being that of a poor woman who, moved by the impulse of pity, did her best to help a fellow creature in distress' (*ibid.*, p. 397).

13 Gamble was in hospital for four months and spent another twenty-six days in a convalescent home (*ibid.*, p. 388). He was operated on four times. A member of the Commission compared the injury to his having fallen upon a railing (*ibid.*, p. 793). There was an additional rupture to an artery lying between the urethra and the rectum. In the words of the house surgeon at the London Hospital, he was 'permanently damaged' (*ibid.*, p. 79).

14 *Ibid.*, p. 389. 'The sergeant (Sheedy) stood there and said, "That is enough – you have done enough to him." Witness (Gamble) did not say anything but only shouted. He heard the sergeant telling him to stop – "You have done quite enough." The constable did not stop for a little while.'

15 Joseph Wiltshire, a seventeen-year-old, who was living in a Brick Lane lodging house and sold papers into the early hours (*ibid.*, pp. 780–9). Joseph helped Ethel to get George Gamble to the London Hospital. The elderly person did not appear before the commission. But, in addition to Mrs Franks (see below), four

residents testified that they had been woken up by the noise and saw part of the assault.

16 A fellow patient at the London Hospital brought the case to Timewell's attention. Timewell wrote formally to the Commission of Police two days after Gamble came out of hospital. At the tribunal's hearings the Vigilance Society set out to show that PC Ashford had been guilty of wrongful assault and that the commissioner had failed to investigate the case with the thoroughness it deserved.

17 *Ibid*., pp. 793–8. Mrs Annie Franks, whom the Commission and later the courts recognised as the crucial witness: 'The importance of Mrs Franks' evidence is due to the fact that it is the evidence of an obviously respectable and perfectly intelligent person, who speaks to something to which she could hardly be mistaken. Such an incident as that of being awakened in the middle of the night by groans, and finding a man lying in the road with a policeman standing over him, is not easily forgotten . . . there seems to be no reason for doubting the good faith of this witness, and her manner in the witness box impressed us very favourably' (*ibid*., p. 394). And, 'She struck us as a calm and capable woman' who was 'thoroughly trustworthy' (cf. Ethel Griffiths) and 'completely disinterested' (*ibid*., p. 397).

18 Cf. the later occasion when Wensley tried to pull Arthur in with two young van-drivers who had been stealing van-loads of goods from the North London Railway at Broad Street, using faked loading papers. See pp. 165–6.

19 See *Daily Mail*, 27 September 1906 and *Daily News* same day, p. 9. 'Mr. Cluer said that Constable 47 H. R. had not said anything about an attempted rescue. Either the witness had added it or the other constable had forgotten it.' Under cross-examination by Arthur two of the three police witnesses placed the incidents 40–50 yards apart. They also disagreed on which ear PC 47 had been struck. The hearing took place on 26 September 1906 and is described by the Royal Commission who had the benefit of Cluer's notes (*Royal Commission on the Metropolitan Police*, pp. 330–4). Cluer himself had already given evidence and was not recalled as a witness in Arthur's case. Perhaps it was regarded as indelicate and demeaning to bring a magistrate into individual cases. Cann's story that Arthur had hit him was supported by two constables, one of whom was Ashford (*ibid*., p. 333).

20 *Ibid*., p. 334. 'Mr. Cluer dismissed the charge, saying that there could be no doubt P.C. Cann was assaulted, but the defendant Harding's witness, and particularly the manager of the tavern, proved conclusively that he never went to the crowd or the

constable. The defendant then said, "May I ask what protection I have against the police?" And Mr. Cluer replied, "Your best protection is a magistrate at this court."' Part of Arthur Harding's fame and notoriety at this time arose from his ability to press home the implications of a case like this – particularly those in which the police had been outmanoeuvred or appeared in a bad light. Most persons with a criminal record would have been relieved to get off and would have left it at that. In effect the question thrown at Cluer turned Arthur's defence into an attack on the police. It pushed Cluer into a corner by asking him either to attack the police, or to assert the independence and rights of his court – which he did.

21 Arthur comments, '[It was] the worst thing I ever did when I went up to the tribunal. It put every policeman – good or bad – against me.' He recalls that he was advised by the Borstal Assocation 'to get out of England and give them time to forget you'. (Additional information, December 1977.)

22 'P.C. Ashford guilty of the misconduct alleged, but in kicking Gamble did not intend to do him the serious injury which resulted' (*ibid.*, p 409), and 'P.C. Ashford and Sergeant Sheedy were guilty of the misconduct alleged against them respectively.' Sheedy was guilty because he failed to stop the assault or to make any report to a superior. The police investigation by Inspector Hewison which got no further than ascertaining that Gamble's name was not listed at the London Hospital – due to a clerical error he had been admitted as 'Pearce' – 'did all that could be reasonably expected' (*Royal Commission on the Metropolitan Police*, p. 410).

23 *East London Observer*, 31 October 1908, p. 7, col. 3, and *Old Bailey Sessions Papers*, vol. 149, 1908, pp. 840–53. A summons against Ashford was obtained immediately the Royal Commission published its findings. At the Old Bailey his counsel tried to defend his client in two ways. He attempted to blacken the characters of Gamble and Ethel Griffiths, using those parts of the tribunal's findings which were unfavourable to them. For example, the commissioners knew that the couple had lied about their relationship to one another, and they had written down Ethel's evidence because she was a prostitute. Counsel also claimed that there had been no proper identification of Ashford as *the* constable who had kicked Gamble. In his summing up the Common Sergeant, Sir Albert Bosanquet, advised the jury to give no weight to what Ethel had told them. Nevertheless, he emphasised the case was important not only because Gamble's injuries were serious but because 'the attack on Gamble was by a

man who had the power of the law at his back'. The jury was out for two hours. Ashford was found guilty and sentenced to nine months with hard labour (*The Times*, 16 September, 1908, October 24 and 26). The Court of Criminal Appeal refused him right to appeal.

24 The 'Crimes Act' charge described in footnote 2.

25 This is the case described on pp. 164–5.

26 Rutter, according to Arthur Harding (November 1977), along with 'Jew Boy' Stevens 'hated Wensley like poison'. Both of them refused to leave the pantechnicon van covering Exchange Buildings during the preliminary stages of the Sidney Street siege. Rutter, in particular, seems to have fed Arthur opinions and information about the police. Rutter is mentioned by Wensley (*Detective Days*, p. 88) as being involved in the case of the Reuben brothers. And he was involved with Wensley, then Detective Inspector, Brogden and Dessent, and Smart in the case of the receiver who also arranged robberies and even lent the operators vans to remove the stolen goods (*Hackney Gazette*, 5 August 1907, p. 3).

27 Harry Simmons, 188 Jamaica Road (1912–52). For the year 1911 the shop is listed as A. Simmons & Co.

28 Joseph Barker, undertaker at 71 Church Street from 1891 to 1911 and then (1912–13) at 129 Bethnal Green Road.

29 E. H. Pickersgill.

30 Wensley, *Detective Days*, p. 32: 'It was the Seaman affair that first brought me into personal touch with Sir Melville Macnaghten. It began an understanding between us that was of immense value to me.' 'It also brought me into personal contact with Sir Melville Macnaghten . . . a fact which had some influence on my future career' (p. 23). '[He] showed an almost paternal interest in my work . . . [which] was calculated to give a human and inspiring tone to our relationship' (p. 33). For the chase over the roofs see ch. 3, pp. 21–31. And the meeting with Sir Melville – 'Quite unexpectedly he strolled into the Leman Street Police Station and it happened that I was the only C.I.D. officer there at the time' (p. 32 again).

31 Thomas Divall, local inspector from 1902 to 1906 at Whitechapel or 'H' Division which took in Leman and Commercial Streets together with Stepney (Arbour Square) and Shadwell police stations. The title 'local' became 'divisional detective' inspector around 1910. As third in the divisional hierarchy below superintendent and chief inspector and Wensley's immediate superior, Divall was well placed to veto the younger officer's promotion. In *Detective Days* Wensley writes, 'My chief was not sympath-

etic. "It's no use coming to me", he said bluntly. "I shan't recommend you. I'm not going to have you transferred after I've taught you all you know. You must wait till a vacancy occurs in this division."' (p. 33). Before this Divall had made it difficult for Wensley to get into the CID: 'yet, somehow, I remained a uniformed constable. Transfer to the Criminal Investigation Department depended upon the recommendation of the divisional detective inspector . . . and I was not regarded with any particular favour by the officer who held that position' (p. 10). Nevertheless, Wensley succeeded Divall in 1907 when the latter was moved to Hackney ('J' Division) where he was again local inspector. In 1913 Divall became chief inspector in the Criminal Investigation Department at Scotland Yard. This was the year that Wensley became Chief Inspector at Whitechapel for his part in the siege of Sidney Street. The title *chief* detective inspector was held by no other divisional officer at the time and meant that he maintained the same prestige as his old chief. Divall disappears from the police lists in 1914. Three years later Wensley became chief inspector at Scotland Yard and in 1926 chief constable. Divall has left an autobiography of first-class interest to students of East End history and of the London underworld – Tom Divall, *Scoundrels and Scallywags*.

32 This seems to confuse the post of chief constable of whom there were five (covering twenty-two local divisions grouped into four and one for the CID) with Wensley's chief inspectorship at Whitechapel, the reward for his part in the siege of Sidney Street and the fame which sprang from it. What was unique about Wensley was not this questionable fame but 'that I should ultimately be the first detective of modern times to be given the rank of Chief Constable' (*Detective Days*, p. 216) at a time when the highest posts in London were monopolised by former army officers.

33 Wensley, *Detective Days*, pp. 105 and 106. The words quoted here are not exact, e.g. Wensley writes 'teach *them* a lesson' and the sentences appear on different pages. Discussing the Royal Commission, which gets half a page, Wensley rehashes his own evidence and seems to have written his account with the report at his side.

34 Frederick Porter Wensley (1865–1949). Came from Somerset to London to join the Metropolitan police in 1887. In the next year he was drafted into the East End to take part in the hunt for Jack the Ripper. Moved to Whitechapel in 1891 where he became a detective and rose to the rank of detective inspector, and, after Sidney Street, chief detective inspector. In 1916 Wensley went to

Scotland Yard, becoming head of the Criminal Investigation Department in 1921. In 1926, three years before retirement, he was made Chief Constable, one of four posts directly below the Commissioner of Police. Wensley's fame came from the Turner Street murders which took place in 1896; the Vendetta affair; Sidney Street when he chased a dangerous man over the rooftops; and the arrest and trial of Steinie Morrison ('one of the most troublesome prisoners with whom the prison authorities ever had to deal' (Wensley, *Detective Days*, p. 131). After his move to Scotland Yard he took part in and charge of a large number of murder hunts including the cases of Madame Gerard and Edith Thompson. However, his greatest contribution was as one of the 'big four' in reorganising the Yard to move more quickly and effectively against organised crime, and in setting up the Flying Squad. Unfortunately Wensley's autobiography has little to say about developments in police work. He seems to have had great skill in questioning suspects and in the cat-and-mouse games which were a part of this. And he lays stress, as one might expect in the East End, on the use of informers. Even as late as 1928 a member of an official inquiry censured his part in the questioning of a young man in a Scotland Yard inquiry into perjury (P.P. 1920 (3147), XII, *Report of the Tribunal (on) . . . Interrogation of Miss Savidge by the Police*, p. 32).

35 Another version of the story is related earlier on p. 192.

36 Wensley's appearance before the Royal Commission was brief but devious: '22496. (Mr. Eldon Bankes). In his examination-in-chief Harding suggested that you had said to him . . ."Well, Harding, we will have you for another offence". . . . (Wensley replied) I said nothing of the kind. 22497. Is that absolutely untrue? – Absolutely untrue. 22499. (Earl Russell). Did you not say something of that kind to him . . . – No.' So far so good. But now Sir David Brynmor Jones decided to join in. '22504 (Chairman). Had you been acquainted with Harding before? I had seen him. I knew him by repute. 22505. That is not an answer to my question. Had you known Harding before? – Yes. 22506. Personally? – Personally' (*Royal Commission on the Metropolitan Police*, p. 545).

37 Norman Lucas, *The Flying Squad*, 1968, ch. 3 ('The Squad – World War II', pp. 52–67), confirms that forged coupons were a major problem during the war. In 1939 the squad had 18 cars, 2 taxis, a van and 50 detectives to cover an area of 700 square miles. See pp. 55ff on rationing cards.

Chapter 16   Marriage

1 See immediately below.

2 Edward Greeno, *War on the Underworld*, 1961, p. 21. All Greeno
  says is: 'The same Bethnal Green villains invaded a club in
  Maiden Lane, Strand, and stabbed one of the Sabini boys to death
  and, on a later occasion, threw another on the fire.' The sentence
  also appears in the *News of the World*, 8 November 1959. The
  words which Arthur Harding repeats appear in neither source.
  (Greeno's articles in the *News of the World* ran from 1 November
  1959 until 14 February 1960.)

3 The 'athletic outfitters' situated between Hatton Garden and
  Leather Lane beside, as Arthur mentions, the Prudential's red-
  tiled gothic building, and now overtaken by office development.

4 Preliminary hearing, *The Times*, 21 December 1921. The constable 'saw the men surround an unattended taxicab in Holborn
  on the night of December 10, and one of them got up and turned
  the starting handle. When he told them he was a police officer he
  was knocked down and became unconscious. His jaw was frac-
  tured.' The magistrate discharged the other two men. The appeal
  four months later was not reported in *The Times*.

5 Milly's father, Alfred, first appears in the West Ward rating
  books in 1915. This means the family moved into the Gardens
  between 1910 and 1915 – roughly ten years after the Hardings.
  According to Arthur Harding, Alfred thought the railway was
  the top of the world (February 1978).

6 Strictly speaking in Bunhill Row at the back of Bunhill Fields
  running between Old Street and Chiswell Street. For many years
  until it moved out of London in the mid-1960s de la Rue's carried
  on an important part of their banknote printing at this address.
  They had been there since 1833, two years after Thomas de la
  Rue had patented his first embossed playing card in 1831 (Lorna
  Houseman, *The House that Thomas Built*, 1968).

7 The house continued to be rented under the name of Mary
  Harding until after 1930. The 1935 rating books record only
  surname and No. 5 is listed simply under Harding.

8 That is on the corner of Satchwell Rents and Bethnal Green
  Road, seven numbers down from the Gardens.

9 I can find no reference to Bryant in the directories' listing of
  Metropolitan police officers.

10 According to Arthur, Gardiner and Moey Levy's club was opposite Middlesex Street over a big confectioner's shop.

11 Francis Henry Cassels, born 1910, now senior circuit judge,

Inner London Crown Court. Cassels was called to the bar in 1932. This suggests Arthur's date is wrong.

Chapter 17   Wardrobe dealing

1 Chapter 1, note 16. Although the name was changed shortly before Arthur Harding was born it is likely that the older name continued to be used.
2 John Pearson, *The Profession of Violence*, 1973, for a different account of the family history.
3 The name by which Mount Street was known in the Nichol. Later it was changed to Swanfield Street. Earlier references speak of 'Friars Mount'.
4 At No. 234, close to St Matthew's Row. Sidney Smith is listed as trading here since 1960. However, before this, they seem to have carried on business in Buckfast Street starting around 1954.
5 At 8a under the name of Alfred Smith from 1926 to 1931 or 1932.
6 Chapter 1, note 17. According to the *Post Office Directory* the Morgans were shutting up shop around the time that Alfred Smith was getting going in Chilton Street. Mrs Morgan bought up many houses in Essex Street, a well known rooming area of Hoxton. Two sons managed them for her. (Additional information, February 1978).
7 The 'Prince's Head' was one of the large number of pubs closed by the Liberal government in the years leading up to the First World War. (Additional information, February 1978.)
8 No record of the business survives in the directories. It would have been impossible to list every small business carried on from home in this way.
9 Selby's fame dated from much earlier than this. In 1908 (*Hackney Gazette*, 11 November) he was commended along with Detective Sergeants Bishops, George Stephens (*sic.*), Laing and Leach and Detectives Cleary by the Clerkenwell magistrate as 'among the best known and most respected of the officers known to him, and he had commended them often and often'. Four men with 'terrible records of crime having been proved against them' were captured breaking into the British Premium Tea Co. Stephens (*sic.*) and Selby, disguised as printers' labourers, saw the van with thieves in it arrive. Bishop dodged into a jewellers close by and changed clothes, emerging as a shop assistant, and Stephens fought one of the thieves using truncheon against jemmy. Another of the thieves fell 50 feet off the roof and was later found unconscious in a yard at the back of the premises.

10 Moses, whose business is listed in the directories at 12 Harrow Alley (now Palace) from 1914 to 1933.

11 According to Arthur, Joey Lyons probably lived at Brighton. He would have come up to London to deal at Exchange Buildings and to wait for the hawkers to bring in what they had collected. Fifteen shillings was paid for 'auction' suits i.e. things he would later sell in suburban areas around Epping and further out in East Anglia, and five shillings for repairs, pressing and cleaning which was done by Russian and Polish Jews roundabout. In Arthur's words 'they worked to get five shillings out of the suit brought to them, and then he would work to get five shillings' out of the reconditioned garment. It should be remembered that the suits were not shabby cast-offs but more likely to be business or Sunday suits bought from (say) Hector Powe. The dealers in Exchange Buildings were many and they were specialised. 'What I liked about them was this,' comments Arthur, 'if you had a dozen suits no one would undercut anyone else – once an offer was made. If he said £15 he meant £15.' (Additional information, January 1978).

12 'Jew Boy' Stevens.

Chapter 18   Domestic life and social change

1 Harris Lebus, cabinet-makers in Tabernacle Street and Paradise Street (or Place) on the boundary of Shoreditch and Finsbury (1885–1955) – less than half a mile from Finsbury Square. They can be traced back to 1873 and to an address at Wellclose Square, south of Cable Street, under the name of Lewis Lebus.

2 No. 406 – James Brooke and Sons, house furnishers (1923–35), two streets down from Wilmot Street. They also seem to have had a shop from the early 1920s at Broadway, London Fields where several pianoforte manufacturers are listed.

3 Mrs Casey is not listed in the rating books. However, her house adjoined a timber-yard and may have been listed elsewhere or under another name. 'Walk' refers to Gilbraltar Walk, the first thoroughfare to the west of the Gardens.

4 The 'Blade Bone' to the east and 'Well and Bucket' to the west were almost equidistant from the gardens. The closest pub, the 'Gibraltar' in Gibraltar Walk, is not mentioned. Originally this was joined to the gardens by a short passage. However, some time after the Hardings moved into one of the three tenements lying beyond the cottages the police had it closed off and a street-lamp installed at the entrance on Bethnal Green Road. In

1908 when Arthur was arrested on Wensley's Crimes Act charge he was followed by the two detectives who took him in charge from the gardens which had been under continuous police observation for about a week.

5   For most of the period there seems to have been three. Amos Saunders, the Hardings' landlord, J. J. Avery who owned six of the cottages opposite the Hardings and Worbys, and J. Donn who owned the remaining of these together with the three tenement buildings at the northern end of the gardens. The original row of cottages which followed the line of a footpath through fields were built between 1799 and 1819. Around 1900 the row to the west were owned by the Commercial Building Society who may have built them. (Bethnal Green Rating Books for these years.)

6   Appears in the rating books in 1925 and 1930 but not 1935.

7   They first appear in the rating books in 1935.

8   West Bethnal Green ward rating books list: Henry Mason 1920, Mary Mason 1925 and 1930, and Mason 1935.

9   Cf. rating books: Alfred Worby No. 4 – 1915, 1920, 1925, as Alfred Worley (*sic.*) 1930 and Worley (*sic.*) 1935.

10   Henry Davis listed at No. 19 (or, following the more common-sensical numbering in the text, No. 4) in 1925, 1930 and 1935.

11   Henry Daniels at No. 18 (No. 8) in 1925, 1930 and 1935.

12   Albert Gibbs at No. 21 (No. 11) in 1920 and 1925; Mrs Albert Gibbs in 1925.

13   At No. 23 (No. 13) Elizabeth Assen (*sic.*) 1930, corrected to Mary Asser in 1935.

14   Mrs Dugard at No. 24 (No. 14), listed under George Dugard or Dugard in 1925, Caroline Dugard in 1930, Charlotte Dugard in 1935.

15   Charles Whitehead at No. 27 (No. 17) in 1925, 1930 and 1935.

16   At No. 25 (No. 15): William Marsden 1920, Charles Marsden 1925 and 1930, Mrs Marsden 1935.

17   In 1930 listed as occupied by James Allcorn who was Mighty's husband, and in 1935 under Harding.

18   No. 4: 1920 Alfred Worby, 1925 Alfred Worby, 1930 Alfred Worby, 1935 Worby.

19   Arthur Howard is first listed in the West Ward rating books in 1930. The couple occupied two rooms on the first floor of the first tenement. The name also appears in 1925 and 1935.

Chapter 19   The Gold Rush

1 Between Kettering and Corby.
2 Golding & Co., Silversmith, 20 Clerkenwell Road, from around 1930 to 1936 when the branch was closed or merged with its antique silver business in Wardour Street.
3 There seems to be no reference in the *Leytonstone Independent* of 1935 to these proceedings.

Chapter 20   A shop in Brick Lane

1 'Harding, A. Second hand clothes dealer' listed in *Kelly's* at 250 between Padbury Court and Ducal Street from 1951 to 1961. This is a little later than the text appears to indicate.
2 Mile End Waste, an area of Mile End between Charringtons and Mile End Station.

Chapter 21   Politics and philosophy of life

1 In the 1890s the *Star* was the organ of the 'Progressives' (liberal-radical) on the London County Council.
2 In his autobiography, *Forty Years in and out of Parliament*, 1947, pp. 91–2, Sir Percy writes: 'Sir Matthew Wilson was a major in the Army, a great sport, and knew a lot about horses, anyhow much more about them than politics. He had a cheerful attractive personality. His friends called him Scalters Wilson, while in Bethnal Green he was popularly known as "the Major". . . . It soon got about that Wilson was not assiduous in his attentions to his parliamentary duties, but he did know how to make himself liked. One man I met in the street wished me luck at the election, but when I asked if he were going to vote for me he replied in the negative. "You see, Mr. 'Arris, Mr. Wilson he gave my child 'alf a crown, and 'alf a crown is 'alf a crown."'
3 Sir Matthew's son, Sir Martin Wilson, cannot confirm this. Nevertheless he remembers that his father 'was very interested in the costers who gave strong support when he was electioneering' (personal communication, October 1977).
4 There is no record of Wilson having spoken in parliament on the coster issue. Nevertheless, like his successor Sir Percy Harris, he would be in constant contact over licences and traffic regulations with the Commissioner for Police and perhaps the Home Office.
5 East London's working men's clubs already had a well developed

liberal-radical character in the 1880s. John Taylor, *From Self-Help to Glamour; The Working Men's Club, 1860–1972*, History Workshop, Oxford, 1972.

6 Tom Brookes (died 1954), Mayor of Bethnal Green who sat for twenty-eight years on its council and for six years before that as a vestryman. He was three times chairman of the Works Committee and chairman of the Public Health Committee when the Brady Street Clearance Scheme was carried out. His only defeat in the West Ward was at the very first metropolitan council elections. He lived for forty years at 263 Brick Lane and was a staunch temperance advocate. He attracted attention in the national press in 1936 when he attended a Buckingham Palace Garden party and then hurried back to Bethnal Green to do another job of chimney sweeping – a trade he had done since he was twelve. In a *News Chronicle* interview (7 November 1931) he noted that there had been a decline in domestic fires due to redevelopment and that he was sweeping chiefly in large City offices.

7 Rev. R. C. Jones, Vicar of St Paul's in Virginia Road. Jones continued the earlier tradition of High Church evangelism. In the middle 1930s (the *Star*, 31 March 1936) more than 1,000 people attended Sunday-night service and attendances of 700 at week-night services were common. His greatest achievement was a holiday home near Chelmsford which provided over 1,000 Bethnal Green children with a fortnight's holiday each year.

8 The reduction in the number of licences had in fact been going on for some years. For some local examples, see *Hackney Gazette*, 28 November 1906, p. 3, col. 7; *Eastern Post*, 30 March 1907.

9 For Rocker, see Rudolf Rocker, *The London Years*, 1956, and W. J. Fishman, *East End Jewish Radicals 1854–1914*, 1975.

10 Harry Louis Nathan (1889–1963), first Baron Churt. Solicitor with volunteer regiment background and links with an enormous number of voluntary bodies. As a young man, Nathan was honorary secretary of the Brady Working Lads' Club, the oldest and largest Jewish Lads' Club in London. He was Liberal MP for Bethnal Green from 1929 until 1933 when he crossed the floor of the Commons to oppose the National Government. In 1934 he joined Labour, moving to Central Wandsworth until 1940 when he made way for Ernest Bevin thus gaining his peerage. In the post-war Labour government he was first an under-secretary of state for war and then minister for civil aviation. His links with charities included hospitals, cancer research, the Jewish Board of Deputies and serving as Chairman of the Isaac Wolfson Foundation. Harry Gosling lost at Lambeth North in 1910. He lost

again, this time to a Coalition Conservative, at Middlesex Uxbridge in 1918, and yet again to a Conservative at Lambeth Kennington in 1922. He then transferred to Stepney, Whitechapel and St George's, winning in a by-election in August 1923. He held on to the seat in 1923 and in 1924 where he was opposed by H. L. Nathan. Gosling, a waterman, and one of the leaders of the 1889 dock strike, published a fine autobiography, *Harry Gosling, Up and Down Stream*, 1927.

11 Percy Harris (1876–1952), MP for Bethnal Green South West 1907–18, 1922–34 and 1946–9, and, after boundary changes, for Bethnal Green 1949–52. Percy's views were formed as a member of the Progressive Party on the LCC. This mixed group of Liberals, radicals, labour representatives and Fabians, where Sidney Webb and Will Crooks rubbed shoulders with T. McKinnon Wood and Sir Algernon West, provided him with an ideology and an apprenticeship to politics which served him for forty years. After the Liberal Party had disappeared from County Hall, leaving him as a sole reminder that they had ever existed, Harris told the *News Chronicle* (26 February 1946), 'I am standing because there is a desire in the district that I should stand. People want the personal and human touch I have always used.' How he did this and how his supremacy was maintained is revealed by occasional glimpses in the local press. For example as president of the Master Association of the Furniture Trade 'he could well remember a stormy meeting at the back of Shoreditch Church when the formation of the Assocation was proposed' (*Hackney Gazette*, 21 February 1947). The mixture of vigorous but old-fashioned progressive politics with intense small-scale local politics was ideally suited to the conservative and precarious world of Bethnal Green.

12 For Alf Flockhart, see Robert Benewick, *The Fascist Movement in Britain*, 1972, and Colin Cross, *The Fascists in Britain*, 1961.

13 Jeffrey Hamm, Welsh schoolmaster, British Union member in Harrow before the war. On release from detention joined the Royal Tank Corps (Colin Cross, *The Fascists in Britain*, 1961, p. 200). Hamm's British League of Ex-Servicemen was the first attempt after the war to rally Mosley's fragmented support. It held open-air meetings in the East End, mostly at Ridley Road. At these Hamm would publicly call for Mosley to return to politics. At one of these meetings Hamm's head was split open by a brick (Skidelsky, *Oswald Mosley*, p. 490). When the Union Movement was formed in 1948 Hamm became a leading office holder in it and 'the main active force' (Robert Skidelsky, *Oswald Mosley*, 1975).

Index